Railways and International

This new volume of essays by expert scholars shows how the construction and expansion of the railways represents a key factor in understanding international politics from 1848 to the end of the Second World War.

While the effect of railways on economic development is self-evident, little attention has been paid to their impact on international relations. This is unfortunate, for in the period from 1848 to 1945 railways were an important element in the struggle between the Great Powers. These essays provide in-depth analyses of railways as objects of political and economic Great Power rivalries and as tools of power projection, strategic mobilization and imperial defence. The book demonstrates the strategic significance of railways and reaches conclusions that can be applied to other technological innovations.

This book will be of great interest to students of international history, military history and strategic studies.

T.G. Otte is Lecturer in Diplomatic History at the University of East Anglia. He is the author (with G.R. Berridge and Maurice Keens-Soper) of *Classics of Diplomatic Theory* and the editor of *Military Intervention: From Gunboat Diplomacy to Humanitarian Intervention*, and *Personalities, War and Diplomacy*.

Keith Neilson is Professor of History at the Royal Military College of Canada, where he teaches military and diplomatic history. He is the author of *Strategy and Supply: The Anglo-Russian Alliance 1914–1917* and, most recently, of *Britain, Soviet Russia and the Collapse of the Versailles Settlement, 1919–1939*, and has edited several collections.

Routledge Series: Military History and Policy
Series Editors: John Gooch and Brian Holden Reid
ISSN: 1465–8488

This series will publish studies on historical and contemporary aspects of land power, spanning the period from the eighteenth century to the present day, and will include national, international and comparative studies. From time to time, the series will publish edited collections of essays and 'classics'.

Railways and International Politics

Paths of Empire, 1848–1945

Edited by T.G. Otte and Keith Neilson

Routledge
Taylor & Francis Group

LONDON AND NEW YORK

First published 2006
by Routledge
2 Park Square, Milton Park, Abingdon, Oxon, OX14 4RN

Simultaneously published in the USA and Canada
by Routledge
711 Third Avenue, New York, NY 10017

*Routledge is an imprint of the Taylor & Francis Group,
an informa business*

First issued in paperback 2012

Typeset in Times New Roman by
Newgen Imaging Systems (P) Ltd, Chennai, India

British Library Cataloguing in Publication Data
A catalogue record for this book is available from the British Library

Library of Congress Cataloging in Publication Data
A catalog record for this book has been requested

ISBN 13: 978-0-415-34976-5 (hbk)
ISBN 13: 978-0-415-65131-8 (pbk)
ISBN 13: 978-0-203-35023-2 (ebk)

Publisher's Note
The publisher has gone to great lengths to ensure the quality
of this reprint but points out that some imperfections in the
original may be apparent

Content

Contributors

Nigel Brailey recently retired as Lecturer in History at the University of Bristol. having specialized in modern Asian history and Western imperialism in Asia. Among his publications are *Thailand and the Fall of Singapore* (1985) and *The Satow Siam Papers* (ed., 1997).

F.R. Bridge is Professor Emeritus in International History at the University of Leeds, specializing in Austro-Hungarian foreign policy. His publications include *Great Britain and Austria–Hungary, 1906–1914* (1972), *From Sadowa to Sarajevo* (1972), *The Habsburg Monarchy among the Great Powers* (1991) and (with Roger Bullen) *The Great Powers and the European States System, 1814–1914* (2nd edn, 2005).

John Fisher is Lecturer at the University of the West of England, Bristol, specializing in British foreign and imperial policy in Central Asia. His publications include *Curzon and British Imperialism in the Middle East, 1916–1919* (1999), *Gentlemen Spies* (2002) and *Paris Peace Conference – Peace without Victory* (ed., 2001), and he has published widely in academic journals.

Anthony J. Heywood is Senior Lecturer at the University of Aberdeen and specializes in East European and Russian history. His publications include *The Russian Revolution of 1905* (ed., 2005) and *Modernising Lenin's Russia: Economic Reconstruction, Foreign Trade and the Railways* (1999).

Greg Kennedy is Senior Lecturer at the Joint Services Command and Staff College (King's College London), specializing in twentieth-century British strategy, foreign and naval policies. Among his publications are *Anglo-American Strategic Relations and the Far East, 1933–1939* (1999), *Far Flung Lines* (ed., 1996), *The Merchant Marine in International Affairs, 1850–1950* (ed., 2000), and *British Naval Strategy East of Suez* (ed., 2005).

Keith Neilson is Professor of History at the Royal Military College of Canada, and specializes in nineteenth- and twentieth-century Anglo-Russian/Soviet diplomatic and strategic relations. Among his publications are *Strategy and Supply: Anglo-Russian Relations* (1984), *Britain and the Last Tsar, 1894–1917*

(1995), *Britain, Soviet Russia and the Collapse of the Versailles Order, 1919–1939* (2006) *Coalition Warfare* (ed., 1983), *Go Spy the Land* (ed., 1992), *Navies and Global Defence* (ed., 1995), *Military Education* (ed., 2002) and *The Office: The Permanent Under-Secretary for Foreign Affairs, 1854–1945* (co-author, forthcoming).

T.G. Otte is Lecturer in Diplomatic History at the University of East Anglia, specializing in Great Power relations, 1856–1914. His publications include *Military Intervention* (ed., 1995), *Personalities, War and Diplomacy* (ed., 1997), *Classic Guides to Diplomatic Theory* (co-author, 2001), *The Makers of British Foreign Policy* (ed., 2002), *The Office: The Permanent Under-Secretary for Foreign Affairs, 1854–1945* (co-author, forthcoming). He is also Associate Editor and Reviews Editor of *Diplomacy & Statecraft*.

Dennis E. Showalter is Professor of History at Colorado College, specializing in German military history. Among his many publications are *Tannenberg* (1990), *The Wars of Frederick the Great* (1996), *History in Dispute: The Second World War* (2 vols, 2000) and *The Wars of German Unification* (2003).

Martin Thomas is Senior Lecturer in European History at the University of Exeter, specializing in twentieth-century international history and French military and imperial strategy. His publications include *Britain, France and Appeasement* (1996), *The French Empire at War, 1940–1945* (1998), *The French North African Crisis* (2000), *International Diplomacy and Colonial Retreat* (ed., 2001) and *The French Empire between the Wars* (2005).

Neville Wylie is Lecturer in Politics at the University of Nottingham, specializing in twentieth-century international history and intelligence studies. His publications include *Britain, Switzerland and the Second World War* (2003) and *European Neutrals and Non-Belligerents during the Second World War* (ed., 2001), as well as numerous articles in scholarly journals. He is also Reviews Editor of *Intelligence & National Security*.

1 'Railpolitik'

An introduction

Keith Neilson and T.G. Otte

> The locomotive was the greatest thing of the age. With it man conquered space and time.
>
> Stephen E. Ambrose[1]

With the railway came the modern age. The advent of the railway had a greater and more immediate impact than any other technological or industrial innovation before or since. Railways, Max Weber noted in the early twentieth century, 'have been the most revolutionary instrument that history records as regards the economy, and not merely transport'.[2] In the wake of the fast growth of the railways from the 1840s onwards, there came the development of modern capitalism, and the formation of modern societies and nations. The railways transformed, redefined and expanded the limits of the civilized world.

The economic impact of the nineteenth-century steam-powered transport revolution has been the subject of numerous academic studies, and it also gave rise to the original counterfactual approach to the study of history.[3] The introduction of railways followed different paths in different countries, though certain common pattern emerged which had a bearing on the political and strategic utility of the railways. It will suffice to concentrate here on the three most significant cases, Britain, Germany and Russia.

Britain played a pioneering role in the development of modern railways. The new mode of transport boosted the concentration of British industry.[4] Railways provided the most significant stimulus for the metal producing and processing branches of industry. But they also marked an important new departure. As metal and coal producing industries grew, so their heavier investment needs contributed to the formation of corporations and joint stock companies. Engineering, machine and tool-making firms made important inroads into the great industrial cities. Especially during the 'railway mania' in the mid-1840s, railway-building projects became the object of great financial speculations – and failure, as the case of the Yorkshire 'railway king' George Hudson illustrated. The 'railway boom' of 1844–7 was far more volatile than earlier booms, and probably played a decisive role in the cyclical fluctuations of the British economy.[5] Parliament passed the necessary legislation for the construction of 270 new railway lines in the peak year 1846 alone. During these years a total railway capital of £133 million was raised. In 1847 over £40 million was invested, about 7 per cent of Britain's national income. This tide of capital investment was slowed down by a significant credit crisis. Railways already had the potential to influence the international economic situation through the London financial market.[6] British railway building in those years even spread across the Channel to Belgium and northern France, so much so that the liberal Belgian Prime Minister Jean-Baptiste Nothomb warned: 'We are going to become a province of England.'[7]

Construction proceeded at a brisk pace. Between 1846 and 1848, 2,600 miles of railway lines were opened; by 1851, 6,300 miles were in service; and by 1870 the total mileage had reached 13,400. In 1900, Britain's railway network extended to some 18,700 miles.[8] The fact that, in mid-century, over 100 Members of Parliament had substantial financial interests in railway concerns is indicative of the overall importance attributed to the development of railways by the country's élite.[9] This attraction continued throughout the nineteenth and twentieth centuries. Large aristocratic landowners and politicians, like the Earl of Derby or the Duke of Devonshire, derived a significant portion of their income from railway properties. Others, like the Marquis of Salisbury, augmented theirs through directorships of railway companies, while the seriously wealthy W.H. Smith made his by exploiting station platforms and foyers.[10] In the second half of the 1840s railway investment amounted to some 55 per cent of gross capital formation. In the years following the 'boom', the railways ceased to be an engine of growth, but they remained an important supporting sector. In the 1850s and 1860s the share of railway capital as a percentage of British gross capital had sunk to between a fifth and a quarter, though between 1863 and 1866 Parliament still authorized some £150 million to be spent on the railways.[11]

The growth of the railway network facilitated the rise of industrial centres in the provinces and of the great international seaports. Crewe and Swindon emerged as railway towns where engines and rolling stock were built. Middlesborough and Barrow-in-Furness rose from tiny rural communities to become the mid-Victorian 'boom' towns, made possible by a combination of natural resources, rail transport and access to the sea. The railways transformed Britain's landscape and society. Rail transport determined Victorian urban development, especially the growth of the suburbs. Conversely, once thriving rural market towns fell into decay if they remained unconnected – something neatly illustrated in one of Trollope's Barchester novels by the fate of the market town of Courcy, whose centre shifted from the old market to the new railway station some distance away.[12]

The Victorian railway station was one of the 'key buildings of the age'. In newly incorporated Barrow, the Corporation met in the railway offices, until the new town hall was built. Railway stations were the cathedral buildings of the nineteenth century, monuments to industrial and social progress. As the *Yorkshire Post* commented in 1866: 'Railways and the electric telegraph have established a frequency of locomotion and circulation of ideas which rob country society of all its inertness and stagnation which were once its peculiar characteristics.'[13] Yet, the spread of railways also stoked fears of change. In Cambridge, the University's vice-chancellor insisted that the new railway station be built at exactly one mile's distance from Senate House, lest the city be invaded by Sunday trippers!

If Britain was a pioneer in the development of railways, there were similar developments in other countries. But there were also significant differences. While the British railways were financed by private investors, state governments played a more important role in continental Europe. In Germany 'railway development was effecting a mighty transformation in economic life', as the nineteenth-century historian and prominent nationalist propagandist Heinrich von Treitschke observed.[14] Already in 1828, the Prussian finance minister Friedrich Christian Adolph von Motz, the creator of the German *Zollverein*, had considered the scheme for a railway line connecting the Rivers Rhine and Weser, and thence to the North Sea, thereby avoiding the Dutch Rhine tolls.[15] The railway era started fitfully in the second half of the 1830s. Ministerial coolness and official suspicions of private enterprise eased only in the 1840s. Following the consolidation of her state finances in 1842, Prussia gave government guarantees to construction companies. As a result the length and the density of the Prussian railway network grew rapidly. If in 1840 there were a mere 115 miles in service, by 1847 the network had grown to 1,506.3 miles. By 1850, 1,834.7 miles were operational, and in 1860, 3,580.5 miles. At the beginning of the so-called Great Depression in 1873, Prussian railways extended some 8,986.1 miles; on the eve of the First World War they had reached 22,744.5 miles.[16]

Eighteen forty-six was a 'boom' year also in Germany. The railway sector was the 'pace maker' of economic growth in this early stage of German industrialization, and surpassed all other sectors until the 1880s. As in Britain, large corporations and joint stock companies played a major role in railway construction. Prussian railway capital accounted for more than half of Germany's total gross capital; and the railways remained the lead sector in Prussia's industrialization.[17] Net investments in the railways in Germany were constant at about a fifth to a quarter of the total German gross capital from 1850 until the late 1870s, a figure roughly comparable to the figures for Britain after the 'railway boom'.[18] And, as in Britain, railways became the objects of financial gamblings, as the spectacular rise and fall of Prussia's own 'railway king', the British-trained Dr Bethel Henry Strousberg, illustrated.[19]

In contrast to the development of railways in Britain, the Prussian government exercised close supervision over all construction projects to avoid wasteful competition and to provide adequately for economic and strategic necessities. The latter consideration grew steadily in importance.[20] Still, the efforts to gain control over all lines running through Prussian territory did not always succeed in reducing wasteful competition. A dispute with the Saxon government in 1860–1, the so-called *Eisenbahn-Krieg*, led to the creation of two railway hubs in close geographical proximity at Leipzig and Halle, where one would have sufficed.[21] Initially, the government in Berlin had encouraged the building of essential lines through guarantees of interest or financial devices, but had relied on private enterprise to raise the capital necessary for the construction of the lines and to carry their business management. In the 1850s, under the commerce minister August von der Heydt (1848–62), the Prussian government sought to gain direct possession of or control over as many railways as possible. By 1860, more than half of Prussia's railways had either been nationalized or placed under some form of government supervision. This policy was reversed in the early 1860s under Prime Minister Otto von Bismarck. In order to finance the 1866 war, von der Heydt, by now finance minister, sold off some 4.5 million *Thalers* of railway stocks and shares in government ownership during the war and a further 13 million after the war. Such sacrifices paid off, for the Prussian government increased its rail network after the successful war by taking over the railways in the annexed territories.[22]

Economic and military strategy remained blended in Prussian railway policy. After 1866, the government began to search for ways of bringing the railways on Prussian territory under its control. Bismarck saw in them the sinews of Prussia's economy in peacetime and of her armed might in times of war. He was determined that they should belong to the state.[23] It was a reflection of the central role of the railways in Germany's industrial development, but also during the wars of 1866 and 1870–1, that German state governments began to purchase privately owned lines. Still, the full nationalization programme was not passed into law until December 1879.[24] While in the 1870s the majority of lines were in private ownership, there were hardly any private lines left by 1890. The Prussian state railways operated a model system, reliable, efficient and economical. In this fashion, the Prussian state (but also the other larger German states) acquired effective instruments of state intervention in the economy; they also acquired highly profitable concerns that raised a significant portion of government revenues. In the 1897–8 Prussian budget net railway receipts of Mk 266.6 million were more than half the government's total revenue of Mk 527.9.[25] The nationalization of the railways also made the Prussian state the largest employer in Germany, responsible for some 700,000 people on the eve of the First World War. And since the railway workers and clerks were subject to almost military discipline and banned from trades union activities, the railways also buttressed the existing political order of Imperial Germany.[26]

The mixture of private and government enterprise, of economic and politico-military considerations, also characterized the growth of the railways in Tsarist Russia. Here, too, there was initially ministerial suspicion of this new means of transport. Tsar Nikolai I's finance minister, Count Igor Frantsevich Kankrin, opposed railway projects as they would lead to 'frequent and useless travel, thus fostering the restless spirit of our age'.[27] It required the shock of the Crimean War to alert St Petersburg to the potential of the railways. Tsar Aleksandr II declared in a *ukase* in early 1857 'that our fatherland, equipped with abundant gifts but divided by huge spaces, especially needs suitable communications'.[28] Russian railway construction after the Crimean War was financed largely through foreign loans. Mainly French capital funded the Grand Société des Chemins de Fer Russes that built a number of arterial lines, which served both economic and military needs.[29] In consequence, Russia's finance ministers played a key role in the development of the country's railways. Mikhail Khristoforovich Reutern, finance minister between 1862 and 1878, was instrumental in consolidating Russia's overstretched budget and introduced technical innovations into financial administration. He promoted railway construction through different schemes of concessions and guarantees of minimum interest on capital investments.[30] This was the 'pioneer era' in Russian railway building, dominated by socially non-distinct and unscrupulous financiers, assisted by corrupt but technically competent engineers. One such beneficiary of the 'boom' was P.G. von Derviz, who, having received railway concessions from Reutern as an old schoolmate, sold up at a profit and spent the rest of his life in ostentatious indolence.

While Reutern held the finance portfolio, the Russian Empire's railway network expanded from 2,200 miles to 14,200 miles. Although this was modest in relation to the size of the Empire, and although the companies were often inefficiently managed and wasteful, railway construction marked the beginnings of an industrial infrastructure. Moscow and St Petersburg were connected by rail, and the capital also with Warsaw and Vienna. From the 1870s onwards lines were pushed forward into the Ukraine, the Caucasus and Central Asia. The railway system covered around 1,408.7 miles in 1861, but after three 'feverish' bouts in 1868–71, 1877–9 and 1885–7 extended to some 17,776.5 miles.[31] The fact that these bursts of railway-building activity coincided with periods of international tensions is suggestive of the strategic impetus behind Russia's railway programme. The effect of the railways in the 1860s and 1870s was 'truly revolutionary in that they stimulated an internal and foreign market for grain'; they also stimulated domestic steel production.[32]

As had been the case in Western Europe, the substantial financial requirements of the railways led to an enmeshing of engineering interests with financial and stock exchange activities. Under Reutern's 'liberal' economic policy the construction and management of railways lay in the hands of private enterprise. One of the most significant 'railway magnates' of this era was Jan Bloch (later Ivan S. Bliokh), a financier of Polish-Jewish extraction, who acquired the Odessa Railway in 1877 and combined it with other lines in his possession to form the Southwestern Railway Company. Bloch's network covered the grain centres of the western Ukraine and Poland from the Baltic to the Black Sea, and linked up with the German and Austro-Hungarian railways.[33] Crucially, he selected able men to operate the company for him. Ivan Alekse'evich Vishnegradsky, a high-ranking official and head of St Petersburg's prestigious Technological Institute, was made a director of the company, in which role he proved himself to be a skilful operator on the stock exchange, until, in 1887, he was appointed finance minister. Bloch's business manager was Sergei Iulevich Witte, whose experience in private business would later be crucial when he became, first, head of the Railway Department of the Russian finance ministry, before succeeding Vishnegradsky as minister in 1892.[34]

Witte is widely credited with reforming Russia's chaotic railway system. However, Reutern's 'liberal' railway policy was already gradually being replaced from 1877 onwards, largely in reaction to strategic and foreign policy considerations.

The over-extension of Russian supply lines and the slow pace of transporting troops and matériel during the Russo-Turkish War of 1877 had demonstrated the insufficiency of the existing railway network for military purposes. This, combined with the diplomatic setback at the Berlin Congress in 1878, underlined the urgent need for a clearer direction in the government's railway policy. The construction of strategic railway lines to the west and south was regarded as an urgent necessity, while increased debts on account of the war with Turkey and the subsequent collapse in agricultural prices added to Russia's financial difficulties.[35] However, the changes introduced under Reutern's two successors Nikolai Khristianovich Bunge (1882–6) and Vishnegradsky (1896–92) were piecemeal, and lacked systematic coherence. In 1880 only 6 per cent of all lines were operated by the government, rising to 13.3 per cent in 1886 and 34.7 per cent in 1891.[36]

Under Witte Russia's railway development gathered pace and gained greater coherence. Railways were no longer directed solely for profit, but became instruments of state policy to service economic and military needs. Witte purchased privately owned railway companies for the state at a greater pace than Bunge had, and at high prices to encourage Russian entrepreneurship. By 1903, nearly 70 per cent of all lines were in the hands of the state. Between 1893 and 1900 the Russian government invested 2,226.6 million roubles in the railways. During the Witte period the railway network more than doubled in size, from 18,134.6 miles in 1891 to 36,689.1 miles in 1906. Witte's 'system' had a stimulating effect on the Russian economy. The intensive programme of railway construction created a steady demand for the products of the mining and metallurgical industries. Railway construction provided some 37 per cent of the total Russian market for pig iron. While Russian domestic production had met only about 41 per cent of domestic demand, in the 1890s this had risen to 73 per cent.[37]

The construction programme also helped to open up backward areas to industrial development. The Ekaterinoslav or 'Catherine Railway' (1885), for instance, which connected the capital with Krivoi Rog in the Dniepr bend, and formed a link between the iron of Krivoi Rog and the coal of the Donets, laid the foundations for the development of the Donbas area, later to become the industrial heartland of the Ukraine.[38] Much of the expenditure for railway building and equipment came from the St Petersburg government, and this was a key factor in attracting foreign, and especially French, investment in Russian industry. Foreign investments brought advanced technological know-how and management skills, while French loans and investments became the mainstays of the Russian economy before 1914.[39]

Witte's programme of encouraging Russia's industrial development is often associated with the construction of the Trans-Siberian railway. The project predated Witte's arrival at the finance ministry and had been dominated by strategic and political motives, but Witte also introduced economic considerations into its planning. In Witte's grand design the Trans-Siberian line was the crucial link between Russia and the Far East; it was to be the vehicle of Russia's *pénétration pacifique* of East Asia.[40] The Trans-Siberian project was part of a wider programme of laying double tracks on existing lines, shortening connections and building branch lines to the West and South of the Urals. Between 1896 and 1902 on average 1,250 miles of new track were opened per annum. Between 1891 and 1902 the network increased by some 17,000 miles, 5,400 of these in Asiatic Russia. Nevertheless, the Trans-Siberian line was a 4,000 mile 'monster devoid of purpose'.[41] What began as a gigantic engineering project ultimately produced an economic and strategic railway mouse. The continued constraints on the Russian exchequer limited the amount of money that was spent on the project. Major population centres were avoided in order to shorten the line, safety standards were relaxed, inferior construction materials were used, curves were sharp and gradients often too steep. This markedly reduced the average speed of trains, and the line could only accommodate a low volume of traffic. Ultimately, the line did not serve Russia's military requirements, nor did it allow for the full development of Siberia's vast natural resources.[42]

His Trans-Siberian grandiloquence notwithstanding, Witte's railway policy was more successful in western Russia, where he concentrated the bulk of railway investment. Yet even here only a quarter of all lines were double-tracked, and the investments yielded no rapid returns. By 1899, Russia's railways had run up debts of 70 million roubles, and no net profit was recorded until 1911. On the eve of the First World War, as Anthony Heywood's study in this collection shows, the concept of 'strategic railways' was still not fully developed. Rail transport remained the weakest link in Russia's military preparedness, especially when compared with Germany or Austria–Hungary. To some extent, then, Witte's railways 'were more expensive than the autocracy could afford and less extensive than it required'.[43]

The connection between economic and politico-military considerations, which the German and Russian cases in particular demonstrate, is crucial for a proper understanding of railways as an instrument in the tool kit of the Great Powers in the second half of the nineteenth and first half of the twentieth centuries. Industrialized Europe and North America extended their imperial influence in the half century before 1914 by building railways. The railways had already demonstrated their potential to transform industrialized economies, 'and once the trunk-lines had been completed at home with profits, railway mania spread abroad'.[44] In the process, the profit motive was fused with strategic calculations, and the Great Powers began to play out their rivalries and project their imperial strategies along railway tracks. Strategic railways became a tool of Great Power politics. *'Railpolitik'* became a corollary to *realpolitik* calculations. As the war correspondent George Lynch commented on the eve of the Russo-Japanese war, '[t]he path of Empire is along the railway track'.[45] Railway concessions and construction loans became means of 'pegging out claims', spheres of influence in overseas areas.

Historians and political scientists have advanced a range of interpretations of and theories on the connection between imperial expansion and economic motivations. Crucially, the two were fused together by the transport and technological revolutions of the mid-nineteenth century. The locomotive, the steamship and the telegraph shrank time and space within and between regions.[46] As steam power conquered the world, empires could be extended and profits be sought on a global scale. Railways were both instrument and generators of informal empire-building; they were a function of European expansion. Lord Salisbury's prognostication in 1871 was prescient: the less advanced countries 'are marked out by the destinies of the world for destruction.... The greater organisation and greater means of locomotion of the present day mark out the future to be one of great empires'.[47]

The potential power of the railways was demonstrated on a vast scale in the era of transcontinental lines.[48] Their construction was followed by colonial partitions. The superstructure of the Raj was bolted onto India's extensive railway network. The northwestern frontier, in turn, was defended by means of a series of strategic railways against the threat posed by Russian railways coming down from the Caspian Sea or Tashkent towards the Afghan and Persian frontiers.[49] As the chapters by John Fisher and Keith Neilson in this volume show, imperial states-man like Lord Curzon were acutely aware of the railways' potential value for the defence of British imperial interests in India and Central Asia. Delimiting railway spheres of influences proved a useful, if unwieldy, diplomatic means of managing the often antagonistic relations between these two Asiatic Powers.[50]

Lines connecting the central European capitals with Constantinople dissected the Balkans peninsula and raised the spectre of partition there. The first projects here commenced in the late 1860s with Baron de Hirsch's Oriental Railway.[51] Given the potential for Great Power clashes in this sensitive region, the later project of the Berlin–Constantinople–Baghdad Railway became a major source of tension in relations between Germany, Britain and Russia, while Austro-Hungarian schemes for a line linking Bosnia with the Salonica railway caused frictions between Vienna and St Petersburg, as Roy Bridge's study here shows.[52] Thus, the 'Great Game' in Asia or increased rivalries in the Balkans and the Near East were projected along steel tracks that connected imperial expansion in the geostrategic periphery of Europe with calculations of national defence in Europe.

Transcontinental routes were not confined to the East. In tropical Africa, too, projects were designed to connect the supposedly rich mineral reserves of central Africa with the seaports or to link the great lakes and rivers by rail so as to monopolise the anticipated trade of the unknown hinterland. Such expectations gave rise to Cecil Rhodes' dream of a Cape–Cairo line or French projects for a line connecting the North African colonies with Lake Chad. In general, the risks for private enterprise were too great in such African ventures, and the strategic imperatives usually not strong enough, so that these projects never left the drawing board. One notable exception, however, was the British Uganda Railway, the one truly strategic railway project in tropical Africa. Control over the Uganda protectorate and the railways there was an integral part of British efforts to shield the Upper Nile Valley against the designs of other powers in order to keep British rule in Egypt on a firm footing.[53]

In this process of imperial extension, governments tended to harness private railway capital to the needs of imperial strategy. Conscripting, in Lord Salisbury's phrase, 'patriotic capitalists' was preferable to doling out imperial subsidies.[54]

If the locomotive was an engine of imperial expansion, railways were also sources of imperial rivalries. Above all they had significant territorial implications: the construction of a line required the political backing of the host government; territorial concessions with financial guarantees were then needed to exclude competing lines by other foreign powers so as to ensure future profits and thereby attract the necessary longer-term investments. This dynamic gave rise to a distinct type of 'railway imperialism', adding a new dimension to overseas expansion and projecting it on a vast canvas.[55] Railway lines created forms of informal imperial influence in pre-industrial societies. In most cases this gave a foreign power a monopoly position, though in 1880s Siam, for instance, Belgian, British, French and German bidders were competing against each other for state railway contracts.[56] Indigenous élites fully appreciated that, in the absence of railways, their countries would remain economically backward and could not be made subject to modern administration. Also, as Martin Thomas' examination of the problems surrounding the Hijaz railway in the 1920s shows, railway projects were not merely tools of foreign imperial extension, but also significant in contests for supremacy between rival regional élites or dynasties. Yet, introducing technology was expensive, and fraught with risks too large for local capitalists to undertake rail projects.[57] As Russia's railway development had shown, railways rarely produced a profit until well after the lines were completed. As a result the governments of the Balkan states, Turkey or China, for example, became increasingly dependent on foreign loans, while in the Argentine politics became to a large extent 'railway politics'.[58]

For European financiers and the governments of railway-building countries alike, railways were a symbol of industrial prowess and progress. But the railways also carried the hopes of many European liberals for political progress. In 1837 the satirical writer and liberal journalist Ludwig Börne pointed to the 'immense political consequences (of the railway). It will break the neck of all despotism, and wars will become completely impossible'.[59] Liberal optimism had got the better of a realistic appreciation of the military potential of the locomotive. That potential was first demonstrated during the politically disturbed 1840s. When revolutions swept through continental Europe in the spring of 1848, many revolutionaries arrived at Berlin by train, and when in the following year an armed revolutionary insurgency took place in the southwestern German state of Baden, a railway game of 'cat-and-mouse' ensued, as the commander of the Prussian troops observed: 'The insurgents disperse into forests and mountains, the unreliable Baden troops are put on trains, and so also evade persecution. The insurgents are in possession of 44 locomotives and 480 wagons. This type of warfare will end only when we have taken possession of the whole railway line'. In the same year Russia moved 30,000 troops by rail to Hungary to quash the revolutionary movement there, so saving her conservative ally Austria from collapse.[60]

Railways continued to demonstrate their military value. In October 1850, during the Austro-Prussian 'Olmütz crisis', the Austrians mobilized and concentrated their forces in Bohemia. In 26 days, they moved 75,000 men, 8,000 horses, 1,800 artillery pieces and carriages, and 4,000 tons of supplies via a single track line from Hungary and Vienna to the Silesian frontier. This ostentatious demonstration of Vienna's resolve forced the Prussians to disengage. It also marked the birth of modern military transport and logistics.[61] During the Crimean War, a makeshift line was constructed by the firm of Peto, Brassey & Betts between the harbour at Balaclava and the main siege encampments at Sevastapol. At its peak it transported some 700 tons per diem. It proved vital in the allied logistics effort, bringing up heavy siege equipment, but acting also as the first ever hospital train.[62] In 1859, during the Franco-Sardinian war with Austria, the Paris–Lyons–Méditerranée (PLM) railway company helped the French to gain an early numerical advantage over the Austrians in northern Italy. In the course of 86 days the PLM transported 604,000 troops and 129,000 horses to the theatre of war, though in the absence of proper coordination the troops were often without their full equipment.[63]

It was in the 1860s that the full potential of the railways was grasped by military planners. The key experience was the American Civil War, the first proper railway war. Railways gave the Union army a significant logistical edge over the Confederate forces, and Union generals used railways as strategic and tactical tools. The railways also ensured that this conflict became a truly continental one, for without them the war would have been confined to the Eastern seaboard. Northern victory was based on an extensive rail network and an ability to harness greater industrial power and logistics skills available within the railways to create an integrated supplies and construction service. In 1860, the Union's network extended to some 21,978 miles, the South's to a mere 9,010 miles, and most of that was disjointed, with several different gauges in use, and with no sufficient or skilled labour force to operate it. As a result of such shortages, much of the Confederacy's tracks, engines and rolling stock were cannibalized to maintain a skeleton network. The fact that only 19 out of a total 470 locomotives produced in the United States in 1860 were built in Southern workshops is an indication of the Confederacy's industrial inferiority.[64]

An imbalance in resources alone did not readily translate into military superiority. Material resources, transport and logistics still needed to be integrated into strategy and tactics. Yet, the railways did allow the North to mobilize her greater economic and manpower reserves more speedily and direct them more efficiently towards the battle zones. From the outset, railways played a major role in particular battles. During the early stages of the conflict the Baltimore & Ohio Railroad Company saved an almost defenceless Washington, DC, against advancing Confederate columns. Ironically, it was the Confederate General Joseph E. Johnston who first made use of railways, moving some 6,000 men by the Manassas Gap Railroad on the eve of the first Battle of Bull Run in July 1861. It was a sign of things to come.[65] Within eighteen months of the outbreak of the war, the Union government had reorganized the existing railway network on an integrated war-footing. Conversely, the failure of Federal troops in April 1862 to destroy the Confederate rail link between Atlanta, GA, and Chattanooga, TN – the famous 'Great Chattanooga Locomotive Chase' – undoubtedly prolonged the South's ability to sustain its war effort. The Union general Grenville Dodge was the former chief engineer of the Union Pacific and one of America's great railway builders. By June 1862 he was writing to his wife: 'I am at my old job again – railroading.'[66] Thomas A. Scott, Assistant Secretary of War, used his former professional experience as superintendent of the Pennsylvania Railroad Company to form an army railway corps. Another railway man, Daniel C. McCallum, general superintendent of the Erie Railroad Company, took charge of the Northern railways for much of the conflict, and turned them into an integrated, efficient, mostly double-tracked and fully standardized network – before the war there had been no standard gauge or fuelling systems. McCallum's US Military Railroads, a branch of the War Department, possessed 400 engines, 6,000 carriages, and a work force of 17,000. It also had a reputation for civil-engineering excellence, most famously by building a 400 ft long bridge high above the Potomac creek within less than 40 hours, a feat which allowed for a line to be carried through directly to George Gordon Meade's army at Gettysburg.

The Union generals William T. Sherman and Ulysses S. Grant made full use of their rail superiority. It enabled them, in July 1863, to transport 10,000 men in four days from central Kentucky to Vicksburg, itself an important Confederate railway junction. In the summer of 1864, the Chattanooga line, now in Union hands, supported Sherman's Atlanta campaign in the rear of the Confederate army.[67] Sherman's destruction of Southern railway installations at this stage of the war robbed the bulk of the Confederate forces under General Robert E. Lee of secure supplies. In the end, it was the greater skills of the Union forces in making strategic use of railways that led to the Confederate surrender at Appomattox in April 1865.

If the American Civil War was a first demonstration of the military capabilities of the locomotive, it was the Prussian wars of 1866 and 1870 that made the European Great Powers take note of railway warfare. The use of the railways by the Prussian army has become especially associated with the name of Field Marshal Helmuth von Moltke, chief of the Prussian general staff after 1857, even though Moltke only gradually came to appreciate the strategic value of the railways. Moltke had that Napoleonic obsession with time and speed. He hoped to shape the still largely privately operated Prussian railway network to suit the country's military needs.[68] The use of railways would expedite mobilization and deployment of the army, and so optimise Prussia's chances of success. For Moltke, railways were the great facilitator, allowing for the resort to armed force where previously this would have been unrealistic. Prior to the Austro-Prussian War of 1866, he had identified Austria's inferior rail network as her main weakness. Moltke had five railway lines at his disposal to concentrate his forces along the Saxon and Bohemian frontiers. The Austrian commander, Field Marshal Ludwig Ritter von Benedek, by contrast, had only one line available to deploy his main force in Bohemia: 'We shall concentrate within three weeks all our forces, the enemy his in six weeks.'[69] The availability of several lines also allowed Moltke to disperse his troops and concentrate them in three separate army groups instead of one large, and therefore less mobile force. To an extent Moltke was forced to do so, as Prussia mobilized after the Austrians. Timing and coordination were paramount, not least because there was the real possibility of a French intervention in the conflict. The Prussian war plan envisaged an *Eisenbahnaufmarsch* along the five railway lines as axes of advance. This entailed the close coordination of railway timetables to allow the forces to advance separately before concentrating at a specified point in close proximity to the enemy's forces. The railway lines allocated to each army corps during the *Aufmarsch* phase processed between eight and twelve trains per diem; the concentration of troops was completed within eight days. All in all, 197,000 men, 55,000 horses, and 5,300 vehicles of all kinds were moved in 21 days. The mobilization was not flawless. The ability of the railheads to receive and process troops and supplies had been underestimated. As a result, traffic on the five lines was severely congested and supply lines were stretched.[70] Nevertheless, Moltke was able to combine his three armies at the crucial moment, giving him an overwhelming force which achieved victory at Königgrätz/Sadowa.[71]

The 1870 war with France has often been described as the definitive event in rail warfare. The success of the highly trained and specialized Prussian general staff – Moltke's 'demi-gods' – in speedily mobilizing the troops and transporting them to the front created a legend, the 'railway myth', as Dennis Showalter demonstrates.[72] Greater centralization of the general staff meant that the Prusso-German armies were able to complete the *Aufmarsch* of 480,000 troops in the Rhineland in three weeks via six lines. Mobilization took place in one continuous phase from 15 July 1870. Rail concentration began on the eighth day of mobilization, and on 3 August, the nineteenth day of mobilization, the main forces were assembled and ready to move.

If the German mobilization was speedier and more efficient, the French had the better rail network. The French railways were better geared towards war. There was a fuller integration of timetables; the lines were mostly double-track, and had more rolling stock and faster trains. What logistical advantages could be derived from this were lost through the dispersal of the army. The roots of France's defeat were political rather than military. Fear of domestic unrest had persuaded Napoleon III to garrison regiments far away from their recruiting areas lest they be infected by local discontent. Mobilization, therefore, involved a cumbersome double journey to the regional depots and then back to the prescribed areas of concentration. A large of body of troops was thus on the move on the railways, which were not properly under the control of the army's *Intendance*. Overstretch of the railway system was the result, congesting lines and disrupting supplies.[73] A good knowledge of the French railways, moreover, allowed Moltke correctly to anticipate the enemy war plans. On 4 August, with German concentration nearly completed, the French had not yet fully mobilized. When on 6 August 1870, the twenty-third day of mobilization, the French army went into its first battles at the Spichern Heights and at Fröschweiler, it had 270,000 men under arms. The Germans had by then mobilized 462,000 troops. Half the French reserves had not yet been mobilized, and most regiments lacked supplies and vital pieces of equipment.[74]

France had been goaded into a war for which she was not prepared. Moltke's speedy and relatively smooth *Aufmarsch* undermined what plans the French generals had devised. Having lost the initiative right at the opening of the war, they never regained it, and were forced into fighting a series of defensive and disjointed battles. Still, for all Moltke's emphasis on the railways, once the trains had disgorged their loads onto the battlefields, there was no more role for them. There was no proper transport and logistics coordination in the German army.[75]

The Franco-German War had demonstrated the potential edge railways could give army commanders. Warfare had become rail warfare. This had wider ramifications for Great Power strategies, not least in that it reduced the strategic advantages Great Britain had previously enjoyed as a result of her naval supremacy.[76] The 1870 war had also underlined the need for the specialized skills involved in harnessing the railways to military needs. It was a lesson Russian generals had failed to learn. In the 1877 Russo-Turkish War, they found the incompatibility of the narrower gauge of the winding Turkish railway lines in the Balkans with the Russian broad gauge an almost insuperable obstacle. Ten weeks of loading and unloading trains slowed down the Russian columns, overstretched their supply lines, and contributed to Russia's military and financial exhaustion at the end of 1877, a circumstance which forced her to yield to international diplomatic pressure and give up most of the territorial gains made during the war.[77]

Railways played a central part in some of Britain's colonial campaigns at the end of the nineteenth century. Field Marshal Sir Horatio (later Earl) Kitchener, aided by his chief engineer Lieutenant Percy Girouard, who had been trained on the Canadian Pacific Railway, re-conquered the Sudan in 1896–9 by building railway lines and moving troops and supplies by steamboat on the River Nile.[78] In the Boer War, railways were similarly key to the pursuit of dispersed Boer forces and to transporting supplies for the British army in the *veldt*. However, the British commander, Field Marshal Earl Roberts, never fully understood the importance of the railways, and the single-track, narrow gauge line in the Orange Free State was repeatedly sabotaged by Boer commandoes.[79]

Both the importance and the limitations of the railways were demonstrated in the Russo-Japanese War in 1904. In an attempt to apply the presumed lessons of the German successes in 1866 and 1870, Russian generals commandeered all the trains on the Trans-Siberian railway. Yet, without any prior planned coordination this merely served to restrict the mobilization of the Russian army. The railways had developed their own strategic logic. Applying this logic required managerial skills and industrial discipline of which the autocratic regime was incapable. To compound matters, 5,000 miles of the line were still only single track, and there were two significant gaps in the line. It took the Russian troops six weeks to reach the front, where Russia's problems were exacerbated by Japanese disruption of the existing Far Eastern lines.[80]

If the Russian generals had failed to grasp the need for proper training and planning as a prerequisite for the strategic use of railways in war-time, the German army high command ignored the railways' inflexibility in 1914.[81] As Dennis Showalter argues here, in German military thinking after 1871 railways 'became...the touchstone of military effectiveness'. The elder Moltke's successors had lost nothing of their illustrious predecessor's obsession with speed. Field

Marshal Count Alfred von Schlieffen came to regard railways as crucial. State secrets, he noted, could be extrapolated from a railway map: 'In the age of railways the *Aufmarsch* of every army is conditioned and shaped by those tracks of steel.'[82] In his last official memorandum of December 1905, outlining a possible strategy for a two-front war, which would later become known as the 'Schlieffen Plan', he envisaged an arc-like sweeping movement of the German right wing through the Low Countries. This would allow the advancing columns to use especially Belgium's dense rail network as a connection between the German and French systems, whilst avoiding protracted siege warfare along the heavily fortified Franco-German border. It was, thus, in Gerhard Ritter's trenchant criticism, 'for technical reasons due to the railways' that the whole breadth of neutral Belgium had to be crossed in the event of a war with France.[83] While there is evidence to suggest that the December 1905 memorandum was not so much an operational 'plan' as an analysis of a given strategic problem,[84] the principal parameters of Schlieffen's recommendations were not modified, even though the Great General Staff kept revising it every year. Indeed, when at the end of March of each year the mobilization plan was finalized, railway considerations remained paramount. As Wilhelm Groener, head of the railway department and one of the keenest intellects on the staff (and also one of Schlieffen's most ardent disciples), later reflected, the German railway corps was to move ahead of the mass of the German army to take possession of and to make useable the enemy's rail system. What Schlieffen envisaged was not so much a 'Super-Cannae' as a perfected Sedan, moving over one million troops via a sophisticated, modern and closely integrated rail system.[85]

Such considerations imposed their own logic on German crisis diplomacy in 1914. Under the Schlieffen 'Plan' mobilization had become deployment. There was no longer an interval between the two; there were no more opportunities, as there had been in previous decades, for diplomacy to launch a last-minute effort to avert war. Thus, when on 1 August 1914, Kaiser Wilhelm II thought he had secured British neutrality in the forthcoming war, provided Belgian neutrality was observed by Germany, his euphoria was dashed by the chief of staff, the elder Moltke's nephew. The war plans allowed for no last minute alterations; success depended entirely on speedy mobilization; stopping mobilization meant losing time, and this would reduce what chances of success there were. Even though Moltke and Groener were doubtful about aspects of the 'plan', railway time-tables had come to dominate strategic thinking and political decision-making.[86] Political considerations apart, it was the potential capacity of the railways for efficient mass transport that undermined the 'plan'. While seven German armies (some 1.6 million men) could be moved to the concentration area, once the troops moved away from the railheads, they could no longer be supplied by rail. Thus, the more men were moved to the front, the slower their advance through Belgium would become.[87]

Once the fronts had stabilized and the opposing armies settled down to a war of attrition, the immense industrial and logistics infrastructure in their rear was crucial for the continuation of the war. The battle zones in the West covered an area with the densest rail network in Europe. Both sides laid hundreds of miles of additional standard and narrow gauge lines to reinforce the strength of defensive positions. In the end, the gradual wearing out of the German rail system contributed to the German collapse in 1918.[88] Given the importance that had been attached to railways at the outbreak of the war, it was perhaps appropriate that the armistice of November 1918 was signed in a railway carriage.

August 1914 was the last time that railways played a major part in the mobilization for war, but not in strategic thinking. As Keith Neilson and Greg Kennedy show, railways remained a significant matter for British imperial defence in the Middle East until the 1930s, while the Chinese Eastern Railway (CER) was viewed by British defence planners as a barometer for measuring the stability of Soviet–Japanese relations in East Asia. Still, at the outbreak of the Second World War road transport had become the principal vehicle of mobilization and concentration.[89] Germany's lightening successes in 1940, however, had a pertinent epilogue. The signature of the 1918 armistice had been a symbol of Germany's military humiliation. To wipe it out, Adolf Hitler insisted that the French surrender was signed in the same carriage and on the same spot at Compiègne. The railway carriage itself was then transported to Germany, and stored in a tunnel in the hillsides of Thuringia. So powerful was its symbolic value that a special detachment of the SS blew it up in April 1945, shortly before the arrival of US troops in the area. Never again should Germany be forced to submit to another surrender in the same carriage.

Although railways played no significant role at the outbreak of the war, the railway network of the Axis Powers was nevertheless vital for their war efforts, and if the Allies had targeted more of their air power on destroying that network the German war machinery might well have ground to a halt earlier. As it was, as Neville Wylie demonstrates, Swiss willingness to let German trains pass through Switzerland's Alpine passes and tunnels allowed the *Wehrmacht* to continue fighting in northern Italy until April 1945, thereby creating unique problems as well as opportunities for the government in Berne. More poignantly, the German-controlled rail network of central and Eastern Europe was the key to the lethal efficiency of the Holocaust.[90]

With the end of the war, the era of rail warfare also came to an end – a point forcefully underscored by the first East–West stand-off in the early Cold War. The Soviet blockade of West Berlin severed all rail links between the former German capital and the Western zones of occupation. The Western response, the 'Berlin airlift', demonstrated that railways were no longer indispensable. For nearly a century railways had been a central part of the infrastructure of empire and a vital tool of modern warfare. In both these roles railways developed their own technical and politico-strategic logic which imposed itself on international politics. The 'path of empire' may now no longer run along the railway track, but the railways' impact on Great Power politics and strategy holds important lessons for the impact of more recent technologies on the logistical and strategic underpinnings of contemporary international relations.

Notes

1 S.E. Ambrose, *Nothing Like It in the World: The Men Who Built the Transcontinental Railroad, 1863–1869* (New York, 2000), p. 21.

2 M. Weber, *Wirtschaftsgeschichte: Abriss der universalen Sozial- und Wirtschaftsgeschichte*, ed. S. Hellmann and M. Palyi (Munich and Leipzig, 1925), p. 255.

3 R.W. Fogel, *Railways and American Economic Growth: Essays in Interpretative History* (Baltimore, MD, 1964).

4 E.J. Hobsbawm's argument that the railway 'boom' of the 1840s solved 'the crisis of the first phase of British capitalism' is now largely regarded as something of an over-statement, cf. E.J. Hobsbawm *Industry and Empire: From 1750 to the Present Day* (Harmondsworth, repr. 1977 (pb)), p. 114.

5 A.G. Gayer, W.W. Rostow and A.J. Schwartz, *The Growth and Fluctuation of the British Economy, 1790–1850* (2 vols, Oxford, 1953), vol. i, pp. 304–18; also R.A. Church, *The Great Victorian Boom, 1850–1873* (London, 1975), pp. 30–4.

6 F. Crouzet, *The Victorian Economy* (London, repr. 1991), pp. 285 and 299–301; G.R. Hawkes, *Railways and Economic Growth in England and Wales, 1840–1870* (Oxford, 1970), p. 205; L. Girard, 'Transport', in H.J. Habakkuk and M. Postan (eds), *The Cambridge Economic History of Europe*, vol. vi/1 (Cambridge, 1966), tab. 41, p. 228.

7 As quoted in Girard, ibid., p. 235; S.G. Checkland, *The Rise of Industrial Society in England, 1815–1885* (London, 1964), pp. 36–7 and 139; cf. E. Witte and J. Craeybeckx, *La Belgique politique de 1830 à nos jours: Les tensions d'une démocratie bourgeois* (Brussels, 1987), pp. 54–6.

8 B.R. Mitchell and P. Deane, *Abstracts of British Historical Statistics* (Cambridge, 1962), pp. 225–6.

9 The number of MPs with railway interests were in 1847: 86, 1857: 98, 1859: 111, 1865: 160, cf. J.A. Thomas, *The House of Commons, 1832–1901: A Study of Its Economic and Functional Character* (Cardiff, 1939), pp. 7–9.

10 M. Bentley, *Lord Salisbury's World: Conservative Environments in Late Victorian Britain* (Cambridge, 2001), pp. 106–7; J.V. Beckett, *The Aristocracy of England, 1660–1914* (Oxford: Blackwell, 1986), pp. 238–61.

11 Checkland, *Rise of Industrial Society*, pp. 137–9.

12 *Dr Thorne* (London, 1947 [originally published 1858]), pp. 160–1; cf. A. Briggs, *Victorian Cities* (Harmondsworth, 1968 (pb)), pp. 241–76; S. Pollard, 'Barrow-in-Furness and the Seventh Duke of Devonshire', *Economic History Review*, 2nd ser., vol. viii, no. 3 (1955), p. 214; O.S. Nock, *The Great Western Railway in the Nineteenth Century* (London, repr. 1972), pp. 48–59.

13 Briggs, *Victorian Cities*, pp. 29 and 357; cf. also D. Read, *The English Provinces, c. 1760–1960: A Study in Influence* (London, 1964), pp. 244–6.

14 *Treitschke's History of Germany in the Nineteenth Century*, ed. W.H. Dawson (7 vols, London, 1919), vol. vii, p. 277.

15 Schuckmann and Motz to Prussian Ministry of Foreign Affairs, 22 May 1828, in W. von Eisenhart–Rothe and A. Ritthaler (eds), *Vorgeschichte und Begründung des Deutschen Zollvereins, 1815–1834: Akten des Deutschen Bundes und der europäischen Mächte* (3 vols, Berlin, 1934), vol. iii, no. 568.

16 The Prussian railways constituted over half the German network; figures from H.-U. Wehler, *Deutsche Gesellschaftsgeschichte, 1700–1949* (4 vols, Munich: C.H. Beck, 1987–2003), vol. ii, p. 615, and vol. iii, pp. 69–70; and *Statistisches Jahrbuch für das Deutsche Reich 1913* (Berlin, 1913), p. 120.

17 For statistical details, cf. Wehler, ibid., vol. ii, pp. 623–4; also W. Sombart, *Die deutsche Volkswirtschaft im Neunzehnten Jahrhundert* (Berlin, 1903), pp. 277–87; R.H. Tilly, 'Capital Formation in Germany in the Nineteenth Century', in P. Mathias and M.M. Postan (eds), *The Cambridge Economic History of Europe*, vol. vii/1 (Cambridge, 1978), tab. 98, p. 416.

18 Railway capital thereafter steadily declined, but still amounted to 7.9 per cent of gross capital formation in 1913; cf. Wehler, *Gesellschaftsgeschichte*, vol. iii, tables 50 and 74, pp. 43 and 582; and Tilly, 'Capital Formation', tab. 100, p. 418.

19 J. Borchart, *Der europäische Eisenbahnkönig Bethel Henry Strousberg* (Munich, 1991), and M. Ohlsen, *Der Eisenbahnkönig Bethel Henry Strousberg: Eine preussische Gründerkarriere* ([East] Berlin, 1988).

20 This is comprehensively treated in D.E. Showalter, *Railroads and Rifles: Soldiers, Technology and the Unification of Germany* (Hamden, CT, 1975).

21 W.O. Henderson, 'Die Rolle Preussens bei der wirtschaflichen Einigung Deutschlands', in M. Schlenke (ed.), *Preussen: Politik, Kultur, Gesellschaft* (Reinbek bei Hamburg, 1983), pp. 216–17.

22 A. Bergengrün, *Staatsminister August von der Heydt* (Leipzig, 1908), pp. 163–92, 165–9 and 326–38.

23 H. Böhme, *Deutschlands Weg zur Grossmacht: Studien zum Verhältnis von Wirtschaft und Staat während der Reichsgründungszeit, 1848–1881* (Cologne, 3rd ed. 1974), pp. 380–2.

24 F. Stern, *Gold and Iron: Bismarck, Bleichröder and the Building of the German Empire* (London, 1977), pp. 210–17; A. Mitchell, *The Great Train Race: Railways and the Franco-German Rivalry, 1815–1914* (New York, 2000), pp. 121–7.

25 G.A. Ritter and J. Kocka (eds), *Deutsche Sozialgeschichte: Dokumente und Skizzen*, vol. ii, *1870–1914* (Munich, 1974), pp. 91–2. In 1850, 54.7 out of a total 1,843.7 miles in Prussia were under government control; by 1910, only 6 per cent (mostly smaller branchlines) were privately owned.

26 At the end of 1911 there were some 713,000 railway employees in Prussia, a significant increase since 1899, when there were 520,000, cf. *Statistisches Jahrbuch 1913*, p. 121; *Statistisches Jahrbuch für das Deutsche Reich 1901* (Berlin, 1901), p. 44.

27 As quoted in W.E. Mosse, *An Economic History of Russia, 1856–1914* (London, 1996 (pb)), p. 19.

28 *Ukase*, 26 Jan. 1857, as quoted in T.H. Von Laue, *Sergei Witte and the Industrialization of Russia* (New York, 1969 (pb)), pp. 6–7; M.C. Kaser, 'Russian Entrepreneurship', in Mathias and Postan (eds), *Cambridge Economic History*, vol. vii/2, pp. 461–3.

29 Earlier railway loans had been issued by Mendelssohn & Bleichröder and by Barings, cf. P. Ziegler, *The Sixth Great Power: Barings, 1762–1929* (London, 1988), pp. 172–6.

30 O. Crisp, *Studies in the Russian Economy before 1914* (New York, 1976), pp. 22–3.

31 R. Portal, 'The Industrialization of Russia', in Habakkuk and Postan (eds), *Cambridge Economic History*, vol. vi/2, p. 813.

32 Crisp, *Studies*, p. 17; Mosse, *Economic History*, p. 60.

33 Kaser, 'Entrepreneurship', pp. 463–5.

34 Mosse, *Economic History*, p. 90; Laue, *Sergei Witte*, pp. 42–6.

35 Reutern opposed war as financially ruinous, cf. B. Jelavich, *Russia's Balkan Entanglements, 1806–1914* (Cambridge, repr. 1992), pp. 172–3; J.W. Kipp, 'Strategic Railroads and the Dilemmas of Modernization', in D. Schimmelpenninck van der Oye and B.W. Menning (eds), *Reforming the Tsar's Army: Military Innovation in Imperial Russia from Peter the Great to the Revolution* (Washington, DC, and Cambridge, 2004), pp. 98–9.

36 Figures from C. Trebilcock, *The Industrialization of the Continental Powers, 1780–1914* (London, repr. 1994), pp. 223 and 235. For details on Bunge and Vishnegradsky, cf. ibid., pp. 226–31; also Kaser, 'Entrepreneurship', pp. 464–5.

37 Crisp, *Studies*, 24–5; Mosse, *Economic History*, p. 90; Trebilcock, *Industrialization*, pp. 231–6.

38 Portal, 'Industrialization', pp. 818–20.

39 Here especially Crisp, *Studies*, chs. 6 and 7; D.W. Spring, 'Russia and the Franco-Russian Alliance, 1905–1914: Dependence or Interdependence?', *Slavonic and East European Review*, vol. lxvi, no. 4 (1988), pp. 564–92; P. Gatrell, *Government, Industry and Rearmanent in Russia, 1906–1914: The Last Argument of Tsarism* (Cambridge, 1994), pp. 313–17.

18   *Keith Neilson and T.G. Otte*

40 Memo. Witte, 6 Nov. 1892, as quoted in B.A. Romanov, *Russia in Manchuria, 1892–1906* (New York, repr. 1974), p. 2.
41 Trebilcock, *Industrialization*, p. 234; also Mosse, *Economic History*, pp. 105–6.
42 S.G. Marks, *Road to Power: The Trans-Siberian Railroad and the Colonization of Asian Russia, 1850–1917* (London, 1991).
43 Trebilcock, *Industrialization*, p. 235. Useful comparative data can be gleaned from R. Pipes, *The Russian Revolution, 1899–1919* (London, 1992 (pb)), pp. 206–7.
44 R.E. Robinson, 'Introduction', in C.B. Davis and K.E. Wilburn Jr. (eds), *Railway Imperialism* (Westport, CT, 1991), p. 1.
45 G. Lynch, *The Path of Empire* (London, 1903), p. xv.
46 D.R. Headrick, 'The Tools of Imperialism: Technology and the Expansion of European Colonial Empires in the Nineteenth Century', *Journal of Modern History*, vol. li, no. 2 (1979), pp. 231–63.
47 Salisbury speech in the House of Lords, 6 Mar. 1871, *The Times* (7 Mar. 1871).
48 D.W. Roman, 'Railway Imperialism in Canada, 1847–1865', in Davis and Wilburn (eds), *Railway Imperialism*, pp. 7–20. At the close of 1907, there were 601,808 miles of railway lines in service in the world. The mileages per continent were as follows: Europe, 199,371; America, 309,974 (of these 236,452 were in the United States); Asia, 56,181 (of these 29,893 were in British India and 8,373 in Russia beyond the Urals); Africa, 18,516; and Australia, 17,766, cf. R. Morris, 'Railways: General Statistics', *Encyclopaedia Britannica* (29 vols, New York, 11th ed. 1910–11), vol. xxii, pp. 822–4.
49 J.S. Cotton, 'Industrial and Economic Conditions', in A.J. Herbertson and O.J.R. Howarth (eds), *The Oxford Survey of the British Empire: Asia* (Oxford, 1914), pp. 167–9; also, P.J. Cain and A.J. Hopkins, *British Imperialism: Innovation and Expansion, 1688–1914* (London, 1993), pp. 334–8.
50 K. Neilson, *Britain and the Last Tsar: British Policy towards Russia, 1895–1917* (Oxford, 1995), pp. 199–203 and 279–88; D.W. Spring, 'The Trans-Persian Railway Project and Anglo-Russian Relations, 1909–1914', *Slavonic and East European Review*, vol. liv, no. 1 (1976), pp. 60–82.
51 K. Grunwald, *Türkenhirsch: A Study of Baron Maurice de Hirsch, Entrepreneur and Philanthropist* (Jerusalem, 1966), pp. 28–62; K.E. Born, *International Banking in the 19th and 20th Centuries* (Leamington Spa, 1987), pp. 44–5.
52 E.M. Earle's study remains the only comprehensive, though by now dated, examination of this politically important project, *Turkey, The Great Powers and the Baghdad Railway* (New York, 1923); P.M. Kennedy, *The Rise of the Anglo-German Antagonism, 1860–1914* (London, 1990 (pb)), pp. 262–6 and passim.
53 R.E. Robinson and J. Gallagher (with A. Denny), *Africa and the Victorians: The Official Mind of Imperialism* (London, 2nd ed. 1981), ch. 12; J. Darwin, 'Imperialism and the Victorians: The Dynamics of Territorial Expansion', *English Historical Review*, vol. cxii, no. 3 (1997), pp. 634–6.
54 Salisbury to Curzon, 30 May and 4 June 1898, Curzon Mss, British Library, Oriental and India Office Collection, Mss.Eur.F.111/1B; cf. D. McLean, 'Finance and "Informal Empire" before the First World War', *Economic History Review*, vol. xxix, no. 2 (1976), pp. 291–305.
55 Robinson, 'Introduction', p. 3.
56 N. Brailey, 'The Scramble for Concessions in 1880s Siam', *Modern Asian Studies*, vol. xxxiii, no. 3 (1999), here especially pp. 522–35.
57 For a case study, cf. D. Charlesworth, 'Rich Peasants and Poor Peasants in Late Nineteenth-Century Maharashtra', in C. Dewey and A.G. Hopkins (eds), *The Imperial Impact: Studies in the Economic History of Africa and India* (London, 1978), here pp. 105–8.
58 H. Feis, *Europe: The World's Banker, 1870–1914* (New York, repr. 1965 (pb)), pp. 293–310 and 342–60; R. Owen, *The Middle East in the World Economy, 1800–1914* (London, 1998), pp. 191–9; D.C.M. Platt, *Latin America and British Trade, 1860–1914* (London, 1972), pp. 65–72.

59 As quoted in W. Minaty (ed.), *Die Eisenbahn* (Frankfurt, 1984), p. 34.
60 Roon to wife, 1 July 1849, in A. von Roon, *Denkwürdigkeiten aus dem Leben des General-Feldmarschalls Kriegsministers Grafen von Roon: Sammlung von Briefen, Schriftstücken und Erinnerungen* (2 vols, Breslau, 1892), vol. i, p. 225; cf. I.W. Roberts, *Nicholas I and the Russian Intervention in Hungary* (New York, 1991).
61 J. Niemeyer, *Das österreichische Militärwesen im Umbruch: Untersuchungen zum Kriegsbild zwischen 1830 und 1866* (Osnabrück, 1979), p. 162; J. Angelow, *Von Wien nach Königgrätz: Die Sicherheitspolitik des Deutschen Bundes im europäischen Gleichgewicht, 1815–1866* (Munich, 1996), pp. 155–6.
62 T. Royle, *Crimea: The Great Crimean War, 1854–1856* (London, 1999 (pb)), p. 257.
63 C.W. Robinson *et al.*, *Warfare in the 19th Century* (London, 1914), pp. 139–40; D. Gates, *Warfare in the Nineteenth Century* (London, 2001), pp. 61–2.
64 Gates, *Warfare*, p. 123.
65 H. Hattaway, *Shades of Blue and Gray: An Introductory Military History of the Civil War* (Columbia, MO, 1997), pp. 48–50.
66 J.R. Perkins, *Trails, Rails and War: The Life of General G.M. Dodge* (Indianapolis, 1929), p. 123.
67 D. Evans, *Sherman's Horsemen: Union Cavalry Operations in the Atlanta Campaign* (Bloomington, IN, 1996).
68 Grosser Generalstab (ed.), *Moltkes Militärische Werke*, vol. iv/1, *Moltkes Kriegslehre: Die operativen Vorbereitungen zur Schlacht* (Berlin, 1911), pp. 204–58; M. Salewski, 'Moltke, Schlieffen und die Eisenbahn', in R.G. Foerster (ed.), *Generalfeldmarschall Moltke: Bedeutung und Wirkung* (Munich, 1991), pp. 90–4. For an excellent discussion of the wider context, cf. S. Förster, 'Helmuth von Moltke und das Problem des industrialisierten Volkskriegs im 19. Jahrhundert', ibid., pp. 103–15.
69 Moltke to Stosch, 24 Apr. 1866, Grosser Generalstab (ed.), *Moltkes Militärische Werke*, vol. i/2 (Berlin, 1896), pp. 150–1.
70 Showalter, *Railroads*, pp. 59–61; [S.] von Schlichting, *Moltke und Benedek: Eine Studie über Truppenführung* (Berlin, 1900), p. 4.
71 M. van Creveld, *Supplying War: Logistics from Wallenstein to Patton* (Cambridge, repr. 1991 (pb)), pp. 84–5; H. Blankenburg, *Der deutsche Krieg von 1866: Historisch, politisch und kriegswissenschaftlich dargestellt* (Leipzig, 1868), pp. 208–11.
72 For the trend towards specialization, cf. M. Messerschmidt, 'Die politische Geschichte der preussisch–deutschen Armee', in *Militärgeschichtliches Forschungsamt* (ed.), *Deutsche Militärgeshichte, 1648–1939* (6 vols, Munich, 1983 (pb)), vol. ii, pp. 323–5; also M. Howard, *The Franco-Prussian War: The German Invasion of France, 1870–1871* (London, 1962), pp. 61–2. For an instructive impression of the differences between 1866 and 1870, cf. Freiherr von Werthern, *General von Versen: Ein militärisches Zeit- und Lebensbild* (Berlin, 1898), pp. 87–8.
73 For a thorough analysis of the French mobilization and the role of the railways, cf. G. Wawro, *The Franco-Prussian War: The German Conquest of France in 1870–1871* (Cambridge, 2003), pp. 48–9; also A. Guérin, *La Folle Guerre de 1870* (Paris, 1970), pp. 74–6. The absurdity of the French dispositions was already noted by Friedrich Engels in the *Pall Mall Gazette* (29 July 1870), in idem, *Notes on the War: Sixty Articles Reprinted from the "Pall Mall Gazette,"* ed. F. Adler (Vienna, 1923), p. 1.
74 Howard, *Franco-German War*, pp. 42–3. For some of the intelligence aspects, cf. L. von Schlözer, *Generalfeldmarschall Freiherr von Loë: Ein militärisches Zeit– und Lebensbild* (Stuttgart, 1914), pp. 65–7; T. Krieg, *Constantin von Alvensleben, General der Infanterie: Ein militärisches Lebensbild* (Berlin, 1903), pp. 79–94.
75 For a critical examination, cf. Creveld, *Supplying War*, pp. 103–8.
76 [C. à C. Repington], *Imperial Strategy, by the Military Correspondent of "The Times"* (London, 1906), pp. 180–210; also 'Militair–Eisenbahnen 1876', in H. von Löbell (ed.), *Jahresberichte über die Veränderungen und Fortschritte im Militairwesen 1876* (Berlin, 1877), pp. 380–405; C.J. Bartlett, 'The Mid-Victorian Reappraisal of Naval

20   *Keith Neilson and T.G. Otte*

Policy', in K. Bourne and D.C. Watt (eds), *Studies in International History: Essays Presented to W. Norton Medlicott* (London, 1967), pp. 189–208.

77 [Repington], *Imperial Strategy*, p. 194; R.L. DiNardo, 'Russian Military Operations in 1877–78', in B.K. Kiraly and G. Stokes (eds), *Insurrections, Wars and the Eastern Crisis in the 1870s* (Boulder, CO, 1985), pp. 125–40.

78 C. Falls, 'The Reconquest of the Sudan, 1896–9', in B. Bond (ed.), *Victorian Military Campaigns* (London, repr. 1994), pp. 287–8.

79 E.M. Spiers, *The Late Victorian Army, 1868–1902* (Manchester, repr. 1999), p. 322.

80 There is as yet no full study of the transport services on both sides. Some useful insights may be gleaned from A. Kearsey, *A Study of the Strategy and Tactics of the Russo-Japanese War, 1904* (Aldershot, s.a. [c. 1919]), pp. 18 and 26–7: also B.W. Menning, *Bayonets before Bullets* (Bloomington, IN, 1992), pp. 152–99; D. Schimmelpenninck van der Oye, 'The Russo-Japanese War', in Kaplan and Higham (eds), *Military History*, pp. 183–201.

81 A. Bucholz, *Moltke, Schlieffen and Prussian War-Planning* (Providence, RI, 1991). pp. 232–4; S. Förster, 'Der deutsche Generalstab und die Illusion des kurzen Krieges, 1871–1914: Metakritik eines Mythos', *Militärgeschichtliche Mitteilungen*, no. 54 (1995), pp. 79–94.

82 A. von Schlieffen, 'Cannae (I)', *Vierteljahreshefte für Truppenführung und Heereskunde*, vol. vii, no. 1 (1910), p. 15.

83 G. Ritter, *The Schlieffen Plan: Critique of a Myth* (London: Oswald Wolff, 1958), p. 45.

84 T.M. Holmes, 'Classical Blitzkrieg: The Untimely Modernity of Schlieffen's Cannae Programme', *Journal of Military History*, vol. lxvii, no. 3 (2003), pp. 745–7; idem, 'The Real Thing: A Reply to Terence Zuber', *War in History*, vol. ix, no. 1 (2002), pp. 111–20; T. Zuber, 'The Schlieffen Plan Reconsidered', ibid., vol. vi, no. 2 (1999), pp. 262–305.

85 W. Groener, *Lebenserinnerungen: Jugend, Generalstab, Weltkrieg*, ed. F. Freiherr Hiller von Gaertringen (Göttingen, 1957), p. 73; also anon., 'Die Rolle der Eisenbahn in der modernen Kriegsührung', *Kriegstechnische Zeitschrift*, vol. x, no. 10 (1908), pp. 441–6.

86 D. Stevenson, 'War by Timetable? The Railway Race before 1914', *Past & Present* (1999).

87 Creveld, *Supplying War*, pp. 119–20. On the congestion on the railways cf. A. von Kluck, *Wanderjahre–Kriege–Gestalten* (Berlin, 1929), pp. 171–5.

88 D. Stevenson, *1914–1918: The History of the First World War* (London, 2004), pp. 182–3; Groener, *Lebenserinnerungen*, pp. 268–78 and 442; M. Kitchen, *The Silent Dictatorship: The Politics of the German High Command under Hindenburg and Ludendorff, 1916–1918* (London, 1976), pp. 249–51.

89 Brauchitsch, 'Aufmarschanweisung "Gelb"', 24 Feb. 1940, in H.-A. Jacobsen (ed.), *Dokumente zur Vorgeschichte des Westfeldzuges, 1939–40* (Göttingen, 1956), no. 19, pp. 64–8; for a detailed discussion, cf. K.A. Maier *et al.*, *Das Deutsche Reich und der zweite* Weltkrieg (8 vols, Stuttgart, 1979 et seq.), vol. ii, pp. 99–104 and 269–76.

90 G. Fleming, *Hitler and the Holocaust* (Oxford, 1986 (pb)), pp. 142–3. For a general discussion along popular lines, cf. J. Westwood, *Railways at War* (London, 1980), pp. 185–219.

2　Railroads, the Prussian army, and the German way of war in the nineteenth century

Dennis E. Showalter

From the Peace of Frankfurt in 1871 to the outbreak of the Great War, the German army in particular was generally accepted both at home and abroad as embodying a particular 'genius for war' in its modern, technological form. An increasing body of recent scholarship, however, suggests that technology, broadly defined, was incorporated into nineteenth-century Germany without significantly modifying its antirational, nostalgic aspects. In that context the army became an unstable synergy of retrograde and progressive elements. Feudalism, absolutism and authoritarianism were juxtaposed to an increasing rationalization of the details of war preparation and war fighting – a cognitive dissonance never resolved.[1] Antulio Echevarria asserts the 'regeneration and reaffirmation' in German military planning of an essentially irrational, heroic-vitalist 'warrior identity' that reflected 'despair' at confronting the demands of twentieth-century conflict.[2] Stig Foerster argues specifically that the German General Staff consciously plunged German into war in 1914 despite knowing it would not and could not be the short conflict that was the only kind of war the Second Reich stood a chance of winning.[3]

Railroads played a significant physical and psychological role in this development. After 1871 railways became not merely the key to military planning but the touchstone of military effectiveness. They were expected to compensate for diplomacy that made virtually certain Germany would face a two front war. They were expected to compensate for domestic policies that left Germany with an army smaller in proportion to its population than France, so exponentially weaker compared to its prospective enemies that war plans became increasingly risky. Concentration on improving railway effectiveness took precedence over considering developments in weapons systems, communications technology, even alternate means of transportation. General Staff officers measured their worth in terms of their ability to save minutes off train schedules.

The overall result was a pattern of foreshortening that virtually guaranteed escalation of any serious crisis into full-scale war. The German railways, originally regarded as enhancing flexibility, became the focal point of a doomsday machine that in 1914 would enmesh the rest of Europe in its timetables, and take it down the track to catastrophe. The purpose of this essay is to present the matrix of that development: the integration of rail transportation into Prussia's military system and the Prussian way of war.

The process involved five stages. From ad hoc beginnings during the revolutions of 1848, railroads became part of the army's plans for concentration in the 1850s, culminating in the mobilization of 1859. In 1866, they played a crucial role in buying time for a government unwilling to go to war until its hand was forced beyond denial. In 1870 railroads took a crucial step towards their eventual central position in the German doomsday machine, enabling the strategic concentration that underwrote Prussian operational plans for war against the French Empire. In that war railroads also demonstrated their capacities and limitations as a logistical tool, foreshadowing the gridlocks of August 1914. And finally, but by no means marginally, railroads were at the centre of an approach to partisan war that provided the matrix for two world wars' worth of atrocities which remain an ineradicable stain on what passes for German military honour.

I

Prussia's historic military culture shaped and reflected a state grand strategy based on deterring war by cultivating the ability to win wars quickly and decisively, then negotiating peace on specific, mutually acceptable, terms. Properly demonstrated, the combination of fighting power and diplomatic moderation was expected to prevent a defeated foe from trying conclusions a second time.[4]

The introduction of railroads into Germany in the 1830s offered possibilities of solving two fundamental obstacles confronting that approach. One was geographic: Prussia's three-sided exposure to France, Austria and Russia. Railways provided the ability to shuttle troops from one potential front to another. The second was institutional: Prussia's army after the reforms of the Napoleonic Era depended on mobilized reservists. Railroads offered a force multiplier, enabling citizen armies to be concentrated in roughly the same time frame as the professionalized forces of the other powers, structured for the purpose of making war from a standing start.

The limited carrying capacity of the early track systems sharply restricted their capacity to move other than token amounts of troops or material. As late as 1836 a pamphlet accurately demonstrated that a war-strength Prussian corps could cover in sixteen days' marching a distance that would require twenty days by rail.[5] But a General Staff that based increasing amounts of its everyday work on mathematical calculation and linear projections found no difficulty accepting the postulate that railway networks were only going to become denser and more extensive with the passage of time.

Not until 1849, however, were the military possibilities of German railroads put to a practical test. A major problem of German governments for over a year had been how to deploy forces large enough and reliable enough to overawe or suppress revolutionaries without running the risk of having the troops either trigger an outbreak by their presence, or be influenced by their potential enemies. Since the risings of 1849 were largely urban, troops could be moved from city to city without risk of ambushes or demolished tracks. They could be unloaded in areas held by government forces rather than go into action directly from the trains.

The nature of urban warfare limited the need for cavalry and artillery, and for elaborate logistic arrangements: the host government could supply rations.

The Saxon capital of Dresden was a centre of revolutionary activity and liberal activism, and the Prussian government offered assistance in any counter-insurgency operations. Massive public protest against the Saxon King's rejection of a German constitution led on May 3 to the organization of a Committee of Public Safety accompanied by large-scale rioting. Prussia promptly despatched a three-battalion task force. Its strength was not particularly impressive, but the troops arrived in Saxony by rail virtually overnight, and played a crucial role in destroying the uprising before it could organize coordinated resistance.[6]

Similar, larger task forces rode rails all over Germany in succeeding months. Most of a division was deployed in Schleswig–Holstein and Hamburg. Two provisional corps went south and carried the weight of suppressing revolution in Baden. A half-dozen battalions were stationed in Frankfurt after the National Assembly evacuated the city. Success against the German Revolution was achieved, however, at the price of completely disrupting the army's organization. In contrast to Austria before 1848 or the Kingdom of Italy after 1871, the Prussian army was not organized with preserving domestic stability as a primary focus. And as the flames of revolution faded to embers, a Prussian War Ministry desperately attempting to untangle and restore its orders of battle confronted a new, potentially far more serious crisis.

Growing friction between an assertive Prussia and a revived Austrian Empire determined to reassert its dominance north of the Inn River brought the major German powers to the brink of war. In May 1850 the Prussian army began concentrating troops in the south. One hundred seventy-five thousand men and 500 guns were under orders for Prussian Saxony and nearby points, and the War Ministry sought to move as many of them as possible by rail. The result was compounded confusion. Since no plans existed for systematic military use of the railways, responsibility was assumed by the Ministry of Commerce. Troop trains were fitted into regular schedules on an ad hoc basis, moved at seeming random along single-track lines from point to aimless point whose only common feature was the absence of food, water and latrine facilities.

Most of Prussia's active regiments had still not returned to their home districts, and stray detachments of reservists could be found at railway stations all over Prussia, sometimes seeking their parent units and sometimes hoping the affair would be settled by the time they reached them. It took two months to concentrate 60,000 men around Torgau – without much regard to where that force could move next, or whether it could eat once it arrived. An army corps was responsible for mobilizing over a thousand men in its logistics formations. The total peacetime cadre was two officers and one NCO! Depots fleshed out the army's trains by disposing of their castoffs: the slow-witted, the intractable, the incompetent. Small wonder that supply units gridlocked as wagons broke down, and horses died at the hands of men unaccustomed to caring for any animal larger than a house pet.[7]

Meanwhile Austria was preparing to deploy over a third of a million men, its own troops plus contingents from Bavaria and Wuerttemberg, on an arc from

Moravia through Bohemia into Saxony, and westward towards Hesse. Austrian operational planning depended heavily on railroads initially to secure interior lines of operation, then once the fighting started take the Prussians in the rear or 'do anything circumstances allow'.[8] Austrian supply systems and Austrian troop movements, while anything but flawless, also proved superior to their Prussian counterparts. The result was a compromise settlement, the Peace of Olmuetz – generally regarded in Prussia as an avoidable humiliation.[9]

In its aftermath Prussia's army, specifically its general staff, paid increasing attention to railroad technology as a force multiplier. The experience of 1850 demonstrated that complex machinery made its own laws. Railroads challenged fundamentally the vitalism that had been so important to the military reform movement at the turn of the century. Iron and steel were indifferent to *Bildung*. Appeals to patriotism and threats of punishment were useless in the face of hotboxes, broken axles or tracks that led nowhere operationally useful. And should technical difficulties be overcome, bringing the largest possible forces to the largest rail junctions nearest a potential threat merely postponed strategic and operational decisions. An army of a hundred thousand strong advancing on a common axis could not really march. Instead it inched cross-country, using every accessible track and cowpath to move the food and forage on which its effectiveness depended. Even paved roads were not intended to stand the kind of day-in, day-out battering delivered by artillery pieces and heavily loaded wagons.

These factors made calculation and preparation the keys to the successful utilization of railroads for military purposes. Based on its performances in 1849 and 1850, Prussia's army was unlikely to manage its mobilization and concentration successfully by applying the 'muddling through' (system D) of which France boasted. Prussia had nothing like France's cadres of experienced old soldiers who could improvise, make do, or go without. Indeed, part of the implied contract between the Prussian state and its conscript reservists involved providing boots that fit, uniforms that did not dissolve in the first rainstorm, and regular deliveries of reasonably edible food. Studies of the breakdowns of discipline in 1848–50 suggested strongly that specific problems of command and administration were more common catalytic events than any commitment to revolutionary ideals or hatred of the possessing classes. And while the General Staff's competences and capacities to overhaul the entire army were limited, it was in a position to improve its use of railroads for concentration, transport and supply.[10]

One legacy of the Napoleonic era had been an emphasis on 'genius' as an indispensable quality of generalship. Even in Prussia, where the retaming of Bellona had been such a high priority, mass-produced competence was not regarded as a complete substitute for great captains.[11] A certain randomness was an acceptable price for giving genius a chance to unfold – even when, like the proverbial second marriage, actual results too often indicated the triumph of hope over experience. Things began to change in 1857 when Helmuth von Moltke was appointed provisional Chief of the Prussian General Staff.

Moltke was particularly interested in railroads. an experience that confirmed his position that optimum utilization of this new means of transportation required long-term, large-scale planning. Apart from these professional considerations Moltke, like most new men in senior positions, wished to make a quick, sharp impact. Railways were a useful entering wedge – one, moreover, not directly challenging any other military or civilian bureau. In March 1858, the General Staff issued its first general policy statement on the use of railroads for large-scale troop movements. The autumn manoeuvre(s) of that year featured the movement of 16,000 men of V and VI Corps from the manoeuvre(s) ground to the base area around Liegnitz, in Silesia. Moltke had played a generally prominent role in the exercises, the first Chief of Staff to do so, acting as an umpire and spending enough quality 'face time' with William that the Regent confirmed his appointment as permanent after the manoeuvre(s).[12]

The manoeuvre(s) of 1858 also highlighted in Moltke's mind the need for continuous coordination among the Ministries of War, Interior and Commerce if railroads were to institutionalize their growing capacity to move men and material. That concept, however, was at significant variance with a long Prussian history of ministerial autonomy and collegial decision-making.[13] The normal pattern of cooperation involved specific coordination on particular issues. Moltke instead saw the General Staff as the potential, and the logical, vector of permanent administrative cooperation in this area – not least because it had surplus bureaucratic capacity. The General Staff's Second Section was in charge of evaluating Prussia's possible military involvement in southern Europe: Switzerland and Italy. Whatever may have been the contingencies forty years earlier, the prospects of direct Prussian commitment to either theatre were sufficiently remote that in 1859 the section was reconfigured, becoming responsible for mobilization planning and given a special department of railway affairs.

That reorganization followed Prussia's second mobilization of the decade. In 1859, as its confrontation with Piedmont escalated, Austria sought support in Berlin. The diplomatic prospects of serving as Austria's faithful second at the price of an autonomous sphere of influence north of the Main were balanced by advocates of rejecting participation in what seemed to critics a fiasco with its roots in Vienna. To complicate matters further, Prussian Prince Regent William possessed a conscience better able to generate questions than to resolve them. He sympathized in principle with Austria, but was willing neither to deliver that state from its own behaviour nor exploit its position for Prussia's advantage.

As the crisis deepened, War Minister Eduard von Bonin took counsel with Moltke on the practical problems of implementing a mobilization. Prussia, Moltke believed, could best contribute by moving as many troops as rapidly as possible to the line of the lower Rhine, as a deterrent to French initiatives against Germany and a warning against committing too heavily in the Italian peninsula. It would require, he wrote on March 14, six weeks to concentrate a quarter-million Prussian troops on the Rhine and Main. At least two weeks could be saved by double-tracking some existing lines and completing another dozen already projected or under construction. Might the Ministry of Commerce be pressured to expedite the processes?

The War Ministry, reluctant to act in the absence of a policy decision, refused even to raise the subject. The Commerce Ministry replied politely that it was always willing to discuss with the General Staff all issues affecting the military use of Prussia's railroads – a piece of bureaucratic boiler plate that left no one ignorant of its real meaning. Meanwhile, as Austrian requests for Prussian support turned into increasingly strident demands, William hung back in the breeching. Beginning on 22 April he ordered the army placed on a war footing but held in its garrisons. Only the Austrian defeat at Magenta decided him in favour of mobilizing six corps on 14 June and sending them west as a warning to Napoleon of the risks of pressing his success too far.

Moltke and his subordinates had done enough preliminary negotiating with the appropriate ministries of Prussia and the other north German states that the first troop trains were scheduled to depart on 1 July. Then the Foreign Ministry complicated matters by urging William not to act so strongly without direct support from the German Confederation. The movement was cancelled, then restored. But on 4 July, when William ordered five corps to the Rhine, the rolling stock collected to support the original movement had been scattered across Prussia to meet regular scheduling requirements. It would take, Moltke reported, at least eleven days before any large-scale movements could begin. The subject became moot when on 11 July Austria and France concluded at Villafranca an armistice that for all practical purposes ended the war. William held his own troops at the ready till 25 July, then ordered demobilization to begin.[14]

II

The most obvious lesson of the mobilization of 1859 involved the absolute necessity of regulating in detail and in peacetime the administration of railways used for military purposes. In the aftermath of Villafranca Moltke proposed the creation of permanent committees including General Staff officers and civil officials. The relevant ministries cooperated with good will – particularly since a working time limit of three weeks was established for the completion of rail transport from mobilization areas to zones of concentration. This removed the uncertainty that had so plagued Ministry of Commerce officials in the spring of 1859: the problem of sustaining an increasingly rail-based economy without knowing what track lines and how much rolling stock would be available when, or for how long.

The foreshortened transport time was accompanied by a series of administrative reorganizations. A unit system was introduced, with war-strength infantry battalions, cavalry regiments, and artillery batteries each moved by a single train. Since military traffic had priority during mobilization, neither long halts nor repeated loading and unloading would be necessary. That was expected to facilitate maintaining discipline – an issue whose significance was increased by the reduction of notification time for callups from five days to one, and the decision to load units at as many sites as possible rather than foot-march them to rail centres. Since 1815 supporters of Prussia's reserve system had been able to cite the lapse of time between mobilization and deployment as a kind of safety valve, giving units an opportunity to shake down under operational conditions before going into action. Now that lead time was being reduced to the vanishing point, and war was projected as 'come as you are' – warts and all.

Nor were these innovations mere paper-framed recommendations. In July 1859, V Corps executed a practice mobilization along the new lines. The exercise was successfully completed in twenty-nine days. V Corps's location in the rural east and its high proportion of Polish recruits, who bore reputations as stupid and refractory, hardly made it a likely showcase for high-technology operations.[15]

Improving Prussia's military reaction time was by no means regarded as an unmixed blessing. Since the end of the Seven Years' War a century earlier, the Prussian army had been regarded by the Prussian government as a deterrent force whose presence in the right numbers in the right place at the right time was part of a carefully calibrated response to a particular situation. If all went optimally that response would fulfil the state's policy aims without firing a shot. The mobilizations of 1850 and 1859 had been ordered in that context, and for all their flaws had been ultimately successful in that context. The General Staff's new mobilization proposals, once implemented, at best were certain to diminish diplomatic flexibility. At worst they risked escalating crisis into war by provoking or frightening the adversary into a military response.

France, Moltke responded, was the main objective threat to Prussia and the German Confederation – not from the ambitions of its government, not from any moral or ideological grounds, but because of the nature of its military system. Strategically and tactically, French doctrine emphasized the offensive. The French army, with its large cadres of professional soldiers, requiring no lengthy and complex mobilization to reach war footing, was well matched to the doctrine. The French rail network possessed the capacity to move large forces east, and to sustain them once they reached the theatre. While the administration of the railroads currently left much to be desired, it was in the highest degree imprudent to assume improvements would not be forthcoming.

Moltke believed the most probable French initiative would involve an offensive into south Germany to destroy its armies and secure the advantage of inner lines *vis-à-vis* Prussia and Austria. Only two Prussian corps were based near the threatened area. These could not be reinforced in peacetime by units from other regions without risking a repetition of 1850's confusion when it became necessary to call up reserves. Prussian strategy therefore must be based on an initial defence, holding the Rhine while concentrating along the Main for a counterattack – preferably in cooperation with other Confederation forces. The Chief of Staff's position was clear. Flexibility as traditionally defined was a snare and a delusion against an army able to make war from a standing start and a state able to send its strike forces into battle behind locomotives.[16]

In February, 1861, the German Confederation created a special commission to evaluate the German railway system from a military perspective. The body was dominated by its Austrian chair and his Prussian counterpart. Each man reflected his army's institutional and psychological approach to the technical aspects of military reform. Captain Wilhelm Ritter Gruendorf von Zebegeny was a self-christened progressive who had developed an autodidactic interest in technologies from small arms to steam engines. Primarily a staff officer, a military courtier in what might for Austria be called the good sense of the term, he had positioned himself as one of the token technocrats in the Habsburg army's higher circles: frequently called upon to explain some new tool of war to an old general. Hermann Graf Wartensleben-Carow had begun his career as an officer of cuirassiers, the heavy cavalry with a deserved reputation as the starchiest and most retrograde element of the Prussian army's mounted arm. Assigned to the General Staff's Second Section before it concentrated exclusively on mobilization planning, he caught Moltke's eye during the manoeuvre(s) of 1858 for his reliability, energy and capacity for hard work.

Wartensleben, a War Academy graduate, acquired his knowledge, and developed the mind-set to use it, on the job. In 1859, when Moltke needed plans for coordinating railway transport in a hurry, Wartensleben prepared them with a minimum of paperwork. He was the General Staff's acknowledged expert on railway issues – a career move as far as might be imagined from his days as a hard-riding subaltern of cavalry. Instead he became the first of the 'demigods', the group of junior officers with aristocratic pedigrees and deep roots in the system that Moltke shaped to the measure of his ideas, and who served as his nervous system in the army at large.[17]

Gruendorf, Wartensleben, and their colleagues, one Bavarian and one Hanoverian, spent several months travelling around Germany, discussing the actual and potential capacities mission eventually recommended creating a central Confederation authority to supervise and coordinate the work of the military and civilian agencies operating individual routes. It prepared as well detailed plans for the concentration of Confederation forces in the west in case of a war with France. This theoretical exercise was the first comprehensive plan for the military use of the entire German railroad network. It seems almost superfluous to add that Wartensleben did most of the detail work. What, after all, was the purpose of having a Prussian on the commission, if not to make the figures come out properly?[18]

III

The small scale and slow pace of the Schleswig-Holstein operations during 1864 put no serious direct strains on the Prussian railway network. Instead Moltke increasingly concentrated on developing a war plan against the Habsburg Empire, which in the calculations of Chancellor Otto von Bismarck had replaced France as Prussia's most likely immediate enemy. At this stage of his career Moltke was anything but a nuts-and-bolts technocrat. The precondition of his operational plan was diplomatic: guaranteed French and Russian neutrality, thereby obviating the necessity for securing Prussia's eastern and western frontiers. That was Bismarck's job, which he eventually fulfilled. Moltke's was countering what he considered the certainty of an Austrian deployment in Bohemia.

Thrusting into Prussia's heartland like a knife blade into an exposed armpit, that province was the only theatre where war between the German powers promised a quick decision. It offered the Habsburgs two major possibilities: an attack into Silesia or a drive north towards Torgau, with the eventual objective of Berlin. Moltke assumed Austria would choose the Berlin option. That initiative suited the Austrian army's emphasis on dash and aggressiveness. Since, moreover, the Prussian capital was unfortified, loss of a single battle could force a Prussian retreat into Pomerania, with corresponding risks of intervention by the flanking powers presumably neutralized by Bismarck's diplomacy.

Moltke proposed to counter Prussia's geographic disadvantage by using the railroads to concentrate eight of Prussia's nine corps against Austria. A single active corps supported by reserves and reinforced by Prussia's small north German clients would contain the Habsburgs' south German allies. That manoeuvre(s) in turn required maintaining the initiative: moving maximum forces into the theatre of operations as quickly as possible. It was for that reason that Moltke pushed for constant last-minute fine-tuning of the mobilization plan. It was for that reason as well that he fixed the major concentration sites at Dresden and Goerlitz: south Prussia's major railway centres, each served by several double-track lines and each with extensive maintenance facilities. He proposed to concentrate three corps concentrate around each city. The remaining two would deploy in Silesia. Should Austria drive on Berlin as he expected, the Chief of Staff projected a major battle and a quick decision. If instead the Habsburg army thrust into Silesia, the Prussians could use their rail network to shift their main force sideways into the threatened province. They could also throw the dice for high stakes and attack into Bohemia, along the direct route to Vienna.[19]

Austria's cabinet, after months of temporizing, backing and filling, decided on 21 February 1866, that it was appropriate to begin overt military preparations for a war that no one in Vienna regarded as imminent. The first orders were only sent a week later, and then to regiments in the east of the empire. That was the kind of measured escalation great powers had practiced since the Renaissance. Horses purchased, reservists recalled, regiments dispatched to the frontier – all were pawn moves in a wider game, designed in this case to convince Bismarck that discretion was the better part of policy. At the same time it was necessary to show the Empire's intentions were ultimately serious. That involved concentrating the main army in Bohemia, as Moltke expected. Austria, however, had one railway line leading into the projected theatre of operations. Prussia had a half-dozen. Austria was larger than Prussia. Its transportation network was less developed. Particularly in the Empire's southern and eastern regions, the roads and railroads to move troops and supplies quickly did not exist. When all the math was done, the general staff reported that Austria would need ten to twelve weeks to bring decisive forces into Bohemia. The challenge was to accomplish as much of the concentration as possible without provoking hostilities.[20]

As negotiations between Vienna and Berlin continued, Moltke adjusted and readjusted his plans for the railroads to compensate for the time he saw being lost.[21] Since before his assignment to the general staff Moltke had argued autonomy of movement was the operational essence of the army corps system. He warned against being seduced by railroads into massing too many troops in a too-small area, leaving them tied to railheads and strangled by limited road networks. His final pre-war proposal, however, divided the army into two equal forces: four corps going to Prussian Saxony, four more to Silesia. Given Austria's steadily increasing strength in Bohemia, only by taking maximum advantage of Prussia's rail network and sacrificing the original strategic concentration in Saxony was it now possible simultaneously to cover Berlin and Breslau, and position the largest force possible opposite Bohemia in the shortest possible time.

Prussia's King William was viscerally hostile to the concept of a German Civil War that he believed could benefit only democrats and Frenchmen. Time and again Bismarck was able to stimulate anger at particular Austrian behaviour; time and again did the anger dissipate with Bismarck's departure from the royal presence. Moltke's repeated reminders that Prussia was losing the initiative had more intellectual than emotional impact on a monarch formed by a different culture of time. Not until mid-March would William authorize even limited reinforcement of the fortresses in Silesia. When on 27 April Vienna ordered mobilization for the 'North Army' in Bohemia, William took a week to respond. Even then he did no more than order the mobilization of five of Prussia's nine corps, while refusing to approve their concentration against Austria.

William sought, in other words, to give Austria every opportunity either to back away from the crisis or to take such a plainly false step that European neutrality would not depend entirely on Bismarck's gossamer web of negotiation and innuendo. While beginning to comprehend the time/space/mass relationships Moltke was at pains to explain, the King did not understand why railway movement orders could not be drafted after a formation was mobilized and ready to take the field. In his mind that represented a desirable refinement of the strategy of 'gradual escalation' with which he was more comfortable, morally, militarily and politically, than with Moltke's developing concept of war by timetable.

Prussian mobilization plans in 1866 were far from the elaborate interlocking structure of 1914. They were in fact sufficiently flexible to support William's sense that they could play a part in deterring war as opposed to initiating it. Only in mid-April was the redoubtable Wartensleben transferred to Berlin as head of the General Staff's Railway Section. Not until 1 May did he present a specific proposal for establishing mixed military-civilian 'line commissions' to control and coordinate movement on the route networks leading into the proposed theatre of operations. Moltke at this stage of his career did not consider it his place to convince the king of anything. He was still breaking new ground both for his office and himself, and the air was thin at these high altitudes of state policy. As the king remained reluctant to take the final step into war, the chief of staff responded by focusing his efforts downward, doing everything possible to adjust train schedules and rolling-stock allocations to William's decisions.

It required a total of nine separate orders, issued between 3 May and 24 May, to bring the whole army under the colours and set it in motion. This was a far cry from the single-step action for which Moltke had hoped and advocated. It nevertheless represented the beginning of the process of identifying mobilization with

concentration and concentration with action that over the next half century came
to dominate the thinking of every general staff in Europe. With his hopes for
systematic, simultaneous deployment gone, Moltke concentrated on moving
individual corps into the theatre of operations as rapidly as possible.

Despite some problems caused by senior officers attempting to modify
schedules, nowhere was the rail network overloaded beyond the line commissions'
ability to compensate. Destination points were able to cope with the limited
number of trains that arrived on any given day, and to keep men, animals, supplies
and equipment from piling up haphazardly at the railheads. Arrangements for
feeding men and horses were correspondingly effective. Since 1806, 1815 and
even 1848 Prussia's subjects had moved steadily towards becoming citizens, who
sought reasons they could understand for risking their lives and sacrificing their
wages.[22] The sense of order and control as one approached the sharp end did much
to instil confidence at all levels of an essentially untested army.

Far more serious seemed the circumstances imposed by the spacing of southeast
Prussia's smaller railway hubs at intervals along the frontier. Moltke's transport
plan initially distributed seven and a half corps like beads on a string around a
400 kilometre arc from Silesia to Saxony. Civilian and military analysts described
the chief of staff as resorting to a cordon deployment in the worst fashion of those
superannuated generals who had proven such obliging enemies of the young
Napoleon. Moltke confidently answered that the rail concentration was only the
first stage of the army's deployment.[23] On 29 May three divisions from the
Rhineland, somewhat grandiloquently dubbed the Elbe Army, began assembling
around Torgau. From Prussian Saxony II, III and IV Corps, the First Army, shifted
eastwards towards Goerlitz. First Corps simultaneously moved from Goerlitz into
Silesia to reinforce the two corps, V and VI, already on the ground.

These lateral movements reduced the deployment arc by one-quarter – but it still
extended over 300 kilometres. Moltke might have made a case in the high councils
to which he now had access for the risks of further delay. Instead he accepted them,
sending the Guard Corps from Berlin to reinforce the Second Army forming in
Silesia, but simultaneously warning the army's chief of staff against making any
decisions that might unleash a war as yet undecided upon by the King.[24]

That left Moltke with three widely spaced groupings. Elbe Army's three divisions were at Torgau. First Army's six divisions stood 150 kilometres eastward at
Goerlitz. Eight more divisions were in Silesia with the second Army – almost
200 kilometres' distance from the First Army. By now any chances for a defensive campaign were long gone. Even William understood that Prussia would have
to advance into Bohemia, no matter what Benedek decided to do, in order to have
any hope of concentrating its forces. Moltke assured his King that whether the
Austrians turned towards Silesia or confronted the forces in Prussian Saxony, they
would be enmeshed in an operational net. Things did not go as smoothly as all
that in succeeding weeks. But if the outcome of the Bohemian campaign was
determined on the battlefield of Koeniggraetz, its structure was established by the
Prussian Army's use of the state's railroads.[25]

IV

The run-up to war in 1866 resembled a test of nerves between Old West gunfighters. The Franco-Prussian War began almost on duelists' terms. Neither party had a significant advantage in mobilization; neither had undertaken preliminary preparations. It was a classic 'come-as-you-are' collision, and as such its initial advantages rested with the French. That was the kind of conflict around which France's military system had been developed and refined since Waterloo. The Prussians, playing catch-up, compensating for instant readiness with speed and system, had shown what they could do in 1866 against an army configured similarly to the French, albeit one that in hindsight seemed a second team. To participants and observers alike, *retiarius* now faced *secutor*: a contest of asymmetric military systems whose outcome was anybody's guess.

Moltke's understanding of the relationship between war and policy grew steadily more focused during the 1860s. As chief of staff he accepted a sharp distinction between the two spheres. In peacetime the army's job was to plan and prepare for the next war. It was the government's task to establish that conflict's paradigms and define its parameters.[26] After 1866 Moltke accepted Bismarck's assurances that he faced a single-contingency military situation; planning a war against France. Like all of Prussia's wars, it would have to be decided quickly – more quickly, however, than usual. While Bismarck's diplomatic virtuosity might give Moltke an initial free hand operationally, the Chancellor's international constructions were as fragile as they were elaborate. That meant the war's true objective must be the French army. Decisively defeating it was the best way to convince other powers, Austria in particular, to let half-drawn swords return to the scabbards. And the best way to engage the army was to advance on Paris. The heart of France and of the Second Empire, Paris could not be sacrificed in a strategic withdrawal that in any case was foreign to the French way of war.

The next question was how best to achieve the campaign's projected political/military goal? Insofar as a single war plan ever held sway in Imperial councils, France's strategy prior to 1870 was projected as defensive: drawing the Prussians into the natural killing ground on the French side of the frontier.[27] The diplomatic situation as it developed in 1870, however, seemed to demand the quality the French army was most supposed to embody: quick reaction. A thrust into Germany and an impressive victory or two won from a standing start might well convince Italy and Austria to jump on the Second Empire's bandwagon. A French invasion was also expected to cause the south German states to think twice about involving themselves in Bismarck's war.[28] In the summer of 1870 strong political and journalistic warnings were raised everywhere south of the Main against blindly rushing into a second great-power conflict in less than five years.[29] Nor could the still-untempered North German Confederation reckon automatically on internal stability in the face of a French blitz.[30] Attacking across the Rhine from a standing start to open the campaign offered France, in short, the same kind of prospect as beginning a fight with a kick to the groin.

France's railway network, arguably the best in Europe from a military perspective, was eminently capable in material terms of supporting such an initiative. As a pre-war German study noted, almost two thirds of its lines were double tracked. France had a third more rolling stock per track mile than Prussia. Stations in the French eastern provinces were larger, marshalling yards better equipped, than their German counterparts.[31] Commercial and military interests were generally considered compatible. In 1856, for example, the war ministry subsidized the fortification of part of a line from Paris to Muhlhouse in Alsace. In 1863 the government agreed to compensate the Eastern Railway Company 62,800 francs for building what was essentially a complex of unloading facilities for military trains. The result was a regional network of lines along the eastern frontier, connecting the major fortresses and facilitating the lateral movement of troops and connected to a larger rail web extending outward from the hub of Paris.[32]

Moltke thus faced two diametrically opposing prospects. The French army might cross the Rhine and hit the Prussians while they were still unloading their troop trains. Or the French might assume the natural defensive positions in which the region abounded, meet the Prussian advance in a series of encounter battles, then counterattack a weakened, confused enemy. His response represented a major contribution to the development of what has been called 'operational art', the shadowy level between strategy and tactics – which depended heavily on the railroads.[33]

Moltke initially expected to have about 360,000 men for his offensive, plus whatever the south Germans might provide – superior numbers, but not exactly overwhelming for an attacker, and certainly not the three to one advantage conventional wisdom recommended for an attack. He planned to concentrate in the Rhineland/Palatinate area of Prussia. The initial centre of gravity, the *Schwerpunkt*, would be around Homburg, where two armies – in the event a single, oversized second Army – would advance in two echelons, ready to attack to the front or swing to either flank. On the right, a First Army of two corps would cover the Second's advance and be ready to act offensively against the French should an opportunity arise. A Third Army, concentrating somewhat further south than the other two, would advance northwest into Alsace on the left. Its strength was initially set at two Prussian corps, with a third to follow and the south German contingents adding what amounted to two or three more if they showed up. Like the First Army, the Third was to serve as a flank guard and itself engage a French flank should opportunity offer.

Geographically this meant swinging the main Prussian force south of the French fortress complex at Metz, then advancing northwest towards the Moselle between Luneville and Point-à-Mousson. A major battle should take place before reaching the river, Moltke believed, and 'thereafter nothing can be predicted in detail'.[34] His concept is often cited in general works as illustrating the chief of staff's familiar aphorism that no plan survives contact with the enemy. It also embodied Moltke's accompanying contention that therefore the initial plan must be a good one! He recognized the risks of gridlock inherent in deploying forces of the size at his disposal in a relatively small sector on a relatively narrow line of advance: the sixty or so miles between Metz and the Vosges Mountains. His projected counter was to maintain tight control of the advance for as long as possible, Moltke proposed to regulate corps and division marches in the theatre of operations to the point of providing regularly updated timetables for the advance from the assembly area – tables so detailed as to specify the locations each corps would reach on a particular day, thereby facilitating mutual support, and mutual cooperation against French flanks.[35] Control was the best available safeguard against the campaign's developing a continuous front, with Prussia's three armies pushing the French back steadily enough – but too slowly to fulfil the war's policy objectives.

Moltke's operational plan correspondingly depended on the railroads. Where in 1866 he had improvised existing lines and based his plan on the extrinsic deployment that resulted, his concern before 1870 was to funnel as many men and horses as possible into a relatively small area on Prussia's western border as quickly as possible. That was easier said than done – not least because the patterns of railway construction in Germany had for thirty years clearly favoured north-south lines as offering commercial advantages obvious enough to overcome enduring southern particularism in railway matters.[36]

At the heart of the restructuring was the Railway Section of the General Staff. After 1866 its establishment was increased and its position enhanced – to a point where officers in the planning sections at times complained that the railway tail was wagging the operational dog. But newly promoted Colonel Baron Hermann Wartensleben-Carow and his 1868 successor Major Karl von Brandenstein understood how to work with a railroad system that included over fifty separate lines, some public, some private and others a mixture of the two. In November 1867, corps headquarters received detailed mobilization instructions, providing for the mobilization and dispatch of each subordinate unit. A Military Transportation Plan established rail schedules for the entire army. Three permanent Line Commands were created, with ten more to be added in wartime. One for each major east–west rail route in the North German Confederation, to coordinate movement, maintenance and administration of specific rail networks during mobilization. Integrating general staff officers with civilian administrators and technicians, they heralded the synergy of bureaucracy and technology that for the next century defined the nature of war. The new organization removed the major obstacle to rapid long-distance troop movement: using the tracks of several companies with different ownership structures in the same operation. In case of war, the civilian authorities would work under military command. Another harbinger of total war was the complete suspension of civilian traffic during mobilization. Never before had a government asserted the power to control the movement of its citizens in such detail as a matter of routine.

Tested in a November 1867 war game, the Military Transport Plan required thirty-two days to move the Prussian field army into its designated zone of operations in the west. A year later that time had been reduced to twenty-four days. By 1870 it was twenty days. As the declining rate of improvement suggests, fine-tuning was becoming increasingly important. Enough slack must remain in the schedule to enable the process to continue without disruption. Prussian troop trains did not move particularly rapidly. In some cases at least during the mobilization of 1870, it was possible for men to jump out of the train, grab a loaf of bread or a can of coffee from civilian bystanders, and catch up with their assigned boxcar – all without attracting serious attention from an unsympathetic sergeant. What was important was that the trains move systematically, reach their destinations predictably, and unload in safety.[37]

Increasingly Moltke accepted the Railway Section's recommendation that it was preferable to concentrate at the principal railheads – behind the Rhine if necessary – and temporarily sacrifice German territory rather than risk disruption or disorder in unloading and returning the trains.[38] Moltke accepted as well the accompanying argument that the army should move in echelons rather than risk straining a rail network that, even under the diplomatic conditions of the late 1860s, did not add lines or tracks for strategic reasons. No fewer than 7 of the North German Confederation's 27 active divisions remained behind when the first trains rolled west in 1870. One of them was assigned the mission of defending the western coast against any French attempts to use their superior navy to support amphibious operations. The other six – I, II and VI Corps – were left in their peacetime districts not for security reasons *vis-à-vis* Austria, though Moltke had considered that issue, but because moving them immediately from West Prussia, Pomerania and Silesia risked overstraining the carrying capacities of the railroads further west. Given the actual speed with which they were eventually moved to France, those three corps might be called a second strategic echelon. Moltke, however, would have preferred if possible to have them closer at hand than the specialists' timetables allowed.[39]

The nature of the Prussian mobilization system helped explain the refusal of the general staff and the war ministry to react to reports that the French were gaining the initiative by transporting reservists from Algeria, or moving supplies from one point in eastern France to another. When the order for mobilization was issued, the Prussians had no fewer than six organized rail routes, each able to handle two or three corps in succession: eighteen trains a day over double-track lines, twelve on single-track routes. Beginning on 15 July, over 1,500 trains reached their destinations, discharged their cargoes, and – not least – turned around and went back for another load. By 3 August, the nineteenth day of mobilization, the field force was ready to advance. And a mere lieutenant-colonel had directed the whole process: Freiherr Karl von Brandenstein, the first third-generation general staff officer who had made his military career with the railroads. Moltke trusted him implicitly; Albrecht von Roon complained that because of the youngsters, as War Minister he had too little to do! Even when allowances are made for hyperbole, the mobilization and concentration of the Prussian army in 1870 marked the beginning of a new era of warmaking, with administrative preparation and peacetime planning at least as important as operational virtuosity. But when it was all over, sighs of relief went up from a good many desks![40]

The south Germans had three lines of their own, running from Augsburg, Noerdlingen and Wuerzburg to the southern sector of Moltke's designated zone of concentration. The success of those three states in keeping pace with the Prussian concentration, over railroads with a generally lower carrying capacity and without the elaborate Prussian staff organization supporting the operation, should not be dismissed in a footnote. It demonstrates the significant improvement in the operational effectiveness of all three armies – and suggests as well that the military establishments of Baden, Bavaria and Wuerttemberg were anxious to demonstrate that they were more than mere spear-carriers for their larger ally across the Main.[41]

V

Ironically, just as the south German contingents demonstrated that they could keep pace with Prussia in at least the early stages of mobilization and concentration, Moltke's operational plans encountered an unexpected snag. In 1866 the general staff's elaborate railway timetables had not included post-mobilization logistics. Instead each corps was responsible for keeping itself supplied. In earlier wars that meant living off the countryside by purchase and requisition. But neither Prussian Saxony nor Silesia produced much in the way of agricultural surplus relative to the high numbers of men and horses the railways delivered. As much to the point, corps quartermasters preferred to deal with contractors they knew, firms from their home districts. There seemed no reason why the railroads could not be organized to forward supplies as they had earlier moved men, on a district basis. Railway tracks seemed a kind of magic carpet that would for the first time free armies from both the limitations of fixed bases and the exigencies of requisitioning.

Results in practice proved far different. Perhaps a bit of peculation might have been welcome in a context where quartermasters, determined to keep the men and animals depending on them well-fed, purchased and forwarded such huge quantities of food and forage that the processing systems were swamped. In contrast to mobilization, no central authority was responsible for controlling shipments and establishing priorities. The War Ministry neither prepared schedules for supply trains nor designated depot areas. The railroads assumed responsibility only for delivering goods – not unloading or storing them. Moltke, believing Wartensleben was too valuable to leave behind in Berlin, took him into the field as his operations officer, leaving the general staff correspondingly rudderless in railway matters.[42]

The results included freight cars arriving in the theatre from as far away as Cologne, loaded to the limits with completely inedible loaves of bread baked at regimental depots. Other freight cars sat for days awaiting the few labourers available in the context of a campaign that virtually ignored administration along the lines of communication. Local military commanders were often long-retired majors and lieutenant colonels whose active service had been spent in the cavalry and whose ranks were too low for them to generate results by intimidation. About half the army's supply columns were composed of civilian farm wagons whose durability and weight-carrying capacities were overextended by the demands of keeping fed the constantly-advancing forward units. Nor did horses from civil life, accustomed to regular food and dry stabling, respond well to field service conditions. Some Prussians fought the battle of Koeniggraetz on empty stomachs, comforted only by the announcement of their commanding general that 'God who feeds the sparrows will also provide for us.'[43]

The logistical shortcomings of the Koeniggraetz campaign did not go unnoticed by Moltke and his subordinates. After the war Brigadier General Albrecht von Stosch, Second Army's chief quartermaster in 1866, was appointed to overhaul the Military Economy Department. Stosch was as close to a Renaissance professional as the Prussian army developed in the nineteenth century, with a breadth of administrative talent that eventually made him an effective minister of the new German navy. He also believed in militarizing management as far as possible. In contrast to Wartensleben, he sought to remove civilian officials and civilian contractors from the supply system. Too many of his military appointments were officers partially disabled by wounds or illness, with no other obvious qualifications as administrators. Too many of the civilians responded by what one authority calls 'inner emigration', a pattern of working to rule that boded ill in any emergency situation.[44]

Stosch did much to improve the organization of the army's logistics. Instead of moving the bulk of the army's provisions by rail from the interior of Germany, he established a general principle of obtaining supplies locally, in 'enemy country', by requisition and purchase. Even with a reduced burden of food and forage, however, the problem of transportation in advance of the railroads remained. Since combat units had priority and the wagons and draft horses of each corps were in its later rail echelons, supplies delivered to railheads could initially be distributed only on an improvised basis. The more troops that assembled in the zone of concentration, the less possible it was to meet their needs from local resources. Once the advance began matters grew worse as supply trains clogged roads and obstructed junctions far beyond the capacity of the relatively few military police to resolve. Empty wagons were arguably more of a problem than the loaded ones that received what priorities there were. Too often instead of returning promptly to the depots established along the rail lines, supply columns found themselves diverted to the least desirable routes: roads that were little more than local trails, that broke down quickly under the pounding of heavy wheeled traffic. The Third Army in particular lagged well behind Moltke's original schedule, in part because of the difficulties posed by the poorly organized supply trains of its two Bavarian corps, but even more because of the relative scarcity of any kinds of secondary roads along its axis of advance.[45]

VI

The central logistical role railways played in 1870 generated another unforeseen consequence for the Prussian army. Since the sixteenth century a consensus had developed in Europe that civil populations were required to remain conspicuously aloof from any kind of hostilities. A Prussian decree of 1867 was typical in establishing armed civilians as subject to the death penalty. Other authorized responses to civilian resistance included destroying buildings from which shots were fired, taking hostages for the good behaviour of a community, and levying punitive contributions on an offending place or region. All three were applied almost from the war's beginning.[46] All were intended in principle as measured deterrents, not only suppressing misguided individuals by limited applications of force, but encouraging communities to suppress their own hotheads with no subsequent questions being asked. In the circumstances of 1870, however, none seemed sufficiently effective to secure order in the German rear – in particular, to protect the railroads that seemed increasingly vulnerable as they grew more necessary to German operations extending into the heart of France.[47]

The classic image of the franc-tireur is of a townsman or peasant tending peacefully to business by day and scourging the invader by night. Reality was far less dramatic. One French prefect summarized it nicely:

> Your fatherland... only expects that each morning three or four resolute men will leave their village and go where nature has prepared a suitable place for hiding and for firing on the Prussians without danger.[48]

Against outposts, patrols and supply columns, trained soldiers able to shoot back, such 'pure' partisans were little more than a nuisance, especially when their activities were uncoordinated with any wider efforts.[49] The idea of cutting railroads was correspondingly obvious.

Loosening or removing a few lengths of rail, even burning a small bridge, had nuisance value, and little more. Railway demolition in the American Civil War had proven a task sufficiently complex that it took armies years to learn it. Small partisan groups operating on their own usually had neither the equipment, nor the know-how, nor usually the time to do more than temporarily interrupt service.[50] Initially, effective demolitions were usually the work of retreating regulars – as at Nanteuil, on the main route to Paris, where a half dozen professionally sited mines blocked a long tunnel with loose sand. When later sandslides made repair impossible, it was necessary to build a bypass that was not completed until 22 November: a major contribution to the delay in bringing up material for the bombardment of Paris.

The Third Republic's operations against the railroads had greater success in the Vosges, where legendary guerrilla leader Giuseppe Garibaldi conducted a seminar in large-scale irregular warfare. Partisans blew up railroad bridges and sabotaged tracks, on one occasion sending three scarce locomotives into the Meuse. The Germans took hostages. Prominent citizens were required to ride the locomotive or the forward cars. Flight cost 1,200 francs for a first offence. A second was worth 5,000 francs and a prison term to be served in Prussia. If a train was derailed near a town, the inhabitants were fined 25,000 francs. The Germans dispatched 'flying columns' only to see them embarrassingly outmarched and outwitted.

The French railroads' total loss in damages as calculated after the war amounted to thirty-three million francs – not a bagatelle, but hardly a budget-wrecker either.[51]

Railway service, particularly on the main lines connecting Germany with Paris, was affected far less by partisans than by traffic jams. Depots in Germany tended to push trains forward with little concern for when or whether they could be unloaded. A frontloaded army organization provided no labour formations for such mundane tasks. The heavy operational concentrations of troops around Metz, then Sedan, further exacerbated crowding. Tracks were blocked as far back as Frankfurt and Cologne. As early as 5 September, over 2,300 freight cars of supplies for the Second Army alone were in place on five different rail lines. Between the 1st and the 26th of October, 29 of 292 trains sent from Wissembourg to Nancy – a routine regional run – never arrived.[52]

No officer was likely to step forward and claim responsibility for that degree of rear echelon chaos. It was far easier to file reports blaming partisans – whose activities were in fact often a final straw for overworked and overstressed train crews and administrative personnel. A rifle slug ricocheting off a locomotive or a loosened rail spotted in time to avoid derailment could be enough to produce demands for action from the civilians who made the railroads run. Increasing numbers of these were German, around 3,500 by the end of the war, and they were not shy about asserting that being shot at was not part of their job descriptions. The train crews, moreover, were responsible to the Ministry of Commerce, not the Ministry of War. The resulting jurisdictional squabbles only exacerbated friction on the ground, and increased demands to do something about the guerrillas.

Partisans everywhere in France took notice. On 22 January 1871, a raiding party of about 400 franc-tireurs came sixty miles to strike the town of Fontenoy-sur-Moselle. They took the small garrison by surprise, destroyed a key viaduct on the rail line to Paris, and withdrew. It was a partisan operation in the classic sense: a bolt from the blue in an area generally considered quiet, producing concrete results and demonstrating that there was no safety anywhere.

The Germans who reoccupied Fontenoy understood the message. They burned the town. According to French sources they also executed civilians, throwing corpses and perhaps wounded, into the fires. Moltke ordered official reprisals: formal executions, and a fine of ten million francs imposed on Toul, the nearest large community. When a demand for French workers to repair the damage went unheeded, the occupation authorities shut down the entire *departement's* factories and workshops, then forbade paying unemployed workmen. The Germans, one might say, had learned their lesson as well. Fontenoy was at once a signpost and an open door to a way of war that would come to grim fruition in the next century.[53]

The Prussian/German army of 1870 had only an attitude towards partisans. In 1914 it had a doctrine. In 1939 it had an ideology. In the early stages of the First World War, reports of civilian guerrilla activity quickly reached senior command levels and led to direct orders for reprisals.[54] The Prussian/German army of 1870 had only time enough to develop an approach towards partisans. In 1914 it had a doctrine based on that approach: a doctrine of immediate, massive repression. In the early stages of The Great War, reports of alleged civilian guerrilla activity during the invasion of France and Belgium quickly reached senior command levels and led to direct orders for immediate, large-scale reprisals. In little more than a month, 6,500 civilians were deliberately killed. Between 15,000 and 20,000 buildings were destroyed. By 1939 the army would have an ideology – one not merely legitimating but requiring the systematic application of violence and brutality against conquered peoples whether or not they resisted in arms. In five years it would lay waste a continent. And the railroads were a catalyst.

Conclusion

The military parameters of what Allan Mitchell calls 'the great train race' were so well established in Germany by 1871 that the next four decades amount to an extended footnote. Improvements in track design and roadbed configuration enabled ever greater 'concentrations of heavy, high-speed traffic on a given set of lines. Improved communications facilitated control and timing of traffic. The growing bureaucratization of Germany's railway system provided an organization increasingly capable of collaborating effectively with the military on long-range planning.

That reflected and reinforced developments in professional preparation and career patterns that conditioned even officers assigned to the Great General Staff to accept rather than question the army's order of things. The new men were also significantly more ready than their predecessors to concentrate on performing as capably as possible the tasks to which they were assigned, as opposed to looking beyond pigeonholes and 'thinking outside the box'. In a sense the ethos of the officer corps began taking on some of the creed of railroad procedure – continued, reliable and predictable service independent of any specific individual.[55]

This 'railway mentality' in turn fostered an offensive approach to war in two ways. Most obvious and most often cited was the encouragement of war by timetable. The schedules of train movements, prepared in peacetime with such increasingly elaborate care, could not be altered lightly. Quite apart from the actual difficulties involved in such a process, the years of time and effort spent developing the administrative structure of mobilization generated their own momentum and their own mind-set. The most familiar illustration of this came on 1 August 1914, when William II, his spirits temporarily buoyed by hopes of French neutrality, announced to his Chief of Staff that now all Germany needed to do was concentrate its entire strength against Russia. Moltke the Younger, insisting that the result would be mass chaos, responded with a nervous collapse. After the war a senior officer on the General Staff's Railway Section, outraged by the implied slur against his bureau, demonstrated in a Teutonically learned monograph that such a shift had indeed been possible – in theory.[56]

'Theory' is the key word. Perhaps the redeployment might have been strategically, politically or even morally preferable to the alternative that was actually implemented. But when facing an ultimate professional challenge, officers who had spent careers specializing in detail, saving kilometres and hours from particular schedules, were psychologically unlikely to imagine, much less seriously consider, scrapping their life's work in response to a mere change in external circumstances. That was even more the case when they were convinced that their planning had given Germany, if not a recipe for victory, then certainly the best chance for victory it was likely to have in the contexts of August 1914. Their mistake had a century's worth of consequences.

Notes

1 Jeffrey Herf, *Reactionary Modernism: Technology, Culture and Politics in Weimar and the Third Reich* (Cambridge, 1984). See also Avner Offer, 'Going To War in 1914: A Matter of Honor?' *Politics and Society*, 33 (1995), 213–14; and Christian Mueller, 'Anmerkungen zur Entwicklung von Kriegsbild und operativ-strategischem Szenario im preussisch-deutschen Heer vor dem Ersten Weltkrieg', *Militaergeschichtliche Mitteilungen* LVII (1998), 371–83.
2 Antulio Echevarria, 'On the Brink of the Abyss: The Warrior Identity and German Military Thought before the Great War', *War & Society*, 13 (1995), 23–40.
3 Stig Foerster, 'Der deutsche Generalstab und die Illusion des kurzen Krieges, 1871–1914. Metakritik eines Mythos', *Militaergeschichtliche Mitteilungen*, 54 (1995), 61–93.
4 Dennis Showalter, 'German Grand Strategy: A Contradiction in Terms?' *Militargeschichtliche Mitteilungen*, 48 (1990), 65–102.
5 *Ueber die militaerische Benutzung der Eisenbahn* (Berlin, 1836).
6 Rolf Weber, *Die Revolution in Sachsen 1848/49: Entwicklung und Analyse ihrer Triebkraefte* (Berlin, 1970), is a general history from a GDR perspective. Cf. the articles in *Dresden Mai 1849: Tagungsband*, ed. K. Jeschke, G. Ulbricht (Dresden, 2000).
7 Cf. Hermann Rahne, *Mobilmachung* (Berlin, 1983), p. 16 ff.; and Curt Jany, *Geschichte der koeniglich-preussische Armee*, 2nd edn, E. Jany, Vol. V (Osnabrueck, 1967), p. 184 ff.
8 Chief of Staff Field Marshal Heinrich Hess to General von der Mark, 27 Nov., 1850, in *Feldmarschall Hess. Schriften*, ed. M. Rauchensteiner (Osnabrueck, 1975), pp. 229–30.
9 Cf. Julius H. Schoeps, *Von Olmuetz nach Dresden: 1850–51; ein Beitrag zur Geschichte der Reformen am Deutschen Bund* (Cologne, 1972); Roy A. Austensen, 'The Making of Austria's Prussian Policy, 1848–1852', *The Historical Journal*, 27 (1984), 861–76; and Anselm Doering-Manteuffel, 'Der Ordnungszwang der Staatsystems: Zu den Mitteleuropa-Konzepten in der oesterreichisch-preussiscnen Rivalitaet', in *Die Herausforderung des europaeischen Staatensystems. Nationale Ideologie und staatliches Interesse zwischen Reatauration und Imperialismus*, ed. A. Birke, G. Heyemann (Goettingen, 1984), 119–40.
10 Cf. Michael Salewski, 'Moltke, Schlieffen, und die Eisenbahn', in *Generalfeldmarschall von Moltke: Bedeutung und Wirkung*, ed. R.G. Foerster (Munich, 1992), pp. 89–102; and Moltke's '1869 Instructions for Large Unit Commanders', in *Moltke on the Art of War*, ed. D.J. Hughes (Novato, CA, 1991), pp. 171–224.
11 Dennis Showalter, 'The Retaming of Bellona: Prussia and the Institutionalization of the Napoleonic Legacy', *Military Affairs*, 44 (1980), 57–63.
12 Eberhard Kessel, *Moltke* (Stuttgart, 1957), p. 202 *passim*; Rahne, 23 ff.
13 Reinhold Dorwart, *The Administrative Reforms of Frederick William I of Prussia* (Cambridge, MA, 1953); and Hans Rosenberg, *Bureaucracy, Aristocracy, and Autocracy: The Prussian Experience, 1660–1815* (Cambridge, MA, 1958), present patterns of a system that endured well into the nineteenth century.
14 Kessel, 265 ff. Hans Kentmann, 'Preussen und die Bundeshilfe an Oesterreich im Jahre 1859', *Mitteilungen des Oesterreichischen Instituts fuer Geschichtsfoerschung, Ergaenzungsband* 12 (1933), 297–415, remains a useful overview.
15 Rahne, 25 ff., Kessel, 272 ff.
16 Moltke's memorandum of spring 1860 is in Helmuth von Moltke, *Militaerische Werke*, 13 vols in 4, Part 1, *Militaerische Korrespondenz*, ed. *Grossen Generalstab, Kriegsgeschichtliche Abteilung*, 4 vols (Berlin, 1892–1902), III, 16 ff.

17 Hermannn Graf von Wartensleben-Carow, koengl. Preuss. General der Kavallerie; ein Lebensbild, 1826–1921, ed. E. Graefin v. Wartensleben (Berlin, 1923).

18 For the commission's work see the engaging, not always entirely accurate Gruendorf von Zebegeny, Memoiren eines oesterreichischen Generalstaeblers 1834–1866, ed. A. Sanger, 2 ed. (Stuttgart, 1913), I. 158 ff.; Kessel, 234, 308–9; and the Bericht ueber die Leistungsfaehigkeit der Deutschen Eisenbahnen zu militaerischen Zwecken erstattet durch die…Specialcommission (Frankfurt, 1861). W. Kousz, 'Wilhelm Ritter Gruendorf von Zebegeny', Dissertation, Vienna, 1967, corrects in pedestrian fashion its subject's more extreme overstatements.

19 MMW, 1, II, 21–45. Cf. Wolfgang von Groote, 'Moltkes Planungen fuer die Feldzug in Boehmen und ihre Grundlagen', in Entscheidung 1866, ed. U. von Gersdorff (Stuttgart, 1966), p. 94, Kessel, 437 ff.

20 For Austria's mobilization in 1866 see Geoffrey Wawro, The Austro-Prussian War: Austria's War with Prussia and Italy in 1866 (Cambridge, 1996,) p. 57 ff.; and Antonio Schmidt-Brentano's more favorable treatment in Die Armee in Oesterreich; Militaer, Staat und Gesellschaft 1848–67 (Boppard, 1975), p. 155 ff.

21 For the following cf., inter alia, Kessel, 437 ff.; Arden Bucholz, Moltke and the German Wars, 1864–1871 (New York, 2001), p. 112 ff.; and Dennis E. Showalter, 'Mass Multiplied by Impulsion: The Influence of Railroads on Prussia's Planning for the Six Weeks War', Military Affairs, 38 (1974), 62–7.

22 Stig Foerster, 'Militaer und Staatsbuegerliche Partizipation. Die Allgemeine Wehrpflicht im Deutschen Kaiserreich, 1871–1914', in Die Wehrpflicht, ed. R. Foerster (Munich, 1994), pp. 55–70.

23 Moltke to Steinmetz, June 1, MMW, 1, II, 186–7.

24 Karl Leonhard Graf Blumenthal, Journals of Field-Marshal Count von Blumenthal for 1866 and 1870–71, ed. A. von Blumenthal, tr. A.D. Gillespie-Addison (London, 1903), p. 14 passim; Kessel, 456.

25 Dennis Showalter, Railroads and Rifles. Soldiers, Technology, and the Unification of Germany (Hamden, CT, 1975).

26 Rudolf Stadelmann, Moltke und der Staat (Krefeld, 1950).

27 La Guerre de 1870, in La Guerre de 1870–71, ed. by the Section Historique de l'IÉtat-Major de l' Armée, 31 vols (Paris, 1901–13), I, 79 ff., reprints part of the most comprehensive prewar strategic proposal.

28 The new approach is summarized in Napoleon III, Des Causes qui ont amenes la capitulation de Sedan (Brussels, 1871), pp. 4–5.

29 E. Weis, 'Vom Kriegsausbruch zur Reichsgruendung. Zur Politik des bayerischen Aussenministers Graf Bray-Steinburg im Jahr 1870', Zeitschrift fuer bayerische Landesgeschichte, 33 (1970), 787 ff.; presents the high politics of the strongest of the southern states. Erich Schneider offers a case study in public opinion with 'Die Reaktion der deutschen Oeffentlichkeit auf den Kriegsbeginn. Das Beispiel des Bayerischen Rheinpfalz', in La Guerre de 1870/71 et ses consequences, ed. P. Levillain, R. Riemenschneider (Bonn, 1990), pp. 110–57.

30 Alf Luedtke discusses 'The Permanence of Internal War: The Prussian State and its Opponents, 1870–71', in On the Road to Total War. The American Civil War and the German Wars of Unification, 1861–1871, ed. S. Foerster, J. Nagler (Cambridge, 1997), pp. 377–92. Cf. Stewart A. Stehlin, 'Guelph plans for the Franco-Prussian War', Historical Journal, 13 (1970), 789–98.

31 H.L.W., Die Kriegfuehrung unter Benuetzung der Eisenbahnen (Leipzig, 1868), p. 74 ff.

32 See especially Alan Mitchell, The Great Train Race; Railways and the Franco-German Rivalry, 1815–1914 (New York, 2000), p. 31ff.; and F. Jacquemin, Les Chemins de Fer pendant la Guerre de 1870–71 (Paris, 1874), p. 111 ff.

33 Michael D. Krause, 'Moltke and the Origins of the Operational Level of War', in Generalfeldmarschall von Moltke, ed. R. Foerster (Munich, 1991), pp. 141–64, is a useful introduction.

34 Moltke's plan of campaign for 1870 has been the subject of near-theological exegesis. His 'Erste Aufstellung der Armee', begun in the winter of 1868–9 and most recently reworked in July, 1870, is in *MMW*, 1, III, p. 114 ff. Cf. the memo of May 6, 1870, in *ibid.*, 131 ff. The quotation is on p. 132. Among the many analyses, Bradley J. Meyer. 'The Operational Art: The Elder Moltke's Campaign Plan for the Franco-Prussian War', in *The Operational Art: Developments in the Theories of War*, ed. B.J.C. Mc Kercher and M. Hennessy (Westport, CT, 1996), pp. 29–49; Kessel, 538 ff.; and Bucholz, *Moltke and the German Wars*, 155 ff. stand out for perception and clarity.

35 *MMW*, 1, III, 133.

36 Mitchell, 65.

37 Cf. Wolfgang Petter, 'Die Logistik des deutschen Heeres im deutsch-franzoesischen Krieg von 1870–71', in *Die Bedeutung der Logistik fuer die militaerische Fuehrung von der Antike bis in die Neuzeit*, ed. *Militaergeschichtliches Forschungsamt* (Bonn, 1986), p. 109–33; Rahne, 52 ff; and Arden Bucholz, *Moltke, Schlieffen*, and *Prussian War Planning* (New York, 1991), p. 48 ff.

38 Kessel, 548.

39 Ibid., 537–8.

40 The most detailed account is Gustav Lehmann, *Die Mobilmachung von 1870* (Berlin, 1905). Rahne, 59 ff., is a good modern overview. Cf. Conrad von Hugo, 'Carl von Brandenstein, Chef des Feldeisenbahnwesens und engster Mitarbeiter Moltkes 1870–71', *Wehrwissenschaftliche Rundschau*, 14 (1964), 676–84.

41 L. Sukstorf, *Die Problematik der Logistik im deutschen Heer waehrend des deutsch-franzoesischen Krieges 1870/71* (Frankfurt, 1994), p. 64 ff., surveys the south German mobilizations and concentrations. Cf. K. Thoma, 'Die Eisenbahntransporte fuer Mobilmachung und Aufmarsch der K. Bayerischen Armee 1870', in *Darstellungen aus der Bayerischen Kriegs-und Heeresgeschichte*, 5, ed. K.B. Kriegsarchiv (Munich, 1896), 151–81.

42 Kessel, 456 ff.

43 Wolfgang Foerster, *Prinz Friedrich Karl von Preussen: Denkwuerdigkeiten aus seinem Leben*, 2 vols (Stuttgart, 1910), II, 109.

44 For Stosch's achievements see Petter, 'Logistik', 115 ff.

45 See particularly Sukstorf, 114 ff.; and for details *Truppenfahrzeuge, Kolonnen und Trains bei den Bewegungen der I. und der II. Deutschen Armee bis zu den Schlachten westlich Metz, Kriegsgeschichtliche Einzelschriften*, 17, ed. Grosser Generalstab (Berlin, 1895).

46 Frederick III, *The War Diary of the Emperor Frederick III, 1870–1871*, tr. and ed. A.R. Allinson reprint ed. (New York, 1988), p. 95.

47 Georg Cardinal von Widdern, *Der Krieg an den Rueckwaertigen Verbindungen der deutschen Heere 1870–71*, 5 vols in 8 (Berlin, 1893–1899); and *Der kleine Krieg und der Etappendienst*. 2 ed. rev. (Berlin, 1899), incorporated a wealth of narrative data; Bernhard Winterhalter, 'Die Behandlung der franzoesische Zivilbevoelkerung durch die deutschen Truppen im Kriege 1870/71', Dissertation Freiburg, 1952, provides the framework of laws and regulations that shaped much, though not all, of the army's behaviour. Cf. as well Mark Stoneman, 'The Bavarian Army and French Civilians in the War of 1870–71', MA thesis, Augsburg, 1994; and Ferdinand Thiebault, 'Der Krieg in franzoesischer Sicht', in *Entscheidung 1870*, ed. W. von Groote, U. von Gersdorff (Stuttgart, 1970), p.165 ff.

48 Quoted in Geoffrey Best, *Humanity in Warfare* (London, 1980), p. 198.

49 Paul B. Hatley, 'Prolonging the Inevitable: The Franc-Tireur and the German Army in the Franco-German War of 1870–71', Dissertation, Kansas State University, 1999.

50 An excellent case study in the limits of anti-rail operations at this period, even when undertaken by large forces, is David Evans, *Sherman's Horsemen. Union Cavalry Operations in the Atlanta Campaign* (Bloomington, IN, 1996).

51 Jacquemin, 316 ff., also lists the sites of destruction and damage.

52 Martin van Creveld, *Supplying War. Logistics from Wallenstein to Patton* (Cambridge, 1977), pp. 94–5.
53 The most detailed account of the raid and its aftermath is Herman Kunz, *Der Ueberfall bei Fontenoy sur Moselle am 22. Januar 1871* (Berlin). The French versions include Amadée Brenet, *La France et l'Allemagne devant le droit international pendant les operations militaires de la guerre de 1870–71* (Paris, 1902), p. 12 ff. and H.Genevois, *Les Coups de main pendant la guerre* (Paris, 1896), p. 111 ff., Cf. *MMK*, 1, III, 531–2.
54 John Horne and Alan Kramer, *German Atrocities 1914: A History of Denial* (New Haven, CT, 2001), p. 98 ff.
55 Mark R. Stoneman, 'Buegerliche und adelige Krieger: Zum Verhaeltnis zwischen sozialer Herkunft und Berufskultur im Wilhelminischen Armee-Offizierkorps', in *Adel und Buergertum in Deutschland II: Entwicklungslinien und Wendepunkte im 20. Jahrhundert*, ed. H. Reif (Berlin, 2001), is a pathbreaking analysis of the simultaneous development of professionalization and bureaucratization.
56 Annika Mombauer, *Helmuth von Moltke and the Origins of the First World* War (Cambridge, 2001), p. 216 ff.; and for the refutation, H. von Staabs, *Aufmarsch nach zwei Fronten* (Berlin, 1925).

3 'The most catastrophic question'

Railway development and military strategy in late imperial Russia

Anthony J. Heywood

The relationship between railways, state and empire in late tsarist Russia became distinctively ambiguous. A fundamental lesson of the Crimean War was the economic, political and military urgency of creating a public railway network. During the following half-century the development of a common-carrier system of some 70,500 route km duly facilitated economic modernization, increased central control over the periphery, abetted diplomatic resurgence, and furthered imperial expansion.[1] By 1913, the railways were the empire's 'arteries': much faster than the few waterways and roads, and far less susceptible to winter disruption, they handled most long-distance freight and passenger traffic. Yet by this juncture their construction expenses had helped burden Russia with a huge foreign debt without clearly finishing the job: many more lines were still deemed essential. Meanwhile, the projection of Russian power into Manchuria through the building of the trans-Siberian route in 1892–1905 contributed to the outbreak of the Japanese war in 1904, with traffic difficulties at Lake Baikal becoming a symbol of the empire's disarray. A railway strike in October 1905 even threatened to topple the autocracy. Above all, the railways failed, for most observers, to cope with the huge demand for transport in the First World War. Exacerbated by poor management and pre-war underdevelopment, their problems impaired the army's ability to fight, and spurred crisis in the rear. The resultant price inflation and food shortages helped to spark the February 1917 revolution in the capital, Petrograd (formerly St Petersburg), which ousted the autocracy. In short, to mix medical metaphors, the empire's apparently sclerotic arteries proved to be its 'Achilles Heel'.[2]

This picture highlights the immense significance of railway transport in imperial Russia. But how valid are the criticisms? Regarding the world war, for example, some historians now see the railway problems as merely part of a general political and economic collapse. The network coped adequately with peacetime demand, but not with a long war which no one had predicted; in the circumstances, railway performance was very creditable. For instance, network management by the Ministry of Ways of Communications (MPS) was hindered by the assignment of nearly one-third of the mileage to direct army control, and especially by the army's hoarding of freight wagons on those lines. The government failed not only to address these problems, but likewise to define locomotive, wagon and rail production as a defence priority. Yet the railways shipped a record amount of freight in 1915 and again in 1916. The food shortages were arguably more a product of poor local distribution from urban warehouses.[3]

Seeking to extend this debate, this chapter revisits 'Russia's most catastrophic question': the military's concern that insufficient and uneven development of the transport infrastructure represented a 'sword of backwardness' which greatly restricted military planning.[4] The discussion focuses on the western areas of the empire during the last decades before 1914. The first two sections survey the relevant railway and military contexts: network growth, patterns of ownership and management, the procedure for evaluating proposals for new lines, and the ethos of Russian military planning. The third section discusses the army's railway analysis in terms of the network's military tasks in the event of war, alleged railway deficiencies, and the military implications of those problems. The final section uses a 1912 proposal for a new trunk route to highlight these issues in planning practice. Amid confusion about the meaning of basic concepts like 'strategic railway', the army's evaluation of underdevelopment was probably exaggerated. Moreover, military interests shaped Russia's western system to a much greater extent than has been realised: the army's wounds from the 'sword of backwardness' were partly self-inflicted.

The railway context

For all the fame of the trans-Siberian project, the Russian empire's public railway system was concentrated with most of the population in European Russia, Poland, Finland and the Caucasus, with much of the construction occurring in two 'booms' somewhat later than in European rivals like Britain and Germany. The first public railway opened in 1837, at roughly the same time as the first lines of Germany, France and Austria–Hungary. But by 1854 only about 1,000 route km were in operation, including the 650 km St Petersburg–Moscow line known as the Nicholas Railway in honour of the reigning tsar. Thanks to a 'boom' in the 1860s–70s the operational mileage leapt to about 20,000 km. These lines mostly formed a basic system radiating from Moscow towards the iron ore deposits of the Urals, the coal, ores and new heavy industry of the Donetsk basin (Donbass) in the south, the grain of the Volga region and Ukraine, and ports on the Baltic and Black sea coasts. Investment in new lines declined somewhat in the later 1870s and remained modest through the 1880s. But a second 'boom' in the 1890s boosted the route mileage to 58,400 km by 1903. Now the empire had a system which was approaching the most distant borders in Central Asia and the Far East. After a dip in investment during the early 1900s another investment 'boom' began in about 1907, with over 27,000 km of new routes authorized by 1916 despite disruption caused by the First World War. As of 1913, the empire had about 70,500 route km, of which 52,854 km (75 per cent) were in European Russia and Poland.[5] In absolute terms the mileage was similar to Britain, Germany and France, though these countries were far smaller and had largely completed their trunk routes by the 1870s.

Essentially there were four related reasons for the fitful pattern of development: geographical challenges, the socio-economic environment, state officialdom's deep-rooted suspicion of private enterprise, and concern about foreign control. By the 1840s most governments in western Europe had conceded, reluctantly or otherwise, that the construction of a national railway network required large-scale private investment. But the Russian government resisted this conclusion for much longer, even though the vast distances implied huge costs. Alarmed by financial scandals in the first projects, aware of the scarcity of domestic venture capital, and resistant to foreign control of Russian railways, the government accepted the slower rate of progress implied by reliance on state funds. For years there was virtual stagnation because Count E.F. Kankrin, Minister of Finances in 1823–44, convinced the tsar not to fund railways with state borrowing. Policy changed only when the Crimean débâcle inspired a sense of urgency and desperation. The consequent openness to private capital, including foreign loans and investment, duly delivered the first 'boom'. But soon this policy caused alarm. More scandals, with bankruptcies and the expense of ill-advised state guarantees, helped reinvigorate suspicion of the private sector and foreign ownership. Now the state sought to become the dominant player in ownership as well as regulation. Over the next thirty years, at enormous expense, it funded the majority of new projects, nationalized many private lines, and encouraged the consolidation of other private lines into a few large companies, which the state would purchase at the end of their concession. The modesty of investment in the 1880s reflected the government's need to rebuild the state finances after the war of 1877–8 with Turkey; the frenzy of the 1890s marked the determination of I.A. Vyshnegradskii and especially S.Iu. Witte, Ministers of Finances in 1886–1903, to promote rapid industrialization. By 1910, however, this control strategy had created such a financial burden that, despite MPS opposition, private capital was accepted for the next phase of railway construction.[6]

Proposals for new railways were evaluated within a hierarchical state committee structure.[7] The model established by the 1870s survived, with refinements, until 1917, and is best illustrated for present purposes with the institutions used in 1899–1917. Projects were normally initiated by, or in conjunction with, the MPS Directorate for Railway Construction. An initial land survey, which required government permission, was used for preparing technical and financial-economic proposals. Once these proposals had been provisionally agreed within or with the construction directorate, the technical aspects underwent preliminary assessment by a committee of senior railway engineers known as the MPS Engineering Council, which often stipulated significant changes. The financial-economic document went to an inter-departmental committee called the Commission for New Railways. This committee was based in the Department of Railway Affairs at the Ministry of Finances, and had voting members from all the main ministries, including the Ministry of War and Ministry of the Navy.[8] Here local government and private interests had their main opportunity to make representations, after which the committee debated the proposal's economic, political, military and other implications behind closed doors. Competing proposals for a given route were normally discussed together. The result was a policy recommendation which guided the compiling of a draft law by the MPS and Department of Railway Affairs. According to a statute of 1892, in force until 1906, state-promoted schemes and large private schemes generally went forward to the Committee of Ministers, and were referred to the State Council's Department of the State Economy if public money was required; approved projects then went to the tsar for ratification as law. After 1906 proposals wholly financed by private interests were assessed by the State Council's Second Department, usually in the presence of relevant ministers, including the Minister of War. Meanwhile projects requiring state expenditure were analysed by the new elected consultative parliament, the State Duma. As before, the tsar provided final authorization. Then began the detailed planning, including more surveys and a revised technical plan.

The most important and difficult step in this ladder was the Commission for New Railways. The Engineering Council caused inordinate delays on occasion, and Duma representatives generally relished opportunities to inconvenience the regime by challenging expenditure proposals. But the Commission for New Railways was the main forum for the interplay of departmental and other interests. This was the point at which the relative importance of economic and military priorities was assessed. Moreover, a firm recommendation from this committee was unlikely to be overruled unless there were potentially major financial implications for the treasury. Thus, if there were competing proposals for building a given route, the losers could not expect much joy from appeals to the committee's chair, the Minister of Finances, or the State Council.

One should clarify here the military's institutional place in railway development debates. Numerically, the position of the military representatives in the Commission for New Railways appears weak. The ministries of finance, ways of communication, trade and industry, and internal affairs each had five members, though the finance team was strongest, for the director of the Department of Railway Affairs was the *ex-officio* chairman. The audit ministry, known as State Control, had four members, while the War Ministry and the agriculture directorate each had two members; the Navy Ministry, the State Chancellery and the Ministry of the Imperial Court each had just one member. But the military ministries could bring further representatives to specific debates, albeit in a non-voting capacity. Their ministers could participate in the debates of the Committee of Ministers or Council of Ministers, as well as in the State Council's sessions. And in the last resort they also had ministerial access to the tsar, which they did use. In institutional terms there is no reason to conclude that they were excluded from the process.[9] Whether their voice was heeded, and if not, why, are separate questions to which we will return below.

The military context

During the late nineteenth and early twentieth centuries Russian military planners contended with an ominous strategic environment. Defending a vast territory, they identified serious dangers on all sides: the alliance of Germany,

Austria–Hungary and Romania in the west; the Ottoman Empire in the south; the growth of British influence in Afghanistan and potentially in Central Asia; China, which was succumbing to West European influence and with which Russia shared a long but very exposed border; and the rise of Japan with imperial ambitions. By the 1890s the Main Staff defined the Triple Alliance of Germany, Austria–Hungary and Romania as the most potent threat. But after 1905 the military authorities were also inclined to expect more Japanese aggression. Basing their plans on worst-case scenarios, they wanted the capacity to fight simultaneously on two fronts, which they expected to be in the West and Far East.[10]

This aim constituted an extraordinary challenge.[11] Army strategists expected a short war with a decisive battle very soon after the start of hostilities. Rapid troop mobilization and deployments were thus essential for victory.[12] This perspective was reinforced for Russia by an accord with France to attack Germany as soon as possible in the event of war, which dated from the birth of the Franco-Russian alliance in the 1890s. Yet it was seemingly compromised by chronic problems. Russian generals regarded the quantity and quality of their manpower as insufficient, their transport system as underdeveloped, and their funds as inadequate. Moreover, after 1905 they had to balance their western and eastern needs. The loss of the Baltic and Pacific fleets in 1904–5 left two coasts and the capital exposed. Yet urgent naval reconstruction required huge investment, and the vast distance between the two prospective fronts rendered quick transfers of troops impossible even in ideal conditions. Iu.N. Danilov, deputy chief of the General Staff in 1909–14, was perhaps a little melodramatic in recalling 1906–10 as 'the period of our complete military helplessness', but he did have a point.[13]

For decades, until about 1909, the Russian army's response was essentially cautious. This course was set in the early 1870s following Prussia's crushing defeat of France. Especially influential was an analysis by Major-General N.N. Obruchev, who argued that Germany and Austria–Hungary would probably act in coalition in the event of war with Russia, that each had numerical superiority over the Russian army, and that they could mobilize in less than half the time needed for Russian mobilization. Hence it was vital for Russia to strengthen her defences. She should construct new fortresses and some 7,000 km of strategic railways, expand the army, and deploy larger forces in and next to Poland to reduce long-distance troop movements during mobilization. If war occurred, the army would mobilize as quickly as possible so as to thwart an enemy offensive and, when and where appropriate, conduct offensive and/or counter-offensive operations.[14] Aspects of this approach (known as the Miliutin–Obruchev system) were later changed, but the underlying ethos of caution remained intact despite even the 1892 agreement with France. Indeed, following the losses and dislocation of the Russo-Japanese War, this defensive mentality was even stronger for some years.[15]

But from about 1911 a more aggressive strategy was devised for which alleged railway underdevelopment was a critical aspect. Adopted in 1912, the plan involved two offensives on diverging trajectories, against Germany and Austria–Hungary respectively, and the commitment to begin the offensive against Germany from the fifteenth day after the declaration of mobilization. On both counts the plan was risky: the two attacking forces would be vulnerable to counter-attack in the gap emerging between them, and the attack would begin before the completion of Russian troop mobilization and concentration. Despite progress in building strategic railways since the 1870s, the network was still considered inferior to German and Austro-Hungarian railway capability, and only minimally adequate for supporting the war plan now being adopted. A programme of railway investment to speed up mobilization was negotiated in 1912–14, but it was not scheduled for completion until 1917. Indeed, the outbreak of war in 1914 prevented it from being submitted to the Council of Ministers for formal endorsement.[16]

This abandonment of long-standing caution has prompted much scholarly debate about motives and responsibility. For example, Menning has argued that the plan was an opportunistic compromise between Danilov and General M.V. Alekseev, the chief of staff for the Kiev military district.[17] For our purposes two questions arise. First, army agreement to advance against Germany from M+ 15 begs the question of whether perhaps the army was more sanguine about railway support than has been assumed. Second, did the Russian army reluctantly agree to French pressure for this offensive timetable on condition that France provided loans for building strategic railways, as various Russian and Soviet sources have claimed, or was the loan merely a convenient excuse for the acquiescence, as J. Snyder has suggested?[18] Whichever interpretation is accepted, alleged railway deficiencies were potentially a political weapon. In that light, how should we assess the Russian army's analysis of, and responses to, the military-strategic railway situation for the western frontier?

The army's railway analysis

To define a 'strategic railway' in imperial Russia is more difficult than one might expect. A lay observer might reasonably assume, and the Russian public undoubtedly did assume, that all trunk routes and many secondary lines were strategically significant. But up to 1914 the army took a much narrower view.[19] In fact, the railways would have just two main jobs in the event of conflict, which reflected the expectation of an early decisive battle and a short war. The first was to move the troops from assembly points to the concentration areas during mobilization; for the western border, this task focused attention on about eight trunk routes from such cities as St Petersburg, Moscow, Orel, Kursk, Poltava and Odessa. The other task was to maximize the army's scope for operational manoeuvre by enabling troops to be moved between different sectors of the front; in the west the necessary railways were mostly shorter secondary and local routes in Russian-controlled Poland and on, very crudely, a north–south axis in the vicinity of Russia's frontiers with Poland and Austria–Hungary, where the miltary landscape was complicated by the vast Pripiat marshes.[20] Accordingly, army planners identified 'strategic railways' and assessed their adequacy primarily in relation to these two tasks. Outside this framework, and hence not treated by the military as 'strategic railways', were most lines in the rear, including those geared to the industrial and civilian needs of major cities like Moscow and Petersburg.[21]

Relying mostly on broad international statistical comparisons, the army consistently perceived alarming backwardness in railway infrastructure and equipment right up to 1914. As Table 3.1 shows, on the eve of the First World War Russia seemed far behind Germany and other powers on such criteria as mileage per capita and square kilometre of land, quantity of locomotives, and quantity of freight wagons. To match Germany's infrastructure, it was claimed, the Russian network would need expansion to about 200,000 route km. Especially worrying were comparisons of the quantity of trunk lines to the frontier area, especially double-track lines, and their traffic capacity. As of 1909, Germany, Austria–Hungary and Romania had eighteen, fourteen and four lines to their border with the Russian empire, whereas Russia had ten, seven and two respectively.[22] The implication was that Germany and Austria–Hungary could concentrate their troops near the border far more quickly than Russia. Yet Russia could not easily overcome her disadvantage. Military issues, the strategists complained, were being neglected in railway planning in favour of economic criteria. Insufficient state funds were being released for the improvements and new lines required for military purposes.[23] And, ironically, the construction of more lines in border areas might do more harm than good by assisting an enemy advance.[24]

The army's policy responses were, until about 1912, a combination of adaptation, caution, investment, and pressure for change. The peacetime deployment of troops was designed to minimize the need for railway capacity during mobilization. Until 1910, for example, regular army units were mostly deployed near the frontier, and the railways' main task during mobilization was to bring in reservists. Meanwhile the army's demands for more investment were mainly designed to

Table 3.1 Public railways of European powers and the United States, 1910

	European Russia	*Austria– Hungary*	*Germany*	*France*	*Great Britain*	*United States*
Route mileage, versts	50,453	40,002	54,521	37,893	35,291	360,067
Of which double/ triple track, versts	13,737	4,516	21,393	16,602	19,726	38,259
Locomotives	16,930	10,806	27,042	12,840	22,840	58,947
Locomotives per route verst	0.34	0.27	0.50	0.34	0.65	0.16
Freight wagons	400,022	249,177	604,677	348,714	786,819	2,213,236
Wagons per route verst	7.93	6.29	11.17	9.19	22.30	6.15
Train-versts operated (mill.)	322.0	269.5	643.4	362.9	638.6	1,843.8
Employees per route verst	13.3	10.2	12.8	8.9	no data	4.7

Source: *Statisticheskii sbornik Ministerstva putei soobshcheniia za 1913 g., vypusk 141, chast' 3* (Petrograd, 1916), pp. XII–XXI, cited in A.M. Anfimov *et al.* (comps and eds), *Rossiia 1913 god: Statistiko–dokumental'nyi spravochnik* (St Petersburg, 1995), pp. 113–14; 1 verst is 1.06 km.

speed up mobilization by increasing trunk route capacity from the interior towards the border. The desired measures included new lines and improvements such as double-tracking. Indeed, the war ministry encouraged French pressure on the Russian government to authorize more strategic railways, possibly – as noted above – to the extent of agreeing to attack Germany after M+15 in return for a railway loan. As for new routes in the frontier area, the army's characteristically cautious policy for many years was normally to resist proposals. And this opposition was actually very successful, however much the army felt neglected in railway development planning.[25]

The more offensively oriented 1912 war plan involved important policy changes regarding railway construction. Much more money was to be assigned for developing and improving 'strategic railways' over the period 1913–17. This change was due partly to French pressure on the Russian government to launch an offensive against Germany very soon after the outbreak of war, and to strengthen the railways for that purpose – circumstances in which the war ministry happily linked its alliance commitment to railway investment and a French loan.[26] In 1912, therefore, the ministry compiled a list of its top priorities across the empire, costed at roughly 650 million rubles, for inclusion in the 1913–17 railway development and improvement plan. The MPS, broadly sympathetic but dubious about certain details, suggested that an inter departmental commission be formed to agree a programme of militarily essential work. This body duly began functioning in November 1913, by which time the war ministry had expanded its list to about 1,240 million rubles.[27] Eventually, the railway improvement and development plan included some 470 million rubles for military needs – roughly 72 per cent of the war ministry's opening gambit, and 17 per cent of the plan's total budget of 2.8 billion rubles.[28] With regard to the western areas these works were mostly designed to speed up transit for troop mobilization; the war ministry did not change its defensive policy regarding local lines in the frontier area until January 1914.[29]

To what extent, then, can we endorse the military's railway analysis? The first point to make is that, although the task of maintaining Russia's security was daunting, historians have strongly criticized the army's strategic planning. It has been argued that the defensive plans were overcautious, based on exaggerated notions of the threats. On one occasion, for instance, the General Staff assumed simultaneous conflict on virtually all sides, prompting the respected analyst A.A. Kersnovskii to remark that only a Martian attack was discounted.[30] As for the ill-fated 1912 plan, Menning writes of its 'tragically flawed strategic design that helped lead to the catastrophes of 1914 on the Russian front'.[31] Aspects of the more detailed planning have likewise been disparaged. For example, the Russian war games assumed that Germany would advance, and ignored the possibility that Germany would not move – the eventuality of August 1914. Also, the war games usually excluded railway transport issues, despite their centrality to the mobilization effort.[32]

Curiously, military historians have been much less critical of the army's railway analysis. In particular, the claim of railway underdevelopment has remained largely unchallenged. W.C. Fuller notes that the Austro-Hungarian and German railway networks 'consistently outclassed' Russia's network between the 1870s and 1914.[33] Similarly, Luntinen accepts the French verdict that much more investment was needed to bring the network to the level needed for enabling a successful offensive against Germany, and their verdict that lack of money was the reason for 'the defect'.[34] The only important criticisms of the army's stance have concerned the narrow concept of 'strategic railway' and the lack of railways near the border. But even these points have mostly been confined to brief notes in a few Soviet and émigré works of the 1920s and 1930s.[35] Now, to such criticisms we add the argument that the army's view of railway underdevelopment was probably exaggerated, and that its policy responses may also merit thorough reassessment.

The narrow definition of railway military tasks affected both development and operation. It encouraged an unfortunate tendency at the MPS for 'strategic railway' to imply a state-funded loss-making line. True, economic and military imperatives coincided in the case of east–west routes which had good commercial prospects. But cross-country and local routes in the frontier area were another matter. They were rarely seen as commercially viable during the mid-to-late nineteenth century, and because neither the MPS nor the war ministry wanted the financial burden of building and operating military lines, such routes did not get built at that time; later the war ministry opposed the construction of such routes for fear of aiding the enemy. As for prospective wartime railway operation, the lack of a broader view of the front and rear as an integrated military-economic system ensured that the military plans underestimated the importance of industrial and civilian supply routes in the rear. For example, war with Germany would probably close the Baltic Sea to the shipments of British coal on which the Russian capital relied for most of its fuel needs, and would force their replacement by Donbass coal – a substantial and potentially disruptive new south–north traffic flow.

Furthermore, the use of international comparisons to identify underdevelopment was problematic. The statistics appeared to provide an objective comparative picture, with at least a basic indication of foreign capabilities and strengths (or weaknesses). They appeared, crucially, to support the military's case for substantial investment, and, one might add cynically, to identify a potential scapegoat in the event of trouble. But they could also mislead. The army authorities largely ignored the methodological problems inherent in making very broad comparisons. Potentially huge variations in context could severely restrict the data's comparability, especially in the geographical, socio-economic, technical and military-strategic circumstances. And if we look closely at examples of these contextual issues, we can suggest that Russia's strategic railway disadvantage for *defence* of the western frontier may have been much less than the army perceived.

For a start, the range and character of the data were potentially misleading. For the western frontier, comparisons with Germany, Austria–Hungary and Romania were natural. But, for the empire as a whole, how does one explain the usual absence of data for the Ottoman Empire, the perennial foe in the south? In fact, as of 1912, the Russian General Staff was confident that it had superior rail access in the Caucasus, and was seeking certain new lines so as to maintain superiority and offensive capability in the light of projects like the Berlin–Baghdad route.[36] Similarly, the comparisons neglected the Far East, where railway density was low everywhere. Perhaps, then, these omissions reflected concern about dilution of the 'underdevelopment' thesis. As for the data's character and comparability, the methods of compiling statistics could vary considerably. For example, the usual Russian figure for network route kilometres concerned only the common-carrier railway system, and excluded such things as narrow-gauge feeder lines in the Baltic provinces and Poland, which could be important as field railways.[37] Were the same criteria used for the German, Austro-Hungarian and Romanian data?

Similarly, one must query the criteria for comparisons with specific countries. Russia's low railway density becomes much less striking as an indicator of backwardness if one remembers that much of the Russian territory would remain sparsely populated because of its inhospitable geography. Zaionchkovskii, writing in the 1920s, acknowledged this difficulty by removing certain northern regions from his statistics. But one suspects that this point should be taken much further. It certainly seems absurd to extrapolate from German data on this basis, as the Russian General Staff evidently did in all seriousness, that Russia needed a public network of some 200,000 route km to match Germany's provision.[38]

Broad socio-economic comparisons have suggested Russian weakness relative to her rivals. Yet one needs to know why patterns of railway development differed in the frontier areas. The explanations may well be local factors devoid of specific military significance. For instance, differences between Germany and Russia in the pace of development stemmed partly from their radically different investment philosophies: the former encouraged private capital in most regions, whereas the latter relied on state finance from the 1870s. The associated planning philosophies also differed: the German army was much less involved in railway development planning for the frontier area than its Russian counterpart.[39] Moreover, in Germany there were few geographical obstacles, land was cheap, and the country was well situated to benefit from international transit traffic.[40] In Silesia, Germany had the advantage of coal extraction as an obvious commercial objective for private railway investment, irrespective of strategic issues. Indeed Silesia was the third busiest region of German railways in 1913.[41] By contrast, large railway profits were not expected for most of Russian-held Poland, which was mainly agricultural plain with a lower population density; the analogous Russian mining area was the Donbass, which did gain a dense railway net.

Technical comparisons can be especially troublesome, as the following five examples show. First, famously, gauge difference was relevant. The story that defence concerns explain why Russia adopted a gauge of 1,524 mm (five feet) instead of the emerging European norm of 1,435 mm is apocryphal.[42] But the result obviously favoured Russia for defence purposes to some extent, though the same point applied for Germany and Austria–Hungary. Second, Russia probably made greater progress than her rivals in equipment standardization and unified management. Standardization efforts were under way by the early 1870s, and were intensified after the transport chaos of the 1877–8 war with Turkey. In

Germany, by contrast, such measures were delayed by the local 'particularism' of German states.[43] Third, the crucial question of line capacity must be related to the availability of rolling stock; in reality, because the Russians glossed over such nuances with a crude rule-of-thumb analysis, French experts concluded that the Russians were overestimating Austro-Hungarian railway capacity.[44] Fourth, the quantities of rolling stock need to be related to equipment quality and traffic demand. On both these counts the Russian difficulties were probably exaggerated. For instance, the army believed that the locomotive situation on the eve of the First World War was deteriorating because the stock quantity was declining; in fact, the introduction of new 'powerful' locomotives was permitting the MPS to withdraw large numbers of obsolete low-powered designs. As for traffic, stock shortages did occur, generating much adverse publicity. However, they were periodic and localized rather than all-embracing, and the railways generally carried the traffic on offer.[45] Fifth, route and stock capacity were also a function of what was carried. The designation '40 people or 8 horses', found on wagons throughout Europe at the time, did not simply indicate a dual use for the rolling stock; it also had implications for line capacity. In practice, a Russian cavalry division required four times as much railway capacity as an infantry division. Had the Russian army reduced its reliance on cavalry, it could have moved many more infantry units much more quickly during mobilization.[46]

Finally, if we look at the central European strategic transport context, the railway comparison can seem much less unfavourable for Russia for three reasons. One is that Germany and Austria–Hungary also faced potential war on two fronts, respectively against France and Russia, and against Serbia and Russia. The second reason is that, ironically, Russia's apparent railway inferiority encouraged the German high command to feel reasonably secure in East Prussia and Silesia. And the third reason is that, like their Russian counterparts, the Germans regarded their railway network as problematic. They considered it sparse in the east, though adequate thanks to its greater density compared to Russian Poland. But the east–west axis was weakened by the lack of a Berlin orbital railway, which was not completed by 1914 (the Moscow equivalent was opened in the early 1900s). In the west, industrial Westphalia was well served, but funds were lacking for more crossings of the River Rhine for military purposes. Crucially, there was only one junction – Aachen – on an 80-mile front to handle the troop concentration for the attack on Belgium; and correspondingly the rapid success of this invasion would depend heavily on capturing intact the tunnels and bridges of the Liège junction. This bottleneck had important repercussions for Russia. Within the Schlieffen concept of a knock-out blow against France, and given Germany's defensive strength in East Prussia and Silesia, it helped produce the plan whereby Germany's rolling stock would be concentrated in the *west* during mobilization.[47]

The result was a tragic irony for Russia. Although Russia had less railway capacity than Germany for troop concentration, she would be making much greater use of that capacity than would be the case in eastern Germany. However, the delicate balance would be upset if Russia significantly improved her net of 'strategic railways', for the German command would feel much less secure. Yet the Russian General Staff's *perception* of underdevelopment did lead, from about 1912, precisely in that direction. The Germans duly became more apprehensive about how much more quickly Russia could mobilize. By 1917, they feared, Russian mobilization would take only three days longer than German mobilization if no major changes were made in Germany. Since the Schlieffen Plan could not succeed in those circumstances, Russian railway-building may have encouraged Germany's readiness to fight in 1914.[48]

The Russian perception of underdevelopment was perhaps more justified in relation to an immediate Russian offensive. Railway capacity determined the speed with which troops could be concentrated, and the network of 1912 simply could not complete both its own mobilization (needing perhaps ten days) and the movement of sufficient troops in time for the offensive scheduled to follow M+15 in the new war plan. But this point too must be caveated. In railway terms an offensive meant far more than just mobilization. Since the technology favoured a defender over an attacker, a certain advantage was automatically conceded to Germany and Austria–Hungary.[49] Moreover, the gauge difference would form an additional barrier. If the Russians broke through, their forward units would soon be far from the nearest Russian-gauge railhead, with all the supply difficulties which that implied. In other words, no matter how well Russian railways were developed, and how quickly Russia mobilized, her offensive could still be badly disrupted by railway problems in enemy territory.

The army's perceptions of obstacles to overcoming railway underdevelopment may also require reassessment. For example, one must question the fundamental charge that the Commission for New Railways hindered strategic railway development by prioritizing commercial concerns. Many railways were built primarily for strategic purposes from the 1870s, and a large budget was being drafted in summer 1914 in the light of the new war plan. The commission generally accepted the military's objections to projects for western border areas. In any case, the military's use of a narrow definition of 'strategic railway' was bound to make investment in such lines seem small compared to overall railway investment. And from 1900 the government excluded the commission from discussion of the army's highest priority proposals: Orenburg–Tashkent, Bologoe–Sedlitskaia, the Amur railway (a northern bypass, on Russian territory, for the exposed Chinese Eastern Railway across Manchuria to Vladivostok), and Petrozavodsk–Murmansk.[50] Interestingly, line promoters and other non-military interests tried to strengthen their position by reference to military arguments, using a much wider definition of 'strategic railway' than did the military. Nor should one assume that these military arguments were monolithically self-evident: there were major differences of opinion. And as our case-study will show, there are grounds to suspect that the military was somewhat lethargic in defending its interests in the planning process.

Similarly, it was misleading for the military to argue that insufficient state funds were allocated for its railway needs. Clearly the army's opposition to private investment restricted the options. Moreover, although France gave several loans for strategic railway construction directed primarily against Germany, the Russian army chose to use much of this money in relation to Austria–Hungary.[51] In any case, the military had the option to allocate some of its own budget for railway construction. The fact that it evidently did not do so was, ultimately, a matter of the general squeeze on resources, the ministry's spending priorities, and the army planners' relative lack of interest in railway logistics. Like ministries the world over, the Russian war ministry was playing budgetary politics.

Finally, the worries that line development in border areas would aid an enemy advance were probably exaggerated. Obviously, the Russian side stood to benefit from any lines built if its army managed to hold the border or even advance. It might also benefit to a certain extent from the gauge difference in any defensive actions on Russian territory. An enemy advance could be slowed by even partial destruction of railway infrastructure – a delay which could prove useful though probably not decisive. The complete dismissal of this option was a sign of the army's deep-seated caution, and possibly of an expectation of retreat. Ironically, the later private interest in building lines here would not have undermined the military budget. On balance, in terms of utility during a conflict, one suspects that the benefits would have outweighed dangers.

What, then, of the army's policy responses to 'underdevelopment' in relation to the western border? The initial, purely military measures did address the main perceived difficulties, but later changes tended to exacerbate them. First, the defensive posture adopted for several decades until 1912 was appropriate for the available railway net. However, the 1912 plan represented a big risk in transport terms until the planned investment could enable much quicker troop mobilization. Second, the associated tactic of adjusting the deployment of forces to minimize transport needs was also, for many years, beneficial for prospective railway operation during mobilization, as noted above. But again, later changes – in this case, from 1908 – negated some of that benefit by requiring greater use of transport, notwithstanding the more easterly points now designated for the troop concentrations during mobilization.

The policy of blocking railway construction in forward areas may have been counterproductive. It did achieve its aim of ensuring that few lines were opened in these areas for many years. And it yielded a notable strategic benefit – albeit unintended and unappreciated – in that the Germans felt more secure through their sense of logistical superiority. However, the limited rail network in frontier areas restricted the military's options for operational manoeuvre by rail. Moreover, the policy's reversal from about January 1914, and the subsequent flurry of development interest and activity in the area, alarmed the Germans by threatening quickly to eliminate their superiority. Thus, paradoxically, it actually increased the level of danger to Russia. If, at this juncture, mobilization was effectively an act of war, so too – almost – was this amount of new preparation. Had construction of these lines started earlier at a slower pace, the German reaction could conceivably have been more relaxed.

Generally, the existing literature lacks analysis of the military's efforts to secure more investment in strategic railways, promote specific routes, or obtain improvements such as double-tracking. For example, how should we interpret the budget of 470 million rubles negotiated in 1914? Detailed research is needed, especially regarding the early 1900s and the efforts of 1912–14 to identify the priorities. The next section of this chapter contributes an analysis of the planning discussions about a 1912 proposal to build a trunk route from Orel, south of Moscow, to the Baltic coast. Concentrating on the Commission for New Railways, it shows how the issues discussed above were reflected in the day-to-day practice of railway development planning. It reveals that the army's definition of 'strategic railway' led it to oppose this important extension to the national network, to the military's own potential disadvantage.

Economics, military policy and railway development: a case study

The aftermath of the Russo-Japanese War was an auspicious time for private proposals for a railway from Orel to the Baltic coast. Elements of the state bureaucracy, especially in the Ministry of Finances, were warming to the use of large-scale private finance for the first time since the 1870s. The MPS staunchly resisted this change, but it had no realistic alternative funding for all the projects which it deemed essential. Importantly, this route figured in the five-year railway development plan compiled by an interdepartmental conference in 1908, it bisected many districts which lacked easy access to the rail network, and official permission for surveys was granted in February 1911.[52]

In the event the Commission for New Railways considered three such proposals during 1912–13. The first was submitted in late 1911 by the entrepreneurs N.A. Vasil'ev and K.E. Iurkovskii. They had surveyed a route of some 975 km from Orel through Viaz'ma, Nelidovo, Toropets, Kholm and Dno to the old coastal city of Narva (now Tallinn). The Department for Railway Affairs hoped that the commission could consider this proposal in October 1911 alongside a 'rival' Moscow–Revel' project. But since the paperwork was not completed in time, it deferred the Orel–Narva discussion, hoping in the meantime to hear whether the Council of Ministers supported the commission's rejection of the Moscow–Revel' proposal as uneconomic. The second project was a late entry in May 1912 from the military engineer V.K. Fel'dt and his business partner F.A. Tsekhanovskii. Canny publicists, they called it the Peter Railway to exploit the kudos of Tsar Peter the Great and echo the prestigious Nicholas Railway. It followed a similar route from Orel to Nelidovo, but then took a more easterly course, running via the ancient city of Novgorod to a new terminus in the capital (overall length excluding branches: 921 km). Finally, when the commission began its hearings, the private Moscow–Vindava–Rybinsk Railway Company (MVR) announced its own scheme. Its submission in October 1912 showed a route which, north of Nelidovo, was situated between the other two plans, passing to the west of Novgorod so as to join the company's existing tracks at Tsarskoe Selo for the last few miles to St Petersburg (overall length excluding branches and other lines: 907 km).[53]

The commission's deliberations proceeded according to the normal routine. They commenced with formal hearings in which the promoters outlined their projects and local interests made representations; these meetings were held in late May and mid-December 1912. Then the committee discussed the evidence at length during December 1912, March 1913 and April 1913, including further submissions from the various parties in the later meetings.[54] The process was unusually protracted for several reasons. The first was the need to accommodate the late bids, as well as some reworking of the Orel–Narva plan. Second, the case was complex: the route had high priority, there were multiple proposals, and numerous parties gave evidence. Third, the discussions produced ideas for related projects, mainly to improve access to Revel', which the candidates were required to investigate. Finally, there was the practical obstacle that scheduling extra meetings was difficult because of the commission's heavy workload.

Military considerations were broached at the outset both by promoters and by representatives of local interests. For example, the Narva route's promoters stressed that if the Nicholas Railway had insufficient capacity in the event of war with western powers, their line could move troops and supplies to the coast for defending the capital. Similarly, defenders of the interests of the town of Belyi in Smolensk province claimed that the Narva route had prime strategic importance because it would cross the majority of lines from Moscow to the western border, and would be the nearest main route to the Gulf of Finland.[55] Meanwhile the MVR asserted that its proposed 424 km connecting link from Valdai via Novgorod to Taps would provide alternative winter access to Revel' port while St Petersburg was ice-bound, and would allow rapid movement of troops from Novgorod province to the Gulf together with a convenient supply route for them from the upper Volga region.[56] Essentially the same point was made by delegates from Novgorod in support of a connection from the Peter Railway; they also reminded the commission that the regauging of their narrow-gauge link to the Nicholas Railway would benefit army traffic.[57] Especially pertinent, in the light of future events, was the concern of the St Petersburg city authorities about the capital's reliance on British coal, the supply of which had recently been disrupted by miners' strikes. It was vital to facilitate the use of Russian coal in Petersburg by reducing domestic transport costs, primarily through creating a shorter railway route from the Donbass:

> In the event of military difficulties it will be critically important for St Petersburg to have Russian coal, so that if [British coal] becomes unavailable the city's water supply, trams, factories, artillery institutions and the Navy do not find themselves in a difficult situation. The matter of reducing the cost of transporting Russian coal is a matter of state significance.[58]

On occasion such discussions were quite involved, though not necessarily well informed. In this instance we have a full record of the military-minded justification for the Narva line which a delegate from the town of Kholm presented at an associated session of the Petersburg Regional Committee for Regulating Shipments.[59] Prince K.M. Shakhovskoi commenced by offering his own overall strategic analysis. It was essential, in his view, for the state's system of strategic railways to be coordinated with the defensive and offensive plans of neighbouring states. Germany's plan in alliance with Austria, he asserted, had been to leave a few troops in the east, defeat France quickly, and then attack Russia. Therefore Russian strategic routes needed to connect the centre of country with the western border, 'although we would have enough time for gathering our forces where needed'. In this scenario, a large German assault on the Baltic coast had been impossible thanks to Russia's Baltic Fleet and Germany's engagement on two fronts with relatively limited forces. However, he continued, German plans had probably changed. Germany was building fortresses on the French border, and having strengthened that area, might attack Russia first. Noting the increase of German forces in the east from eighteen to twenty-three corps and the Austrian increase from fourteen to eighteen corps, Shakhovskoi gave full rein to his imagination, and warned that Russia should fear a major German attack on her Baltic coast, which could threaten St Petersburg and the rear of the western army. The situation was serious given the Baltic Fleet's weakness since 1905, the defencelessness of the coast, and the lack of suitable railways apart from the Petersburg–Narva–Revel' route.

How, then, did the military representatives react to such arguments? Except for a statement by the Ministry of Trade and Industry, the commission's minutes do not identify the views of particular ministries. However, records of the State Council show that the army strongly preferred the ill-fated Moscow–Revel' route.[60] Projects for Moscow–Revel' dating from 1902 and 1904 had been rejected by the Commission for New Railways in 1907, and the Revel' project which the commission rejected in 1911 was dismissed by the Council of Ministers on 17 May 1912. But the war ministry kept faith, and objected to the Orel projects as rivals, even though it did not include Moscow–Revel' in its own 1912 list of military priorities. It did not protest formally against the commission's verdict in favour of the MVR's plan in 1913, nor when the Council of Ministers referred this project to the State Council in 1914.[61] But the day before the State Council's meeting, scheduled for 14 June, the war minister, V.A. Sukhomlinov, requested a postponement until the Moscow–Revel' route could be considered as an alternative. Rebuffed, Sukhomlinov lambasted the Orel project in the meeting:

> From the perspective of state defence tasks these lines cannot meet the needs of the army and navy ministries for moving troops, materials and supplies to the city of Revel', which is set to become not just a base for the Baltic Fleet but also a first-rank land fortress, defending access to the capital. The indicated needs can be met appropriately only by building a Moscow–Revel' main line, which the Orel–Petersburg and Smolensk–Iur'ev routes cannot replace at all in this regard. He felt obliged to state this view now, he said, so that when Moscow–Revel' was discussed in the future, no one could argue that these other lines made it unnecessary.[62]

The Commission for New Railways supported the MVR's project mainly on financial grounds. The minutes and related correspondence show that it reaffirmed its opposition to the Moscow–Revel' project as hopelessly uneconomic.

Its comparative analysis of the three Orel proposals concentrated on expected construction costs, commercial traffic and revenue forecasts, and so forth. The question of how much traffic – and hence income – the existing state-owned network would lose to the newcomer was especially delicate: were the tariff advantages for both the mining industry and St Petersburg outweighed by the revenue losses for the state-owned system, which was under intense pressure to cut costs and improve efficiency? Ironically, from this perspective of state-private competition, the commission was less concerned with underdevelopment than with, in its terms, overdevelopment. Finally, the choice of the MVR implied another, less obvious opportunity for a significant saving, for the state could obtain improved terms for its scheduled buy-out of the MVR at the end of the company's operating concession.

The supremacy of such matters over the army preference for Moscow–Revel' may appear to confirm the military's general allegation of economic bias in railway planning. Yet this conclusion would be unjustified, as the commission worked hard for a sensible compromise. It could not be expected to favour an 'uneconomic' alternative which even the war ministry had not registered as a military priority. Indeed, rejecting the Moscow–Revel' route, most members evidently disagreed with the war ministry about Revel's strategic needs. For the commission the strategic priority was links to the naval base at Kronshtadt and to the Urals region, which could be best provided through double-tracking the Petersburg–Narva–Revel' coastal line – a measure which the military did regard as a priority. As for bringing troops to Revel', it was better to have a connection to Pskov and Iur'ev from the Orel route – an argument which the military representatives apparently accepted in the debate as a workable compromise.[63] Indeed, one suspects that the designation of the Iur'ev connection as an essential component of the Orel–Petersburg scheme reflected the commission's concern to accommodate the military's position as well as possible within a sustainable financial framework.

Thus, ironically, the military rejected arguments which were proved correct in 1914–17. It ignored warnings that the Nicholas Railway might be overwhelmed in the event of war. And there can be no doubt that for the actual circumstances of 1914–17 a direct Moscow–Revel' route would have been far less useful than a line from Orel to Petrograd via Viaz'ma. The former would perhaps have relieved some of the strain on the east–west routes supporting the front-line army, as well as providing additional support for defence of the Baltic coast. But the army did not actually need more long-distance east–west capacity either during or after mobilization, except for the evacuation in 1915. Meanwhile an Orel–Viaz'ma–Petrograd line would have relieved the intense pressure on the Nicholas, Moscow Ring and Moscow–Kursk railways, which formed the main route north of Orel for the vital grain, coal, ore and manufactures traffic from the Ukraine to the capital. In reality, this Moscow route became one of the most important traffic bottlenecks in 1915, and a favourite target for critics of the railways.

To this day there is no line from Orel to the Baltic coast through Viaz'ma. Although the State Council approved the MVR's project, it left open a number of decisions about the precise route – for example, whether to pass through Belyi or Demiansk. Naturally, these debates were delayed by the outbreak of war, and local interests took every opportunity to keep lobbying. Not until 16 December 1916 did the State Council deliver its final verdict, with ratification by the tsar on 9 February 1917 – just a fortnight before the revolution started.[64] Some construction work was started during the civil war, but it was soon abandoned, and was never resumed.

Conclusions

Surprising as it may seem, fundamental concepts such as 'strategic railway' and 'underdevelopment' were not clearly defined in railway development planning in late imperial Russia to 1914. Expecting a short war, the military regarded 'strategic railway' in terms of just two tasks: the movement of troops to the forward concentration areas during mobilization, and the transfer of units between parts of the front-line. Logically the military assessed network development in these terms too. By contrast, non-military interests such as private promoters and city authorities tended to take a broader view of military needs as part of their effort to maximize institutional support for (or against) a particular investment proposal. Included in their arguments were such issues as support for the industrial economy and civilian population during a conflict. In other words, non-military interests emphasized concerns which the military neglected and which, of course, became critical during the First World War.

Undoubtedly the European network of the Russian Empire, including the western borderlands, was underdeveloped to at least some extent. Aside from other evidence, the large volume of private investment proposals on the eve of the First World War bespeaks this. But the extent of underdevelopment surely requires reassessment. Even in its own terms – the two strategic tasks – the army's pre-war assessment seems exaggerated and misleading. Its statistical comparisons were beset with methodological pitfalls, especially concerning the multiple contexts. Exactly why the army analyses glossed over these issues is a matter for more detailed research. But one can suggest that two factors may prove especially important: the underlying caution of the pre-1912 war plans, and budgetary politics.

Similarly, the army's explanations for the 'underdevelopment' which it perceived were also exaggerated and misleading. The army's complaint that it had no voice in railway development planning is untrue: it had representatives at all key stages of the process. Moreover, military concerns were not simply ignored: objections to projects in frontier areas were certainly heeded, and the Orel case shows that the Commission for New Railways tried hard to accommodate military interests when rejecting the army's clear preference for a different project. On this basis one should be wary of the military complaint about undue preference for economic criteria in railway development planning. Indeed our case-study reveals that this allegation may conceal such embarrassments as civilian disagreement with the army's strategic analysis *per se*. One can agree that a shortage of money restricted the speed at which military priorities could be met. But how much did it really undermine strategic railway development, especially in the empire's last years? Budget limits were and always will be a fact of bureaucratic life, and they should not be allowed to distract attention from the reality that the war ministry gave other issues greater priority. In fact, the main non-geographical reason for the lack of local lines in the frontier area was the army itself; the war ministry could have chosen to invest more of its own budget in supporting strategic railways, especially short local lines, if it believed they were so important. Further to the rear, the military opposed at least one project which could have immense value in a prolonged conflict in favour of a scheme which did not figure in even its own list of strategic priorities.

In this light we can conclude that there were fundamental problems with the way in which the tsarist military expected to use railway technology to assist imperial defence. Its interest in measures to quicken the pace of troop mobilization made great sense for the paradigm of a short war and decisive battle. But its failure to think beyond this paradigm – in retrospect, very surprising given its customary relish for worst-case scenarios – prevented it from seeing important challenges in the rear. Rather than blame the Russian railways for failing to cope with a long, all-encompassing conflict which not even the military experts predicted, we should consider why indeed the army failed to plan for this most catastrophic scenario.

Notes

I am very grateful to O.R. Airapetov, E.P. Consey, C. Divall, B.W. Menning, J.N. Westwood and the staff of the Russian State Historical Archive (RGIA) in St Petersburg for assistance in the preparation of this chapter. Some of the cited sources were consulted during visits to Russia funded by the Royal Society as part of work on a biography of the engineer Iu.V. Lomonosov; I am very grateful for this support.

1 The term 'public' is used here in the sense of publicly accessible common-carrier transport, as distinct from non-public railways such as a factory's internal lines. A common-carrier railway had a statutory obligation to ship all traffic on offer. For mileage details by 1913, excluding Finland, see *Statisticheskii sbornik Ministerstva putei soobshcheniia za 1913 g., vypusk 141, chast' 1* (Petrograd, 1916), pp.2–25, also cited in A.M. Anfimov and A.P. Korelin (comps and eds), *Rossiia, 1913 god: Statistiko-dokumental'nyi spravochnik* (St Petersburg, 1995), pp.110–12. Note that by 1913 there were some fifteen local feeder railways (2,644 route km), mostly narrow-gauge lines in Poland and the Baltic Provinces, which were not part of the common-carrier network, but which were publicly accessible.

2 For a general history of Russian railways see J.N. Westwood, *A History of Russian Railways* (London, 1964). The Achilles heel metaphor was popularized by the Soviet historian A.L. Sidorov in his account of the war years: 'Zheleznodorozhnyi transport Rossii v pervoi mirovoi voine i obostrenie ekonomicheskogo krizisa v strane', in *Istoricheskie zapiski*, Vol. XXVI (Moscow, 1948), pp.3–64. For a good example of such criticisms in an authoritative Soviet work of military history see K. Ushakov, *Podgotovka voennykh soobshchenii Rossii k mirovoi voine* (Moscow-Leningrad, 1928), pp.13–15, 105–7.

3 See in particular J.N. Westwood 'The Railways', in R.W. Davies (ed.), *From Tsarism to the New Economic Policy: Continuity and Change in the Economy of the USSR* (Basingstoke, 1990), pp.169–88; and J.N. Westwood, *Railways at War* (London, 1980), pp.148–9. Some

of these points are conceded in a thoughtful analysis of the war years by an army insider and post-revolutionary émigré, S.A. Ronzhin: 'Voennye soobshcheniia i upravlenie imi', in *Sbornik zapisok otnosiashchikhsia k russkomu snabzheniiu v velikuiu voinu* ([San Francisco], 1925), pp.123–55.

4 For the two quotations see respectively: A.M. Zaionchovskii, *Podgotovka Rossii k imperialisticheskoi voine: Ocherki voennoi podgotovki i pervonachal'nykh planov, po arkhivnym dokumentam* (Moscow, 1926), p.55; B.W. Menning, *Bayonets before Bullets: The Imperial Russian Army, 1861–1914* (Bloomington, IN, 1992), pp.116–17, 120, 122. On the issue more generally see, for example: Zaionchkovskii, *Podgotovka Rossii*, pp.44–5, 55–60, 78–80, 122–40; N. Stone, *The Eastern Front, 1914–1917* (Abingdon, 1976), pp.32–3; P. Luntinen, *French Information on the Russian War Plans 1880–1914* (Helsinki, 1984), especially pp.26, 31, 191–3, 195–6.

5 For an exhaustive record of lines and opening dates see G.M. Afonina (comp.), *Kratkie svedeniia o razvitii otechestvennykh zheleznykh dorog s 1838 po 1990 g.* (Moscow, 1995). Mileage figures tend to vary between sources. For instance, slightly lower figures for 1837–1913 were recorded in V.I. Shapiro (ed.), *Statisticheskii ezhegodnik na 1914 g.* (St Petersburg, 1914), p.663, cited in Anfimov *and Korelin, Rossiia, 1913 god*, p.109. The 1913 total for European Russia (excluding Finland) is taken from *Statisticheskii sbornik Ministerstva putei soobshcheniia za 1913 g., vypusk 141, chast' 3* (Petrograd, 1916), pp.XIII–XXI, cited in Anfimov and Korelin, *Rossiia, 1913 god*, pp.113–14. The third 'boom', often overlooked because of the war, is detailed in 'O deiatel'nosti Komissii o novykh dorogakh' [circa January 1917]: RGIA, f.268, op.3, d.1372, ll.2–7ob.

6 For detailed analyses see R.M. Haywood, *The Beginnings of Railway Development in Russia in the Reign of Nicholas I, 1835–1842* (Durham, NC, 1969), and *Russia Enters the Railway Age, 1842–1855* (Boulder, CO, 1998); B.E. Hurt, 'Russian Economic Development, 1881–1914' with Special Reference to the Railways and the Role of the Government (unpublished PhD dissertation, University of London, 1963); S.G. Marks, *Road to Power: The Trans-Siberian Railroad and the Colonization of Asian Russia, 1850–1917* (London, 1991).

7 This paragraph and the two following ones are based on numerous contemporary sources, such as: S.K. Kunitskii (ed.), *Kratkii istoricheskii ocherk deiatel'nosti Inzhenernogo soveta za XXV let s 1892 po 1917 g.* (Petrograd, 1917), especially pp.1–14, 51–65; archive files of the Commission for New Railways, including organizational correspondence 1911–13: RGIA, f.268, op.3, dd.832–834; 'O deiatel'nosti Komissii o novykh dorogakh' [circa January 1917]: RGIA, f.268, op.3, d.1372, ll.1–15; *Obzor deiatel'nosti Vtorogo departamenta Gosudarstvennogo Soveta po rassmotreniiu del o chastnykh zheleznykh dorogakh za vremia s 1906 po 1913 god* (St Petersburg, 1914), especially pp.5–16; *Zhurnaly Vtorogo Departamenta Gosudarstvennogo Soveta sessii 1913–1916 g.* (St Petersburg/Petrograd, 1914–17); *Gosudarstvennaia Duma, sozyv IV, sessii 1–4, 1912/13–1915/16: Zakonoproekty Ministerstva putei soobshcheniia*. For descriptions of the main institutions of state power see A.S. Turgaev (ed.), *Vysshie organy gosudarstvennoi vlasti i upravleniia Rossii, IX–XX vv.: Spravochnik* (St Petersburg, 2000).

8 The other main concern of the finance ministry's railway department was tariff policy.

9 On this point see, for instance, W.C. Fuller Jr, *Strategy and Power in Russia, 1600–1914* (New York, 1992), pp.439–40.

10 See, for example, F.F. Palitsyn and M.V. Alekseev, 'Doklad o meropriiatiiakh po oborone Gosudarstva, podlezhashchikh osushchestvleniiu v blizhaishee desiatiletie' [St Petersburg, 1908], pp.7–9.

11 Analysts such as S.K. Dobrorol'skii have concluded, indeed, that the army leadership was deluding both itself and the whole state: *Mobilizatsiia russkoi armii v 1914 godu: Podgotovka i vypolnenie* (Moscow, 1929), pp.62–3.

12 For a comparative study of French, German and Russian offensive planning see J. Snyder, *The Ideology of the Offensive: Military Decision Making and the Disasters of 1914* (Ithaca, NY, 1984).

13 Iu.N. Danilov, *Rossiia v mirovoi voine* (Berlin, 1924), p.32, cited in B.W. Menning, 'Iu.N. Danilov and M.V. Alekseev in Pre-1914 Russian War Planning', *International Historical Review*, Vol. 25, No. 4 (December 2003).

14 Menning, *Bayonets before Bullets*, pp.19–23.

15 Palitsyn and Alekseev, 'Doklad o meropriiatiiakh', pp.38–41; Zaionchovskii, *Podgotovka Rossii*, p.31.

16 Snyder, *Ideology of the Offensive*, pp.157–98; Menning, 'Danilov and Alekseev'; 'O deiatel'nosti Komissii o novykh dorogakh' [circa January 1917]: RGIA, f.268, op.3, d.1372, l.7ob.

17 Menning, 'Danilov and Alekseev'.

18 Snyder, Ideology of the Offensive, pp.181–2.

19 Zaionchkovskii, *Podgotovka Rossii*, p.123.

20 For a detailed description of relevant lines, stretching back to Moscow and St Petersburg, see Ushakov, *Podgotovka*, pp.49–63.

21 Ronzhin, 'Voennye soobshcheniia', p.133; N. Vasil'ev, *Transport Rossii v voine 1914–1918 gg.* (Moscow, 1939), p.62.

22 Zaionchkovskii, *Podgotovka Rossii*, pp.123–6, 130, 134–9. See also Ushakov, *Podgotovka*, p.15.

23 Private funds were expected to be unavailable in any event because most strategic lines would not be commercially viable.

24 Zaionchkovskii, *Podgotovka Rossii*, p.57.

25 For instance: Menning, *Bayonets before Bullets*, pp.117–20; Snyder, *Ideology of the Offensive*, pp.171–2, 181–2; Zaionchkovskii, *Podgotovka Rossii*, pp.57–8, 128, 130–2. For an example of army opposition to a specific railway project see P.A. Stolypin–V.N. Kokovtsov, 19 May 1909: RGIA, f.268, op.3, d.1643, ll.1–2. This intriguing policy is noted briefly by Zaionchkovskii: *Podgotovka Rossii*, pp.57–8, 128; and by Ronzhin: 'Voennye soobshcheniia', p.134. But neither of them analysed it, and subsequently it has usually been neglected. For an example of a recent comment see Fuller, *Strategy and Power*, pp.439–40. The concept was not exclusive to Russia: French generals considered it after the war of 1870–1: Westwood, *Railways at War*, p.65.

26 On French pressure at this time see Zaionchkovskii, *Podgotovka Rossii*, p.127; Luntinen, *French Information*, pp.192–4.

27 The War Ministry's demands at this time are reproduced in Ushakov, *Podgotovka*, pp.187–90.

28 Rukhlov–Kokovtsev, 22 March 1913: RGIA, f.268, op.3, d.1643, ll.200–3; 'Mery po usileniiu i uluchsheniiu seti zh.d. Imperii dlia obespecheniia interesov gos. oborony na piatiletie 1913–1918' [1912]: RGIA, f.268, op.3, d.1643, ll.204–5; [Department of Railway Affairs?] internal memorandum [June 1913?]: RGIA, f.268, op.3, d.1643, l.230; 'Vypiska iz zhurnala Soveshchaniia pod predsedatel'stvom tain.sov. Dumitrashko otnositel'no meropriatii po uluchsheniiu i usileniiu zheleznodorozhnoi seti so strategicheskoi tsel'iu', 30 November, 10, 16 and 28 December 1913: RGIA, f.268, op.3, d.1643, l.242; Dumitrashko-Starynkevich, 18 February 1914: RGIA, f.268, op.3, d.1643, l.241-ob.; [Department of Railway Affairs?] internal memorandum, [March 1914?]: RGIA, f.268, op.3, d.1643, ll.249–50; Department of Railway Affairs internal memorandum, 12 May 1914: RGIA, f.268, op.3, d.1643, l.262.

29 Zaionchkovskii dates this change as January 1914: *Podgotovka Rossii*, p.128. An example of successful army opposition as late as November 1912 was a projected line from Suvalki on the North Western Railway to the German border: S.V. Rukhlov–Kokovtsov, 28/30 November 1912: RGIA, f.268, op.3, d.1643, l.193-ob.

30 Cited in Menning, 'Danilov and Alekseev'.

31 Menning, 'Danilov and Alekseev'.

32 Snyder, *Ideology of the Offensive*, pp.164, 190–2.

33 Fuller, *Strategy and Power*, p.xix.

34 Luntinen, *French Information*, pp.192–4.

35 Zaionchkovskii, *Podgotovka Rossii*, pp.57–8, 128; Ronzhin: 'Voennye soobshcheniia', p.134.

36 'Mery po usileniiu i uluchsheniiu seti zh.d. Imperii': RGIA, f.268, op.3, d.1643, ll.204–5; Zaionchkovskii, *Podgotovka Rossii*, p.80, 130–1; Luntinen, *French Information*, p.130.

37 For mileage details see Anfimov and Korelin, *Rossiia, 1913 god*, pp.111–12.

38 Zaionchkovskii, *Podgotovka Rossii*, pp.124–5.

39 R.E.H. Mellor, *German Railways: A Study in the Historical Geography of Transport* (Aberdeen, 1976), p.4; Zaionchkovskii, *Podgotovka Rossii*, pp.56, 132.

40 W.O. Henderson, *The Rise of German Industrial Power, 1834–1914* (London: Temple Smith, 1975), p.50.

41 Mellor, *German Railways*, p.47. The same source shows Poznan, the Baltic coast, and East/West Prussia as the least busy areas.

42 Haywood, *Beginnings of Railway Development*, pp.112–13, and *Russia Enters the Railway Age*, pp.118–19; Westwood, *Railways at War*, pp.12–13.

43 Westwood, *History of Russian Railways*, pp.81–2, 95–6, and *Railways at War*, pp.89–90, 120; Mellor, *German Railways*, pp.4, 19.

44 Snyder, *Ideology of the Offensive*, p.176.

45 Zaionchkovskii, *Podgotovka Rossii*, p.137; Sidorov, 'Zheleznodorozhnyi transport', pp.12–13 (and citation in Menning, *Bayonets before Bullets*, p.292, note 124); Westwood, 'The Railways', pp.170–8.

46 Ronzhin, 'Voennye soobshcheniia', p.143; Westwood, *Railways at War*, p.139; Stone, *Eastern Front*, p.36.

47 Mellor, *German Railways*, pp.18–19; Snyder, *Ideology of the Offensive*, pp.112, 152, 154; A.J.P. Taylor, *War by Timetable: How the First World War Began* (London, 1969), p.26; H.H. Herwig, *The First World War: Germany and Austria–Hungary, 1914–1918* (London, 1997), pp.59, 75.

48 For example, Taylor, *War by Timetable*, p.89; Stone, *Eastern Front*, pp.40–2; Westwood, *Railways at War*, pp.126–7.

49 On this general point see Snyder, *Ideology of the Offensive*, pp.21–2, 112, 161, and Westwood, *Railways at War*, pp.141–3. The examples from 1914 include France's troop redeployments to meet the German march through Belgium, the German defence of East Prussia, and Russia's response to an Austrian offensive into Poland.

50 'O deiatel'nosti Komissii o novykh dorogakh': RGIA, f.268, op.3, d.1372, ll.1ob-2.

51 Snyder, *Ideology of the Offensive*, pp.181–2.

52 The priority and survey authorization are noted in N.A. Vasil'ev and K.E. Iurkovskii–Minister of Finances [23] July 1911: RGIA, f.268, op. 3, d.1200, l.1; 'Kratkie ekonomicheskie i finansovye dannye k proektu sooruzheniia zheleznodorozhnoi linii Orel–Narva' [1911]: RGIA, f.268, op.3, d.1200, l.174ob.

53 Vasil'ev and Iurkovskii – Minister of Finances [23] July 1911: RGIA, f.268, op.3, d.1200, l.1; Department of Railway Affairs – Vasil'ev and Iurkovskii, 26 July 1911: RGIA, f.268, op.3, d.1200, l.3-ob.; 'Ekonomicheskaia zapiska k proektu zheleznodorozhnoi linii Orel–Narva' [1911], and revised version [February 1912]: RGIA, f.268, op.3, d.1200, ll.33–76, 80–167; Department of Railway Affairs internal memorandum [circa 11 May 1912]: RGIA, f.268, op.3, d.1200, l.334; 'Zhurnal Kommissii o novykh zheleznykh dorogakh po voprosu o sooruzhenii zheleznykh dorog ot g. Orla k Baltiiskomu moriu', 26 May 1913–9 April 1913, p.5: RGIA, f.268, op.3, d.1326, l.3. The spelling Revel' was used by the planners, for which reason it is preferred here to such alternatives as Reval and Tallinn.

54 For full details see: 'Zhurnal Kommissii', pp.1–82, appendices and map: RGIA, f.268, op.3, d.1326, ll.1–81.

55 'Kratkie ekonomicheskie i finansovye dannye': RGIA, f.268, op.3, d.1200, l.178; Zhurnal Kommissii, p.20: RGIA, f.268, op.3, d.1326, l.10ob.; Representatives of Smolensk Provincial Council, Belyi District Council and the town of Belyi – Minister

of Finances [January 1912]: RGIA, f.268, op.3, d.1200, l.223. Similarly strong sentiments were voiced by representatives from Narva and Gdovsk: Zhurnal Kommissii, p.39: RGIA, f.268, op.3, d.1326, l.20.

56 'Zhurnal Kommissii', pp.5, 24: RGIA, f.268, op.3, d.1326, ll.3, 12ob.

57 'Zhurnal Kommissii', p.37: RGIA, f.268, op.3, d.1326, l.19.

58 'Zhurnal Kommissii', p.38: RGIA, f.268, op.3, d.1326, l.19ob.

59 'Popravka v zaiavlenii Predstavitelia Kholmskogo Zemstva Kniazia Konstantina Mikhailovicha Shakhovskogo v zasedanii S.-Peterburgskogo Poraionnogo Komiteta', 26 August 1912: RGIA, f.268, op.3, d.1201, l.2. This committee, which coordinated the organization of railway traffic in the Petersburg area, collected evidence during 1912 in preparation for its own submission to the Commission for New Railways. Kholm was on the route of the Narva line, but not on the other two routes.

60 V.A. Sukhomlinov (War Minister) to N. Petrov (Head, Second Department, State Council), 13 June 1914: RGIA, f.268, op.3, d.1245, l.443; [Second Department, State Council] internal memorandum, [circa 13 June 1914]: RGIA, f.268, op.3, d.1245, ll.445–8; Minutes of Second Department, State Council, 14 and 19 June 1914: RGIA, f.268, op.3, d.1245, ll.506–10.

61 For details of the main objections and suggestions see the Department of Railway Affairs submission to the Council of Ministers, 3 April 1914: RGIA, f.268, op.3, d.1245, ll.89–ob.

62 Minutes of Second Department, State Council, 14 and 19 June 1914: RGIA, f.268, op.3, d.1245, l.508.

63 See [Second Department, State Council] internal memorandum, [circa 13 June 1914]: RGIA, f.268, op.3, d.1245, l.446–7; 'Vypiska iz zhurnala Soveshchaniia pod predsedatel'stvom tain.sov. Dumitrashko', 30 November, 10, 16 and 28 December 1913: RGIA, f.268, op. 3, d.1643, l.242.

64 MPS Directorate for Railway Construction–Second Department, State Council, 19/22 November 1916: RGIA, f.268, op.3, d.1246, l.261-3ob.; Statute from the Second Department, State Council, 16 December 1916: RGIA, f.268, op.3, d.1246, l.285.

4   The Sanjak of Novibazar Railway project

F.R. Bridge

The Sanjak of Novibazar Railway project, publicly announced in January 1908 but first envisaged in Article XXV of the Treaty of Berlin, was never to come to fruition. Yet its relevance to the theme of 'railways in international history' is undeniable, above all thanks to its contribution to the polarization that culminated in the final catastrophe of the nineteenth-century European states system in 1914.[1] Certainly, as a scheme that hardly even reached the drawing-board stage – indeed, one which was, as will be seen, unrealistic from the start – the Sanjak Railway made no impact whatever on material developments in that Balkan storm-centre whence the Great War arose. It was to make a significant impact, however, on the perceptions and misperceptions of the decision-making elites, their assumptions about the threats they faced, and the measures they felt constrained to take, whether in response or preemptively, to counter these perceived threats. Although the dramatic events of the summer of 1914 seem at first sight to have little to do with the Sanjak Railway crisis that had briefly preoccupied the Powers some six years previously, that the events of in that summer should have been viewed in quite such cataclysmic terms was by no means unconnected to the impact on mentalités in Vienna, St Petersburg and London of the Sanjak Railway crisis of 1908.

   Although 1914 was the first – and last – occasion on which the Habsburg and Romanov empires went to war with each other, their interests in south-east Europe had begun to diverge in the eighteenth century, when the Austrians had ceased to support Russia in her wars against Turkey. From their point of view, the inert Ottoman state was infinitely preferable as a neighbour to anything that might replace it – obstreperous, and potentially irredentist, Russian satellite states or the Russian military colossus itself. Since their expulsion from Italy and Germany in the 1860s, the Habsburgs had been particularly sensitive to the danger that Russian domination of the Balkans might expose them yet again to that disastrous combination of irredentist nationalism backed by a first-class power, this time with terminally fatal consequences for the great power status of the Monarchy – encircled by Russia, excluded from its colonial markets in the Balkans, and at the mercy of irredentist neighbours. The Russians, for their part, could not contemplate the domination of any other Power than Turkey over the approaches to the Straits at Constantinople, through which passed the grain exports of southern Russia so essential to her financial and military viability, indeed, to her very existence as a great power. As a result, the two powers found themselves entangled in a clash of two defensive strategies: the more the Austrians sought security through keeping the Balkans out of Russia's orbit, the more desperate became Russia's efforts to secure the causeway to the Straits by establishing her influence over the peninsula. It was, indeed, its very defensive character that made the problem so dangerous, and so intractable. But in the Near East, neither power felt it could allow the other to achieve the security that came from political domination without fatally jeopardizing its own vital interests.

Yet, for over half a century after the Crimean War the great powers managed to avoid going to war with each other over their conflicting interests in the Near East. Certainly, they were fortunate in that the simple fact that the Ottoman Empire continued to function as an invaluable shock-absorber in the states system, under rulers who skilfully manoeuvred to maintain their independence by involving as many powers as possible in their affairs, affording to all a measure of influence and security and ensuring that none would be confronted with the stark choice between total retreat and war. (It is perhaps significant that within a year of the disappearance of this stabilizing element from south-east Europe the states system broke down in general war.) The powers themselves made their own contribution, however, by generally accepting this situation and cooperating to maintain a status quo, which, if ideal for none, was at least tolerable for all; and even on those occasions when Panslav pressures threatened to drive St Petersburg into a bid for control of the Balkans, the states system proved flexible enough to enable the status quo powers, notably Austria–Hungary and Great Britain. sometimes with the acquiescence of Germany and the support of Italy, to force Russia back into line.

The most effective devices for defusing the potentially explosive Eastern Question, however, were the agreements reached directly between the two chief contenders, Russia and Austria–Hungary, founded on monarchical solidarity and the fear that a war would destroy the social order in both empires. True, even these agreements could only mitigate, not remove, the underlying conflict of interests; they all ended in recriminations – in 1878, 1887 and 1908 – when one party or the other appeared to be tampering with the status quo to its own advantage; and it then generally took some time before mutual confidence recovered to an extent that permitted a renewal of cooperation. After 1908, of course, time was exactly what the two powers were not vouchsafed before the sudden disappearance of the Ottoman Empire in Europe rendered the Eastern Question itself infinitely more dangerous. Yet, for over a decade at the turn of the century, it seemed that the Austro-Russian Entente of 1897, a realistically modest arrangement for practical day-to day cooperation, cutting across formal alliance structures and taking a lead in organizing the Concert, had given the lie to Bismarck's famous prophecy to Albert Ballin: 'I shall not live to see the World War; but you will, and it will start in the Near East.'

It is in terms of its contribution to the deterioration of the international situation between January 1908, when the Sanjak Railway project was announced, and the start of the world war in the Near East in 1914 that the project acquires its significance for international historians. Those years saw the final collapse of Austro-Russian cooperation in the Eastern Question, the deepening of British suspicion of Germany and of its supposed cat's paw, Austria–Hungary; and the corresponding intensification of cooperation between London and St Petersburg, which in turn heightened German paranoia about isolation and encirclement. To all of these ominous developments – and to the weakening of the Concert generally – the Sanjak Railway affair made its baneful contribution.

Right from its inception in the great Eastern crisis of the 1870s the Sanjak Railway project bore witness to Austrian nervousness about the threat posed, not only to Turkey, but to the Dual Monarchy, by Russia and her Balkan clients. Initially, Andrássy[2] had relied on the Three Emperors' League to safeguard Austro-Hungarian trade and influence in the Balkans without the burden of annexing more south Slavs persuading the Russians to agree to the Monarchy's acquiring control of Bosnia and the use of military and commercial routes through the Sanjak of Novibazar, the strip of territory that linked Bosnia to the rest of European Turkey and separated Serbia from Montenegro. When in March 1878, however, Russia broke loose, and the Panslav Treaty of San Stefano established an autonomous Bosnia and simply handed over the Sanjak to Serbia and Montenegro, the Austrians redefined their own objectives more forcefully, insisting on clear territorial access to the western Balkans, and mobilized the British and the Concert to secure international recognition for them at the Congress of Berlin.

Thus, by the Berlin Treaty of 28 July 1878 the Sanjak remained in Turkish hands and Austria–Hungary acquired the right to occupy Bosnia and to maintain garrisons in, and to have military and commercial routes through, the Sanjak. Already on 13 July Andrássy had managed to extract from the Russians a promise not to oppose even its eventual occupation; but his objective was still essentially defensive. As he later explained[3] to the council of ministers, any occupation of the Sanjak would not be 'a stage in the march on Salonica as public opinion wrongly conceives it,' but simply a means of 'protecting our position in Bosnia'. For the Sanjak was to Bosnia and the Herzegovina what the Straits were to the Black Sea: a gateway to the east which must be kept open. If Serbia and Montenegro acquired it, Bosnia would become a *cul de sac*, not a base for Austro-Hungarian influence in the Near East; a Turkey completely cut off from Austria–Hungary would not long survive; while, worse still, if Serbia and Montenegro took the Sanjak, they might unite to form one big Slav state, which would in due course cast its eyes on Bosnia and Dalmatia.

Partly thanks to these arrangements, the threat to the Monarchy's interests in that particular quarter abated for the rest of the century. Altogether, while they could never afford to relax their vigilance, the Austrians managed by dint of a number of economic and political devices and a variety of diplomatic combinations, to safeguard their position throughout the Balkans. When the British under Gladstone proved a disappointment, the Three Emperors' alliance of 1881 restored cooperation with the Russians, who even consented to the Monarchy's eventually annexing Bosnia and the Herzegovina – although as regards the Sanjak they refused to go beyond their 1878 promise to acquiesce in its eventual occupation. Not that the Austrians were for the moment inclined to do more than maintain the status quo in that quarter: they had no immediate plans for a railway network even in Bosnia, let alone the Sanjak. Such railway building as the relatively impecunious Monarchy promoted in the 1880s related to the more crucial north–south route from Vienna and Budapest through Belgrade and Sofia to Constantinople, in which Serbia, Bulgaria and Turkey had been obliged to coop-erate by the terms of the Treaty of Berlin. Concurrently, the Monarchy's alliances and trade treaties with Serbia and Romania and its commercial links with Bulgaria kept those states out of the Russian orbit, and Vienna could rest content with the existing railway connection to Constantinople. Even when Russia's abortive attempt to seize control of Bulgaria in 1886 destroyed the Three Emperors' Alliance, the Austrians managed to devise, in their 'Mediterranean Entente' with Great Britain and Italy (supported, for a few years in the early 'nineties, by Germany) a fairly effective means of holding Russian influence at bay.

By the mid-1890's, a number of changes on the international scene led them to reconsider their position. On the one hand, were problems in the local Balkan arena, as the Balkan states began to find unfettered Austrian domination irksome and moved towards a balancing posture between the two rival great Powers. On the other, the Monarchy's former supporters, increasingly absorbed in naval and overseas activity, no longer seemed to offer the same degree of support: and if the British were beginning to distance themselves from an Ottoman Empire stained with the blood of Armenians, the Germans were actively cultivating St Petersburg in an effort to counteract the new Franco-Russian alliance. Nor could the Monarchy itself, about to descend into a maelstrom of racial conflicts that would over the next ten years both paralyse the parliament in Vienna and threaten the very fabric of the Dualist system, defend its interests with confidence should a crisis arise. Even so, two factors might yet offer the Habsburgs a hope of salvation. In the first place, Russia, increasingly preoccupied with the Far East, had certainly no desire to see the Near Eastern Question opened up for the time being; in the second, the Turks not only weathered the Armenian crisis, but managed, in the war of 1897, to inflict a resounding defeat on their Greek attackers and to demonstrate that their Empire was still a going concern. The Greco-Ottoman war transformed the Eastern Question. Whereas the notion of an agreement reconciling Austrian and Russian interests in the event of disappearance of Turkey had been regarded in Vienna, as late as the tsar's visit of August 1896, as a virtual impossibility, if the status quo could prove a viable basis, something might indeed be done. This, the Austrians set out to explore during Franz Joseph's return visit to St Petersburg in April 1897. The upshot was the Austro-Russian Entente of 1897 that served for over ten years – and more successfully than any of its precursors – to eliminate the Eastern Question as a potential source of war between the great powers.

Compared with its predecessors, the Austro-Russian Entente of 1897[4] was a rather loose informal arrangement, and rested, not on one agreed text but on an exchange of dispatches between the two governments. Their common resolve to work together to maintain the status quo in the Balkans and refrain from interfering in the internal affairs of the Balkan states was both uncontroversial and a notable step forward. Their commitment, should the maintenance of the status quo prove impossible, to reach an agreement about the future political configuration of the peninsula and impose it on the other powers was more problematical. In fact, any attempt to alter the status quo risked exposing the underlying conflict of interest between them; indeed, it was on this rock that the Entente was eventually to founder. For example, the Austrians insisted that in the event of the collapse of Turkey, they must retain Bosnia, the Herzegovina, and the Sanjak, indeed, that they enjoyed since 1881 the right to annex Bosnia whenever they wished; whereas the Russians objected that these questions, like the Straits question, could only be settled by the Concert; and that the exact territorial extent of the Sanjak had yet to be defined. For the time being, neither party needed to press the issue; but from the start, the Entente of 1897 rested on an equivocation.

Even so, the practitioners of the new Entente policy in Vienna – the Emperor, his foreign minister, Count Agenor Gołuchowski and the officials of the Ballhausplatz were agreed that the potential benefits it offered in terms of relief from confrontation with Russia outweighed the rebuffs that they soon had to accept from their obstreperous Balkan neighbours in the name of non-intervention. By the end of the century, while Romania remained loyal to the alliance, Bulgaria was, like Montenegro, firmly in the Russian camp, and Serbia was moving in the same direction. It was, indeed, partly in response to these trends, and to Italy's awakening interest in the *altera sponda* – Montenegro and Albania – that Gołuchowski moved in 1900 to safeguard the Monarchy's strategic and economic interests in the Western Balkans by developing at least the Bosnian railway network. For him, the issue was one of the highest policy. It was militarily of the greatest importance that the Monarchy should be in a position to send troops speedily to the frontiers of the Sanjak. It was, moreover, desirable to have a railway connection with Turkey independent of the Balkan states – the existing line to Constantinople ran through Serbia and Bulgaria – both to strengthen the Monarchy's hand in any commercial negotiations with those states and to counter the threats from rival schemes to its trade and its 'predominance' in Macedonia.

The upshot was, however, only to throw into stark relief the extent and limitations of the détente. The Bosnian network itself was not to be completed until 1905, and no concrete proposals were made at this stage for its extension into the Sanjak of Novibazar. Yet the mere rumour of such a possibility[5] now drew from the Russian embassy a warning that this would contravene the principle of the maintenance of the territorial status quo; and while this elicited a careless assurance from a Sektionschef to the effect that the Monarchy could not build railways in foreign territory, Gołuchowski was immensely put out at what he saw as a Russian attempt to whittle away Austria–Hungary's rights. In November he sharply reminded the Russian ambassador that the Bosnian railways were a purely internal affair, and would have been built twenty years earlier if the money had been available. As for the Sanjak, the Treaty of Berlin had given the Monarchy a clear right to build railways there by agreement with Turkey alone. Such railways had nothing whatever to do with the Entente of 1897, which was concerned with the political status quo.[6] Even so, that eventually the Bosnian network, once completed as far as Uvac on the northern boundary of the Sanjak, would be linked to the Turkish line from Mitrovitsa, at the southern end, to Salonika was, in Gołuchowski's view, 'obvious'. Further desultory discussions about a such a project at the end of 1902 again came to nothing, however, in the face of Russia's frowns and Germany's ostentatious refusal of support.

In the event, the Entente not only survived, but prospered during the next three years,[7] thanks both to the accentuation of the trends that had fostered it in the first place – the prospect of political deadlock in Hungary and of war in the Far East – and to alarming developments in Macedonia. There, Christian terrorist bands, encouraged by co-religionists in the Balkan states, were resorting to violence against the Ottoman authorities and against each other, in the hope of forcing the Great Powers to intervene in the manner of the 1870s. The upshot, however, was great power intervention in a very different sense, when Russia and Austria–Hungary seized the lead in the Concert with the Mürzsteg Punctation of October 1903, inviting the other powers to join them in imposing on the Sultan a programme of reforms designed to uphold the status quo in Macedonia by making life tolerable for the Christian inhabitants. Although this failed to check the terrorists, the reforms, implemented under the leadership of the Austro-Hungarian and Russian ambassadors at Constantinople, at least testified to the determination of the Concert to do something to contain the crisis. Meanwhile, on the wider political scene, an Austro-Russian neutrality treaty of October 1904 emphasized their special relationship within the European states system; just as they were relatively unaffected by the crisis between their western allies over Morocco in 1905–6. Not for nothing, it seemed, were they known in the diplomatic parlance of these years as 'the Entente Powers'.

Even so, by late 1907 developments had occurred that made the future of the Entente somewhat problematical. First, the trade embargo – or 'Pig War' with which Gołuchowski responded to Serbia's attempt to free herself from commercial dependence on the Monarchy called forth a stream of denunciations of Austria–Hungary – and of the Entente – in the Russian press. Second, with the establishment of a constitutional regime in Russia, and (at least as regards the discussion of foreign affairs) a free press, the slavophile voice of 'unofficial' Russia was heard more loudly – while that of the advocates of monarchical solidarity at court was temporarily muted. The replacement of the traditionalist bureaucrat Lamsdorff as foreign minister by Izvolsky, a 'westerner', who was both close to liberal elements in the Duma and inordinately sensitive to press criticism, underlined these trends. Even so, the simplistic view that Izvolsky set out to make up for Russia's Far Eastern disasters by challenging Austria–Hungary for mastery of the Balkans is not supported by the evidence.[8] On one thing the decision-making elite in St Petersburg was unanimous: Russia needed peace to stamp out the embers of revolution at home; and was in no position to challenge anybody. On the contrary, Izvolsky spent the next two years conciliating as many powers as possible: in the summer of 1907 agreements with Great Britain and Japan were followed by an agreement with Germany to maintain the status quo in the Baltic; and he was determined to have no truck with what he regarded as

British 'attempts to form rings round Germany'. It is true that, like his predecessor, who had begun to fear that, with Russia so weakened by war and revolution, the dual control established with Austria–Hungary in Macedonia might mean in effect Austro-Hungarian control; and like Lamsdorff, he drew in other Powers, particularly Great Britain, into the discussions at Constantinople. When he met Aehrenthal in Vienna in September, however, he not only reaffirmed his devotion to the Mürzsteg programme, but talked of extending the entente to cover some of the future possibilities left in the air in 1897.

True, Aehrenthal had had to abandon the hopes he had entertained on moving from the St Petersburg embassy to the Ballhausplatz in October 1906, of transforming the Entente into a full-blown Three Emperor's Alliance directed from Vienna; nor had his efforts to stiffen Izvolsky against radical proposals of the British, whether at the Hague Peace Conference or in the ambassadorial conference on Macedonian reform made much headway in the face of Izvolsky's balancing policy. Even so, as the discussions on Macedonian judicial reform got under weigh at Constantinople, and although the Russian ambassador, Zinoviev, was proving increasingly susceptible to British, rather than Austrian, advice, Aehrenthal held on to the Entente. Certainly, he remained truculently impervious to German pressure to abandon the reforms: that might only provoke the Balkan states to desperate measures and drive the Russians altogether into the arms of the British.[9] The drift of Russian policy was nevertheless perhaps a factor – along with recent French and German commercial activity[10] – in the timing of his decision at the end of 1907 to instruct the Austrian ambassador at Constantinople, Margrave Pallavicini, to take up the matter of the Sanjak Railway with the Turks. As he later explained[11] to Berchtold in St Petersburg:

> Sooner or later we should have had to consider whether we should continue to work together with Russia, who had fallen under English influence, in the Balkans. It was indeed my intention to carry on as long as at all possible, but at the same time I was determined, in view of the realities of the situation, to lose neither time nor opportunity to stand up for our interests, so long neglected, in the Balkans.

Already in the previous spring a series of conferences[12] in the Ballhausplatz had recommended the construction of a number of Balkan railways in the first place because the recently completed Bosnian railway network terminated in a *cul de sac*; in the second, because the construction of rival schemes for transverse railways, giving the Balkan states access to the Adriatic independently of Austro-Hungarian territory would be 'contrary to our most vital interests'.[13] As, however, the *Drang nach Westen* on the part of the Balkan states was a natural 'healthy' tendency, Aehrenthal decided that the old policy of hindering its realization was in the long run doomed to failure.[14] It would be infinitely preferable to canalise the movement through Austrian-occupied territory – for example by connecting a Serbian railway with the Bosnian line to the Adriatic, drawing the kingdom back into the economic orbit of the Monarchy and rendering superfluous any projects for a Danube–Adriatic railway skirting Austria–Hungary. Meanwhile, a line from Uvac through the Sanjak of Novibazar, linking the Bosnian railway network to the Turkish line from Mitrovitsa to Salonika, would further the Monarchy's own political and economic influence in Albania and Macedonia; and an extension of the Southern Dalmatian railway through Montenegro to Scutari would counter Italy's ambitions. As, however, to press for the Sanjak Railway alone might push 'the political aspect too much into the foreground' it was considered advisable 'to stress the commercial aspect' and present Constantinople with a whole package of projects, including a link between the Turkish and Greek lines at Larissa (in which the western powers too might participate).[15]

In the event, none of these railways was ever to be built; and as regards the financial aspect to the question Michael Behnen's exhaustively researched account[16] may fairly be regarded as definitive. In the first place, it appears that although 1904–8 was a boom period and competition would initially have been minimal, Austro-Hungarian high finance, trade and industry, were fully occupied in the Balkan states, Europe and overseas, and quite uninterested in risky investments in such a politically unstable area as European Turkey. In the second place, the ruling authorities in the Monarchy were not well equipped to mobilize the financial backing they desired. In stark contrast to, say, France, the Monarchy was completely lacking in any coordinating centre linking foreign policy decisions and economic activity; and the dislocation was hardly mitigated by the social gulf reflected in the personnel of the foreign office and that of the banks and industry. In practice, the banks would only consider Aehrenthal's schemes if they were offered hefty state guarantees at a level quite beyond the resources of the Austrian and Hungarian governments. It was in vain that Aehrenthal tried to reassure the latter that the Sanjak Railway, linked to the narrow-gauge Bosnian lines, would not compete with their existing route to Constantinople;[17] and scolded the agrarians for opposing the Serbian link and jeopardizing the Monarchy's 'trade and also political influence in the Balkan peninsula, where we ought to be concerned for our influence and predominance (*Vorherrschaft*) as our most natural market, against powerful competitors.'[18] As the British ambassador noted: 'there is not much imperial feeling in Austria. It is a country where each party and each nation fights for its own hand.'[19] Finally, whereas the powerful competitors appreciated the importance of collaborative action – as in the four-power syndicate behind the rival Danube–Adriatic scheme – and even Aehrenthal was prepared to contemplate it in the case of his Greek and Montenegrin projects, his insistence on treating the Sanjak Railway as exclusively the Monarchy's affair was, given the latter's impecunious circumstances, hardly conducive to its realization.[20]

If the lack of effective financial backing from its originators was not enough to doom the Sanjak Railway project, the surveyors who in the spring 1908 started work in an impossibly mountainous terrain amidst a decidedly hostile population had not got far before revolution broke out at Constantinople (16 July). Now even the Old Regime had a deeply ambivalent attitude towards railway construction in

European Turkey. It was all very well for liberals and modernizers in the west to laud the advance of civilization – as Noel Buxton observed in the *Westminster Gazette*, a propos the Sanjak Railway, 'The more railways there are in such a place, the better'[21] – a doctrine that even the British and Izvolsky, despite their objections to this particular project – were also prepared to endorse.[22] As far as the Sultan was concerned, however, it was perhaps in his interests, as a German military attaché observed, to oppose all new railway construction 'because the present quite inadequate means of communication in Macedonia can be regarded as a natural defence of European Turkey against the intrusion of foreign operations'.[23] The Young Turk regime was, if anything even more suspicious of foreign tutelage. By August their press was reporting a Turkish member of the surveying commission as saying that the Sanjak Railway was 'of little interest to Turkey and will . . . only be taken up after the construction of other more important lines'.[24] In September the Minister of Works informed Pallavicini that although the Sanjak Railway might be militarily and politically important, 'the reports of the Turkish delegates about the economic advantages which the railway might offer in the next few years, and its profitability, were negative'.[25] It could therefore not be dealt with before March, and then only if Austria–Hungary participated, not indirectly, but directly and to the tune of seventy million francs. Despite the deep frost that descended over Austro-Turkish relations in the Bosnian crisis, and despite the renunciation as part of the settlement, of Austria–Hungary's rights in the Sanjak, inconclusive, Austro-Turkish negotiations over the financing of the railway project continued to make fleeting appearances in the correspondence of the Ballhausplatz. In March 1912, Pallavicini was at pains to contradict Austrian press reports that the project had been 'totally dropped': the Turks were not in fact opposed to it; the question was 'purely a matter of money'; but there could equally be no question of a Turkish financial guarantee, nor would any foreigners be prepared to make loans to Turkey 'for a railway line that will be solely in our interests.'[26] Berchtold does not seem to have followed the matter up, however, before the Serbian and Montenegrin occupation of the Sanjak consigned the Railway project finally to the archives.

Perhaps, as Michael Behnen suggests,[27] it was this tale of failure that as early as 1908 drove Aehrenthal and his colleagues to resort to blatantly imperialist ventures to uphold the social and political status quo by force. Perhaps it was rather, like the humiliations Berchtold was to suffer in the scramble for spheres of influence in Asia Minor, yet another demonstration of the Monarchy's apparent inability to compete in the modern world that by 1914 convinced its rulers that it was in danger of dropping out of the ranks of the great powers.[28] Most immediately, the impact of the Sanjak Railway affair was felt in terms of great-power alignments. On the one hand, that it had put an end to that positive Austro-Russian cooperation that had lately done so much to stabilize the Near East; that it brought the Anglo-Russian Asian agreement of 1907 'to Europe'; and that it intensified Great Britain's growing suspicions of Germany can all be relatively easily demonstrated – as can the fact that these far-reaching consequences resulted to a great degree from its entanglement with the Macedonian reform negotiations. On the other hand, the nature of that entanglement has been so misunderstood and misinterpreted in contemporary reports and in – especially Anglo-Saxon – historiography as to render it perhaps the most controversial aspect of the whole affair.

Relations between the ambassadors at Constantinople and the Sultan were at a critical stage at the end of 1907.[29] The Sultan was not only threatening to veto the ambassadors' proposals for judicial reform, the next item on the Mürzsteg agenda, insisting that supervision by the Christian powers of the judicial machinery in Macedonia was incompatible with his position as Caliph. He was also making difficulties over the renewal of the mandates for the European personnel already engaged in supervising the gendarmerie and the budget of the province. He was encouraged in his resistance by the Germans ambassador, Marschall von Bieberstein, who also convinced the Kaiser that the reforms were only making matters worse, undermining the morale of the Ottoman authorities and encouraging the Christians to look abroad for salvation. Indeed, in January 1908 William II even tried to mobilize his friend, Archduke Franz Ferdinand, to get Aehrenthal to abandon the judicial reform altogether.[30] This advice Aehrenthal, always inordinately sensitive to anything smacking of German tutelage, dismissed out of hand as a German attempt 'to seize control of the whole Turkish affair to the detriment of ourselves and Russia'.[31] He felt it essential to press on with the Mürzsteg programme, if only as a restraint on the more radical British radicals and warlike elements in the Balkan states; and he was determined to secure both the judicial reform and the mandates. Indeed, while Pallavicini at Constantinople was toying with the idea of offering concessions over the reform in order to secure the mandates, Aehrenthal was quite unyielding, suggesting instead to Izvolsky; that the great powers should over awe the Sultan by demonstratively and simultaneously withdrawing their ambassadors.[32]

It was in fact simply a coincidence that in these very weeks Aehrenthal, having enlisted the support of Germany (alone among the powers), at last persuaded the Turks to agree to preliminary studies for the construction of a railway through the Sanjak.[33] Certainly neither he nor Pallavicini seems to have made a connection between this issue and the reforms that were pre-occupying the concert. Pallavicini's arguments were couched in terms of Austria–Hungary's rights under the Treaty of Berlin and he was at pains to reassure them that the railway was not intended as a first step on the fabled 'march on Salonica' (after all, if the Monarchy were planning to attack Turkey it would be on a much wider front that the Sanjak that its *'Millionenheer'* would appear).[34] True, while he admitted that he had been keen to take advantage of the psychological moment, when Turkey, under pressure in the matter of reform, 'seems to be setting certain hopes on us' he was equally emphatic that he had 'obviously' done this 'without holding out any hopes to the Turks that we should prove more yielding in the matter of judicial reform'.[35] Nor was there even a hint of such a suspicion in Paris and London when Aehrenthal informed them of his intentions in the middle of January[36]: on the contrary, the French foreign minister volunteered his 'energetic support' at Constantinople, while Grey's permanent undersecretary, Sir Charles Hardinge, while asking for time to consult his maps, was almost equally forthcoming (even though Aehrenthal was in fact only seeking British support for his Greek project).[37]

Russian reactions were very different – not surprisingly. It was all very well for the Austrians to argue that their railway projects, being 'solely economic'[38] had nothing to do with the political status quo enshrined in the Entente of 1897; and to wax indignant at 'Izvolsky's lamentable attitude... Does he really think that we are compelled by the Entente to renounce all activity in the field of trade and communications?'[39] After all, as Pallavicini frankly admitted, the Monarchy's 'prime objective' in the Balkans was 'to develop our commercial interests as far as possible, which must obviously go hand in hand with the development of our political influence in these lands'.[40] At Constantinople, Zinoviev, was, according to his Italian colleague, Marquis Imperiali, already 'secretly attempting to make the thing come to nothing' and warning of the threat to Italy from 'this Austro-German push in the direction of Albania'.[41] True, in response to Berchtold's first confidential communications on 26 January Izvolsky made no reference to the Entente, and merely expressed his surprise and '*inquiétude*' that the Austrians had chosen such a moment to approach the Sultan: the powers ought to be demonstrating their solidarity in the face of his obstructionism – an argument that, as the ambassador pointed out, would preclude any power from ever seeking a concession from Turkey, the reform negotiations being now a permanent feature of the diplomatic scene at Constantinople.[42] Aehrenthal, for his part, assured Izvolsky that he was not intending to yield an inch in the matter of reform, adding that it was not the railway project but a display of Russian opposition to it that would put the concert in jeopardy.[43]

Just such a display followed inexorably on Aehrenthals' public announcement of his railway schemes, in a speech to the Delegations on 27 January. Moreover, the Entente itself now came into the firing line, as the Russian press denounced Izvolsky as the dupe of his Mürzsteg partners; and when Berchtold reminded him of his duty 'to guide, not to follow the press', the minister promised to do his best to hold to the Entente '*malgré la bombe qu'on lui avait lancée entre les jambes*'.[44] For the moment, he could do little else: although there is Russian evidence to suggest that he was already seeking a pretext to abandon the Entente,[45] the emergency council of ministers that met to discuss the crisis on 3 February, vetoed his proposal to turn from Austria–Hungary to Great Britain: this would risk opening up a struggle over the Eastern Question that Russia in her exhausted state was in no condition to face.[46] Even so, Berchtold was beginning to fear that the minister's endless lamentations, and especially his gloomy insistence that the Entente could now only survive if the judicial reform negotiations were brought to a successful conclusion might be 'a first step towards the denunciation of the Entente'.[47]

Russian suspicions that Aehrenthal was about to sabotage the reforms in order to secure the Sanjak Railway is not supported by Austrian archive evidence. On the contrary, on 30 January he instructed Pallavicini to abandon all thought of offering concessions over judicial reform in order to secure the mandates, precisely because it might fuel unfounded suspicions in St Petersburg.[48] After all, in his speech to the Delegations he had proclaimed not only his railway projects but his determination to carry out the Mürzsteg programme. Indeed, it was this that most impressed Baron Marschall and his Turkish friends. According to the former, the Grand Vizier had been aghast to find Aehrenthal so stubborn in his pursuit of reform just when Turkey was showing herself so accommodating over the railway.[49] Not that this stopped the Sultan from issuing on 4 February an *iradé*, authorizing preliminary survey operations in the Sanjak. Perhaps this was, as the British suspected, a calculated move to fan the flames of dissention in the concert[50]: certainly it provoked the Russian press to redouble its attacks on the Entente. At this critical moment, much would depend on whether, as Pallavicini prophesied on 5 February, 'in the meeting of ambassadors that takes place today the Judicial Note will in all probability be signed'.[51] He was reckoning without Marschall who, as doyen, would preside over the meeting and who, according to his Italian colleague, was already irritated with Baron Aehrenthal, 'saying to me, "If he expects me to support his reform, he is in trouble. I have no desire to ruin my position with the Sultan pour des bêtises... in the next meeting I shall speak even more plainly than I did in the last one." '[52]

The broad outlines of the crucial ambassadors' conference of 5 February – which lasted for four hours but for which no minutes were kept – have been known since the publication, in the official collections of documents, of the reports of the German, French and British ambassadors; and they are substantially confirmed by the reports of their colleagues in the Italian, Russian and Austrian archives. When Marschall, after subjecting the Austro-Russian draft reform note to minute and withering criticism, finally declared that while, as doyen, he would present it to the Sultan, he could not support it, his demoralized colleagues –who had all been instructed to sign and present the note – unanimously decided nevertheless to ask their governments to abandon it. The details of each ambassador's role are, however, less clear. The fullest and most trustworthy report is that of Marschall,[53] who had nothing to hide, and was, indeed, boastful about role in this 'most interesting' meeting. It is significant that he singled out for particular praise his equally Turcophile French colleague: 'M. Constans was superb.'[54] The other ambassadors, by contrast, were embarrassed by the fact that they had disobeyed their instructions, and all attempted – but always with a striking lack of precise evidence – to divert responsibility for the fiasco onto their colleagues. According to the Italian ambassador's report,[55] for example,

> The Austro-Hungarian ambassador withdrew into a silence, from which we dimly discerned the concordance between his views and those of Baron Marschall. ...[But] in the present state of affairs, with Germany hostile, Austria hesitant, and France rather reluctant to support coercive measures. [the outcome was] the only decent way out.

According to his British colleague, Sir Nicholas O'Conor,[56]

> The other ambassadors considered that...[Marschall's] attitude placed them in a difficult position and greatly altered the situation. ...I did not see my way, in the face of the negative attitude of the Russian and Austrian ambassadors, to put myself forward.

Most definite was Zinoviev's report, which was also unique in pointing the finger directly at Austria–Hungary[57]:

> Since the time when the question of reform was raised, political circumstances and, above all, the grouping of the Powers has changed.
>   Germany...comes forward as an open opponent of judicial reform. Austria, for her part, has entered into a secret agreement with the Porte, by virtue of which she decided to sacrifice the judicial reform in order to obtain the Sarajevo–Mitrovitsa railway link, which the Sultan had stubbornly opposed for more than a quarter century.

Pallavicini's account[58], by contrast, was unique in emphasizing the role of O'Conor:

> The attitude of the English ambassador during the conference leads one to conclude that in the judicial reform question he must have substantially different instructions than those which have guided him so far. Sir N. O'Conor...showed himself strikingly forthcoming regarding all the proposed changes coming from the German ambassador. He was also one of the first to agree to Baron von Marschall's final proposition. It seems now, therefore, that people in London...are not willing to push the matter to a head. M. Zinoviev too proved from the start extremely yielding...
>   Under these circumstances it would have been not only impolitic (*unpolitisch*) on my part but also quite pointless to push myself forward particularly.

Not surprisingly, Aehrenthal made the most of Pallavicini's information in his attempts to rehabilitate himself in St Petersburg and London. Boldly, he called on the British to explain their new instructions to O'Conor, and proposed that the governments should overrule their ambassadors and press ahead with the judical reform.[59] Most important, Berchtold was to make clear to Izvolsky[60]

> that the difficult position the ambassadors got into at Constantinople is not in any sense attributable to any connexion with our railway project, but rather to other known factors and also to the unexplained change of mind of Sir N. O'Conor, who managed to influence his colleagues, including M. Zinoviev.
>   In view of this and the attitude of M. Constans and Marquis Imperiali it is really inexplicable that people in the St Petersburg foreign office ascribe to us...the intention of leaving the Balkan states in the lurch in the matter of Macedonian reform.

Not that these embarrassing repercussions had led to any slackening of Vienna's determination to pursue the railway project. Indeed, when Aehrenthal reprimanded him for disregarding his instructions over judicial reform,[61] Pallavicini's reply[62] was hardly contrite: in a situation where all the powers were pursuing their separate interest at Constantinople 'we must not deceive ourselves and have to admit that the judicial reform has suffered as a result of our success in the Sanjak railway question' – even though he had refrained from offering the Turks an actual bargain. Given this unprecedentedly rapid success, moreover,

> this question has now undoubtedly become one of our political prestige in the Balkan peninsula. We must, therefore, more than ever strive to pursue the matter to a conclusion. No political consideration and no financial objections must hold us back.

Aehrenthal, while noting with satisfaction the ambassador's avowal 'that Your Excellency established no kind of connection between your attitude in the judicial reform question and your demarches over the iradé', agreed with him about the essential issue: 'the railway question is for us one of such political prestige that it must be pursued regardless of political and financial considerations'.[63]

This being the case, an Austro-Russian clash was now inevitable. Fundamentally, the issue was, as a Russian note of 10 February spelt out, that Russia was confronted by, on the one hand *un avantage considerable économique et politique assuré sur la Péninsule des Balcans à l'Autriche-Hongrie et de l'autre du naufrage du point principale du programme de réforme'.[64]* As Berchtold observed, this showed 'to what degree the old mistrust has been reawakened here, and it will take a lot of time, effort and patience to dispel it'.[65] Of course, the Monarchy's rights under the Treaty of Berlin ruled out any protest against the railway scheme as such – as even Izvolsky had to confess to a furious duma. He concentrated, therefore, on the charge, as he 'insinuated' on 9 February to a horrified Berchtold, 'that we had arranged (*abgekartet*) a diabolical game with Germany at the expense of the judicial reform'; and his exculpatory *'Pas moi, c'est à Constantinople qu'on parle ainsi'*, still left the ambassador with the 'agonizing feeling that he believed this sinister report'.[66] On the following day, therefore, 'after a sleepless night', Berchtold sought out Izvolsky[67] to give him

> in a voice filled with emotion but very clearly 'ma parole d'honneur de gentilhomme' that in all the correspondence I had seen there was not the slightest trace of such an arrangement, and that rather,...Aehrenthal's latest letters complained about Berlin's wavering attitude and stressed that we must continue to stick together with Russia 'pour déjouer les plans de l'Allemagne' and to secure the judicial reform.

It all did no good. Izvolsky had by now lost interest in the Mürzsteg programme. Even the Tsar remarked to Berchtold that it had never been popular with the Russian public; and dismissed his stock-in-trade appeal to monarchical solidarity with a *'moi aussi, je suis Russe'* that convinced Aehrenthal that the government was indeed beholden to nationalist feeling.[68] Within days, Izvolsky rejected Aehrenthal's proposal to press on with judicial reform as pointless, given the open disunity of the concert; and on 17 February told the British ambassador, Sir Arthur Nicolson, that he wanted 'gradually to get out of a dual action with

Austria and to rally himself to a combination of those powers who are sincerely desirous of reforms'.[69]

His words fell on fertile ground in London, where the Sanjak Railway scheme was judged almost exclusively in terms of the collapse of the judicial reform. Although the British had no objection whatever to railway construction in the Balkans as such, the recent fiasco seemed to show the dangers of appealing to the Sultan in favour of any railways whatever; and throughout the summer they held demonstratively aloof from Serbia's efforts to promote her Danube–Adriatic scheme with the assistance of Russia, France and Italy.[70] As for the Sanjak Railway, the British were early convinced of Aehrenthal's duplicity. If Goschen in the Vienna embassy deemed the speedy issue of the iradé 'a trifle fishy'.[71] O'Conor, who even before the ambassadors' meeting, had thought it 'pretty certain that the Austrians have got their price in the extension of their railway to Mitrovitsa'[72] now decided[73] that

> the coincidence of the unusually complaisant attitude of the Sultan and the hesitation of the Austrians to advocate pressure upon the Porte was...so striking that I fear all the water in the Bosphorus will not wash out the stain.

Grey had in fact already decided 'that Austria had played the mean game of driving a bargain with the Porte in favour of her railways at the expense of Macedonian reform'.[74] Hardinge, thereupon summoned the Austria–Hungarian ambassador, Count Mensdorff, and told him straight out that there could be no question of British support for the railway at such a moment.[75] It was in vain that Berchtold pleaded with Nicolson to recognize

> as the representative of the leading *Kulturvolk*, that an empire of 50 million inhabitants with significant agriculture and a highly developed industry cannot remain sealed off on one side from its neighbouring markets and that the Berlin Treaty gave us the right to build the much begrudged railway

While Nicolson admitted all this, he still termed the railway inopportune, adding that his government was 'very angry' with Vienna and regarded 'Austria–Hungary's independent approach to Turkey as the first step towards breaking up the Concert'.[76]

Righteous indignation over the collapse of Macedonian reform was only one of three components in the British reaction to the Sanjak Railway scheme. The significance of Aehrenthal's speech and the violent reaction to it in Russia was not lost on the British: 'The outcome of it all is that the "entente" is off';[77] but there was a distinctly calculating element in their conclusion that the crisis might actually turn out to their advantage. As early as 3 February Hardinge was quick to note that 'the struggle between Austria and Russia in the Balkans is evidently now beginning, and we shall not be bothered by Russia in Asia'[78] – a remark which, in the light of events that were to be 'bothering' the British by 1914 was perhaps somewhat shortsighted. Meanwhile, however, 'the action of Austria and

Germany will make Russia lean on us more and more in future. In my opinion, this will not be a bad thing'.[79] In a minute approved by Hardinge and Grey,[80] Louis Mallet, assistant under-secretary, termed Izvolsky's approach to Nicolson

> a very important development of the Anglo-French and Anglo-Russian agreement policy. Russia is now asking for our co-operation in the Near East. I think that on every ground we should welcome these overtures.

This enthusiasm was strengthened by the third determinant of British reactions to the Sanjak Railway project: the ingrained suspicion of Germany that character-ized the thinking of the rising generation of diplomats and Foreign Office offi-cials. According to Mallet, the Railway was just part of scheme for 'the Germanization of the provinces';[81] and Goschen's reports from Vienna harped constantly on the theme – which also pervaded the reporting of the Times corre-spondent, Wickham Steed – that Austro-Hungarian policy was made in Berlin. True, Goschen could cite a few Austrian critics of Aehrenthal's Railway project to the effect that 'Germany has made a fool of him';[82] but the elaborate theory he expounded to Hardinge in a private letter of 18 February[83] was simply fantasy:

> (The project was an attempt) to test the strength of the Anglo-Russian under-standing...and to ascertain whether its tendency is to spread to the Near East. That is also to my mind the explanation of Germany's part in the affair – as all other explanations such as the desire to upset the Macedonian reform scheme or to get the railway ultimately into her hands scarcely hold water. The Railway is a very distant thing and may be strangled by other lines, while the wreck of the reform scheme could have been achieved by less compli-cated methods. I see that Steed in the *Times* inclines to the last theory and my French colleague and I arrived at the same conclusion some days ago. We were talking of Morocco and the similarity of procedure at once struck us.

Fantasy or not, their recipients deemed such analyses eminently perceptive: 'There can be no doubt that Germany favours the project both commercially and strategically in the contest with the Slavs'.[84] Aehrenthal's counter-charge, that 'England had Germany on the brain' and his somewhat disingenuous claim that Germany had been treated no differently from any other power, cut no ice in London[85]:

> We need not refer to his remarks on English suspicion of Germany. That is our own affair. But it is ridiculous to suppose that Germany was not aware of and approved of the Railway scheme and that it never would have been mooted if Germany had been opposed to it.
> The independence of Austrian policy is a myth in which Baron d'Aehrenthal likes to believe, but we know in what light William II regards Austrian statesmen from his [brilliant second] telegram to Count Goluchowski on the close of the Algeciras Conference.

In this atmosphere, it was hardly surprising that the British determined to give any Russian proposals 'the most sympathetic attention', albeit while professing the need to 'try to maintain the Concert as far as possible' and even to 'proceed with the greatest caution. Open disagreement with Germany and Austria must be carefully avoided'.[86] The same considerations underlay Grey's speech to the Commons of 25 February. True, his blunt reference to a 'new situation' created by the Sanjak Railway project was to come close to causing an open disagreement with Vienna; but he dismissed calls from spokesmen of the Balkan Committee to ignore Austria–Hungary, who had now placed herself out of court; and he stressed the need to act through the Concert, emphasizing that it would be to the Concert that he would be sending a new set of proposals to deal with the chronic disorders in Macedonia.[87] It was significant, however, that it was to St Petersburg alone that he sent an advance draft of these so-called 'March proposals'. As he explained to Nicolson on 26 February[88]:

> I deliberately abstained in my speech last night from hinting at [the] possibility of our cooperating with one power more than another inside the concert; because I think that such co-operation should come about naturally from force of circumstance or identity of views. But this reticence on my part must not be construed as meaning that co-operation with Russia would be at all unwelcome. On the contrary, if M. Izvolsky accepts my views or suggests proposals going some way to meet them our cooperation will certainly be forthcoming.

As drafts and counter-drafts sped between St Petersburg and London without waiting for any Austrian observations, Hardinge admitted that 'our sole purpose is to come to terms with Russia.'[89] Indeed, as he gleefully reported to Edward VII on 21 March, 'the chief characteristic of Izvolsky's scheme is its complete break with Austria in the Balkans, and Aehrenthal will probably be more angry than ever.'[90] This was too much for the traditionalist monarch, who at once protested[91] that

> It will never do to break with Austria, and... [Izvolsky] must be told that we cannot agree to such a proposition, – my personal regard for the Emperor of Austria is so great that I could not sanction a policy that would cause him trouble or pain. Aehrenthal is certainly in an irritable state, but I hope he will calm down.

At this, Hardinge backtracked to the extent of 'explaining' to the king, with Orwellian aplomb, that 'I do not mean that the break between Austria and Russia is complete', but only that Russia, instead of working exclusively with Austria, 'is now working with the other powers and especially with us'.[92] All the same, he was pleased to note to his own satisfaction that 'the Mürzsteg programme is as dead as a door-nail.'[93]

Aehrenthal was not, in fact, inclined to mourn for it. Rather, he professed himself glad to be rid of the wearisome task of alleviating the ills of Macedonia;[94]

and as Izvolsky seemed to be assiduous in eliminating the more radical features of the British scheme he was ready enough to fall in with the various proposals that emerged from the Anglo-Russian partnership. He had no time for Berlin's objections and complaints of encirclement, and sharply reminded the Germans that the present disagreeable constellation had only arisen as a result of their failure to support the Austro-Russian judicial reform proposals in February.[95] But his chief irritation was reserved for the British. According to Goschen,[96] he termed Grey's allusion to the 'new situation' created by the Railway project 'an unfriendly act towards a friendly power': 'In a boiling rage – pale with anger...he called Sir Edward Grey's conduct unfair and banged the table.' The 'utterly false'[97] accusation that Germany was behind the project infuriated him particularly:

> He was perfectly loyal to the German alliance, which he regarded as a necessity for Austria–Hungary, but...the Monarchy should be a strong and independent state, faithful to its allies but subservient to none. It seemed to him hard that after all the insinuation which had so long been rife as to Austria–Hungary being the tool of Germany a move on his part in the direction of complete independence of action should have been seized on as an example of subservience.

In the end, he decided that the British were a hopeless case[98]:

> They regard us as enslaved to Germany and – in a veritably psychopathic manner – discern in everything that happens, and in whatever we do too, a hidden devilry of Germany's machiavellian policy. It was doubtless this interpretation of our Balkan activity, especially in the matter of the Sanjak railway, that was the real reason why people on the Thames received our project with such obvious displeasure.

So long as this attitude prevailed, he told a crestfallen Mensdorff, and so long as the British continued to strive 'to embroil Russia [*Rußland hineinzuinteressieren*] in the Balkans and to compromise her' there was simply no basis for Anglo-Austrian cooperation.[99] Of course, the estrangement became even deeper, when in the Bosnian crisis the British assumed the role of Russia's chief defenders; but even in the few years of détente that followed, the old 'traditional friendship' that had for so long been regarded as the hallmark of Anglo-Austrian relations was never really revived.

Somewhat surprisingly, in view of the violence of the storm that had raged in St Petersburg, Aehrenthal took a more sanguine view of the future of Austro-Russian relations. At any rate, he talked nonchalantly to Conrad about 'a storm in a teacup'[100] and cheerfully retailed to Bülow Berchtold's assessment that 'Izvolsky's bad humour [*Groll*] is now fading away like the distant rumbling of thunder from a gradually retreating storm'.[101] He had himself made a move to improve the atmosphere by publishing an announcement in the official *Politische Correspondenz* of 14 February, to the effect that the Monarchy was well disposed towards all Balkan railway projects – including the Danube–Adriatic schemes favoured by Serbia and her friends.[102] Izvolsky, for his part, all too painfully aware that Russia in her enfeebled state could not possibly gain from confrontations with any power, was reverting to his policy of the previous year, of collecting whatever diplomatic advantages he could from a combination of ententes with as many powers as possible. It was as part of this policy that he now embarked on that series of diplomatic exchanges with the Austrians that culminated in his famous offer to extend the entente to give Russia freedom of passage through the Straits in exchange for the annexation by Austria–Hungary of Bosnia, the Herzegovina and the Sanjak.

It was as a catalytic element in these exchanges that the Balkan railway schemes that have been under discussion made their last significant appearance in international history. It was Izvolsky who took the initiative, in a note of 27 April, questioning the sincerity of Aehrenthal's *Politische Correspondenz* declaration and pointing out that he had himself expressly recognized Austria–Hungary's good right to build the Sanjak Railway, and had always striven to maintain the Entente despite '*maintes difficultés*' and at great cost to his own popularity.[103] He was asking Aehrenthal, therefore, to participate with Russia in a joint demarche at Constantinople to obtain an iradé for the first stretch of Serbia's Danube–Adriatic Railway, from Mrdare to Stimlya. This, Aehrenthal refused: the Sanjak Railway, which Austria–Hungary had a treaty right to construct, had nothing to do with any other power and was in a category of its own from other Balkan schemes, which depended solely on the Sultan. Serbia and her friends would have to be content with the Monarchy's goodwill.[104] He was equally dismissive of Izvolsky's reiterated – and strikingly onesided – demand for a clear expression of support for the Mrdare–Stimlya scheme in return for Russia's continuing to refrain from opposing the Sanjak railway. It was when these exchanges drifted into the area the meaning and scope of the Entente that the Russians moved – dangerously, and eventually fatally – to extend it to cover those delicate future contingencies that had been wisely left in suspense in 1897.[105] The final Buchlau agreement at least resolved the railway question to the extent that Aehrenthal and Izvolsky agreed simply 'to assume sympathetic attitudes towards the railway projects of interest to one or the other.'[106] Izvolsky still remained non-committal, however, about Austrian plans to build a line from Dalmatia along the coast of Montenegro; and the letter he promised to write to Aehrenthal[107] clarifying his position was never written before the storm over the annexation of Bosnia consigned the matter, along with the various Danube–Adriatic schemes and the Sanjak Railway project itself, to the archives.

Yet if the Entente had seemed to come to life again in the summer of 1908, it had been, ever since the Sanjak Railway affair very much a matter of hardheaded political bargaining, completely devoid of those sentiments of conservative solidarity that had inspired it in earlier years.[108] On the contrary, those very negotiations over railways that had acted as a catalyst for the extension of the Entente, had done nothing to dispel the distrust that now permeated Austro-Russian relations. True, that railway construction in the Balkans was so frustrating to all parties owed much to Turkish lethargy and obstruction. For example, when in June a Franco-Russo-Italian syndicate was preparing to put up the money for a Danube–Adriatic railway, the Grand Vizier assured the Austrians that, given the cost of the Sanjak, Hedjaz and Baghdad railways, Turkey simply 'could not and would not build any other lines', particularly the Danube–Adriatic railway.[109] That the Turks, in their efforts to divide the Powers, persistently circulated false information to the effect that the Austrians were angling for a monopoly of concessions in Macedonia only deepened the fog of suspicion between Vienna and St Petersburg.[110]

Even so, it must be said that Izvolsky's complaints about Austrian duplicity, voiced tetchily in Vienna and vociferously in London, were not without foundation. Certainly, Aehrenthal's public declaration of sympathy for rival Balkan railway schemes was disingenuous in the extreme. It was not just that the Austrians were counting on the Danube–Adriatic scheme's succumbing to 'financial and technical difficulties' – if Albanian tribesmen did not actually tear up the tracks; and if it was not altogether 'a dream-construction that is no more likely to be realized than the Channel Tunnel project.'[111] They were themselves still hoping to render it superfluous by reviving their plan for a Serbian line to the Adriatic through Bosnia; or even planned to compete for contracts to build other transverse lines with a view to simply freezing them.[112] Indeed, on 27 February, barely a fortnight after his *Politische Correspondenz* announcement, Aehrenthal expressly instructed Pallavicini 'to work on the Porte with all discretion to ensure that only those communications projects are realized in the Balkans which serve our special interests.'[113] Not that the Austrians could rely with any more confidence on Russian professions of goodwill towards their own projects. At the grass roots level, the Russian consul in Mitrovitsa was said to be stirring up the local Serbian population to harass the Austrian engineers engaged in preliminary survey work.[114] True, St Petersburg promised to call him to order;[115] but the mood of nationalist circles in Russia, was graphically expressed in *Novoye Vremya* of 7 May: 'Seared by the red-hot iron of the Sanjak railway, which is to cut through the very kernel of Serbia, this Balkan Prometheus is once more in agony.'[116]

In these circumstances, it was not surprising that both public opinion and the government in Russia were sufficiently outraged by the annexation of Bosnia as to compel Izvolsky and his imperial master to abandon both Buchlau and the Entente. Not that recent events had predisposed ruling circles in London either to take a more favourable view of Aehrenthal's activities. Izvolsky's complaints about Aehrenthal's double dealing over Balkan railways found a sympathetic ear in the Foreign Office[117]:

> [This] fully justifies everything that was said about Baron Aehrenthal when the railway project was launched – that the Austrians were trying to secure an advantage for themselves at the expense of reform [and their claim to favour all railway building] sounds rather hollow it this information is correct.

It was significant that in October Hardinge's denunciations of Aehrenthal were not confined to the annexation: he had never ceased to 'play the fool' since taking office.'[118] It is also remarkable how the Sanjak Railway project itself, although in reality further from realization than ever in the wake of the Monarchy's seizure of Bosnia, continued to prey on Russian minds. Although abandonment of Austria–Hungary's military rights in the Sanjak had been welcomed in St Petersburg, it did not satisfy Zinoviev: 'His first question' according to Pallavicini 'was "Et votre chemin de fer?" ... The Sanjak railway is still a red rag for M. Zinoviev.'[119] The Buchlau negotiations started, according to Aehrenthal's account, with an hour and a half of recriminations by Izvolsky about events of the previous spring.[120] (Izvolsky wrote of his 'extreme weariness after a whole day spent in very stormy negotiations with Baron Aehrenthal').[121] In the middle of the crisis itself, Berchtold heard that Izvolsky, denouncing Aehrenthal's iniquities all over Paris, was still 'going on about the Sanjak Railway. He will tell his gravediggers about it some day'.[122]

For years after the crisis had ended Izvolsky never tired of regaling his hearers with a catalogue of grievances, and he usually began with the Sanjak Railway crisis. Encountering Sir Fairfax Cartwright, British ambassador at Vienna, at Venice in September 1909, for example,[123]

> Izvolsky began by a long defence of his conduct, starting from the time anterior to the Sanjak Railway business...He described himself as the innocent lamb who had been destroyed by the wicked wolf...
>
> According to Izvolsky towards the end of the year 1907 he had elaborated with Aehrenthal a scheme for Macedonian judicial reforms...; this scheme was ready to be laid before the Sultan when the Sanjak railway concession was sprung upon Russia and Izvolsky discovered that Aehrenthal had been bargaining behind his back with the Porte to obtain this concession in return for a promise that neither Germany nor Austria would seriously press forward the Macedonian reform scheme upon the Sultan. How far all this is...strictly true,...I will not pretend to say, but if Izvolsky had really thought he had been done in this matter he ought to have been doubly careful in striking future bargains relating to Balkan questions with Aehrenthal...

Although Hardinge[124] was now willing to admit to Cartwright that 'Izvolsky was greatly responsible for all the agitation and risks of last winter, owing to his ineptitude and extreme vanity' Aehrenthal's reputation was still under a cloud in London:

> There is no doubt that the Sanjak Railway was the cause of the first breach between him and Aehrenthal, and I have never yet succeeded in fathoming how far Izvolsky was involved or how much he knew beforehand of that undertaking. In any case, he ought to have been much more careful afterwards, if he had already been tricked by Aehrenthal in connexion with the Railway.
>
> [The bitterness between Aehrenthal and Izvolsky is unfortunate: until one goes the situation can hardly improve] I have known them both extremely

well for a great number of years and I would trust neither; but I would sooner trust Aehrenthal than Izvolsky, and I prefer Aehrenthal because he is much the more clever and the less dishonest of the two.

It was more than a question of personalities, however. Even when the Railway faded from the scene, the Russians remained obsessed with the Sanjak, and the possibility that the Austrians might reoccupy it as a first stage on their advance to the Aegean. In 1910, Sazonov was warning the Greeks to look to their armaments, otherwise, *'vous verrez l'Autriche à Salonique'*.[125] In short, fear of the 'march to Salonica' ran like a red thread through Russian diplomacy, from the Racconigi agreement with Italy in 1909 to Sazonov's sponsorship of the Serbo-Bulgarian alliance of March 1912. Only when the Concert ceded the Sanjak to Serbia and Montenegro at the end of the Balkan Wars were these Russian fears finally laid to rest. Not that this opened the way for a return to the Austro-Russian Entente. On the contrary, the Austrians now in turn took alarm at the prospect of a large Slav state sealing them off in the south and, despairing of the Concert, turned their thoughts to desperate measures.

Only six years before, Aehrenthal's announcement of the Sanjak Railway project had been widely greeted with enthusiasm in the Monarchy. If Aehrenthal's venerable mother hastened 'to get hold of the map, to study the route. Your old mother...rejoices in your successes',[126] imperialist circles long thwarted by Gołuchowski's passivity and convinced that 'we must make commercial preponderance in the Adriatic and in the Aegean our...[long-term] aim,...and fight against all those plans whose realization would...cut us off for ever' took new heart.[127] Even Goschen, no great admirer of the Monarchy, was prepared to 'admit that this Railway scheme breathes a spirit of youthful vigour and enterprise into Austro-Hungarian foreign policy which has long been lacking in the annual statements of the minister for Foreign affairs'.[128] Within months, it had all ended in tears; and the events of that spring marked a dangerous step towards the polarization of the states system. When, by 1913 the Balkan Prometheus was unbound, had taken possession of the Sanjak, and was openly talking of the need to prepare for 'the next round' against Austria–Hungary, the inability or unwillingness of the decisionmakers of the Concert to control the situation was not unrelated to their experiences in the Sanjak Railway affair of 1908.

Notes

1 F.R. Bridge and Roger Bullen, *The Great Powers and the European States System, 1814–1914*, 2nd Edn, London 2004, pp. 324 ff.
2 F.R. Bridge, *Austria–Hungary among the Great Powers, 1815–1918*, London 1990, pp. 115 ff.
3 Ibid., pp. 130–1.
4 Ibid., pp. 225 ff.
5 Ibid., pp. 242.
6 [Haus,- Hof- und Staatsarchiv, Vienna] P[olitisches] A[rchiv] [Series] XII/K[arton] 344, Aehrenthal to Goluchowski, No 5C, 19 January 1901.

7 F.R. Bridge, 'Izvolsky, Aehrenthal, and the End of the Austro-Russian Entente', in *Mitteilungen des Oesterreichischen Staatsarchivs*, Vol. 29, 1976, pp. 315–62.

8 Ibid., p. 324.

9 P.A. XII/340, Aehrenthal to Berchtold, No. 1706, 27 November; Szögyény to Berchtold, No. 69A, 24 December 1907.

10 Ibid., Szögyény to Aenrenthal, No. 69A, 24 December 1907.

11 P.A. XII 345, Aehrenthal to Berchtold, No. 184, 18 February 1908.

12 S. Wank, 'Aehrenthal and the Sanjak of Novibazar Railway project: a Reappraisal', in *Slavonic and East European Review*, 42, 1964, pp. 353–69. Arthur J. May, 'The Novibazar Railway Project', in *Journal of Modern History*, 10 (1938) pp. 496–527, Ibid., 'Trans-Balkan railway schemes' in *Journal of Modern History*, 24 (1952) pp. 352–67.

13 PA XII/344, Aehrenthal to Pallavicini, No. 158, 16 February 1907.

14 Ibid., Aehrenthal to the Ministerpresidents of Austria and Hungary, Nos 321, 322, 22 March 1907.

15 Ibid., Resumé of a conference held in the Ballhausplatz, 9 March 1907.

16 M. Behnen, *Rüstung-Bündnis-Sicherheit. Dreibund und informeller Imperialismus, 1900–14*, Tübingen, 1985, esp. pp. 405–76.

17 PA XII/344, Notes to Ministerpresidents, Nos 321, 322, 22 March 1907.

18 A[dministrative] R[egistratur], F[aszikel] 19, Aehrenthal to Beck and Wekerle, Z 14179/HP 28 February 1908.

19 [Cambridge University Library] H[ardinge] MSS, XI, Goschen to Hardinge private, 7 February 1908.

20 M. Behnen, *Rüstung*, p. 419.

21 *Westminster Gazette*, 24 February 1908.

22 PA XII/339, Mensdorff to Aehrenthal, Tel. 9, 19 February 1908.

23 PA XII/344, Schönberg to Aehrenthal, No. 9C, 7 March 1907.

24 PA XII/346, Pára to Aehrenthal, Tel. 29, 24 August 1908.

25 PA XII/346, Pallavicini to Aehrenthal, Tel. 311, 9 September 1908.

26 A.R. Faz, 19, Pallavicini to Berchtold, No. 22D, 20 March 1912.

27 M. Behnen, *Rüstung*, pp. 448–9.

28 F.R. Bridge, ' "*Tarde venientibus ossa*": Austro-Hungarian colonial aspirations in Asia Minor, 1913–14', in *Middle Eastern Studies*, 1970.

29 F.R. Bridge, *Great Britain and Austria-Hungary 1906–1914: a diplomatic history*, (London 1972) pp. 68–76.

30 Nachlass Franz Ferdinand, William II to Franz Ferdinand, 18 January 1908; P.A. I/487, Szögyény to Aehrenthal, Tel. 28, 19 January 1908; *Die Große Politik der Europäischen Kabinette*, (eds J. Lepsius, A. Mendelssohn–Bartholdy and F. Thimme), Vol. 22, No. 7726, Marschall to Bülow, No. 10, 13 January 1908; No. 7720, No. 238, 24 December 1907.

31 PA. I/487, Aehrenthal to Artstetten (Archduke Franz Ferdinand), Tel., 22 January 1908.

32 PA XII/339, Aehrenthal to Szögyény, No. 20, 20 January; to Pallavicini, private, 23 January; to Berchtold, Tel. 20, 28 January 1908.

33 PA XII/344, Aehrenthal to Szögyény, Tel. 9, 11 January 1908; Pallavicini to Aehrenthal, No. 6B, 29 January 1908.

34 PA XII/344, Pallavicini to Aehrenthal, No. 78B, 31 December 1907.

35 Ibid., Pallavicini to Aehrenthal, No. 6B, 29 January 1908; PA XII/339, Pallavicini to Aehrenthal, No. 12B, 19 February 1908.

36 F.R. Bridge, *Great Britain*, pp. 79–80.

37 Isabel F. Pantenburg, *Im Schatten des Zweibundes. Probleme österreichisch-ungarischer Bündnispolitik 1897–1908*, Vienna 1996, pp. 422–4.

38 For example PA XII/345, Aehrenthal to Khevenhüller, Tel. 5, 10 February 1908.

39 Botschaftsarchiv Petersburg, 121, Dumba to Berchtold, private, 31 January 1908, quoted in Isabel Pantenburg, *Zweibund*, p. 420.

40 PA XII/344, Pallavicini to Aehrenthal, No. 6B, 29 January 1908.
41 Italian State Archives, Imperiali to Tittoni, private, 28 January 1908.
42 PA XII/339, Berchtold to Aehrenthal, Tel. 15, 26 January 1908.
43 Ibid., Aehrenthal to Berchtold, Tel. 20, 28 January 1908.
44 Ibid., Berchtold to Aehrenthal, Tel. 16, 29 January 1908.
45 PA IX/162 Khevenhüller to Aehrenthal, No. 35D, 28 November 1908. Peter Botkine, Russian minister at Tangier admittedly 'no friend of Izvolsky. The minister hates him, but he has the personal support of his monarch' – had told Khevenhüller that 'Izvolsky was determined from when he took office to break with us and to engage with England. After Your Excellency's action over the Sanjak Railway he played the astonished, indignant party, and yet he could have known perfectly that the time had come for Austria–Hungary to finalize this railway affair. Botkine told me that he had himself had in his hands the fat file relating to this matter in the Foreign Office in St Petersburg, and to talk of a surprise was the purest humbug. Izvolsky wanted to abandon the Mürzsteg programme and that was a capital error in terms of Russia's interests.'
46 Isabel Pantenburg, *Zweibund*, pp. 420–1.
47 PA XII/339 Berchtold to Aehrenthal, Tel. 26, 5 February; Tel. 27, 7 February 1908.
48 Ibid., Aehrenthal to Pallavicini, private, 30 January 1908.
49 GP 26/2, No. 8691, Marschall to the Wilhelmstrasse, Tel. 258, 30 January 1908.
50 Cf W.M. Carlgren, 'Informationsstykken från Abdul Hamids senare regeringar', in *Historisk Tidskrift*, 1952, pp. 1–5.
51 PA XII/339, Pallavicini to Aehrenthal, private, 5 February 1908.
52 Ministro degli Affari Esteri, Rome, 6 1908/VIII/7 Imperiali to Tittoni, private, 28 January 1908.
53 GP, 22, No. 7732, Marschall to Bülow, No 21, 6 February 1908.
54 Constans, was obsessed with promoting France's financial interests in Turkey, and dismissed the reforms as 'de la bêtise et de la niaiserie' G.P. 26/1, Nos 7702, 7720. Retrospectively, in response to Izvolsky's complaints, he claimed that his 'role in the debate was modest'; but he was unrepentant about the outcome of the conference: *Documents diplomatiques français 1871–1914 2e série, Vol. 11, Nos 274, 32,* Constans to Pichon, Tel. 16, 6 February; No. 73, 30 March 1908.
55 Ministro degli Affari Esteri, Rome, Imperiali to Tittoni, No. 259/94, 11 February 1908.
56 B*[ritish]* D*[ocuments on the Origins of the War, ed. G.P. Gooch and H.W.V. Temperley, Vol.]* V, No. 181, O'Conor to Grey, No. 62, 7 February. 1908.
57 Russian State Archives, A[rchiv] V[neshnoi] P[olitiki] R[ossii], Fonds Kanzelyariya, No. 470 1908. File No. 34, pp. 97–112, Zinoviev to Izvolsky, No. 13, 25 January/ 7 February 1908.
58 PA XII/ 339, Pallavicini to Aehrenthal, Tel. 43, 6 February; No.10A, 12 February 1908.
59 Ibid., Aehrenthal to Mensdorff, Tel. 8, 7 February; to Pallavicini, Tel., 26, 12 February; to Berchtold, No. 183, 18 February 1908.
60 Ibid., Aehrenthal to Berchtold, Tel. 29, 7 February 1908.
61 PA XII/339, Aehrenthal to Pallavicini, No. 180, 16 February 1908; H. MSS XI, Goschen to Hardinge, 21 February 1908.
62 PA XII/339 Pallavicini to Aehrenthal, No. 12B, 19 February; No 13B, 26 February 1908.
63 Ibid., Aehrenthal to Pallavicini, No. 228, 27 February 1908.
64 Ibid., Berchtold to Aehrenthal, Tel. 29, 10 February 1908.
65 PA XII/ 345, Berchtold to Aehrenthal, No. 5, 10 February 1908.
66 Ibid., and Berchtold MSS, Tagebuch, 9 February 1908.
67 Berchtold MSS, Tagebuch, 10 February 1908.
68 PA I/ 484, Aehrenthal to Bülow, 11 March 1908.
69 PA XII/ 339, Berchtold to Aehrenthal, No. 4F, 9 February; Tel. 39, 17 February; [Public Record Office London] F[oreign] O[ffice Series] 371/ [Volume] 581, Nicolson to Grey, private telegram, 17 February 1908 and minutes.

70 PA XII/339 Mensdorff to Aehrenthal, Tel. 9, 19 February 1908.
71 H.MSS, XI, Goschen to Hardinge, private, 7 February 1908.
72 BD V, O'Conor to Grey, private, 4 February 1908.
73 BD V, No. 180 O'Conor to Grey, private, 18 February 1908.
74 BD V, No. 184, Grey to O'Conor, private, 10 February 1908.
75 FO 371/581, Grey to Goschen, No. 18, 10 February 1908; PA XII/345, Mensdorff to Aehrenthal, Tel. 6, 9 February; Tel. 7, 10 February; Tel. 8, 12 February 1908.
76 PA XII / 345, Berchtold to Aehrenthal, No. 6C, 16 February 1908.
77 FO 371/581, Goschen to Grey No. 16, 14 February 1908, minutes.
78 FO 371/581, Nicolson to Grey, No. 59, 30 January, minute by Hardinge, 3 February 1908.
79 Ibid., Nicolson to Grey, No. 63, 4 February 1908, minutes.
80 Ibid., Nicolson to Grey, private telegram, 17 February 1908 and minutes.
81 Ibid., Nicolson to Grey, No. 59, 30 January, and minutes by Mallet, 3 February 1908.
82 H. MSS, XI, Goschen to Hardinge, private, 6 March 1908.
83 Ibid., Goschen to Hardinge, private, 21 February 1908.
84 FO 371/581, Goschen to Grey, Tel. 10, 2 March 1908.
85 Ibid., Goschen to Grey, No. 27, 2 March 1908 minutes.
86 Ibid., Nicolson to Grey, private telegram, 17 February 1908 minutes.
87 Ibid., Balkan Committee to Grey, 24 February; memorandum for the Cabinet, 26 February 1908.
88 Ibid., Grey to Nicolson, private telegram, 26 February 1908.
89 FO 371/582, Nicolson to Grey, private, 13 March 1908. H. MSS, XIII, Hardinge to Goschen, private, 24 March, 7 April 1908.
90 H.MSS XIV, Hardinge to Edward VII, 21 March 1908.
91 Ibid., Edward VII to Hardinge, 24 March 1908.
92 Ibid., Hardinge to Edward VII, 28 March 1908.
93 H.MSS, XIII, Hardinge to Goschen, private, 7 April 1908.
94 PA XII/346, Aehrenthal to Berchtold, private, 31 March 1908.
95 PA XII/343, Aehrenthal to Szögyény, No. 965, 24 June; to Berchtold, private, 14 June 1908.
96 H. MSS XI Goschen to Hardinge private, 6 March 1908.
97 FO 371/581 Goschen to Grey, No. 27, 2 March 1908.
98 PA XII/ 346, Aehrenthal to Mensdorff, No. 502, 23 April 1908.
99 Ibid.
100 *Aus dem Nachlass Aehrenthal*, ed. S. Wank, (Graz, 1994) Vol. II, No. 423 Aehrenthal to Conrad, 17 February 1908.
101 Ibid. No. 426, Berchtold to Aehrenthal, private, 5 March; PA I/ 484 Aehrenthal to Bülow, private, 11 March 1908.
102 PA XII/345, *Politische Correspondenz*, 14 February 1908; Botschaftsarchiv Berlin, 217c, Aehrenthal to Pallavicini, Z 141.81, 27 March 1908.
103 *Ö[sterreich-]U[ngarns] A[ußenpolitik von der bosnischen Krise 1908 bis zum Kriegsausbruch 1914*, eds L Bittner and H. Uebersberger, (Vienna 1930), Vol. 1, No. 2, Russian Foreign office memorandum, 27 April 1908.
104 OUA, 1, No. 3, Memorandum for the Russian government, 1 May 1908.
105 F.R. Bridge, 'Izvolsky, Aehrenthal...' pp. 328–31.
106 OUA 1, No. 79. Aehrenthal Memorandum.[c. 16 September 1908].
107 OUA, 1, No. 103, Aehrenthal to Izvolsky, private, 30 September 1908.
108 F.R. Bridge, 'Izvolsky, Aehrenthal...' p. 326 ff.
109 PA XII/346, Aehrenthal to Conrad, No. 1121, 7 June 1908.
110 For example, PA XII/345, Aehrenthal to Pallavicini, Tel. 29, 19 February 1908; to Berchtold, Tel. 40, 22 February 1908; F.R. Bridge, *Great Britain* p. 99.
111 PA VII/2 217c, Botschaftsarchiv Berlin, Aehrenthal to Pallavicini, Z.14.181/1HP, 27 February 1908; PA XII/345, Khevenhüller to Aehrenthal, No.7B, 19 February 1908.

112 PA VII/2 Botschaftsarchiv Berlin, 217c, Forgách to Aehrenthal, No. 10, 24 February 1908.
113 A.R.F. 19, Fasz. 19, Aehrenthal to Pallavicini, 14181/1HP, 27 February 1908.
114 PA XII/345, Zambour to Aehrenthal, No. 8, 27 February 1908; PA XII/346, Aehrenthal to Berchtold, Tel. 77, 3 May 1908.
115 PA XII/346, Berchtold to Aehrenthal, Tel. 10, 24 June 1908.
116 Botschaftsarchiv Petersburg, Fz. 12, Berchtold to Aehrenthal, No. 24B, 8 May 1908.
117 FO 371/583, Nicolson to Grey, 24 April 1908.
118 GP, 26/1, No. 8989, Metternich to Foreign Office, Tel. 267, 6 October 1908.
119 PA XII/352, Pallavicini to Aehrenthal, 83B, 9 October 1908.
120 OUA 1, No. 79. Aehrenthal Memorandum.[c. 16 September 1908].
121 Izvolsky to Charykov, 16 September 1908 in F.R. Bridge, 'Izvolsky, Aehrenthal', Appendix of documents translated from 'Borba v pravyaschchikh krugakh Rossii po voprosam vneshnei politiki vo vremya bosniiskogo krisisa', ed. I.V. Bestuzhev in *Istoricheskii Arkhiv*, 5 (Moscow 1962), Document 4.
122 *Aus dem Nachlass Aehrenthal*, Vol. II, No. 471, Berchtold to Aehrenthal private, 18 October 1908.
123 H.MSS, XV, Cartwright to Hardinge, private, 20 September 1909.
124 Cartwright MSS, Hardinge to Cartwright, private, 4 October 1909.
125 BD IX/1 No. 186, O'Beirne to Grey, No. 398, 1 October 1910.
126 [Universität Salzburg] Aehrenthal MSS; Maria Aehrenthal to Aehrenthal, 19 February 1908. Aehrenthal himself took a more sober view, thanking his mother for her 'encouraging words... I stand by my principle of doing my duty and leave the rest to the dear Lord God. As always, my wife and children are a comfort and a diversion for me in difficult times'. Ibid., Aehrenthal to Maria Aehrenthal, 22 February 1908.
127 Behnen, *Rüstung*, p. 447.
128 H.MSS, XI, Goschen to Hardinge, 7 February 1908.

5 The railway–oceanic era, the India–China and India–Singapore railway schemes, and Siam

Nigel Brailey

The railway–oceanic era

In 1883, in his celebrated book *The Expansion of England*, Prof. J.R. Seeley made passing reference to a German view of 'stages of civilisation' determined by geographical conditions, commencing with the potamic 'which clings to rivers', the thalassic 'which grows up around inland seas', succeeded finally by the oceanic.[1] Seven years later, in 1890, a rare Japanese student of his at Cambridge, Inagaki Manjiro, a future political activist and diplomat, published a book with Fisher Unwin elaborating the third state of the theory as the 'railway–oceanic' in recognition of the heyday of great railway projects. With the completion of first the American and then the Canadian transcontinental rail lines in 1869 and 1885, and the news of the commencement of a trans-Siberian railway in Imperial Russia, Inagaki suggested that Japan could hope to become 'the Key to the Pacific', lying astride a route ringing the whole northern hemisphere, linked by oceanic steamer services across both Atlantic and Pacific.[2]

The late 1880s in particular, featured a certain perceived trough in world trade which it was felt railway building could stimulate. The Trans-Siberian line was mostly built between 1891 and 1901, on the eve of the climactic Russo-Japanese and 1914–18 wars, and as a rival to the contemporary Trans-Caspian and Orenburg–Tashkent lines of 'Great Game' fame. And at 4,388 miles from the Urals to Vladivostok, it might be counted the supreme expression of this 'railway–oceanic' age.[3] Though the achievement principally of the ambitious Finance Minister, Count Sergei Witte, it was really launched under Tsar Alexander III and his earlier Transport Minister, Admiral Posyet, while Nicholas II when still Tsarevich, in 1890–1, made the long sea-journey to Vladivostok to cut the first sod, and en route was nearly assassinated by a guardsman on parade in Japan in the so-called Otsu Incident. Thereby, at least up to the humiliating outcome of Russia's 1904–5 war with Japan, by personal experience and crisis Nicholas became Asia-orientated or conscious in a way no predecessor of his had been. And the Far East was brought closer to Europe as a whole as never before, the line promising to reduce journey-times from a matter of weeks (via N. America) to hardly more than days.[4] By 1906, on the eve of the development of air travel, there were even visionary ideas of linking the Trans-Siberian with the railways of North America via a tunnel under the Behring Straits.[5]

Leaving aside the railway investment in this period in South America, the Baghdad Railway scheme, various African railways and the dream of a Cape to Cairo line, for some such as Frederick Weld, Governor of the Straits Settlements (Singapore) 1880–7, the prospect had just opened up of becoming part of a great communications link between India and Australia via Singapore comparable with the Trans-Siberian and with, if anything, more far-reaching imperial implications.[6] Responsible for the new Malay protectorates just established on the peninsula, where the railway system, like that of British Burma to the north, was in its early stages, he too visualized ocean-going steamer connections, from Singapore to Australia, to complete the service. To the north, the Malayan line was to be linked with the Burmese, probably requiring the annexation of the intervening Thai territory, even if it meant the French swallowing the rest of the kingdom by way of compensation. And it was supposed that the Burmese system would eventually be linked with that of the Raj proper, all to the metre gauge which was to be adopted in Malaya as in Burma and much of eastern India including in particular, Assam. For that matter, securing control of the whole Malay Peninsula was also likely to block French ambitions led by Ferdinand de Lesseps, currently only intermittently involved with the Panama project, to build a maritime canal across its narrowest portion at Kra which would draw away at least part of Singapore's oceanic trade.[7]

Admittedly it was during the 1880s apparently, that Britain's established pre-eminence in railwaybuilding first really began to be challenged.[8] And if the whole world had hitherto been Britain's oyster in this particular respect, India had been a specially important field for British railway technology. Indeed, Indian Railways, including upto 1947, those of Pakistan and Burma, were long to be the world's fourth most extensive system, not to be overtaken by those of China until 1990, as by then the world's fifth, otherwise only exceeded by the great continental countries of the United States, Russia and Canada, plus a reunited Germany. The Raj was famous for its railways, and it was perhaps as much the product as the reason for them. Planning for the system commenced at the end of the 1840s, under the similarly youthful and resourceful pro-consul forerunner of Curzon, the Marquess of Dalhousie, previously responsible as President of the Board of Trade for the British system. And within thirty years, the lines commenced independently from the original three presidency cities of Bombay, Calcutta and Madras, as well as Karachi and Lahore, had all been linked together, providing so-called grand trunk lines, for instance between Bombay and Madras, Delhi and Calcutta, and even earlier, Calcutta and Delhi. Thereafter, new lines with the notable exception eventually of the narrow gauge line from Calcutta to Assam, were largely a matter of consolidating the existing system.[9]

Thus for the first time, the sub-continent secured the communication system it had always needed to penetrate its inaccessible heart and become a genuine political whole. It was almost as much a strategic achievement as the Trans-Siberian, and a virtual new caste of Eurasians emerged to operate the system, deriving its special status from its role in keeping the Raj functioning right up to independence and partition. The latter is the era of John Masters' *Bhowani Junction* which has some claim to be the most famous railway novel. The tradition has been kept alive since 1947, to such an extent that in recent years, it was to India that Nigeria, Africa's most populous state, turned for the refurbishment of its system.

China and railway development

China was a rather different matter in railway as in other terms. China had anyhow a much stronger tradition than India of political unity and integrity going back before Christ to the beginnings of the Han dynasty. Subsequently the so-called 'dynastic cycle' had featured quite long periods of political confusion, even disunity between dynasties. Both India and China had been subjected in successive centuries to external, essentially alien forces, long before the arrival of Western imperialism. Thus India had been subjected to the Muslim Moghuls in the sixteenth century and China to the Manchus in the seventeenth century. But while the Moghuls collapsed in the face of growing French and British power in the eighteenth, the Manchu Ch'ing were to survive through until the end of 1911. Thus there was by no means the same impulse in China for railways in the nineteenth century, the great era of railway-building. And it was not anyhow colonized, even by the great pioneers of railways, the British.

Although Chinese stonemason labour was apparently being imported into India by the early 1860s for bridge-building,[10] following the defeat of the great pseudo-Christian Taiping rebellion of 1850–64, China's unity had been restored by largely conventional means, and with the assistance of her traditional inland communications, roads, rivers, and canals such as the famous Grand Canal linking the Yellow and Yangtze rivers. As early as 1794, the great Emperor Ch'ien-lung had turned away the 'barbarian' floating industrial showcase brought to China by Lord Macartney as supposedly superfluous to China's needs. And thereafter, the iron roads with their fire-carriages must have been seen as thoroughly alien and unnecessary. Worse, as the nineteenth century wore on, they seem increasingly to have been viewed as instruments of Western imperialism, threatening China's partition and dismemberment. Japan's willingness to adapt to the Western threat was in no way better demonstrated than by her commencing the building of her own railways in the 1870s, but China, like its smaller neighbour known as Siam,[11] at least up to the 1890s, and well into the railway–oceanic age, sought to refuse concessions to Western, mainly British, companies to construct lines.

Thus in 1863, the proposal to build a line from Shanghai to Soochow had been refused by of all people Li Hung-chang, associated with 'Chinese Gordon' in the defeat of the Taipings, and a future viceroy known thereafter as a 'self-strengthener', otherwise relatively sympathetic to Western technology. In 1873, an attempt involving the British Minister, Thomas Wade, to present the young T'ung-chih Emperor with a short line as a nuptial gift was abandoned for fear of rejection. And in 1877, the Chinese Government had bought up another short line from Shanghai to Kangwan en route to Woosung, being constructed by the Jardine Matheson company without authority, and promptly tore up the rails which, along with the locomotives, were deposited on a beach on off-shore Formosa to rust away.[12] A few years later, in 1881 in North China, a colliery line was built under Chinese auspices to the sea at Lutai, and thereafter extended to the port of Tientsin. And both the Treaty of Tientsin that concluded the Sino-French War of 1884–5, and a subsequent Sino-French treaty immediately following the Sino-Japanese war in June 1895, seemed to anticipate French construction of lines across the border from French Indo-china. None were permitted prior to a new agreement in 1898, amidst the new climax of Western imperialism known as the 'Battle for Concessions', but a Chinese railway department was set up in 1891, one year after a similar move in Siam.

As the best explanation of this apparent change of heart, already by the late 1880s, as Inagaki had noted, the Russian Government had been urged to expedite the building of the Trans-Siberian line with an extension across Manchuria to anticipate what were perceived to be Beijing's plans to secure control of the region through its own lines.[13] Thus by the time of the outbreak of the First Sino-Japanese War at the end of July 1894, the Tientsin–Lutai line had been extended beyond the Great Wall, while the connection between Tientsin and Beijing and a further extension into Manchuria were under construction.[14] After the war, first Russia and France pressed on the Chinese a loan of £15.8 million to pay off the initial instalment of their indemnity to the Japanese. Then effectively in return, and in the cause of anti-Japanese collaboration. St Petersburg approached the Chinese for permission to construct the shortcut line, known as the Chinese Eastern Railway, across Northern Manchuria to Vladivostok, which was agreed to on the occasion of Li Hung-chang's attendance at the coronation of Nicholas II in 1896. And lastly, in March 1898, at the same time as the Russians secured the concession of the Liaotung Peninsula, they obtained the right to build a branch down to Port Arthur at its tip. Financed like the Trans-Siberian largely by the French, these lines initiated the 'Battle for Concessions' proper, which featured a virtual frenzy of imperial competition, even if actual construction was not always so prompt.[15] British interests became involved for a time with the Beijing–Manchuria line, unusually, as British activity was otherwise concentrated in the Yangtze valley in central China. Ultimately, as the chances of China's survival improved following the Boxer crisis in 1899–1900, private Chinese interests were allowed to compete, and when, in 1909–10, the Manchu Government offered to secure a new loan from the Western powers against the Chinese lines, the movement that grew into the Revolution of 1909 was launched in protest, and overthrew it in favour of a republic.

Thus the circumstances for railway development, and indeed the opportunities for Western financial interests that pertained finally in China in the years post-1895, were long in coming. And China's refusal to permit trade beyond the ports she was forced by treaty to open after her series of wars with Western powers in the nineteenth century, provoked great frustration. What are still of great interest are the efforts that were made to circumvent Chinese isolationism, as an extension of the growing Western presence in Asia, and their imperial by-products, for instance, in terms of the kingdoms of Burma and Siam bordering on China, the latter being especially pivotal.

Overland access to China was an alternative, and its interior had been viewed as a potential Eldorado for Western trade as far back as the seventeenth century, when the Dutch *Vereenigde Oostindische Compagnie* (VOC) had first attempted to develop the overland 'back-door' route into China from Burma. Very little came of it at the time, and the unsettled condition of this frontier and of mainland Southeast Asia generally through much of the eighteenth century, discouraged further efforts. Similar activity on the part of the Russians to the North was to be handicapped until the twentieth century by Siberia's lack of development. But the Java-focused operations of the Dutch in the East were duly superseded by the India-focused operations of the British. The first two of the three Anglo-Burmese wars of the nineteenth century extended the power of the nascent Raj under the East India Company to the deltas of the Salween and Irrawaddy rivers. This coincided with the growing economic development of the Raj, and interest in the hinterlands of the ports of Moulmein and Rangoon grew rapidly. Prior to the second Burma war of 1852, Britons investigated only the traditional animal-borne trade up to the frontier of China's southernmost province, Yunnan. But after the second war, and with the onset of the railway age even in Asia, an iron road began for the first time to be debated.

While normally classed up to independence in 1947/8 as a part of the Indian system,[16] in fact Burma's railways always remained separate and even neglected like most things in Burma. Thus as late as 1940, one writer comments: 'There were obvious blanks on the railroad map ... and, most remarkable, not one single rail link between Burma and her neighbours, India and Siam.' This might also refer to China as little more difficult of access from Burma than the other two. Apparently, however, such connections 'would have necessitated heavy expenditure – the physical obstacles were overpowering – and would have been of marginal utility.'[17]

This may have been the somewhat unambitious colonial view of the 1930s when air-travel was also expanding fast, but things were seen differently back in the late nineteenth century. Construction in what became, by 1897, the 'Province' of Burma only commenced in 1874 with the Rangoon–Prome line, from the provincial capital to the town at the head of the Irrawaddy delta, completed in 1877. And the line from Rangoon to Toungoo in the Sittang valley was only just completed prior to the Third Anglo-Burmese War.[18] Ernest Satow, as then the British Minister in Bangkok on a visit to the province, travelled over both in July 1885.[19] After the war, the Toungoo line extended in 1889 as the main trunk-route to the captured Burmese capital of Mandalay, still had to compete with the slower but more popular steamer traffic on the Irrawaddy river. Thus for instance J. George Scott, returning in late 1895 to his superintendency of the Northern Shan States after secondment as Britain's Charge d'Affaires in Bangkok, travelled up to Mandalay with his dying first wife by river.[20] A further extension of a sort, effectively a new line, was constructed by 1898 from Sagaing, opposite Mandalay across the river, north to the old Konbaung dynasty home of Shwebo and thence to Myitkyina, giving possible access to both China and, via the Hukawng valley, to Assam.[21] And another line was built up from Mandalay via the great Gokteik viaduct to Scott's headquarters at Lashio in the Shan States, completed in 1902. Other branches were added gradually, including the line, in sections, south from Pegu junction to Martaban and Moulmein, in 1907, and thereafter to Ye. As late as the outbreak of the Far Eastern War in December 1941, the only bridge across the mouth of the Sittang river south of Pegu was that of the railway.

Meanwhile so far as Britain's rivals the French were concerned, the very establishment of their colony of Indochina between 1858 and 1885, largely stemmed from their interest in China, and the prospect of securing the back-door river-routes available. These were respectively the Mekong, explored by the great Lagree-Garnier expedition of 1866–8, ending in descent by the Yangtze to Shanghai, and the Red River, the reason for Francis Garnier's occupation of the citadel of Hanoi near its mouth in 1873.[22] Garnier's death in not dissimilar fashion to Charles Gordon in the Sudan a decade later, provoked a much more immediate response, and the French extinction of Vietnamese independence in 1884–5, but little more. And it was only during the 1890s, that the French began to show serious interest in cross-border railway connections with both Yunnan and Kwangsi provinces in China.

The Burma–China railway schemes

The excitement of the idea of an Indian, or at least Burma rail link with China, and the prospect of it becoming one of the great railway projects of the later nineteenth century, seems evident from the fact that it was being proposed as early as the 1850s. At this point the Indian system itself had only just begun to be built, and the first lines in Burma proper were still years away. Admittedly the emphasis always seems to have been on a freight rather than passenger service, given the largely wild, thinly populated terrain through which it was intended to pass, and its international as opposed to the strategic and nationbuilding character of the Trans-Siberian. But it seems to have been an idea popular in England almost from the start not only with chambers of commerce but certain figures of real standing, including a Duke, and also the third Marquess of Salisbury, prime minister three times over.

The first phase of the scheme might be said to date from 1858 to 1875, following its initial announcement by Captain Richard Sprye formerly of the Indian Army.[23] However, Sprye supported by his two sons appears to have been genuinely active in the campaign only during the first two or three years. Thereafter, it was taken up by a whole set of chambers of commerce in England, various MP's and even *The Times* newspaper, and gave rise to a series of expeditions of exploration. The route Sprye proposed commenced at Rangoon, newly occupied by British forces in 1852, and then turned eastward up the gorgelike valley of the Salween river with its great temperature variations to the Shan State of Kengtung. There, only a relatively narrow tongue of land needed to be crossed to the upper waters of the Mekong flowing out of Chinese Yunnan. The route had the merit of largely by-passing territory controlled by the now quite unstable surviving rump of the Kingdom of Burma but little else.

Advised by people who knew the area at first hand, it seems that the Indian Government preferred the more orthodox and traditional route going back to the Dutch in the seventeenth century.[24] Via Bhamo on the upper Irrawaddy, it was arguably even less suitable for a railway but perhaps that in itself was an advantage in Calcutta's eyes, and also truly minimized the land needing to be crossed. A Muslim rebellion in Yunnan lasting several years delayed any resolution of the matter until 1875, when an arrangement by which an officer from British Burma was due to meet halfway the China-based British consul Augustus Margary, culminated in the murder of the latter just across the Chinese frontier with Upper Burma. Chinese bandits operating with the knowledge of the Yunnan authorities were held responsible and the opportunity was seized to demand the opening to trade of more Chinese riverine ports by means of the Chefoo Convention, the first clear sign of developing rivalry between traditional India-based and the now expanding China coast treaty port interests hitherto held in some contempt by the home chambers of commerce.[25] And no more was heard thereafter of the Sprye Salween scheme.

But the involvement and support of the Marquess of Salisbury, the future prime minister and dominant political figure of late nineteenth century Britain as Secretary of State for India 1866–7 and 1874–8, gave this preliminary stage of the railway project extra significance.[26] And it was during the interval between his two terms as India Secretary that he served three years as Executive Chairman of the domestic British Great Eastern Railway, putting its finances back on a sound footing.[27] Nor, following his resignation from the company in 1872, did he ever lose his interest in railways. Indeed, the proximity to London of his ancestral seat, Hatfield House, made it possible for him to commute daily by train and hansom cab to Whitehall throughout his political career. Admittedly, his friendliness to the Burma–China railway had served little purpose up to this point, and anyhow apparently involved a preference for the Bhamo route. Such was the confidence of the era in its engineering capabilities that nothing seems to have been considered impossible, perhaps demonstrated most clearly with the surmounting of the Western Ghats outside Bombay quite early in the development of the Indian system. In terms of the Burma–China line however, it was the second phase involving a new route, mounted by two initially seconded officials from British Burma, which breathed most life into the idea.

The youthful Archibald R. Colquhoun first made his entry on the scene in 1879 accompanying the mission of Major C.W. Street, Secretary to the Government of British Burma, to the then semi-independent principality of Zimme or Chiangmai in Northern Thailand.[28] This led eventually to the publication of his *Amongst the Shans* in 1885. But in the meanwhile, in 1882, he made his name in rather the same fashion as the famous Australian journalist, G.E. Morrison, a decade later, by means of a cross-country journey from China back into Burma, quickly written up as his *Across Chryse*.[29] What was critical, anyhow, was his association around the same time with his fellow Burma official, Holt S. Hallett, a rather older, rougher man, and an engineer with experience of railway construction back in England.

During 1883–4, Colquhoun enlarged his reputation as a somewhat sensationalist journalist with *The Times*, commuting back and forward between India, China, Siam and Vietnam in the context of the Sino-French war and consequent talk of a French threat to Bangkok. Meanwhile Hallett got on with surveying the route taken by the Street Mission to Chiangmai in 1879.While this also ran up the Salween valley as far as Shwegun, it then branched away from the Sprye route across the mountains to Mae Sariang and Hort on the Ping river, a tributary of the Chaophraya in Siam. Hallett himself continued on beyond Chiangmai as far as Chiangsen on the Mekong, the rest of the route thereafter rejoining that of the Spryes in Yunnan, ultimately, it was hoped, to reach Chungking in Szechwan. And subsequently Hallett came to the conclusion that a better junction with the Ping might be made further south at the larger town of Raheng, so that the line could then bypass Chiangmai via Lampang to its east.

Not until 1890 did Hallett's account of his surveys appear in print, with an appendix detailing widespread chamber of commerce support,[30] by which time the Colquhoun–Hallett, or perhaps more properly Hallett–Colquhoun route, seemed in turn to be on the slide. But its considerable popularity in the intervening years, as maybe the most obviously practicable line for a railway in engineering terms, was clearly largely the product of Hallett's efforts alone. Admittedly he took his explorations no further than the Mekong river at Chiangsen, where he faced country further to the north that was wild and thinly populated, albeit no more so in his view than much of that to be traversed by Russia's Trans-Siberian line. And he made no attempt at costing beyond £1.5 million for the cross-border connection between Moulmein and Raheng. But writing in a period before the idea of the Channel Tunnel attained its first peak of popularity in the early twentieth century, he nonetheless appeared to visualize an eventual link at least with Calais via the Indian system and the Persian Gulf, as an alternative to the prospective Trans-Siberian through northern Eurasia.[31] Simultaneously, Lord Salisbury was also advocating railways in Persia, for general developmental reasons and from a concern to bolster its independence, though thanks to Russian opposition no connection was ever to be built.[32]

By early July 1884, Colquhoun had joined Hallett in Bangkok, and initially both secured the enthusiastic support of the newly arrived British Minister Ernest Satow, and the goodwill of Prince Thewawong, the Siamese Foreign Minister.[33] However, in the process of deciding whether to award the two of them a concession for building a line through Siamese territory and provide financial guarantees, King Chulalongkorn began to stress that instead his priority was a line from Bangkok to Khorat in the Northeast of his kingdom, to strengthen Bangkok authority there in face of French interest in the Mekong valley. Colquhoun's telegrams to *The Times* in London about the French threat even to the Siamese capital heightened the sense of tension. And Satow began to lose patience with Hallett in particular, whom he found contemptuous of the local people he had come to negotiate with. Perhaps most serious of all, the current Chief Commissioner of British Burma, Sir Charles Bernard, an anti-expansionist, began to register his opposition to the project as over-extending British interests in the area, and raising the spectre of an Anglo-French war over Siam, while the Indian Government in Calcutta seems simply to have taken its lead from him.

Among the personages at home in England who nonetheless expressed their support for the scheme at this time were successive Liberal and Conservative Secretaries for India, Lords Kimberley and Randolph Churchill. Lord Salisbury by contrast, given his earlier sympathy for the Bhamo route, was more ambivalent. But the preference of the Thai for a line to Khorat, and evident distrust of one across their northwest through Chiangmai, or alternatively neighbouring Lampang, even if, as the somewhat slippery Hallett assured them, a connection to Bangkok could be added, encouraged rival offers. J.A. Bryce of the Bombay-Burmah Corporation, brother of the Liberal politician James Bryce, was in Bangkok at the same time as Hallett and Colquhoun, promising to undertake a survey of the line the Thai preferred. In late 1887, a London firm named Punchard, McTaggart and Lowther was also showing interest in the same possibility. And in early 1888, this firm despatched to Bangkok a former Governor of the Straits Settlements and empire-builder, himself a trained engineer, General Sir Andrew Clarke. He was to compete with Cromartie Sutherland–Leveson–Gower K.G., the fourth Duke of Sutherland, who made the voyage from England by means of his own yacht, the *Sans Peur*.[34]

The Duke, as Lord Salisbury had been at one time, was a major entrepreneurial figure on the domestic British railway scene, and had been involved with the 'nuptial' railway plan in China in 1873. He was also a friend of the Prince of Wales, the future King Edward VII, whom he had accompanied on a visit to India in 1876, touring around the subcontinent by rail. But the Duke too failed to win over the suspicious Thai, and it was Sir Andrew Clarke who secured the contract to properly survey a line from Bangkok to Chiangmai with a so-called branch to Khorat. And again, in the event, it was not even the General's backers, Punchard, McTaggart and Lowther but the small British Malaya-based company of Murray Campbell which was finally selected to launch merely the Khorat line in 1892, only itself to be ousted in due course, and the line to be completed by the kingdom's newly formed and German expatriate-run Royal Railways Department, with the Chiangmai line still to follow years later. Thus the Hallett–Colquhoun Siam route to China was essentially doomed through the survey contract arranged in 1888.

However, a surprising degree of renewed interest in the Colquhoun–Hallett route was yet to be displayed by the chambers of commerce during 1895–6. Apparently this was prompted by a fear that the Siam crisis that had developed over the previous three years was about to end in French occupation of the kingdom. Hallett was among those whose immediate reaction to the Anglo-French Joint Declaration of January 1896, was that it amounted to an effective partition, and gave British interests a clear run in a supposed western Siam British 'sphere of influence'.[35] That was a sheer misunderstanding, as soon became evident, but one source argues that the British cabinet gave its assent to the Joint Declaration and effective neutralization of Siam only because at that point the Mandalay–Kunlong line now proposed was considered to guarantee eventual rail access to China as an alternative to the Hallett–Colquhoun route.[36]

The trans-Salween Kunlong Ferry route on to Tali in western Yunnan had begun to attract the support of the British Burmese and Calcutta authorities as early as 1886. The annexation of Upper Burma and elimination of the Burmese monarchy following the Third Anglo-Burmese War had freed it of the likely complications of dealing with a third power like the government at Bangkok, though local political disturbances continued until 1890. Thereafter, plans began to be made for the Mandalay–Lashio line en route to Kunlong, involving the great trestle viaduct across the Gokteik gorge hitherto considered almost impassable by such as Holt Hallett.[37] And in 1895, authority was given to commence the line's construction. However, the debate over this decision revealed mixed feelings even in Calcutta, such that the India Office in London began to accuse the Indian Government of having already gone cold over the link with China.

Similar feelings seem evident in the Foreign Office at this time, not least on the part of Lord Salisbury himself, now back in power for his third and final premiership. Indeed it might be said that this fourth and final alternative route, following those via Bhamo, the Salween, and Chiangmai/Lampang, was probably doomed almost as soon as it was considered. By now, there was clearly a growing belief in the prospects for reaching the interior of China from its coast, especially up the rivers from Shanghai and Canton, the Yangtze and Si-kiang. And this was boosted by the formation in London in 1889, of the China Association featuring figures recently returned from Hongkong such as William Keswick of Jardine Matheson and Sir Alfred Dent. The issue is whether those prospects or the difficulties of the Mandalay–Kunlong route were the more influential in causing George Curzon, currently Salisbury's deputy at the Foreign Office, to pronounce against it as early as mid-1896. Long concerned for the strategic aspects of European imperial rivalry in Asia, he apparently concluded nonetheless, two years before his ennoblement and appointment as Viceroy of India, and more than five before he supplied its final coup de grace, that this project was unwise and impractical, 'for engineering reasons, an impossibility'.[38]

Lobbying nonetheless continued right through into 1901 on the part of at least some of the home chambers of commerce and various officials, especially in the India Office and in the province of Burma. This was with respect to one or other of the routes, with support increasingly concentrating on an extension to the Mandalay–Lashio line as the one actually under construction, and thus offering the best chance of something being done. But the era of the so-called 'Battle for Concessions' in China now commenced with the German seizure of Kiaochow on the Shantung peninsula at the end of 1897, and the corresponding Russian occupation of the Liaotung peninsula facing it across the entrance to the Gulf of Chihli in February 1898. This turned attention to China itself as never before, and exposed a new powerlessness on the part of the government in Beijing to resist the penetration of the country by Western commercial interests. Already in May 1898, Lord Salisbury was beginning reluctantly to envisage a partition of China, at least in terms of spheres of influence, a prospect much more alarming than the similar partition of Siam, with Britain restricted just to the Yangtze valley via Shanghai near its mouth. Competition was increasing, in particular with France, which was now attempting to build railways from Indochina across the frontier at Langson into Kwangsi, and Laokai to Kunming, the capital of Yunnan province.[39] And a settlement with Russia was attempted with a view to restricting the Russian presence in the North simply to Manchuria and Northern China. However, the advent of the Boer War in South Africa, distracting and for a time almost prostrating Britain during 1899–1900, handicapped her even in her troop contribution to the suppression of the subsequent so-called Boxer Rebellion. What with Calcutta having already leased out Burma Railways privately in an economy drive back in 1896, and now turning to London for financial support for the extension of the Mandalay railway beyond Lashio, in contradiction of his usually expansionist inclinations, Curzon decided to end the debate. In a speech at Rangoon in November 1901, on a viceregal visit to Burma, he finally dismissed the Kunlong route as 'midsummer madness', and afterwards to the Secretary of State for India in London, Lord George Hamilton, as 'an unprofitable and useless undertaking'.[40] As new international alliances between old enemies impended, China was to be recognized henceforth as an entity and issue in its own right even by the railway planners, not merely an extension of Britain's Indian Empire. As a consequence the idea of a railway connection in what was anyhow becoming a quite different world from the heyday of railway schemes in the 1880s, died probably for ever.

The problem of independent Siam

By contrast Siam continued to figure in terms of international railway connections. So often dismissed over the years as a backwater or 'negligible quantity', it is today the hub of air rather than rail-travel in Southeast Asia. Back in the late nineteenth century, it was the railway and other schemes which pointed up its real strategic significance. It was a matter of the so-called 'Siam Question', how independent so-called Siam was to be dealt with as a problem by the major powers, comparable with the 'Chinese', 'Persian', 'Egyptian', 'Moroccan' and other 'questions' as they were invariably termed. Given the uncertainty of profit and the relative lack of strategic advantage it has been popular in some quarters to regard the Burma–China railway via Siam as never more than a pipe-dream. Even within China, the link between Chungking and Chengtu in Szechwan and Kunming was not completed until the 1970s. But it is not easy to deny its seriousness. The rival link between Hanoi in French Indochina and Kunming, despite the difficulty of the route, was constructed in this era in the interests of politics as well as trade. And in combination with the other schemes it is arguable that the British threat to the kingdom's independence was as great as the better-known threat from France.

What was at issue was the treatment of the kingdom as a 'no-man's-land'. Calculated procrastination by the Thai, and refusal in particular even to finance surveys except for lines of strategic value to themselves, might be considered a major contribution to the maintenance of their independence. Thus the Thai succeeded in excluding two of the great 'railway–oceanic' projects from their territory, the Burma–China line permanently and Burma–Singapore line for at least a couple of decades. This applied quite as much as their similar success in the same period in blocking the project for a maritime canal across the Kra Isthmus leading to Malaya.[41] None of these projects were conceived with Thai interests in mind, or made any reference in their names to Siam and thus the kingdom's sovereign claims to the territories involved. And the stories of other such projects, in particular the Suez and Panama Canals, are evidence enough of the threat they could easily come to represent to the independence of the countries through which they passed.

In India and British Burma, fear of involvement in the defence of Siam against French encroachment seems to have been a major reason for resistance to building even a connecting line up to the Siamese frontier. Indeed figures like Lord Kimberley, back as Secretary of State for India in the first half of 1886, and the Chief Commissioner of British Burma, Sir Charles Bernard, were at that time showing sympathy for the doctrine of 'compensation' by which, leaving aside the allocation of peninsular Siam, the French could be reckoned entitled to the acquisition of the rest of the kingdom to balance Britain's annexation of Upper Burma at the beginning of the year.[42] By contrast concessionaires such as Holt Hallett and the Duke of Sutherland envisaged British control if not rule over Siam, and foresaw a rail connection as likely to contribute to this, with the added advantage of keeping Siam out of French clutches and preserving British predominance in its foreign trade. As with a line down through the Tenasserim coastal province of British Burma to Singapore, such British political control would appear to have been the prime condition for an India/Burma–China link via Siam. But it would probably also have been the instance of such a link had the control been established, almost oblivious to the financial expense. In the last resort, politics and prestige were likely to rule rather than financial gain. In their own interests, the Thai clearly had to guard against the ambitions of both interested Western powers, even if in doing so they laid themselves open to the charge of 'playing off' one power against the other.[43]

Perhaps most intriguing is the evidence that in early 1885, Joseph Chamberlain, a decade later the arch-imperialist himself, apparently advised Prince Pritsdang Chumsai, the senior Thai diplomat in Europe of the time, not to agree even to a British railway concession in his country, for fear of the extra-territorial implications.[44] Extraterritoriality or extraterritorial jurisdiction was a system that had originally developed in the Ottoman Empire by the early nineteenth century, and then spread to the Far East. Via the so-called 'unequal treaties' of the mid-nineteenth century, countries such as China, Japan and Siam were required to exempt Westerners from the due processes of their own legal systems in favour of adjudication by Western consuls. And it was to be expected that any concessions to foreign companies developing projects such as railways and canals would want such arrangements extended to all their employees. including probably natives of the country in question.

More than that, they were likely to demand the application of such extraterritoriality to substantial swathes of territory either side of the canal or even railway-line they were constructing. And finally, as actually happened in the case of Siam in

1886–7, such schemes were likely to be followed up with proposals for extensive territorial concessions with a view to development in a variety of other respects. In the case of Siam, the 'Malay Peninsula Exploration and Development Syndicate' (MPES or MPEDS) aimed in addition to railways, port facilities and a maritime canal, at 'roads, tramways, mines, fisheries, [land] irrigation, reclamation [and] improvement, sewerage, drainage, water supply, gas, hotels, warehouses, markets, public buildings'.[45] The very location of the proposed concession, not far from the frontiers of the British-protected Malay States, along with the omission once again of any reference to Siam in its name, clearly threatened the most dire consequences not only for Bangkok's sovereignty in the area, but the very survival of the kingdom itself.

Equally striking however, is the fact that the real predicament the kingdom sank into in the mid-1890s, did not present the Western concessionaires with any serious new opportunities. In June–July 1893, at the time of the Paknam Crisis when a French naval squadron blockaded Bangkok, Lord Rosebery as Britain's Foreign Secretary, made an initial intervention to discourage French encroachment in eastern Siam. And two years later, by which time he had succeeded Gladstone as Premier, he had to face another confrontation with the French over the principality of Mong Sing on the upper Mekong. He in turn was succeeded by Lord Salisbury returning to power, simultaneously as premier and Foreign Secretary, to resolve the impasse with the French in the January 1896 Joint Declaration. Some passing mention was made of the Kra Canal scheme in these years, but much more of the Burma–China railway. What seems clear nonetheless, is that already by November 1895, prior to the Joint Declaration, Salisbury held out little hope for Siam's long survival, and indicated he believed that railway would simply complicate relations with the French.[46] In early 1896 as already noted, Holt Hallett had renewed hope of building the line through an expected British 'sphere of influence' in Northern Siam, only to have it again quickly dashed. And the kingdom did survive, never to become a Western colony, let alone suffering the partition evidently anticipated by many.

Of particular relevance here is that, whereas in Persia it was principally foreigners, the Russians, who blocked railway development in the late nineteenth century, and permanently, such that it was never linked with India, in Siam it was the locals, but only up to the point at which the great schemes had effectively gone away. Morocco, effectively consigned to France in 1903–4, in the context of the Anglo-French Entente, was held to be 'barbarous' largely, apparently, for its refusal to accept railway development, an important reason why it formed the focus of the Entente 'colonial deal' rather than, as was initially suggested, Siam.[47] Although Anglo-French dislike of the influence of German expatriate employees in the Siamese Railway Department played its part, once the great European projects were frustrated, railway-building, and the development of a Siamese system, remained strictly under the control of the government of the country and up to 1909, unconnected with the lines of any of their colonial neighbours.

At that point, in return for the cession of four of Siam's peninsular Malay states, Britain offered Bangkok a £4 million loan to finance the construction of a new line running right down through the peninsula, to connect the Siamese capital with the expanding Malayan system. That is this revived the spectre of a through connection between Singapore and British Burma, if not also India, briefly talked of in 1895 by such as General Sir Andrew Clarke and Joseph Chamberlain,[48] and the consequent likelihood of Britain claiming the whole of southern Thailand. As recently as 1904, Alleyne Ireland, a leading British scholar of colonial administration, had proposed the separation of Burma from India and its linkage with Malaya, and been supported in this by *The Times*.[49] However, opposition within Indian government circles, concerned that the Raj might lose the Burmese *milch-cow* so valuable to Indian finances, prevented any immediate action. By 1907, the Foreign Office in London had been receiving specific invitations to support a proposal for a Burma–Siam rail-link,[50] the idea was further reconsidered in Indian circles in the early stages of the 1914–18 War, and with the completion in 1917, of the Singapore–Bangkok connection, the ostensibly neutral British Legation in Bangkok in the persons of successive Ministers Dering and Seymour, again took up the idea. Nervous perhaps of provoking suspicions, the Singapore authorities seem to have maintained a low profile.[51] Once again, however, the British authorities in both India and Burma proved unenthusiastic, doing their best to sidetrack the efforts of Prince Burachat, the dynamic new Director of Siam's State Railways, on a trip to Europe. Seymour was soon displaced as Minister in Bangkok and the idea finally died, only to be revived by the Japanese a quarter-century later as the notorious 'Burma–Siam' (or more properly 'Thailand–Burma') 'Death Railway', in the cause of their strategic contingencies following Pearl Harbor. And while previously the preferred junction point had always been Raheng in Upper Thailand, the Japanese chose the different and more difficult route of the Three Pagodas Pass beyond Kanchanaburi alongside the River Kwai (Gweh), a line which again disappeared at the end of the war, mostly dismantled by the British occupationary forces with a view to restoring the colonial lines in Malaya and elsewhere.[52]

But for that matter, the interest of the Thai in what had always been such a politically threatening project must be considered questionable, even that of Prince Burachat, shortly to be promoted Minister of Commerce and Communications. Owing to Anglo-French distrust of the German expatriate influence in the Thai Railways Department, the peninsular line had been built independently of it, with British technology and to the metre gauge, with its own terminus originally at Bangkoknoi in Thonburi, Bangkok's twin city across the river. But the arrangement as such did not long survive the Great War, during which, in 1917, Siam joined the Allies and interned all German citizens including the expatriates of the Railway Department. After the war, under Prince Burachat, it was decided to convert all the lines east of the Chaophraya river to the metre gauge in order to integrate the whole system, while against all expectations (and, doubtless, intentions), 'Phak Tai' proper, the essentially Thai provinces of the peninsula, along with Siam's remaining Malay States, were bound to the rest of the kingdom by the peninsular line as never before. As late as the 1970s, the daily Thonburi–Golok Rapid service linking many city migrants with their homes in the South preserved the memory of the old separate system. But expresses began to run through from Prai (opposite Penang) to Bangkok's central station, and it even became at least theoretically possible later on, to travel from Singapore to China and thence to Europe via the connections with the system in French Indochina, bar only a short river journey from Phnom Penh in Cambodia to My-tho or Saigon in Vietnam. Thereby the very essence of the India–China scheme lost out to Russia's Trans-Siberian connection, which continued to thrive even through the age of developing air travel.

The 'railway–oceanic age' was very important in imperialist terms and clearly merits respect. As for Siam/Thailand, it was precisely its success in restricting these great British projects of the railway–oceanic age, and thereby maintaining its isolation and independence, that preserved its reputation well into the twentieth century as a 'backwater'. As a consequence, it was only to be in the age of air travel, in which the kingdom participated from as early as 1911,[53] that it, or more particularly its capital city, resumed the role of hub of international communication that it had played previously way back in the seventeenth century.[54] In some respects at least, it thereby displaced Singapore, that classic creation of the West which had never realized its hopes of becoming a major rail-centre as well as entrepot port, and restored Southeast Asia's communications to its native peoples.[55]

Notes

1 J.R. Seeley, *The Expansion of England* (London: Macmillan, 1883), p. 87.
2 Inagaki Manjiro, *Japan and the Pacific and a Japanese View of the Eastern Question* (London: Fisher Unwin, 1890), pp. 34, 39–41, 52–4. It was originally written as one of two Cambridge theses under Seeley's supervision but would appear to owe something to Tokutomi Soho's *The Future Japan* (Univ. of Alberta ed., trans. Vinh Sinh, 1989), written five years earlier. See also Iida Junzo, 'Japan's Relations with Independent Siam up to 1933: Prelude to Pan-Asian Solidarity.' Unpub. Bristol PhD., 1991, chaps. 3–4.
3 'It was and probably remains the world's greatest railway project.' J.M. Westwood, *A History of Russian Railways* (London: Allen & Unwin, 1964), p. 122. See also S.G. Marks, *Road to Power: The Trans-Siberian Railroad and the Colonization of Asian Russia 1850–1917* (Ithaca: Cornell U.P., 1991), and J.F. Fraser, 'The Completion of the Trans-Siberian Railway.' *Illustrated London News*, 14 December 1901. The connection around the southern tip of Lake Baikal was only built during the course of the Russo-Japanese War, while further improvements had to be made over several years to its initial flimsy structure.
4 In 1895, Sir Ernest Satow, an acquaintance of Inagaki and Britain's Minister through to 1900 in Japan, and thereafter in China until 1906, though never to travel by the Trans-Siberian, had cut his journey time to his new post by half, from two months to one, by travelling via North America rather than an Italian port, Suez and Singapore. Satow Papers at Kew, PRO 30/33/ 15/7, 17. By 1914, the Moscow–Tokyo journey took 11 days. Westwood, op. cit., p. 122. And by 2002, the plan to connect Seoul with the Trans-Siberian through North Korea promised to deliver South Korean manufactures to Europe in only a quarter of the month still required by sea and at much reduced cost. *The Financial Times*, 10 October 2002.
5 Marks, op. cit., p. 206, and *Illustrated London News*, 24 March 1906. See also issues for 29 February 1908 and 27 July 1907, regarding the Paris–New York road race via the Behring Straits, and the equally visionary plan for a bridge from Key West in Florida to Cuba.

6 See my 'Protection or Partition: Ernest Satow and the 1880s Crisis in Britain's Siam Policy', *Journal of S.E. Asian Studies* 29, 1 (March 1998), pp. 520–2. Cf. R. Ramaer, *The Railways of Thailand* (Bangkok: White Lotus, 1994), pp. 3, 159.

7 See my 'The Scramble for Concessions in 1880s Siam', *Modern Asian Studies* 31, 3 (1999), pp. 520–2. The building of the first rail-line in Selangor State commenced in late 1883. I am grateful to Dr Owen Covick of Flinders University, S. Australia, for evidence of growing interest in this idea in the 1890s.

8 'Railways' in *The Everyman's Encyclopedia*, 4th edn (London: Dent, 1958), vol. 10.

9 M. Satow and R. Desmond, *Railways of the Raj, 1850–1900* (London: Scolar Press, 1980). The Indian trunk lines used the five foot, broad gauge.

10 I.J. Kerr, *Building the Railways of the Raj, 1850–1900* (Delhi: OUP, 1995), pp. 117–18.

11 'Muang Thai' or 'Thailand' was always the indigenous name.

12 N.A. Pelcovits, *The Old China Hands and the Foreign Office* (New York: IPR, 1948), pp. 109–10, 135.

13 Marks, op. cit., pp. 43–5.

14 R.W. Huenemann, *The Dragon and the Iron Horse: the Economics of Railroads in China 1876–1937* (Cambridge Mass: Harvard U.P., 1984), Appendix A. See also E.W. Edwards, *British Diplomacy and Finance in China, 1895–1914* (Oxford: Clarendon Press, 1987), p. 31.

15 The South Manchurian line was to be transferred to the Japanese, along with the Liaotung Peninsula concession, following the Russo-Japanese War.

16 Partition and independence for India and Pakistan occurred in 1947, independence for Burma only following in January 1948. However, some attribute the separation of Burma's railways to 1937, the date of so-called self-government.

17 H. Tinker, *The Union of Burma* (London: OUP, 1967), p. 280. In characteristic Western colonial fashion, the author employs the foreign name for 'Muang Thai', 'the land of the Thai', that is, 'Thailand'.

18 J.S. Furnivall, *Colonial Policy and Practice: A Comparative Study of Burma and Netherlands India* (Cambridge: CUP, 1948), p. 78.

19 Satow Diaries, PRO 30/33/15/9.

20 See A. Marshall, *The Trouser People* (London: Viking, 2002), pp. 284–5.

21 Despite the absence of any alternative link, through Black west-coast Arakan to the rail-head at Chittagong in East Bengal, not even this route to India seems ever to have been seriously considered. This was perhaps due partly to the roundabout route it would have followed, via Ledo, Dimapur, etc. to Calcutta, as well as the malaria-infested character of the Hukawng Pass itself. However, there was also some suggestion of paternalist British official opposition to it as likely to increase the scale of Indian migration to Burma.

22 See H. McAleavy, *Black Flags in Vietnam* and M.E. Osborne, *River Road to China* (London: Allen & Unwin, 1968, 1975).

23 See Pelcovits, op. cit., pp. 112–24, for the most detailed account of the Sprye scheme.

24 Pelcovits, op. cit., pp. 116, 117, 118.

25 Ibid., p. 120.

26 He was still merely Viscount Cranborne during his first term at the India Office. Pelcovits, op. cit., pp. 117, 121, 122.

27 A. Roberts, *Salisbury: Victorian Titan* (London: Weidenfeld & Nicolson), pp. 102–3.

28 Chiangmai, like the other neighbouring 'Western Lao' principalities, was to lose virtually all its autonomy to Bangkok in the context of the events of the subsequent two decades.

29 Published in London: Sampson Low, 1883. *Amongst the Shans* was reprinted by the Paragon Book Corp., New York, 1970.

30 See his *A Thousand Miles on an Elephant in the Shan States* (Edinburgh: W. Blackwood), repr. Bangkok: White Lotus, 1988).

31 Ibid., chap. XXIII. The superiority of the case for the 'Siam' route to China is presented here. Cf. Pelcovits, op. cit., pp. 150–3, for the scale of support in England. Hallett was,

however, somewhat disingenuous in the interview he describes with King Chulalongkorn in his chap. XXVI, when he suggested that if he was also authorized to build a line from Bangkok to Chiangmai, that would represent his main line and the one from Burma a mere branch. Similarly, p. 196, he represents the later Clarke/Punchard, McTaggart and Lowther Bangkok–Chiangmai survey as forming a natural 'portion of the Burmah–Siam–China Railway' when the Siamese Government clearly intended it as an alternative.

32 R. Greaves, *Persia and the Defence of India, 1884–1892* (London: Athlone, 1959), esp. pp. 204–5, 269–70.

33 N.J. Brailey ed., *The Satow Siam Papers* I (Bangkok: Thai Hist. Soc., 1997), pp. 43–72.

34 See Mrs F. Caddy, *To Siam and Malaya in the Duke of Sutherland's Yacht Sans Peur* (London: Hurst and Blackett, 1889, repr. Singapore: OUP, 1992). It was suggested that Prince Thewawong, while in London in 1887 for Queen Victoria's Golden Jubilee, had set up this competition. General Clarke was already familiar to the Thai having mediated a local political dispute back in 1875.

35 'England, France and Siam': Hallett to *The Times*, 20 January 1896.

36 Chandran Jeshurun, *The Contest for Siam, 1889–1902: A Study in Diplomatic Rivalry* (Kuala Lumpur: Universiti Kebangsaan, 1977), p. 250.

37 Hallett, op. cit., p. 431. In the Far Eastern War, 1941–5, this viaduct became an important target for Wingate's Chindit saboteurs aiming to sever Japanese communications with southwestern China. See L. Allen, *The Longest War* (London: Dent, 1984), pp. 127, 136–7.

38 Chandran, op. cit., p. 255.

39 Completed first, the former line eventually ran through to the central Yangtze, but the latter, France's real equivalent to the proposed Burma line, was not properly in service until 1911, and not extended beyond Kunming.

40 Chandran, op. cit., pp. 288, 333. Some diehards such as Sir Charles Crosthwaite, former Chief Commissioner of British Burma, J.G. Scott, now Superintendent of the Southern Shan States based at Taunggyi, or G.C.B. Stirling, his successor in charge of the Northern Shan States based at Lashio (to G.E. Morrison, 1 January 1903. Morrison Papers, Sydney, vol. 47), still refused, apparently for strategic reasons, to recognize the inevitable: 'I give it about two years – i.e. till Curzon goes – till the railway is continued and work started to carry it on to China.'

41 See my 'Scramble for Concessions in 1880s Siam.'

42 Previously, in July 1884, Ernest Satow had supposed that Britain would have to take Upper Burma as compensation for the French annexing Siam. Brailey ed., *The Satow Siam Papers* I, p. 52.

43 Brailey, 'Protection or Partition.' In fact it is questionable whether peninsular Siam which had interested Kimberley earlier as Colonial Secretary, could ever have been left out of the equation. Clearly Kimberley always envisaged that it would become another increment to the British Empire.

44 Brailey, 'Scramble for Concessions in 1880s Siam,' p. 529.

45 Ibid., p. 542.

46 See Pelcovits, op. cit., p. 187, for Salisbury's comments to a sympathetic China Association deputation, and also my forthcoming 'Turn of the Imperial Tide in Asia: Britain, France and the Siam Question, 1897–1905.'

47 See 'Thailand's Appointment with History: "Siam" and the Entente Cordiale', in Winai Pongsripian and Weerawan Ngamsuntikul eds., *Chatusansaniyacharn* (Bangkok: Hist. Commission, 2004), pp. 347–65.

48 Chamberlain to Salisbury, 4 Sept. 1895. Salisbury Papers, Hatfield House. With his appointment as Colonial Secretary shortly before, Chamberlain's stance seems to have taken on a very different character from a decade earlier.

49 Issue of 6 September.

50 Lt Col K.M. Foss to F.O. Under-Sec, 15 Jan. 1907. FO 371/332.
51 For this episode, see PRO files FO 371/3363, 4093, 5369.
52 See Ramaer, op. cit., pp. 57, 60, and my 'The Death Railway in Thai History' in Piyanart Bunnag, F. Knipping and Sud Chonchirdsin eds., *Europe-Southeast Asia in the Contemporary World: Mutual Images and Reflections 1940s–1960s* (Baden-Baden: Nomos Verlagsgesellschaft, 2000), pp. 97–109.
53 E.M. Young, *Aerial Nationalism: A History of Aviation in Thailand* (Washington: Smithsonian Press, 1995), p. 1.
54 See K. Breazeale, *From Japan to Arabia: Ayutthaya's Maritime Relations with Asia* (Bangkok: The Social Sciences and Humanities Foundation, 1999).
55 Cf. T.J.S. George, *Lee Kuan Yew's Singapore* (London: A. Deutsch, 1973), p. 178. on Singapore as a 'neo-colonial beachhead'.

6 'The Baghdad railway of the Far East'

The Tientsin–Yangtze railway and Anglo-German relations, 1898–1911

T.G. Otte

The significance of foreign-built and owned railways for China's development in the late nineteenth and twentieth centuries has been given extensive coverage in scholarly literature. In its broad outlines it is a well-known, if ambiguous, story. It is a story of technological progress (real and imagined), but also of economic and social dislocation. Indeed, the respective costs and benefits of the introduction of railways to the Middle Kingdom have been the subject of a vigorous debate amongst scholars of modern China.[1] The story of China's railways is about more than the economic and social impact of a potent new technology upon an economically backward country. As the first comprehensive account of the development of railway enterprise in China noted, its history 'reflects at once the main characteristics of the Chinese official classes, and the tendency of the Far Eastern policy of foreign powers'.[2] Stubborn opposition by conservative officials and widespread popular resistance meant that the railways made slow progress.[3]

China's defeat in the Sino-Japanese War of 1894–5 marked a crucial turning point. The war revealed to the outside world China's weakness in the face of external pressure. Until the war, her foreign debt had been minimal. Now, the indemnity obligations placed upon her after the war amounted to 250 million Kuping taels, some £38 million. This could only be met through foreign loans. The combination of China's urgent financial needs and the general impression of an overall Chinese malaise, in turn, triggered what the United States minister at Peking, Charles Denby, termed the 'mad scramble for Chinese concessions'.[4]

Persistent opposition to railway construction, especially by foreigners, was not altogether without foundation. The Powers, and especially the three coercive Powers Russia, France, and Germany, whose intervention in 1895 had deprived Japan of some of her territorial gains in the war, began to construct railways on a large scale. Railways very soon become the most high-profile manifestation of foreign presence within the Chinese Empire, closely followed by Christian missionaries. Foreign-owned railways were constructed for political and strategic reasons. They were primarily instruments for establishing and securing spheres of influence. Considerations of commercial profit were of largely secondary importance, as Britain's minister at Peking, N.R. (later Sir Nicholas) O'Conor, observed at the end of the Sino-Japanese War. The railway historian Percy Horace Kent noted in 1907, 'the railway policy of [the triplice]...has been a means to an end, an incident in a larger policy, which can only be described as a policy of colonisation.'[5]

The first railway concession was obtained by France in 1895 in the southern Chinese province of Yunnan, with further concessions being granted in 1896, 1898 and 1899. The governor-general of neighbouring French Indochina, Paul Doumer, stated openly that the planned *Chemin de Fer du Yunnan* was meant to enable France to project her power into southern China. Calculations of profit were of little concern. French regional trade was minimal; indeed, after the completion of its construction in 1910 the railway operated at a loss.[6] By contrast, the mercurial Belgian King Leopold II envisaged the Belgian-built Peking–Hankow and Hankow–Canton lines as '*la colonne vertebrale*' of commerce in the interior of China. As for Russia, the Chinese Eastern Railway (CER), which traversed Manchuria, was a core part of the Russian finance minister Sergei Iulevich Witte's ambitious programme of '*pénétration pacifique*' with the aim of establishing a *de facto* Russian protectorate over Manchuria and northern China.[7]

Britain and Germany also obtained railway concessions. The similarities and differences between British and German railway concessions and those of France or Russia are demonstrated by the Tientsin–Yantgze railway. This was one of the most significant railway projects in China in this period. Yet, a few *en passant* remarks on its general importance apart, no detailed study of this line exists. In fact, it serves as a useful case study to illustrate the nature of British gentlemanly imperialism and German *Weltpolitik* ambitions in China. Its utility is not confined to the affairs of the Far East alone, for it reflects also the changing nature of Anglo-German relations in the period before 1914. This study, then, operates at three levels: (1) the 'geostrategic periphery', or the 'bridgeheads' of Great Power presence in China[8]; (2) the 'metropolitan' dimension of the European chancelleries and banking corporations; and (3) the 'systemic' level of Great Power relations, viz. alliances and treaties.

* * *

The driving force behind the Tientsin–Yangtze railway project were German commercial and political ambitions. Already in the immediate aftermath of the 1894–5 war the *Deutsch-Asiatische Bank* (DAB), a quasi-independent semi-state bank, had sought to negotiate a £60 million loan on condition that £10 million be spent on German machinery. A sum of such magnitude by far exceeded Germany's limited capacity to raise foreign loans.[9] Later in August 1895, the German minister at Peking, Gustav Adolf Baron Schenck zu Schweinsberg, reported on plans by the leading German China merchant firm Carlowitz & Co. to issue a much smaller loan of 30 million taels (around £4.6 million) to build a railway line from Peking's riverport Tientsin to Chinkiang at the confluence of the Yangtze and the Grand Canal.[10] Although the project was pursued for some while, no real progress was made. Matters were brought to a head, however, by the Far Eastern crisis of 1897–8, which was sparked by Germany's seizure of Kiaochow on the Shantung promontory in response to the murder of German Christian missionaries in November 1897.[11] Under the Sino-German convention of 6 March 1898, which brought the crisis to a close, Germany obtained a 99-years lease of Kiaochow Bay with the future naval base of Tsingtao at its heart. The leased territory itself was surrounded by a 30 li (or 50 kilometers-) wide 'neutral zone', in reality an area of more or less direct German rule. In addition, the Chinese government granted Germany a series of mining and railway concessions. There was a linkage between these concessions. The two projected railway lines, from Tsingtao to Tsi'nan, the Shantung provincial capital, with a branch-line to Po-shan, and the other striking southwest to Ichow and beyond to Hsü'chow, traversed the main Shantung coalfields. A further line between the latter place and the provincial capital was to create a German railway triangle in Shantung, with Kiaochow as its natural export harbour. To realize the concessions a DAB-led consortium formed the *Schantung-Eisenbahn-Gesellschaft* (SEB), which was formally established in June 1899.[12]

The government in Berlin regarded these lines as vehicles for the projection of German influence into the hinterland of the naval base. During the talks on the Sino-German convention Edmund von Heyking, the brusque new German minister at Peking since 1896, insisted on Germany's special position in the area. As he impressed upon the German government engineer currently surveying at Hankow, Heinrich Hildebrand, 'Germany regarded the economic development of Shantung province as her sphere of interest.' To his British colleague, Sir Claude MacDonald, he confided that 'commercially Shantung was intended to be a German province'.[13] The soldier-turned-diplomat MacDonald and his first secretary at the Peking legation, Henry Bax-Ironside, warned London that the object of German diplomacy was the creation of 'an "*imperium in imperio*" ' in northern China; any difficulties raised by Chinese central or local authorities would be met with a display of 'the same high-handed methods already employed... in order to coerce the weak Government in Peking'. Such views were echoed in Whitehall by George Nathaniel Curzon, the Parliamentary Under-secretary at the Foreign Office, an advocate of a more forward policy in China: 'The Germans are now asserting a complete monopoly of Shantung.'[14]

There was a complicating factor, for another applicant for the Tienstin–Yangtze railway concession emerged. In 1897, a Chinese merchant, Yung-win, had been granted by the Peking government the right to form a company to construct this railway with the aid of foreign capital. This was fiercely resisted by Heyking, who stressed Germany's '*Vorzugsrecht*' (or preferential rights) in Shantung, in his negotiations with the Tsungli Yamên.[15] The line from Tientsin to the Yangtze was key to the economic and strategic success of the German railway triangle in Shantung province. Without access to the commercial centres in the North around the imperial capital and its river port at Tientsin on the one hand, and to the populous and fertile Yangtze basin on the other, the SEB-run lines were condemned to remain commercially insignificant. By the same token, it was imperative for Germany to ensure that the concession for a line linking Tientsin with the Yangtze was kept out of the hands of another Power. Heyking increased the pressure on the Chinese central government 'under threats of serious consequences'.[16] In early March 1898, he extracted from the Tsungli Yamên an undertaking that no railway would be built through Shantung without prior German consent; that the projected Tientsin–Yangtze line would run through that province; and, finally, that German engineers, matériel and equipment would be employed in the construction of this line.[17] In this manner Heyking blocked Yung-win's railway scheme, but simultaneously ensured that it would go ahead under German auspices.

A further complication now arose in the shape of British intervention. Throughout the Far Eastern crisis the British foreign secretary, the Marquis of Salisbury, had been actuated by concerns that the seizure of Kiaochow and Berlin's assertion of exclusive rights in Shantung were the opening salvoes of a 'policy of grab' by the Powers, and so hasten a partition of China. MacDonald was, therefore, instructed to block Germany's attempts to obtain preferential rights in Shantung.[18] Salisbury's fears were not unfounded. Already in the spring of 1895 there had been a minor diplomatic dispute with Berlin over attempts by German officials in China to supplant Claude William Kinder, the incumbent and very experienced British general manager and chief engineer of the Imperial Chinese Railways, with a German engineer. At the time O'Conor warned that the latter 'would immediately utilise his position not only to substitute Germans for British officials but also to secure for himself and his countrymen if possible the entire control of the railway system of China to the great detriment of Britain.' The development of such new, intimately entwined political and financial rivalries required a new approach by the Foreign Office, embracing more than the purely 'unofficial' means that had been the hallmark of Whitehall support for China commerce in the 1870s and 1880s.[19]

Three years later, MacDonald's intervention in the Tientsin–Yangtze scheme triggered an Anglo-German diplomatic spat at Peking. The matter of the railway concession pitted two rather similar diplomats against each other. The bellicose Baltic baron berated 'Gunboat' MacDonald over his intervention. He dismissed the latter's argument that preferential rights for Germany were an infringement of the most-favoured-nation clause of the 1858 Tientsin treaty; and subsequently sent MacDonald 'a rather intemperate private letter in which he declared my protest to be equivalent to siding with China against Germany.' MacDonald observed to Salisbury that, if Heyking's railway agreement infringed upon the Tientsin treaty, his protest would entitle Britain to compensation in 'the form of concessions to British syndicates of special lines of railway.' Although he was doubtful of the commercial profitability of many of the railway schemes, he advised London to pursue this line with vigour. Since no such syndicate existed, he urged the Foreign Office that one should be formed without delay.[20]

MacDonald's comments chimed in with the views of Salisbury and Curzon. The latter suggested that 'our next step in China should be to get some reliable syndicate to undertake the trunk lines N[orth] and S[outh] from the Yangtze Valley.' Ultimately, Curzon hoped that 'our Yangtze sphere [should] chrystallize into anything like a protectorate, our even an actual possession.'[21] Salisbury's ambitions were more limited. The main obstacle, he noted, was 'to produce a syndicate really willing and able to build a railway in the Yangtze region.' Until one was found, British diplomacy had to block foreign concessions elsewhere. To

Salisbury's mind, railway concessions were primarily diplomatic bargaining chips; and 'patriotic capitalists' were his principal diplomatic tool: 'But we ought to have on the stocks a railway in the Yangtze region; & if any Powers resist the concession to us, we ought to resist concessions of any kind that they ask for anywhere. I see no other mode of fighting the matter.'[22] In a negative sense, resistance by other Powers to British concessions could be utilized to oppose preferential rights for Russia in Manchuria, France in Yunnan and Kwantung, or Germany in Shantung. Put to constructive use, railway concessions might induce the other Powers to acknowledge separate spheres of influence, without the need for a formal, and inevitably messy, partition of China with all its potential for Great Power conflict.

This was sensible enough, but is was also no longer strictly practical politics. In March and April, the twin issues of German preferential rights in Shantung and railway concessions became wound up in the Colonial Secretary Joseph Chamberlain's clandestine alliance talks with Germany. Arthur Balfour, who was deputizing for Salisbury at the Foreign Office, tacitly supported Chamberlain's efforts; and, to facilitate an arrangement with Germany, gave the self-negating pledge demanded by the German foreign minister Count Bernhard von Bülow in return for German acquiescence in Britain's acquisition of a naval base at Wei-hai-Wei on the northern coast of Shantung: Britain would not build a railway from the newly acquired leased territory to the neighbouring treaty port of Chefoo or into the hinterland of the province. Berlin's real aim, Balfour, reasoned was the prevention of the construction of a British-owned railway in the interior of Shantung. Since such schemes were not 'likely in the future', he was prepared to yield to German demands. However, he stipulated that this 'ought more properly be dealt with under the general arrangements governing railway communications in the German and English areas of interest.'[23]

Balfour's overall object, then, did not differ substantially from Salisbury's. However, little progress was achieved in the talks with Berlin. Balfour succeeded in extracting the promise that the projected Tientsin–Hankow line in the central part of the Yangtze basin, which was to pass through the eastern half of Shantung, be exempted from Britain's recognition of German commercial preponderance in that province. As Chamberlain's alliance initiative ran into difficulties, Balfour decided not to continue talks on the delimitation of railway spheres of influence. Instead, he made the pledge requested by Bülow, binding Britain not to construct railways in Shantung, provided the Tientsin–Hankow line was allowed to run through Shantung.[24] Balfour's intervention in the railway question was indicative of the complexity of the issue. Moreover, in balancing British recognition of German commercial preponderance in the province with a special, albeit informal, understanding regarding any railway project linking Tientsin with the Yangtze, he had set the switch for the future course of this scheme.

There was a profound irony in this Anglo-German tug-of-war over railway concessions in northern China. British diplomacy lacked the 'patriotic capitalists' whose services Salisbury required to achieve his strategic objectives in China. On the other hand, Germany's claim to the exclusive right to build the

Tientsin–Yangtze railway belied Berlin's limited capacity to finance such an ambitious engineering project. The claimed railway spheres of influence were paper spheres only, devoid of any practical content or meaning. In a wider sense, this illustrated also the discrepancy between the riches suggested by the contemporary 'myth of the China market' and the altogether more modest and complex reality of late nineteenth-century China commerce.[25]

A joint venture, then, seemed the logical conclusion. There was already the basis for such cooperation. In July 1895, the Hong Kong and Shanghai Banking Corporation (HSBC) had formed a consortium with the DAB with the object of jointly raising Chinese government loans. This cooperation bore some fruit. In 1896, a £16 million loan was issued by the consortium to enable the Peking government to pay the next installment of the indemnity owed to Japan after the war of the previous year. It now seemed as though, in matters of Chinese finance and commerce, Germany had ranged herself alongside Britain. Gustav Detring, the influential German-born ICMCS supervisor at Tientsin, had urged Berlin and London to come to an understanding on the joint financing and construction of Chinese railways. Anglo-German financial prowess would ensure a preponderance by these two countries in the future transport infrastructure and commercial development of China.[26]

Commercial cooperation between British and German firms, nevertheless, was limited. Detring's efforts in this direction were actively opposed by Heyking, who regarded Britain as Germany's principal rival in China and who favoured cooperation with Russia instead. There was a further complication. Under the agreement of 27 July 1895, upon which the HSBC–DAB consortium was founded, both parties enjoyed parity. Any approach by Chinese central or provincial authorities to either partner with a view to concluding a loan would have to be shared with the other. This also included railway and commercial concessions. Heyking's opposition to Anglo-German commercial cooperation, MacDonald's intervention in the Tientsin–Yangtze project, and differences between the two syndicates regarding the third Chinese indemnity loan of 1 March 1898 now soured relations between HSBC and DAB. The latter refused to grant equal rights in Shantung to British firms that were part of the HSBC syndicate. Following an interview between Adolph von Hansemann, the director of the *Disconto-Gesellschaft*, the leading firm within the DAB, and the HSBC's London manager Ewen Cameron, it was agreed that both parties were now free 'to go their own way in negotiating for the construction of railways or other concessions in China'.[27]

Hansemann, one of the leading German investment bankers and active promoter of German colonial expansion, and the DAB were the driving force behind the termination of the 1895 agreement.[28] Hansemann now opened negotiations with A.Yu. Rotshtein (Adolf Rothstein), the Berlin-born first managing director of the Russo-Chinese Bank (RCB), the principal tool of Russia's '*pénétration pacifique*'. Under a preliminary agreement on the joint construction of the Tientsin–Chinkiang railway the northern section of the line from the Hwangho river to Tientsin was allocated to Russia, while its southern section down to the Yangtze basin was defined as the German sphere of interest. Ultimately, the

RCB's limited resources and St. Petersburg's lack of interest rendered the deal abortive.[29]

Hansemann was shrewd enough not to sever all links with his erstwhile partners in London while negotiating with Rothstein. At any rate, MacDonald's intervention had turned the Tientsin–Yangtze railway concession into an object of government policy. On 3 May the German ambassador at London, Count Paul von Hatzfeldt, raised the matter with Francis Bertie, the Assistant Under-secretary at the Foreign Office supervising Far Eastern affairs. MacDonald had not only opposed the German bid for the line, but had demanded it for the British syndicate 'as a political concession'. To maintain friendly relations between the two countries, and to avoid an anti-British backlash in the German public, he urged the British government that MacDonald be instructed 'to drop the demand for the Railway Concession'. Bertie insisted that the agreement between the two syndicates had been terminated following the DAB's refusal to grant equal rights in railway enterprises. The German syndicate had already obtained 'a triangular Railway Concession in Shantung.' Now Berlin wanted 'to get one in opposition to us in the Yangtze Region. Were Germans to have all the Railways?'. In a second interview, Hatzfeldt reiterated German objections to two railway lines being constructed in Shantung in close proximity and so competing with each other. As a possible compromise solution, Berlin might consent to the German railway triangle being connected to Tientsin in the North and the Yangtze basin in the South, 'so that the German Tsinan–Ichow Railway would be the connecting link for Railway communication between Tientsin & Chinkiang. This would in effect be to give running powers over the German line to a Railway from Tientsin to Chinkiang.' Bertie was supportive of such an arrangement.[30]

Salisbury's thinking went in the same direction. He envisaged some form of railway agreement between the two governments, an idea which Balfour had briefly pursued earlier. Under this arrangement the British government and the HSBC would agree that all lines in Shantung should be under German management; profits should be shared equally. In return, all concession in the Yangtze valley should be placed under British management, the companies being registered as British with English names. Such a general arrangement was rejected by Hatzfeldt. Under the Sino-German convention regarding the lease of Kiaochow Germany had obtained 'a special position' in Shantung, which was consequently not unreservedly open to British enterprise. However, as Britain's presence in the Yangtze basin was entirely informal, that region remained open to all foreign commerce. Not surprisingly, Salisbury was unable to assent to this. Hatzfeldt was ready to accept Salisbury's formula regarding the concession for the much shorter Shanghai–Nanking railway along the south bank of the Yangtze, which was then also under negotiation, and which was to be placed under British management.[31] This created a precedent of a kind for a negotiated settlement, though Germany's claim to special position in Shantung remained an obstacle.

In the meantime, the government came under pressure from the China Association (CA), the lobby group of British commercial interests in China, to take more energetic steps to protect Britain's position in the Yangtze region. The

Association's general committee met in early July and addressed a lengthy communication to Salisbury on the subject of British interests in China. The famous letter of 8 July argued that the main threat to British interests was the refusal by the other Powers to recognize the Yangtze as a British sphere. Amongst the many pressing issues, the 'Old China Hands' singled out railway development as the 'question of supreme moment'. Railway rivalries were political, and there-fore materially important. The CA demanded a government guarantee, preferably backed by state aid, to protect British commercial interests in the Yangtze valley.[32] Although the main focus of the Association's concerns was on Russo-French financial and commercial operations in Manchuria and southern China, the letter had implications for the Tientsin–Yangtze project. Under commercial pressure Salisbury was forced to extend the remit of his limited liability policy in the Yangtze, though he refused to accommodate the China Association's demand for a formal guarantee and financial support. It meant that London could not ignore the brewing Anglo-German railway quarrel. Rumours, albeit unsubstantiated, of a Franco-Russian 'grand plan for railways [to be brought] under Russian and French control from Vladivostok to Canton' made a speedy settlement with Germany more urgent.[33]

Both governments desired now to arrive at a solution of the problem. Even Heyking urged Berlin not to oppose Britain in the Yangtze region because there were no substantial German commercial interests in this area, and because London had recognized Germany's preponderance in Shantung. For his part, Bülow was above all anxious that the line be completed, no matter how or under what arrangement.[34] The permanent head of the German foreign ministry, State Secretary Oswald Baron von Richthofen, later elaborated on this point. At the time of the conclusion of the Sino-German convention there had been no reli-able information as to the precise geographical location of the Shantung coal-fields. At that stage London had also not yet recognized Germany's preponderance there. The coalfields had by now been surveyed; and Balfour's recognition of German exclusive rights in Shantung gave Berlin's regional pre-tensions a firmer footing. This placed a premium now on the speedy development of the various railway projects in Shantung so as to give material substance to German claims to a special position in the province.[35]

By mid-July 1898, the DAB and HSBC syndicates had separately applied for the Tienstin–Yangtze railway concession. However, Heyking met with strong resistance by the Tsungli Yamên. The Chinese ministers seemed determined not to allow German participation in the Tientsin–Yangtze project in order to prevent a further strengthening of Germany's hold over Shantung. There was also now United States commercial competition combined with the American govern-ment's refusal to acknowledge German exclusive rights in that province.[36] A break-through came through Arthur Balfour, who once again was in charge of the Foreign Office in July and August. In mid-August he instructed MacDonald to inform the Tsungli Yamên that the railway concession demanded by the British government for the British and Chinese Corporation (BCC), the HSBC's associated company, was also for German and American syndicates, if they desired to participate. On 20 August, MacDonald was informed that, if Berlin insisted that the part of the line passing through Shantung be built with German capital, the British government would not object. Even so, Balfour favoured a joint enterprise, covering the whole line, as the simpler and therefore preferable plan.[37]

On the same day Hatzfeldt called to discuss the matter. Berlin, he reported, was in accord with Salisbury's earlier suggestion that a formal delimitation of respectives spheres of influence was not opportune, and that 'a friendly understanding' on a case-by-case basis was preferable. Hatzfeldt now accepted Bertie's plan of early May. The two syndicates should combine 'on equitable terms', but the main part of the proposed line from Tsinan to Ichow would remain in the possession of the DAB. This accorded with Balfour's instructions to MacDonald of that same day. The rest should be left to the two syndicates. This was the solution Salisbury had favoured from the outset of the dispute which, he suggested, Berlin and London 'should regard as private matter between the two banks'.[38] Of course, since the HSBC were willing 'patriotic capitalists' the pretence that the matter was a private one suited Salisbury's strategic purposes. Nevertheless, the fact that it took over three months to bring the by now increasingly anarchic scramble for the Tientsin–Yangtze concession to a conclusion was indicative of the complexity of Great Power diplomacy and commercial competition in China at this time.

Just as Heyking and MacDonald began to coordinate their steps at Peking, further confusion was caused by unfounded rumours that talks between the two syndicates had collapsed. For the HSBC's part, Ewen Cameron, who was held in high repute in City of London circles as an authority on Chinese finances, was '*most anxious* . . . to act harmoniously with the German Syndicate'. Both Cameron and Hansemann used Alfred de Rothschild, the go-between of the London Rothschilds and various governments, as a mediator to keep the talks going.[39] Through Rothschild's mediation a meeting was arranged in London between Hansemann and Wilhelm Betzold as representatives of the DAB and, for the British side, William Keswick, Chairman of the China Association and a BCC director, and the HSBC's Ewen Cameron and Julius Brüssel, the Hamburg-based agent of the BCC. The London bankers' conference of 1 and 2 September marked a crucial turning point in the scramble for concessions. Although the fiction of a purely private commercial arrangement was maintained, the presence at the meeting of Hatzfeldt, Balfour and Curzon underlined its wider political significance.[40]

The arrangement bound both parties to share the Tientsin–Yangtze concession, and the DAB withdrew its opposition to the BCC project of a Shanghai–Nanking railway line. Crucially, they also agreed on a general delimitation of their respective future railway spheres of interest. The British sphere was defined as the Yangtze valley, the provinces south of the Yangtze as well as Shansi province; the German sphere as Shantung and the Hwang-ho valley. As regarded the Tientsin–Yangtze railway, the arrangement provided for the joint raising of the necessary capital, while its northern portion, from Tientsin to Tsinan on the Shantung boundary was to be built and operated by the German group. The section from there to Chinkiang on the Yangtze river was left to the British consortium. Like Salisbury, Bülow preferred to treat the bankers' arrangement as a private agreement. Despite requests by Hansemann, it did not receive official sanction, though it was recognized by Berlin.[41] In reality, Bülow hoped to keep open the option of a German move on the Yangtze. In so far as the politicians on both sides were concerned, the September agreement was a temporary arrangement of mutual convenience. From London's perspective it helped to consolidate, albeit only informally, Britain's position in the Yangtze. It also furnished a precedent for a similar arrangement with Russia, the first tentative steps towards which had been taken in mid-August by Balfour and the Russian chargé d'affaires in London, Pavel Mikhailovich Lessar. The talks eventually produced the so-called Scott–Muravev agreement of 28 April 1899, which delimited respective British and Russian railway spheres of interest, and so complemented the Anglo-German bankers' agreement of September 1898.[42]

At Peking the British and German ministers jointly pressed the Chinese authorities to agree to a final settlement of the Tientsin–Yangtze railway project.[43] By March 1899, the Tsungli Yamên's resistance began to weaken; on 18 May, a preliminary agreement for the concession of a railway line from Tienstin to Chinkiang and a £7.4 million loan was eventually signed.[44] The preliminary agreement left a number of points yet to be settled. The final amount of the loan depended on the costs involved in surveying the projected track, and so could not be determined in advance. How the loan was to be secured, remained undecided, as did the question of tendering for matériel and equipment.[45] These were potentially divisive issues. The preliminary agreement was the last concession granted by China to foreign governments during the 'battle of concessions'. Negotiations for a final agreement would prove to be even more protracted, subject to changes in China's attitude as well as to changes in relations between London and Berlin.

* * *

The tripartite Sino-British-German negotiations can be divided roughly into two phases. Between 1899 and 1903, before the talks with the Peking government were properly resumed, squabbles between the two syndicates cast doubt on the project's viability. The talks themselves, which commenced in May 1903, were overshadowed by the growing desire of the Chinese to annul foreign railway concessions, and by the emerging Anglo-German antagonism in Europe.

The acute differences between the DAB and HSBC were caused in December 1899 by Hansemann's demands for a redefinition of the sphere allocated to the Germans under the bankers' agreement. His motivations were a mixture of 'imperialist hubris' and fear of commercial competition by a Franco-Belgian syndicate in the Hwangho valley. He was especially alarmed by the activities of the Peking Syndicate. This had been formed two years previously by an Italian concession-hunter, Angelo Luzzati, but was financed largely by British capital. In May 1898 the syndicate had obtained substantial mining rights in Shansi province as well as railway concessions in Shansi and Honan.[46] It was not formally connected to the HSBC, and therefore not party to the bankers' agreement. However, its chairman, Carl (later Sir Carl) Meyer, was a member of the HSBC's London consultative committee. There was also a connection with the Rothschilds, as Meyer had been the first Lord Rothschild's private secretary.

Crucially, through the HSBC and N.M. Rothschild the Chinese Grand Secretary Li Hung-chang had purchased shares in the Peking Syndicate, worth £4,200;[47] and he now supported the Syndicate's plans to build a branchline of the Peking–Hankow railway in Shansi and a second line traversing the Hwangho valley. The latter project led to sharp exchanges between Hansemann and Meyer. In January 1900, Hansemann complained to Julius Brüssel that the Peking Syndicate was acting in breach of the London bankers' agreement. He dismissed Brüssel's argument that the syndicate was not party to the agreement by pointing to Meyer's and the Rothschilds' role in the syndicate. The real bone of contention was Hansemann's implicit contention that under the September protocol 'the British sphere of interest is to be vested solely in these two institutions [HSBC and BCC], to the exclusion of other Britishers.' Hansemann appealed to the self-interest of his London partners: the Peking Syndicate 'would become a dangerous competitor to our Scheme and be in diametrical opposition to the arrangements come to.'[48] Ultimately, Hansemann's attempts to torpedo the Peking Syndicate's plans in the Hwangho valley and to induce Berlin formally to annex that part of northern China were superseded by the outbreak of the Boxer troubles in the summer of 1900. The Anglo-German China agreement of October 1900 placed relations between the two governments and British and German commercial groups on a formal footing. Nevertheless, the October agreement, with its explicit endorsement of the 'Open Door' principle, and the 1898 bankers' agreement provided little more than a quasi-legal umbrella, beneath which the two sides were able to pursue different political and commercial objectives and strategies.[49]

The strongest impetus for a resumption of talks on the final agreement came from the German minister at Peking, Alfons Baron Mumm von Schwarzenstein. In the aftermath of the Boxer troubles he argued that China's current weakness was an opportune moment to finalize arrangements for the Tientsin–Yangtze line. The DAB took up his suggestion, and pressed for negotiations to commence.[50] Additional pressure came from the governor of the Kiaochow naval base, Rear-Admiral Oscar von Truppel. The German naval authorities were determined to turn Kiaochow into a 'German Hongkong'; and key to the economic success of the leasehold was the development of a railway infrastructure. The territory's trade with its western hinterland was river- and canal-borne and oriented towards Tientsin. Any railway development with Peking's riverport at its centre, Truppel argued, would merely reinforce Kiaochow's commercial isolation. It was imperative to construct a line from Tsinan, at the northern tip of the German railway triangle, striking West to Kaifeng in Honan province. This western line had to be completed before the northern connection with Tientsin 'so as to guarantee the colony's [viz. Kiaochow's] economic advantage.' Similarly, the southern extension towards Ichow should not be pursued at the expense of the western line: 'It is to be expected – and this I take to be the main danger of this line – that through a southern extension of the railway network the connection from there to the English line to Chinkiang will divert part of the traffic to the Yangtze bypassing Tsingtao.'[51]

The governor's principal object was the diversion to Kiaochow of all trade in the Shantung and Honan provinces. This required 'railway lines radiating from

Tsingtao to all viable commercial centres', whilst limiting any branchlines or other connections which might divert trade to better located ports in the Yangtze area. Truppel advocated constructing three lines as a matter of priority: a western extension from Tsinan via Yenchow 'into the heart of Honan'; a southern line towards the rich coalfields around Ichow and Ihsien as the territory's main artery; and a northern line 'for the diversion of part of the Chili and Tientsin commerce.' What was missing was the completion of the German railway triangle in the South towards the Shantung provincial boundary, where it was supposed to link up with the British section of the Tientsin–Yangtze line. This was deliberate. Its completion had to be delayed, if not prevented, until Kiaochow was established as the natural export harbour for the whole area between Tientsin and the Yangtze basin.[52]

The DAB's commercial interests and official German policy worked hand-in-hand. The financiers took their lead from the Kiaochow governor. For his part, Truppel and also the commander of the German contingent of the International China Expeditionary Force that had been sent to northern China during the Boxer uprising, Major-General Erich von Falkenhayn, assisted the DAB by detailing officers to survey the projected railway lines.[53] By the end of the summer of 1902, the DAB had concluded its survey, and the legation at Peking pressed for negotiations for the final agreement to commence, a demand to which Prince Ch'ing, head of the reformed Chinese board for foreign affairs, the Wai-wu Pu, acceded. However, the ministers of the board refused to negotiate with the German syndicate separately. Under the 1899 preliminary agreement no concessions could be granted without British participation.[54]

The obvious divergence between British and German commercial interests, however, was a formidable obstacle. The desire of the British group to change the terminus of its section from Chinkiang to Pukow was the least of these problems, though it required German consent. More problematic was the DAB's suggestion that it should now be allowed to conclude a separate final agreement with the Peking authorities. In essence, such an arrangement would have put an end to the preliminary agreement of 1899. Walter Townley, the British chargé d'affaires who took an active part in the railway negiotiations at Peking, warned London that the 'natural objective point' of the German railway enterprise was the Shantung capital of Tsinan. Once this was reached, 'and with their communication to Tientsin they would have a large triangle of railway commanding all the trade of the Gulf of Pechili.'[55]

In light of Truppel's plans Townley's analysis was perceptive. However, as the government had decided to rely on 'willing capitalists' in its efforts to achieve its wider strategic objectives in China, British diplomacy was constrained. By early 1903, the Board of the BCC was no longer 'desirous of a German alliance.' If two separate final agreements had to be negotiated, any future cooperation between the British and German groups would be confined to mutual assistance in issuing bonds for the two sections of the line. There could be no joint issue of such bonds.[56] Keswick and Cameron were ready to accept the idea of separate negotiations. However, they wished to extract from Hansemann a commitment to adhere to the 1898 division of railway spheres regarding the Tientsin–Yangtze line 'and other matters'.[57] Convinced of the Meyer–Rothschild–HSBC connection, Hansemann regarded this as an implicit reference to the Peking Syndicate's concession in the Hwangho valley, and rejected the idea. Talks had now reached a precarious stalemate. Without British concurrence the DAB group could not begin talks for a final agreement on the German section of the railway. For the BCC, the German syndicate had imported extraneous matters into the points at issue; and without an acknowledgement by Hansemann of the continued validity of the preliminary agreement no progress was possible.[58]

Again it fell to Alfred Rothschild to act as mediator. In private talks with Cameron and Keswick the basis of a possible compromise was defined; and on his suggestion the two men, accompanied by Julius Brüssel, travelled to Berlin for direct talks with Hansemann and the Disconto Gesellschaft's legal adviser Curt Erich. The Berlin bankers' conference of 30 March produced a new agreement, binding both sides to commence negotiations at Peking on the basis of identical draft final agreements. The German section would include two branchlines from Techow on the northern boundary of Shantung to Cheng-ting in Chili and from Yenchow to Kaifeng in Honan. The British section would now terminate at Pukow rather than Chinkiang. The 1895 agreement on Chinese loan business was reaffirmed, but not that of September 1898. There would be no railway concession in Hwangho for the Peking Syndicate, and the HSBC and BCC were recognized as 'representatives of all English railway interests in China'.[59] This last stipulation was given practical meaning shortly afterwards when the BCC effectively took over the Peking Syndicate on 8 April 1903: all railway concessions in the Yangtze valley and to the north of it were now combined. This had been actively encouraged by London. The arrangement, as the secretary of the Peking Syndicate, Thomas Gilbert, informed the Foreign Office, 'gives effect to the wishes of His Majesty's Government.' At the end of 1903 Keswick, Meyer and Cameron consolidated the BCC, Peking Syndicate and HSBC interests in the Chinese Central Railways Ltd (CCR).[60] On the German side, the *Deutsch-Chinesische Eisenbahn-Gesellschaft* (DCEG) was formed as the sole German agent in all railway business in China. Fourteen major German banks had raised start-up capital of 1 m Marks (*c*. £48,900) to enable the new company to construct and operate the lines for which concessions had been or would be obtained. The question of the continued validity of the 1898 protocol was deliberately not touched upon at the Berlin meeting.[61] It suited the interests of both sides; uncertainty on this point was preferable to having no agreement at all.

British and German diplomacy now swung into action. At Peking the two chargés d'affaires, Townley and Baron von der Goltz, jointly requested the Wai-wu Pu to begin negotiations.[62] The talks between the Shantung viceroy Yüan Shih-k'ai and Chang Yen-mow for the Chinese government and Heinrich Cordes and Byron Brenan as representatives of the DAB and HSBC respectively commenced in May 1903. Progress was slow, as the Chinese authorities were determined to return all foreign railway concessions to Chinese control at an early stage. Yüan Shih-k'ai especially sought to 'put obstacles in the way of the

German portion of the Tienstin–Chinkiang line'.[63] The BCC also met with strong Chinese government resistance. Prior to the resumption of talks with the Anglo-German group, the Peking authorities blocked plans by the BCC to build a branchline from Tientsin to Paotingfu, the capital of the metropolitan province of Chili. It was an indication of Peking's hardening attitude. Chinese negotiating behaviour further contributed to the prolongation of the talks. Yüan Shih-k'ai refused personally to take part in the talks, and instead nominated two subordinate clerks. As these were not equipped with full negotiating powers, they could act only on Yüan's instructions. These could not be issued until he had reported back to the Wai-wu Pu which, in turn, frequently wished to confer with the Ministry of Commerce (and later the Transport Ministry). As a result the talks were punctuated by intervals of inactivity that lasted weeks, months even.[64]

In the clash between German demands for a speedy conclusion of the talks and Chinese prolixity, the latter invariably prevailed. The two negotiators for the consortia, Byron Brenan, the former consul-general at Shanghai, and the DAB's Tientsin manager Heinrich Cordes, met with two major obstacles at the very outset of the negotiations. The first of these was the Chinese refusal to include the two German branchlines into Chili and Honan provinces in any final agreement. Their inclusion entailed an increase in the projected railway loan. For the German section of the line alone the estimated amount required had been raised to £8 m. Given the financial burden imposed by the 1901 Boxer settlement, the Chinese rejected the DAB's idea of a Chinese government guarantee of the whole of the loan. Peking's resistance to a Chinese loan guarantee was insuperable. Under the 1899 preliminary agreement the Peking government was fully within its rights to refuse the idea. As Mumm observed, the 'enormous greed of the Berlin bank's leaders' had caused the impasse.[65]

To expedite matters, the DAB resurrected the earlier suggestion 'to separate their interests from those of their British associates' in the autumn of 1903.[66] This flew in the face of the Berlin agreement of 30 March 1903, and was at first resisted by Keswick and the BCC. There was some force behind the German argument, as the British minister at Peking, Sir Ernest Satow, pointed out, for the survey of the British section had not even been commenced. No estimate of the total loan required for construction of the entire line was, therefore, available. Under these circumstances, Satow advised, 'lest the Germans should think that we are playing into Chinese hands', the British group should start surveying its section of the line without delay.[67] Since the survey could not be completed before the middle of the year, another bankers' conference was arranged in early February 1904. The London meeting produced a compromise along the lines of the original German suggestion. As the German group was ready to proceed with the financing and construction of its section, both parties would apply jointly and simultaneously for separate final agreements on identical terms. It was also agreed that the German agreement should be finalized regardless of whether the British survey had been completed, provided that the terms of the two separate agreements had been settled. This compromise solution was endorsed by Downing Street and the Wilhelmstrasse.[68]

Diplomatic representations were to no avail. From the outset of the talks the Chinese commissioners refused to discuss separate agreements. This was the second substantive point at issue. In Townley's analysis, their refusal was rooted in Yüan Shih-k'ai's suspicions of the Germans and his 'belief that they are only awaiting a favourable opportunity to adopt in Shantung an attitude similar to that of Russia in Manchuria'. Two separate agreements with the two sections mortgaged separately would merely strengthen German control over Shantung. By contrast, one agreement, carrying with it one mortgage for the whole line, would secure to British bondholders an interest in Shantung. These interests, in turn, would be a form of insurance policy against any possible German aggression. The Chinese negotiators refused to budge, and by early August 1904 the negotiations had reached another stalemate. In consequence, the Disconto Gesellschaft was forced to accept the inevitable, and dropped its demand for separate agreements and a Chinese government guarantee.[69]

Much time and energy had been expended on shunting the talks into the sidings. Although critical of the DAB's attempts to alter the 1899 preliminary agreement, Mumm also apportioned some blame to Satow: 'we suffer as before from insufficient English interest; for the English would no doubt like to see our project fail, and instead of supporting us, they only hamper us.'[70] There was some truth in this, for the Tientsin–Yangtze talks had become wound up in the growing Anglo-German antagonism. In July 1903 a British intelligence report concluded that '[t]he Germans are themselves well on the way to making a second Manchuria in Shantung'.[71] For his part, Satow had always regarded the conclusion of two separate agreements as inimical to British interests. Despite his good personal relations with Mumm, Satow was alarmed at 'hectoring way of Germany'. The British minister and his commercial attaché, J.W. Jamieson, agreed that it was desirable 'to counteract German influence' in Shantung.[72]

Satow's role during this stage of the talks was crucial. The British minister at Peking had become increasingly critical of foreign owned railway enterprise in China. The concessions for the Manchurian, Shantung and Yunnan railways, he observed at the end of 1904, had in fact been granted to the Russian, German and French governments. In the case of the concession for the Peking–Hankow line, the company's largest shareholder was the King of the Belgians. As regarded the Shantung railways, no shares could be purchased on the open market; it was 'essentially a Government enterprise'. As he noted in his diary, 'the taint of politics was over all these r[ai]lw[a]ys'.[73]

To his former American colleague, William Woodville Rockhill, he confessed that '[w]e cannot help the Chinese out of the position they have got themselves into with regard to the Shantung, Manchurian & Yünnan railways. But we ought to use all of our influence to prevent any more political railways being built.'[74] Satow's growing hostility to 'political railways' was largely a reflection of the impact of the Russo-Japanese War. Prior to the clash between the two Asiatic Powers he had been profoundly pessimistic about the future prospects of the Chinese Empire. Japan's success in the war had removed that danger. Indeed, Satow noted the growing strength of Chinese nationalism which took aim at 'foreigners whose only aim for coming to China is to push their trade.' He welcomed China's economic nationalism. At the very least, it offered a useful check against the ambitions of Britain's rivals: 'We have heard a good deal of la conquête paisable de la Chine par le chemin de fer and that is what I am trying to oppose . . . it is necessary for us to be vigilant on behalf of China.'[75]

Chinese negotiators took a more robust stance in the talks with the DAB and HSBC. Satow and Mumm realized that from the winter 1904–5 onwards an arrangement on the basis of the preliminary agreement of 1899 was no longer feasible. At the end of 1904, the DAB made a last attempt to bring the stalled negotiations to a conclusion. Completion of the line, Satow warned, would 'strengthen the hold of Germany over the north of Chihli, and will at the same time complete the German railway system, which, so long as it is not extended beyond Tsinan-fu, is not likely to prove a paying concern.' Private investors were not likely to subscribe to the CCR's southern half. The German portion, he noted, would also 'have the advantage of the traffic between Kiaochou and Tientsin to swell its receipts'; none of that traffic would go via the British section. Under these circumstances only a British government guarantee would make the British portion of the line commercially interesting for potential British investors.[76]

Satow knew that no such guarantee was forthcoming. Lansdowne and the Foreign Office were especially critical of the chronic mismatch between the concession-hunters' appetite for yet more concessions and their often limited capital. The CCR also proved to be an unwieldy tool for British diplomacy, and relations between Satow and the company's Peking representatives were often strained. While the minister was increasingly opposed to the railway project for political and strategic reasons, the CCR began to lose interest in it on commercial grounds. The British group had come to the same conclusion as Satow regarding the commercial advantages of the northern section with its already completed connection to Kiaochow. A final settlement on the basis of the 1899 preliminary agreement was, therefore, no longer acceptable to the CCR. All net profits should be centrally administered, to be divided on a *pro rata* basis depending on the mileage of the two sections. The German negotiator concluded, 'that we shall be punished for having in the meantime constructed the Tsingtao railway, and the English shall be rewarded for having done nothing'.[77]

In March 1905, the CCR finally completed its survey, and the two sides agreed on a complete draft of the final agreement for the Tientsin–Yangtze project. It provided for a £10 m loan, with the German share at £6.5 m. This amounted to significantly more than had been envisaged in the 1899 preliminary agreement. Once again, it was Satow who pulled the brake. The German section would carry the entire through-traffic of the line to Kiaochow, 'and this will cause the British section to be worked at a loss'. German interests in the line were both commercial and political: 'it is doubtful whether, even from a commercial point of view, we have any interests'. In light of the 'altogether disparate' nature of British and German interests, Satow proposed to Lansdowne that British diplomacy should cease actively to support the negotiations. But as the British group regarded the draft agreement as satisfactory, Lansdowne decided that London could not well oppose it now. However, he fell in with Satow's suggestion that the latter 'need not take an active part in the discussions with the Chinese government'.[78]

Without Satow's assistance, Mumm realized, there was little point in resuming negotiations with the Chinese authorities. In this manner British diplomacy had increased its leverage over the Germans. Nevertheless, whilst ostensibly abstaining from any active part in the matter, Satow continued to play a significant role in the background. Following his repeated warnings, the Foreign Office now urged the CCR to ensure that the line was completed in its entirety. It was imperative that the draft agreement would allow for the simultaneous construction and the joint working of the entire line.[79]

Mumm might well complain that the 'perfidy of our official allies' coupled with Satow's 'inertia hampered our energy'.[80] Yet, if the matter was to be moved forward, the German group had to yield to British demands. Accordingly, the text of a redrafted final treaty was agreed to by the two parties in early 1906. By now Sir Edward Grey, Lansdowne's Liberal successor, had ordered a review of British strategy and policy in China. Satow's advice proved decisive in the matter of Britain's future railway policy. The outcome of the Russo-Japanese war had fundamentally altered the strategic situation in the Far East, he observed. Relations with Peking were likely to become more difficult: 'And by "difficult" I mean that China is no longer as ready to submit to all and every demand of the Powers, and unless she gets another knock-down blow, will in future be less and less tractable.' China, he noted, 'has begun to pluck up courage again, not only to refuse further concessions, but also to endeavour to resume those she made during her period of extreme weakness.'[81] On the eve of his retirement from the diplomatic service he addressed a lengthy despatch on the subject of Chinese railway concessions to Grey, and concluded that:

> the policies of 'pacific penetration', 'partition', 'spheres of interest' are dead; and...any offers of spare English capital for investment in Chinese railways...should be regarded as purely commercial undertakings, without any political character. [...] It may even seem a doubtful policy to insist on holding the Chinese government bound to us for ever by preliminary agreements made eight years ago, which either our inertness or inability to procure the necessary capital has hitherto prevented from being carried into effect.[82]

When Satow met with Grey in July 1906, following his return home, both men agreed that 'China had taken a new departure and that for the policy of the big stick we sh[ou]ld adopt a more conciliatory attitude, meeting the Chinese half-way.'[83]

Satow's recommendations were incorporated in Grey's instructions for the new minister at Peking, J.N. (later Sir John) Jordan, which contained guidelines for a new policy of conciliation, tempered by firmness. The further improvement of China's railway infrastructure was of paramount importance to foreign trade. But the British government would not take steps to prevent China from regaining control over the railways. As for the Tientsin–Yangtze railway, given Germany's greater political and economic interests, Jordan was not to take an active part in any talks with the Peking authorities.[84] The new policy of moderation was dictated by the 'logic of facts'. It combined the wider strategic aim of safeguarding British influence in China with economic development and political stabilization. Peking had to fulfil its undertakings with regard to commercial concessions already granted. In return, British diplomacy would 'lend [the Chinese government] a helping hand in their endeavours [to modernize]'. It was, as Grey summarized, 'to some extent a new departure'.[85]

Grey proposed to make concessions in practical matters, whilst at the same time upholding the wider framework of Sino-Western relations based on the 'unequal treaties'. The new policy was an attempt to give practical, political meaning to the the vision of foreign financed railways as a development tool. A memorandum by Robert A.H. Collier (the later Lord Monkswell), of the Far Eastern department, elaborated on the change in British railway policy:

> From the political point of view there can be no doubt that the tendency of railways must be to make the dismemberment of China more difficult. If all points could easily and quickly be reached from all other points by means of railways, the power of the Central Government would be much increased, and the country would be more closely knit together and better capable of withstanding foreign aggression and dealing with internal disturbances.

Since it remained the object of British policy to maintain China's integrity and encourage the further opening up of the country to foreign trade, it was in Britain's interest 'that railways under the control of the Chinese Government should be multiplied.' General control by the Peking authorities was one thing, successful railway enterprise by the Chinese, however, quite another. While British policy towards China became more accommodating, underlying suspicions and assumptions of Chinese backwardness remained: 'such is Chinese nature that it is probable that the Chinese are themselves incapable of successfully building and working a considerable railway owing to the immense amount of dishonest profits that would be made during the process.' Foreign capital, 'involving some sort of foreign control', remained a necessary element in China's railway development.[86]

Like the British, the Germans also had come to reckon with China's new assertiveness. Mumm and his successor, Count Arthur von Rex, advocated greater flexibility and conciliation in pursuit of now exclusively commercial objectives. Accommodation, not confrontation, was required in the post-war era in Far Eastern politics.[87] Direct talks with the Chinese had been in abeyance since 1903, but were resumed in August 1906. At the end of that year, the German and British syndicates finalized their joint position at another bankers' conference at Berlin. The talks with the Chinese delegation slowly edged towards a conclusion, though this was not without several hitches along the way. As Jordan observed in his annual report for 1907, during the negotiations the change in Germany's attitude had been especially noticeable. The German demands, extremely exacting at the outset, assumed in the end the character of concessions to the Chinese, which the British negotiator J.O.P. Bland was inclined to view with some alarm.[88] At one stage British diplomacy threatened to disrupt the talks. Parallel with the Tientsin–Yangtze discussions, Jordan was conducting negotiations for a final agreement for the purely British concession for the Soochow–Ningpo railway. Grey and the Foreign Office accorded greater priority to this than to the Anglo-German project, and Jordan was instructed that progress in the Tientsin–Yangtze talks should not be purchased at the expense of the Soochow–Ningpo negotiations.[89] When at the end of 1907 the final agreement for the Tientsin–Yangtze concession had been intialled, Grey threatened to withhold Britain's signature unless Jordan obtained assurances regarding the Soochow–Ningpo concession.[90] It was only following strong representations by the Keswick and the CCR that Grey revised his stance. On 13 January 1908 the final agreement was eventually signed.[91]

* * *

The 'Tientsin–Pukow Railway Agreement' provided for a £5 m gold loan at a rate of interest of 5 per cent per annum over 30 years, secured against Chili and Shantung provincial customs receipts and internal revenues, and to be used exclusively for the construction of the line. Construction and control of the railway were vested entirely in the Chinese central government. In this respect the final agreement marked an important advance for the Peking authorities in their quest for greater railway autonomy. It went further in accommodating Chinese views on the central question of lenders' control than the recent agreement for the Canton–Kowloon railway which the BCC had concluded in March 1907. Even so. for the construction work Peking had to appoint a German and a British chief engineer, acceptable to the two syndicates. Within their respective spheres the DAB and CCR were to act as agents of the Chinese railway administration and supervise the purchase of all materials and goods required for the construction work. On completion of the work, the Chinese government was to take over the administration of the entire line 'as one undivided government railway', superintended, during the term of the loan, by a European engineer-in-chief.[92] Compared with the preliminary agreement of 1899, the 1908 final agreement was significantly more advantageous to the Chinese. The length of the line had been extended by some 100 km; the construction period was shortened to four years; the loan had also been reduced from £7.4 m to £5 m, and the loan period from 50 to 30 years.

The construction of the German line was begun in June 1908; work on the British section only commenced in the spring of 1909. By March 1913 the whole line was opened to traffic, though the two halves continued to be supervised by two separate boards. The northern section was taken over by the Chinese government after China's entry into the First World War in March 1917. The British section remained under British control. Indeed, by the time the final agreement was signed in 1908 Anglo-German cooperation had passed its high watermark. In 1910 Sir Charles Addis, chairman of the HSBC's London committee, had come to the view that the 1898 London bankers' agreement was 'a figment of the imagination'. Attempts to re-affirm it had foundered on German opposition. The policy of spheres of interest was now dead.[93]

British and German railway diplomacy had undergone a profound transformation. Railways remained a central part of their respective policies, but their overall aims had changed. During the 'scramble for concessions' railways had served German diplomacy primarily as a tool to extend German political and commercial influence in Shantung and its hinterland. After the Russo-Japanese War, German diplomacy shed its political ambitions in the Far East, and acted as the handmaiden of commerce. German enterprise, being efficiently organized, competitive and strongly represented by agents on the ground, was well placed to take advantage of this. For the British, railways were initially a diplomatic instrument to counter any expansionist designs by the other Powers. Cooperation with Germany in the Tientsin–Yangtze project allowed also for some degree of control over the proceedings of the Germans in northern China, albeit through the offices of 'patriotic capitalists'. After Russia's defeat at the hands of Japan, and following Grey's review of British Far Eastern policy, railways continued to be regarded as key to China's economic and political modernization. In the changed circumstances, however, cooperation with Germany was no longer deemed necessary or desirable.

Notes

The transliteration of Chinese names and terms follows the Wade-Giles system rather than the modern *pinyin* romanization to ensure some degree of uniformity with the contemporary sources on which this study is based.

1 For a negative assessment cf. E-tu Zen Sun's classic *Chinese Railways and British Interests, 1898–1911* (New York, 1954), and 'The Pattern of Railway Development in China', *Far Eastern Quarterly*, Vol. xiv, no. 2 (1955), pp. 179–99. For revisionist interpretations, cf. Chi-ming Hou, *Foreign Investment and Economic Development in China, 1840–1937* (Cambridge, MA, 1965), pp. 127–30, and John E. Schrecker, *Imperialism and Chinese Nationalism: Germany in Shantung* (Cambridge, MA, 1971), p. 210. A post-revisionist critique is Ralph William Huenemann, *The Dragon and the Iron Horse: The Economics of Railroads in China, 1876–1937* (Cambridge, MA, 1984), pp. 5–6 and 240–8.
2 Percy Horace Kent, *Railway Enterprise in China: An Account of Its Origin and Development* (London, 1907), p. 1.
3 Hou, *Foreign Investments*, pp. 62–3. For a survey of the construction data see Huenemann, *Dragon and Iron Horse*, appendix A.
4 As quoted in Kent, *Railway Enterprise*, p. 90. On the financial aspects of the treaty and the issue of foreign loans see Hou, *Foreign Investments*, pp. 23–4 and 236, fn. 4; also L.K. Young, *British Policy in China, 1895–1902* (Oxford and Hong Kong, 1970), pp. 26–7; David McLean, 'The Foreign Office and the First Chinese Indemnity Loan, 1895', *Historical Journal*, Vol. xiv, no. 2 (1973), p. 304.
5 Tel. O'Conor to Kimberley (private and secret), 14 May 1895, Kimberley Mss, Bodleian Library, Oxford, Ms.Eng.c.4396; Kent, *Railway Enterprise*, p. 93. For later reflections on the phenomenon, cf. Ronald E. Robinson, 'Railway Imperialism', in Clarence B. Davis and Kenneth E. Wilburn (eds), *Railway Imperialism* (Westport, CT, 1991), pp. 1–5.
6 Michel Bruguiere, 'Le Chemin de Fer du Yunnan: Paul Doumer et la politique d'intervention française en Chine (1889–1902), *Revue d'Histoire Diplomatique*, Vol. lxxxvii,

nos. 2–4 (1963), pp. 23–61, 129–62 and 252–78, see especially pp. 145–52; Hou, *Foreign Investments*, p. 64.

7 Leopold II to Borchgrave, 14 Feb. 1899, as quoted in G. Kurgan-van Hentenrijk, *Léopold II et les groupes financiers belges en Chine: La politique royale et ses prolongments, 1895–1914* (Brussels, 1972), pp. 240 and 225–76; Arthur Lewis Rosenbaum, 'The Manchuria Bridgehead: Anglo-Russian Rivalry and the Imperial Railways of North China, 1897–1902', *Modern Asian Studies*, Vol. x, no. 1 (1976), pp. 41–64.

8 I am following John Darwin's argument, see his 'Imperialism and the Victorians: The Dynamics of Territorial Expansion', *English Historical Review*, Vol. cxii, no. 3 (1997), p. 632; also Rosenbaum, 'Manchurian Bridgehead', pp. 41–64.

9 Tels. Kimberley to O'Conor (confidential), 8 May 1895, Kimberley Mss, Ms.Eng.c.4396, and to Malet (no. 48, secret), 18 May 1895, TNA (PRO), FO 64/1352. On the DAB cf. Maximilian Müller-Jabusch, *Fünfzig Jahre Deutsch-Asiatische Bank. 1890–1939* (Berlin, 1940), and Karl Erich Born, *International Banking in the 19th and 20th Centuries* (Leamington Spa, 1983), pp. 126–8.

10 Vera Schmidt, *Die deutsche Eisenbahnpolitik in Shantung, 1898–1914* (Wiesbaden, 1976), p. 110.

11 A.H. Ganz, 'The German Navy in the Far East and Pacific: The Seizure of Kiaotschou and After', in John A. Moses and Paul M. Kennedy (eds), *Germany in the Pacific and the Far East, 1870–1914* (St Lucia, QLD, 1974), pp. 115–36; T.G. Otte, 'Great Britain, Germany, and the Far Eastern Crisis of 1897–8', *English Historical Review*, Vol. cx, no. 4 (1995), pp. 1157–79.

12 Schrecker, *Imperialism*, pp. 39–40 and 124–7; Schmidt, *Eisenbahnpolitik*, pp. 65–70; Erich Achterberg, *Berliner Hochfinanz: Kaiser, Fürsten, Millionäre um 1900* (Frankfurt, 1965), pp. 71–3; Boris Barth, *Die deutsche Hochfinanz und die Imperialismen: Banken und Aussenpolitik vor 1914* (Stuttgart, 1995), p. 156.

13 Heyking to Hildebrand (no. 277), 4 Feb. 1898, Acten der Kaiserlich deutschen Gesandtschaft in Peking, betreffend Tientsin–Pukou Eisenbahn [hereafter KDGP], Baker Library, Harvard University, Mss.K705.K13/1; tel. MacDonald to Salisbury (no. 48), 19 Feb. 1898, FO 17/1340.

14 Quotes from memo. Bax-Ironside, encl. in MacDonald to Salisbury (no. 38), 26 Feb. 1898, FO 17/1333; and Curzon to Spring-Rice (private), 20 Feb. 1898, Spring-Rice Mss, Churchill College Archive Centre, CASR I/28.

15 Tel. Heyking to Auswärtiges Amt (no. 46), 27 Feb. 1898, KDGP, Mss.705.K13/1; Kent, *Railway Enterprise*, pp. 148–50.

16 Tel. MacDonald to Salisbury (no. 30), 29 Jan. 1898, FO 17/1340.

17 'Minutes of Negotiations on Railway Construction', 4 Mar. 1898, KDGP, Mss.705.K13/1.

18 Note MacDonald to Tsungli Yamên, 3 Mar. 1898, FO 17/1334; memo. Sanderson (on conversation with Salisbury), 23 Dec. 1897, Sanderson Mss, FO 800/2.

19 O'Conor to Kimberley (no. 73, confidential), 6 Mar. 1895, FO 17/1233. On Kinder and his work cf. Lord Charles Beresford, *The Break-Up of China* (London, 1899), 31–9. For official attitudes in the 1880s, cf. David McLean, 'Commerce, Finance, and British Diplomatic Support in China, 1885–86', *Economic History Review*, 2nd ser., Vol. xxvi, no. 3 (1973), pp. 464–76.

20 MacDonald to Salisbury (no. 50), 18 Mar. 1898, FO 17/1334. On MacDonald's energetic efforts during the 'battle for concessions' cf. Margaret H. Wilgus, *Sir Claude MacDonald, the Open Door, and British Informal Empire, 1895–1900* (New York, 1987), pp. 92–4 and 126–69; also D.C.M. Platt, *Finance, Trade, and Politics in British Foreign Policy, 1815–1914* (Oxford, 1968), pp. 283–90.

21 Quotes from Curzon to Salisbury (private), 11 Apr. 1898, Salisbury Mss, Hatfield House, 3M/E/1/118; and memo. Curzon, 12 June 1898, Curzon Mss, British Library Oriental and India Office Collection, Mss.Eur.F.111/78B.

22 Salisbury to Curzon, 30 May and 4 June 1898, Curzon Mss, Mss.Eur.F.111/1B;
   cf. Keith Neilson, *Britain and the Last Tsar: British Policy and Russia, 1894–1917*
   (Oxford, 1995), p. 197. The evidence usefully corrects E.W. Edwards' assessment of
   British Far Eastern policy as being more trade-driven, cf. *British Diplomacy and
   Finance in China, 1895–1914* (Oxford, 1987), pp. 32–3 *et passim*.
23 Min. Sanderson, [4 Apr. 1898], and Balfour to Sanderson, 9 Apr. 1898, Balfour Mss,
   British Library, Add.Mss. 49739; tel. Hatzfeldt to Bülow (no. 77), 5 Apr. 1898, in
   F. Thimme *et al.* (eds), *Die Grosse Politik der europäischen Kabinette, 1871–1914* (40
   Vols., Berlin, 1924 *et seq.*), Vol. xiv/1, no. 3763 [hereafter *GP*].
24 Memo. Sanderson, 13 Apr. 1898, Balfour Mss, Add.Mss. 49739; note Lascelles to
   Bülow, 20 Apr. 1898, in G.P. Gooch and H.W.V. Temperley (eds), *British Documents
   on the Origins of the War, 1898–1914* (11 Vols, London, 1926–38), Vol. i, no. 52 [here-
   after *BD*].
25 Paul A. Varg, 'The Myth of China Market, 1890–1914', *American Historical Review*,
   Vol. lxxiii, no. 4 (1967), pp. 742–58. On the 'miscomprehension' of China's complex
   internal trade system, cf. E.V.G. Kiernan, *British Diplomacy in China, 1880 to 1885*
   (New York, repr. 1970), pp. 251–2.
26 Lascelles to Salisbury (no. 341, confidential), 6 Nov. 1896, FO 64/1379. On Detring
   see Vera Schmidt, *Aufgabe und Einfluss europäischer Berater in China: Gustav
   Detring (1842–1913) im Dienste Li Hung-changs* (Wiesbaden, 1984), pp. 120–9. For
   the 1896 loan, cf. Müller-Jabusch, *Deutsch-Asiatische Bank*, pp. 75–93.
27 Cameron to DAB, 5 Apr. 1898, FO 405/77. For the indemnity loan negotiations,
   cf. Müller-Jabusch, *Deutsch-Asiatische Bank*, pp. 94–7 and 105–7; Barth, *Hochfinanz*,
   pp. 154–8.
28 March to Heyking, 23 May 1898, KDGP, Mss.705.K13/1; memo. Bertie, 3 May 1898,
   FO 17/1359. Barth, *Hochfinanz*, pp. 159–61, comes to a different conclusion, though
   this is based on the German records alone. For Hansemann, cf. his obituary *The Times*
   (10 Dec. 1903), and Achterberg, *Berliner Hochfinanz*, p. 71.
29 Müller-Jabusch, *Deutsch-Asiatische Bank*, pp. 123–5. On Rothstein and the RCB,
   cf. Rosemary Quested, *The Russo-Chinese Bank* (Birmingham, 1977), pp. 5–6 and 29–32;
   Olga Crisp, *Studies in the Russian Economy* before 1914 (London, 1976), pp. 125–6.
30 Mema. Bertie, both 3 May 1898, FO 17/1359; cf. tels. Bülow to Hatzfeldt (no. 129),
   30 Apr. 1898, and reply (no. 104), *GP* xiv/1, nos. 3771–2.
31 Bertie to Hatzfeldt, 5 May 1898, FO 17/1359; tel. Hatzfeldt to Auswärtiges Amt
   (no. 109), 5 May 1898, and Bülow to Hatzfeldt (no. 410), 15 May 1898 *GP* xiv/1,
   nos. 3775 and 3777.
32 Gundry [Hon. Secretary, China Association] to Foreign Office, 8 July 1898, FO
   17/1360. On the meeting and the China Association in general cf. Nathan A. Pelcovits'
   classic *Old China Hands and the Foreign Office* (New York, repr. 1969), pp. 236–8.
33 Memo. Cartwright, 'Peking–Hankow Railway', 9 July 1898, and Mins. Campbell and
   Salisbury, n.d. [9 July 1898], FO 17/1360.
34 Tels. Heyking to Bülow (no. 104), 8 June and *vice versa* (no. 85), 13 June 1898,
   KDGP, Mss.705.K13/1.
35 Richthofen to Heyking (no. A87), 20 Aug. 1898, and tel. (no. 163), 29 Aug. 1898, ibid.
36 Tels. Heyking to Auswärtiges Amt (unnumbered and nos. 125–6), 2, 17 and 19 Aug.
   1898, ibid.
37 Tels. Balfour to MacDonald, 17 Aug. and (no. 261), 20 Aug. 1898, FO 17/1341;
   Heyking to MacDonald, 27 Aug. 1898, KDGP, Mss.705.K13/1; cf. Kurgan-van
   Hentenrijk, *Leopold II*, p. 171.
38 Tel. Hatzfeldt to Auswärtiges Amt (no. 109), 5 May 1898, *GP* xiv/1, no. 3775;
   cf. Balfour to Lascelles (no. 195A), 20 Aug. 1898, FO 244/563.
39 Rothschild to Bertie, 4 May 1898, FO 17/1359 – a point missed by Schmidt,
   Eisenbahnpolitik, pp. 112–13, and Barth, *Hochfinanz*, p. 160; cf. Cameron obituary,
   The Times (11 Dec. 1908).

40 Tel. Balfour to Salisbury, 3 Sept. 1898, Salisbury Mss, 3M/A/96/61; Müller-Jabusch, *Deutsch-Asiatische Bank*, pp. 118–21. For Brüssel cf. Frank H.H. King, *The History ot the Hongkong and Shanghai Banking Corporation*, Vol. i, *The Hongkong Bank in Late Imperial China, 1864–1902: On an Even Keel* (Cambridge, 1987), pp. 225, 590 and 611.

41 Tel. Bülow to Heyking (no. 104), 3 Sept. 1898, and minutes of meeting, 1–2 Sept. 1898, KDGP, Mss.705.K13/1; Bülow to Hatzfeldt, 24 Mar. 1899, *GP* xiv/1, n. *; Philip Joseph, *Foreign Diplomacy in China, 1894–1900: A Study in Political and Economic Relations with China* (London, 1928), pp. 357–9

42 Balfour to Scott (no. 167A), 12 Aug. 1898, FO 65/1551. For the text cf. J.V.A. MacMurray (ed.), *Treaties and Agreements with and concerning China* (2 Vols, London, 1921), Vol. i, p. 175.

43 Tel. Heyking to Bülow (no. 17), 21 Feb. 1899, KDGP, Mss.705.K13/2; tel. Bax-Ironside to Salisbury (no. 150), 19 May 1899, FO 17/1383.

44 Tels. Heyking to Bülow (no. 33), 7 Mar. 1899, and *vice versa* (no. 56), 10 May 1899, KDGP, Mss.705.K13/2; Bax-Ironside to Salisbury (no. 133, confidential), 24 May 1899, FO 17/1374.

45 For the text cf. MacMurray, *Treaties*, Vol. i, pp. 694–6; Kent, *Railway Enterprise*, pp. 260–3. The management arrangements resembled those standard on British railways, cf. George Findlay, *The Working and Management of an English Railway* (London, 1891), pp. 12–24.

46 Barth, *Hochfinanz*, p. 166, summarises Hansemann's 21 Dec. 1899 memorandum. For the Peking Syndicate, cf. MacMurray (ed.), *Treaties*, Vol. i, pp. 700–3; David McLean, 'Chinese Railways and the Townley Agreement of 1903', *Modern Asian Studies*, Vol. vii, no. 2 (1973), pp. 148–9.

47 Li Hung-chang to Rothschild, 6 and 15 Apr. 1899, N.M. Rothschild and Co. Archive, RAL XI/109 and 134. For sketch of Meyer's role cf. King, *Hongkong Bank*, Vol. i, pp. 468–70, and Rudolf Muhs, 'Jews of German Background in British Politics', in Julius Carlebach *et al.* (eds), *Second Chance: Two Centuries of German-Speaking Jews in the United Kingdom* (Tübingen, 1991), p. 185.

48 Brüssel to HSBC, 18 Jan. 1900 (TS copy), FO 17/1436. For the background, cf. Kurgan-van Hentenrijk, *Leopold II*, pp. 348–9.

49 For the text cf. BD ii, no. 17, enclosure. On the negotiations cf. Young, *British Policy in China*, pp. 193–9.

50 Tels. Mumm to Auswärtiges Amt (no. 14), 14 Jan. 1901, and Richthofen to Mumm (no. 9), 18 Jan. 1901, KDGP, Mss.705.K13/3.

51 Truppel to Reichsmarine Amt, 20 Oct. 1901 (copy), ibid., Mss.705.K13/2.

52 Truppel to Mumm (nos G.82 and G. 92), 2 and 10 Feb. 1902, and Falkenhayn to Mumm (no. I6/2776), 14 May 1902, encl. report Captn. Count Verri on surveying of railway lines, n.d., KDGP, Mss/705.K13/3.

53 Mühlberg to Mumm (no. 86), 21 July 1902, ibid., Mss.705.K13/4; also Holger Afflerbach, *Falkenhayn: Politisches Denken und Handeln im Kaiserreich* (Munich, 1996), pp. 45–7.

54 Mayers to Satow, 18 Aug. 1902, Satow Mss, TNA (PRO), PRO 30/33/7/9; Ch'ing to Goltz, 1 Sept. 1902, KDGP, Mss.705.K13/4; also Barth, *Hochfinanz*, p. 280.

55 Townley to Lansdowne (no. 382, confidential), 17 Dec. 1902, FO 17/1527; Keswick [on behalf of the BCC] to HSBC, 16 Jan. 1903 (copy), FO 405/133/53; cf. McLean, 'Townley Agreement', pp. 151–3.

56 Keswick to HSBC, 16 Jan. 1903, FO 405/133/67, encl. no. 1. The extent to which the Foreign Office was bound by decisions by the bankers is indicated in Campbell to BCC, 7 Apr. 1903, FO 17/1597. This also contradicts McLean's argument that there was a new, closer association of the Foreign Office with Chinese finances, 'Townley Agreement', p. 161.

57 Keswick to HSBC, 16 Jan. 1903, FO 405/133/53.

58 Disconto Gesellschaft to Brüssel, 23 Jan. 1903, ibid./67, inclosure no. 7; Keswick to HSBC, 25 Feb. 1903, ibid./160, inclosure no. 3.

59 Memo. Hansemann, 30 Mar. 1903, KDGP, Ms705.K13/4; also Cameron to Bertie, 7 Apr. 1903, FO 17/1598; Müller-Jabusch, *Deutsch-Asiatische Bank*, pp. 155–6; Schmidt, *Eisenbahnpolitik*, pp. 121–2.

60 Peking Syndicate to Foreign Office, 9 Apr. 1903, and Campbell to BCC, 16 Apr. 1903, FO 17/1617; Keswick to Foreign Office, 3 Feb. 1904, FO 405/142/30. The agreement between the BCC and the Peking Syndicate is summarized in memo. Collier and Alston, 'Detailed Memorandum on Railways in China' (confidential), 31 Dec. 1907, FO 371/418/9103.

61 Brüssel to HSBC, 4 Apr. 1903, FO 17/1597; Mühlberg to Mumm (no. A57), 1 June 1903, encl. 'Gesellschafts-Vertrag der Deutsch–Chinesischen Eisenbahn–Gesellschaft m.b.H.', 21 Apr. 1903, KDGP, Mss.705.K13/4; also Schmidt, *Eisenbahnpolitik*, p. 122.

62 Townley to Goltz, 15 May 1903, and Richthofen to Mumm (no. A60), 6 June 1903, KDGP, Mss.705.K13/4; Townley to Lansdowne (no. 209, confidential), 29 May 1903, FO 17/1598.

63 Satow to Lansdowne (no. 311), 23 Oct. 1902, FO 17/1526.

64 There were a dozen meetings between 18 July and 19 Dec. 1903; discussions did not recommence until 23 May 1904, cf. Satow to Lansdowne (no. 284), 5 Aug. 1904, FO 17/1638. For the Paotingfu line, cf. Satow to Lansdowne (no. 347), 19 Nov. 1902, and Townley to Lansdowne (no. 363), 2 Dec. 1902, FO 17/1527.

65 Mumm to Auswärtiges Amt (no. A203), 15 Aug. 1903, KDGP, Mss.705.K13/4; Townley to Lansdowne (no. 288, confidential), 6 Aug. 1903, FO 17/1599; Schmidt, *Eisenbahnpolitik*, pp. 123–4.

66 Tel. Satow to Lansdowne (no. 239), 20 Oct. 1903, FO 17/1603.

67 Tel. Satow to Lansdowne (no. 252), 16 Nov. 1903, FO 17/1599; Satow diary, 21 Jan. 1904, Satow Mss, PRO 30/33/16/7. For the BCC's initial reaction see Keswick to Foreign Office, 23 Oct. and 11 Nov. 1903, FO 405/136/15 and 38.

68 'Memorandum of Agreement respecting Tien-tsin–Yang-tsze Railway', 2 Feb. 1904, FO 405/142/30; tel. Richthofen to Mumm (no. 50), 7 Mar. 1904, KDGP, Mss.705.K13/5.

69 Townley to Lansdowne (no. 273, confidential), 23 July 1903, FO 17/1599; Pourtalès to Mumm (no. A135), 8 Sept. 1904, KDGP, Mss.705.K13/5; cf. 'The Railway Question in China', *The Times* (21 Sept. 1904).

70 Mumm to Klehmet, 6 June 1904, and Satow to Goltz and min. Goltz, both 12 July 1904, KDGP, Mss.705.K13/5. This was a constant theme of his reports, Schmidt, *Eisenbahnpolitik*, p. 124.

71 Report Captn. Barnes [Commanding Officer, 1st Chinese Regt. at Weihaiwei], n.d., encl. in Intelligence Division to Foreign Office, 27 July 1903, FO 405/135/91; Paul M. Kennedy, *The Rise of the Anglo-German Antagonism, 1860–1914* (London, 1987(pb)), pp. 252–4.

72 Satow diary, 16 Dec. 1905, Satow Mss, PRO, PRO 30/33/16/9; memo. Jamieson, 'The Future Prospects of the Leased Territory of Wei-hai-Wei as a Commercial Centre, in relation to the German dependency of Kiaochou and the Province of Shantung in general', 9 Sept. 1904, FO 881/8284.

73 Quotes from Satow to Lansdowne (no. 401, confidential), 27 Nov. 1904, FO 17/1639, and Satow diary, 26 June 1905, Satow Mss, PRO 30/33/16/8.

74 Satow to Rockhill, 22 Dec. 1904, Rockhill Mss, Houghton Library, Harvard, b*46M.386(2879).

75 Quotes from Satow to Grey (private), 15 Dec. 1905, Grey Mss, PRO, FO 800/44; and to Lansdowne (private), 25 May 1905, Lansdowne Mss, PRO, FO 800/121. For a general assessment of Satow's role at Peking cf. my ' "Not Proficient in Table-Thumping": Sir Ernest Satow at Peking, 1900–1906', *Diplomacy & Statecraft*, Vol. xiii, no. 2 (2002), esp. pp. 185–9.

76 Satow to Lansdowne (no. 441, confidential), 28 Dec. 1904, FO 17/1639; cf. Satow to Mumm, 29 Dec. 1904, KDGP, Mss.705.K13/5; cf. Lee En-Han, *China's Quest for Railway Autonomy, 1904–1911* (Singapore, 1977), pp. 160–8.

77 Cordes to Mumm, 2 Mar. 1905, KDGP, Mss.705.K13/6; Satow to Campbell, 11 Aug. 1904, Satow Mss, PRO 30/33/14/14.

78 Tel. Lansdowne to Satow (no. 51), 1 Apr. 1905, FO 17/1674, in response to tel. *vice versa* (no. 62), 31 Mar. 1905, FO 17/1675.

79 Mumm to Bülow (no. A266), 4 July 1905, KDGP, Mss.705.K13/6; Campbell to CCR, 19 June 1905, FO 405/155/116.

80 Mumm to Bülow (no. A360), 25 Nov. 1905, KDGP, Mss.705.K13/6. Mumm's successor later noted that Satow had 'worked against our steps', cf. min. Rex, 4 Apr. 1907, ibid./8.

81 Satow to Grey (private), 31 Mar. 1906, Grey Mss, FO 800/44; Gilbert to Foreign Office, 19 Feb. 1906, FO 405/165/98.

82 Satow to Grey (no. 177, very confidential), 16 Apr. 1906, and min. Grey, 30 July 1906, FO 371/35/18909; also Satow to Campbell, 4 Sept. 1906, FO 371/39/32429.

83 Satow diary, 19 July 1906, Satow Mss, PRO 30/33/16/9.

84 Grey to Jordan (no. 260, confidential), 7 Aug. 1906, FO 371/35/18909; cf. Otte, 'Not Proficient in Table-Thumping', p. 188.

85 Grey to Jordan (no. 298, confidential), 31 Aug. 1906, FO 371/35/29351.

86 Memo. Collier, 'Short Memorandum on Railways in China' (confidential), 31 Dec. 1907, FO 371/418/9109; cf. Niels P. Petersson, 'Gentlemanly and Not-so-Gentlemanly Imperialism in China before the First World War', in Shigeru Akita (ed.), *Gentlemanly Capitalism, Imperialism and Global History* (Basingstoke, 2003), p. 106.

87 Mumm to Bülow (no. A359), 30 Oct. 1905, KDGP, Mss.705.K13/6; Petersson, 'Imperialism in China', pp. 110–11.

88 For the bankers' conference, cf. memo. Collier and Alston, 'Detailed Memorandum on Railways in China' (confidential), 31 Dec. 1907, FO 371/418/9103. Jordan's 'General Report of 1907' gives a detailed account of the talks at Peking, Jordan to Grey (no. 94), 27 Feb. 1908, FO 371/428/13287; cf. Edwards, *British Diplomacy*, pp. 111–12.

89 Tel. Grey to Jordan (no. 38), 10 Apr. 1907, FO 405/180/71; tel. Tschirschky to Rex (no. 32), 11 Apr. 1907, KDGP, Mss.705.K13/8.

90 Tel. Grey to Jordan (no. 136), 10 Dec. 1907, FO 405/181/79.

91 Tel. Jordan to Grey (no. 12), 13 Jan. 1908, FO 371/417/1394; tel. Rex to Auswärtiges Amt (no. 166), 4 Dec. 1907, KDGP, Mss.705.K13/9. For the pressure on Grey, cf. Gilbert to Foreign Office, 12 Dec. 1907, FO 405/181/80.

92 Jordan to Grey (no. 44), 26 Jan. 1908, FO 371/418/5920; MacMurray (ed.), *Treaties*. Vol. i, pp. 684–7; Schmidt, *Eisenbahnpolitik*, pp. 128–30; En-Han, *Railway Autonomy*. pp. 182–3.

93 Addis to Alston, 23 Apr. 1910, and mins. Alston and Campbell, 25 and 26 Apr. 1910, FO 371/851/14208.

7 Lord Curzon and British strategic railways in Central Asia before, during and after the First World War[1]

John Fisher

On 10 May 1911, a despatch was sent from the British Foreign Office in London to Sir George Buchanan, Britain's ambassador in St Petersburg, informing him that his government was ready to agree in principle to a Trans-Persian Railway. Furthermore, Buchanan was told that Britain would sanction negotiations on this matter subject to the following conditions. First, the line would enter the British zone in Persia, created by the Anglo-Russian Convention of August 1907, at Bunder Abbas and not, as the Russian sponsors of the scheme wished, at Kerman. The line would join with the Indian railway system at Karachi and not at Nushki, as its Russian sponsors had hoped. Second, there would be a break of gauge at Bunder Abbas. Third, in exchange for British support, it was expected that Russia would desist from building or supporting the construction of a rail-line in the neighbourhood of the Perso-Afghan frontier. Last, it was hoped that Russia would support applications by Britain to the Persian Government for concessions on several branch lines connected with the larger Trans-Persian project. These lines, which were in southern and central Persia, would connect the towns of Mohammerah to Khoremabad, Bunder Abbas or Chahbar to Kerman, and Bushire to some point on a line from Bunder Abbas via Shiraz to Ahwaz.[2]

All but one of these branch lines and the main section of the Trans-Persian line would lie in the neutral zone of the 1907 Convention and, as such were to be internationalized. The exception, which was entirely in the British zone, was to be an exclusively British scheme. It was a prerequisite that on all lines in the neutral zone, British and British-Indian trade would be guaranteed equality of treatment with other goods, including those of Russia. The telegram outlined, with one exception, the main lines which Britain attempted to build or develop during and immediately after First World War.

By 1911 strategic railways had already featured in British interests in Persia and elsewhere in Central Asia for some time. Indeed, the idea of a Trans-Persian railway was a recurring one which usually took the form of a main trunk line which would traverse the whole of Persia, bearing passenger traffic from Europe to India. During this time railways had also become an important factor in Anglo-Russian relations in the region and in the dealings of those powers with successive Persian governments. Railways had also become to some extent a barometer of Anglo-Russian relations and of the interplay of the strategic priorities of each power. Besides this, they provided a subject of discussion and dissent among strategists in England and India, as well as those who dealt with diplomatic and commercial aspects of the railway question.

From the mid-1860s, French, German, Austrian and British concession hunters had secured the sanction of the Persian Government to develop various lines but not had fructified. In 1872, however, Reuters had secured an effective monopoly on railway construction in Persia and with sole right to build a line from the Caspian to the Persian Gulf. For various reasons, notably the opposition of Russia and of hardliners in the Persian Government, the ambitious scheme also failed and the concession was rescinded. In the remainder of the 1870s, several other concessions of a more modest scale were sought or gained but to little effect in terms of actual railway construction.

During the 1880s British statesmen began to take a close interest in the subject. This was partly because British strategists detected Russian attempts to construct railways to Tehran, into the province of Khorasan, close to the Afghan border, and in a southerly direction to the Persian Gulf. An ineffectual British assurance of protection to Persia in 1888 was followed in 1889 by a declaration by the Shah of Persia that any railway concessions given to other powers in the north would be matched by similar concessions to Britain in the south. In 1890 the Shah signed an agreement with Russia which effectively sterilized railway development in Persia for 10 years. Needless to say, British authorities regarded this, and with some justification, as a cloak for Russian concession hunting and surveying. On the expiry of the agreement in 1900 it was renewed for a further 10 years. The agreement was in 1907 overtaken by the Anglo-Russian Convention, which among other things divided Persia into the three zones, Russian, neutral and British located, respectively, in the north, centre and south-east of the country. By virtue of the convention, Russia agreed not to oppose railway concessions sponsored by Britain in the British zone nor, without previous conversations with Britain, in the neutral zone either.[3]

Yet when war came in the summer of 1914, and indeed for some time before, Anglo-Russian relations in Persia had soured. In the process of concession hunting and pegging out claims, traditional rivalries had resurfaced. Evidently the reasons for this deterioration were much broader than railways alone. Yet in May 1914, Sir Arthur Hirtzel of the India Office observed that it was the issue in Persia on which Britain and Russia were most diametrically opposed.[4] One factor in this was continuing Russian concern that Britain wished any Russian lines built in northern Persia to be connected with the Baghdad Railway; something that would lead to Russian trade being siphoned off towards the Mediterranean rather than its intended outlet in the Persian Gulf. For Britain also, the Baghdad Railway might present a more direct threat if, as the military authorities in India claimed, it was intended as a springboard for greater German activities in southern and central Persia.

Britain was also alarmed by Russian railway construction in Transcaspia. Between the mid 1880s and the turn of the century a branch line of the so-called Central Asian or Transcaspian Railway, had reached the town of Kushk.

According to Lord Curzon, who had traversed the Transcaspian line in 1888, soon after its completion, the construction of the Transcaspian line itself had brought many benefits to Russia, not the least of which was commercial.[5] The completion of the more northerly Orenburg–Tashkent line in 1904 meant that a Russian force invading India through Afghanistan would no longer depend upon supplies and reinforcements coming across the Caspian. As Curzon had predicted in 1889, it was the second arm 'of the forceps, whose firm grip may one day be required to draw the teeth of England in Central Asia.'[6]

Curzon's predilection for viewing international rivalries in the form of a chess board has been commented upon elsewhere.[7] His experience of those rivalries spanned several decades when Russian, then German and then finally Soviet military activities appeared to threaten the safety of the Indian Empire. Curzon had studied and written extensively on the railways as well as broader aspects of strategy and his knowledge of those lines was unparalleled. He was also keenly aware of the factors which had retarded the development of the many railway concessions which, by the 1880s when he first traversed the region, had already been granted to foreign concerns. Among these obstacles he included geography, adverse weather conditions, reluctant foreign investment due to a lack of security and prospects, the opposition in Persia of the Mullahs to British encroachments, and the intrigues of Russia and other countries. Curzon viewed as necessary the construction of railways linking Persia's agricultural, manufacturing and commercial centres. Regenerating Persia in this way would prevent Russian expansion; something which might also be deterred if Britain were to construct a rail line from Baluchistan. Such a line was all the more necessary as Curzon believed it possible that Russia contemplated the construction of lines to Herat and Kandahar in Afghanistan. The construction of the Transcaspian line had, as Curzon noted, led to 'the final Russification of the whole Turkoman Steppes from Khorasan to Khiva, and from the Caspian to the Oxus.'[8] With Russia inexorably pressing down from the north it therefore seemed to him unwise to facilitate this movement on the 'glacis of India' by sanctioning the construction of a mooted Indo-European railway.[9] Within this broader conspectus of international relations the railway had the power decisively to shift the balance of power in Central Asia. It was therefore a vital piece in the matrix of international rivalries.

However, Curzon had also taken a keen interest in the development of the southerly section of the Baghdad Railway, and efforts taken in the years prior to First World War to stem German penetration of Mesopotamia. By 1913, possible German involvement in the construction of the proposed section of the line between Basra and the Gulf led prominent imperialists to be more voluble in their determination to deny Germany a foothold in the Gulf. Curzon was adamant that Germany should be forestalled. Not only was this essential with regard to the maintenance of British interests in the Arab Middle East but also because of the implications for her position in the Persian Gulf and beyond, should Germany also somehow overcome British opposition and bridge the gap between Basra and the waters of the Gulf. However, even if in 1913 German influence in Mesopotamia was not necessarily equated with a threat to India the possibility remained that it would have an impact on Britain's position in Persia in terms of trade and strategic defence.[10]

In conversation with Sir Arthur Nicolson in September 1913, Curzon had noted Germany's recent attempt to obtain a landing place in the Gulf for an overland cable from Asia Minor via Baghdad. As Curzon added, this was proposed on the basis of Germany's claim that she must communicate with East Africa. In his view, this was merely indicative of the 'troublesome future' which awaited the completion of the Baghdad–Basra section of the Railway. As Curzon continued, Germany had outmanoeuvred the Foreign Office where it was felt that, in exchange for the Alexandretta rail and port concession, Germany had surrendered her right to construct the Baghdad–Basra section. However, Curzon noted, Germany was under no obligation having only agreed to consider the idea. Germany, having obtained the Alexandretta concessions and the right to build the Baghdad–Basra section, would exert more influence on the board of the Baghdad–Basra line.[11]

For Curzon and others German ambitions in Mesopotamia during 1913 were overshadowed by Anglo-German rivalry in Persia and in particular by German commercial penetration in the neutral sphere created by the 1907 Convention. By 1913 great efficiencies in existing lines were anticipated and new lines were being built in Transcaspia and Turkestan, and between those regions and Russian lines in European Russia and Siberia. Furthermore, a second strategic line to the Afghan frontier was also anticipated. Assessments of these developments suggested that whilst Britain might not have anything to fear at present, the commercial orientation of existing and developing lines in Central Asia might at a future time be adapted to a hostile strategic use by Russia.

The third and perhaps most important reason for disagreement over railways, and the cause of prolonged discussions, was the issue of the alignment of the proposed Trans-Persian Railway. A formal proposal for such a line had been put forward by a Russian syndicate in 1910. After lengthy interdepartmental debate and public discussion, Britain had insisted that the southern terminus of such a line must not be at a place east of Bunder Abbas. The preferred Russian alignment would have taken the railway through Central Persia possibly with a branch line south from Kerman. The main trunk line would have continued east to Seistan linking with the Indian network and, in due course, with a proposed Russian branch line to Meshed.[12] Whilst some British observers anticipated benefits in terms of improved passenger traffic between Europe and India, these were balanced by continuing suspicions about Russian strategic objectives.

During the discussions about the Trans-Persian Railway from 1910, several positions had emerged. Some, such as George Buchanan, Britain's ambassador in St Petersburg, felt that Britain must not forfeit cooperation with Russia over railways. In his view, the construction of the line was inevitable and for the foreseeable future, Russia appeared not to harbour any hostile designs on India. Furthermore, according to Buchanan the scheme had powerful sponsors in Russia who saw it not only as a guarantee of Persian integrity but also as a means of drawing Russia and Britain together. He continued:

> The emperor himself is interested in it; the Government have given it their support; and many of its original promoters are... the most ardent advocates of an Anglo-Russian understanding. It would be ridiculous to impute to them the Machiavellian design of forging a weapon for a Russian attack on India. They hope, on the contrary, that the projected railway will serve to draw the two countries still closer together, while they believe that it will promote Russian interests by acting as a counterpoise to the Bagdad (sic) Railway. Some of them also, who are opposed to a forward policy in Persia, see in it the best guarantee for the maintenance of Persian integrity.[13]

Buchanan's predecessor, Sir Arthur Nicolson, had argued along very similar lines. In his view, the 1907 Convention, if it were to survive, required nurturing by its parents. Noting his disappointment with the attitude of the Government of India towards the railway, he stated: 'The Russians, so far as I have been able to observe, have buried all the animosities, jealousies and suspicions of the past, and have acted towards us with perfect confidence and loyalty – and I think that their attitude in the Persian question is clear proof of this.' Britain's cooperation with Russia on railways and other Persian matters would, in his view, reduce the likelihood of Russia siding with Germany in the event of Anglo-German hostilities. More immediately, he could see little strategic threat from Russia.[14]

Opponents of the scheme argued that if the negotiations broke down, Russia would by default develop lines close to the Afghan border, a highly dangerous contingency and one which might upset the Amir of Afghanistan. Some argued against prevailing military wisdom which insisted that the line, if constructed, must hug the coastline of the Persian Gulf and therefore be accessible to superior British Naval power. According to Edmund Barrow, an officer with broad experience of Indian defence, Britain could not predict future political alignments and assume that she would invariably be able to bring to bear substantial naval forces there. Equally, should war occur the Makran region would as a battle ground be greatly inferior to Seistan. There was a further risk that if Britain did not endorse the scheme, Russia would oppose a proposed British line running north from Mohammerah, which was intended as a counterweight to an extension of the Baghdad Railway. Others still were sceptical about the whole notion of the line, believing that Russian and British commercial interests would best be served by lines running directly north–south through Persia. The more vital objection, expressed most volubly by the Indian General Staff, and one which recurred during First World War, was strategic. If Russia were allowed to project the Trans-Persian Railway into Seistan, this would enable her in the event of war to turn the Kandahar and Herat lines of advance and to deploy there more troops than Britain could field for the defence of India. It would also facilitate the transit across two waterless deserts of Russian forces to within striking distance of India. Should Britain voluntarily extend her line from Nushki she would not find a suitable point from which to launch offensive operations. If the Trans-Persian line were allowed to link up with the Baghdad Railway then this might provide Germany with a spring board for an assault on India.[15]

These considerations among others led the Government of India to oppose the line reaching the sea anywhere east of Bunder Abbas and also made it unattractive to Russia as a result. The danger of holding to this view was that it would remove scope for Anglo-Russian cooperation on railways in Persia as a whole. Specifically, Britain would lose the ability to influence Russian construction in the northern (Russian) and central (neutral) zones. On the other hand, the Government of India and Sir Arthur Hirtzel also argued against a proposed alignment of the Trans-Persian line which would bring it into the British zone at Kerman.[16] To Hirtzel, writing in January 1913, it had seemed folly to believe that Russia had anything to gain in a commercial sense from extending the line beyond her own sphere. To his mind, Russia's desire to maintain the 1907 Convention was every bit as strong as Britain's. The correct policy would be to stand up to this bluff and prevent Russia attaining a hostile or potentially position.[17]

The strategic importance of Seistan in the defence of British India had been debated at length by the Committee of Imperial Defence (hereafter CID) between 1903 and 1906. One of the key players in that installment of the debate, for most of it as Viceroy of India, was George Curzon. Curzon, as he was occasionally tempted to remind people, had traversed this region and many of the nascent strategic railway lines in Central Asia. In fact, besides some newspaper and magazine articles, he had also written two very long and detailed books in which he elaborated on the subject.[18] Several years later, in 1899 he had explained the strategic importance of Seistan.

> Situated at the point of junction of the frontiers of Persia, Afghanistan and Baluchistan, the future of Seistan affects the destinies of all three countries. Lying as it does almost midway between Meshed and the Persian Gulf, no advance can be made from Khorasan to the sea except through Seistan. Its position upon the exposed flank of Afghanistan would render its occupation of great value to any Power contemplating either a move against that country or an advance upon Khandahar. Nor will it be denied that the Kandahar–Herat line could not be held with safety by India, nor the valley of the Helmand be defended, were a hostile Power in possession of Seistan.

As Curzon continued, the region also possessed many agricultural and other resources. Russian domination there was simply unthinkable.[19] Writing in 1901 about a possible Russian line from Meshed to Seistan, Curzon referred to other objections to the scheme. South of Afghanistan in Baluchistan and Mekran, Russia would be able to stir up trouble necessitating further responsibilities and expenditure for India. In the previous two years Indian trade with Seistan had doubled. Any alteration in this position of preponderance would seriously affect British prestige in Afghanistan and Baluchistan. He added: 'If Great Britain is ever called upon to advance to Kandahar, as she will probably one day be compelled to do, an intolerable state of friction would arise between the Powers that would then control the upper and the lower waters of the Helmand [river]'.[20]

The possibility of a railway linking Quetta, the Indian railhead, and Seistan had been discussed at various stages from the mid-1880s. The idea gained most vociferous support in the late 1880s and in response to Russian advances in northern Persia and on the Afghan frontier. At this early stage the two key diverging elements in future debates of the issue had already emerged. On the one hand, some felt that its completion would effectively counter Russian railway construction and other intrigues on the northern and north-western Afghan frontier, whilst others felt that it would simply stimulate Russian aggrandizement and enhance the ability of Russia to attack or destabilize British rule in India. In any case. as a result of the CID discussions in the first years of the twentieth century, by 1905 a line from Quetta to Nushki, a distance of 98 miles had been completed. Those debates of the CID are worth summarizing here as the key papers submitted at the time were reprinted in the summer of 1916 when India again appeared vulnerable to hostile activity from without.[21]

Some of the key papers were written by Arthur Balfour, the Conservative Prime Minister, who chaired a committee which was charged with investigating the defence of India. Balfour felt that Russia would face considerable difficulties should she advance either by the Afghan cities of Herat and Kandahar or by Kabul. However, the difficulties that she would face were she to advance through Seistan would be even greater and to his mind the supposed strategic and offensive advantages of the 'Russianising' of Seistan were fantasy. For one thing the Helmand Desert would prevent a direct march by Russia on Kandahar. Nor were Baluchistan and Sind viable lines of advance for her. The obvious temptation existed to counter Russian influence in Seistan by extending the Quetta–Nushki railway into Seistan, yet Balfour felt that in the event of war, India could not maintain forces in Seistan for any length of time. If such a line were built by India, the risk was that Russia would reciprocate by running a line south from Meshed and Nasratabad, forming a through connection from Europe to India. If this were to occur then, in Balfour's view, a break of gauge at Seistan would not prevent a Russian invasion nor could British or Indian troops hope to sabotage their own line in time to prevent such an invasion. Russia would simply adapt her rolling stock and proceed unchallenged. Quite simply, any commercial gains to be had from Indian exploitation of Seistan were not worth the candle.[22]

Curzon and Kitchener, then Viceroy and Commander in Chief, of India, respectively, disagreed with Balfour that Russia had little to gain in Seistan. It was precisely as a result of her activities there that, unlike in Afghanistan, were war to break out, she would not have to fight her way through a hostile country to reach India. Both felt that if Russia were to utilize the Quetta–Nushki line, it would probably be to her disadvantage since Indian defences were strongest there. The real danger should Russia become ascendant in Seistan was not, in their opinion, that it would provide an immediate opportunity to invade India via Baluchistan but 'in the opportunities it would provide for unsettling and embroiling the

Beluch border from Seistan through Mekran to the sea.' This would clearly impact on British prestige as well as necessitating costly reciprocal moves by Britain. Equally, if a Russian advance forced Britain to advance to Kandahar and the Helmand Valley this, as Curzon had previously noted, would leave the two powers facing each other on the Helmand River. Such proximity was felt likely to entail a 'greater and perpetual danger of conflict.'[23]

Curzon and Kitchener also disagreed with Balfour's view that Britain would not be able to maintain adequate forces in Seistan in time of war. In fact, surveys suggested alternative strategic points which would enable India to control the whole of Seistan. The most obvious point, according to Curzon and Kitchener, was to obtain from the Amir of Afghanistan, a lease of a portion of the Helmund River or of a larger territory. Britain could then regenerate Seistan or starve it of water. In the former case, they suggested that over 3 million acres of land in Persia and Afghanistan might be brought under cultivation and the population would rise from eighty thousand to 2 million. In either case, whether it was decided to starve or develop the region, the territories would have to be supported by an extended railway from Nushki. However, it would be first and foremost a line of supply and not one that Russia would be able to use for offensive purposes.[24] To this suggestion Balfour simply noted that such an extension would provoke demands for similar concessions from Russia. Furthermore, Balfour felt that such a line would open a third possible invasion route to Russia. However, if India were unable to secure such a lease, then Curzon and Kitchener agreed with Balfour that the extension should not be built as it would most probably provoke rather than prevent Russian construction.[25] If, however, Russia commenced the extension of a line from Meshed, Britain would then have to extend her line, taking advantage of her ability to build more quickly than Russia.[26] Balfour was also deeply sceptical about the idea of utilising a lease on the Helmund River in the manner contemplated by Curzon and Kitchener; namely, to starve to death almost 2 million people in time of peace. That India might be threatened, either by German inspired pan-Islamic propaganda or by enemy military activity in Mesopotamia and Persia, gained credibility partly because of the perceived vulnerability of British interests in Persia and because of consistently unsuccessful attempts to remedy this from within. The interplay between *Drang nach Osten*, the German–Turkish drive to the east, increasing Russian impotence and the internal weakness in Persia and the Caucasian States, provided a backdrop to these discussions about railway development.

Early in 1916 developments suggested that Turkish and German manpower was limited and that extended communications would also work against Turkey. German and Austrian insurgents were marooned in hostile territory and recent intelligence confirmed the loyalties of Afghanistan.[27] By the spring of 1916 the extent to which Russia's increasing internal disruption might affect her impact upon the general conflict remained unclear. Successes against Turkey in Anatolia and Persia, followed by the Brusilov offensive offered hope, but the more sharply focused threat of Germany's eastern ambitions would clearly impact upon railway development.

In the summer of 1916 the Quetta–Nushki line again intruded into policy debates, leading to the reprinting of these earlier memoranda. By this time in Western Persia, a force of roughly 15,000 Turks based in Baghdad had overwhelmed Russian forces under General Baratoff and had penetrated the Persian border. It was expected that this force, which had already reached Hamadan, would cause unrest there and further east. In Central Persia, a force of 500 men under Sir Percy Sykes had reached Yezd with a view to rallying support for Britain. In Eastern Persia a cordon of British, Persian and, ironically, Russian troops had been deployed along a line that included Birjand, Kacha and Robat. The strategic situation had therefore changed to the extent that, besides any future threat to her position from a hostile Russia, until the summer of 1918, Britain had also to consider the threat, real or otherwise, of German and Turkish troops marching towards Afghanistan and India or at least destabilizing Britain's presence in the region by means of sedition.[28]

With the collapse of negotiations for a Trans-Persian line, Russia and Britain again pursued their independent concession hunting with the Shah of Persia. Late in July 1916, it was discovered that Russia hoped to obtain a concession for a branch line from the Trans-Caspian Railway to Meshed.[29] Two days later, the military authorities in India argued for a rapid extension of the broad gauge line beyond Nushki to Dalbandin, a distance of 120 miles. This was due to German–Turkish military advances and intrigues in western Persia, and the inability of the Indian command to supply British forces in Eastern Persia by means of animal transport.[30] Against this the Viceroy, Lord Chelmsford, felt that if it were worth doing at all, the line should be extended the full 360 miles to Robat, which was deemed to have better facilities for a terminus. To enforce his case, the Commander-in-Chief, India, noted that the extension looked beyond the immediate necessities to a time when Britain might again have to actively promote her interests in southern Persia.

Though reluctant to enter hypothetical discussions, the Political and Secret Department of the India Office supported the extension. One reason predominated – that after the war Britain would find that Russia had developed rail lines in Central Persia and these, together with the mooted branch line to Meshed, would give her a considerable advantage over Britain.[31] Further, the department noted:

> from the political point of view it would appear to be wise to lay out our military plans on the hypothesis that within the next half century Kerman will be the junction of lines from Bunder Abbas, Tehran, and Meshed; and if that is so, that we shall be wise to get on the flank of the latter as soon as possible by building from Nushki to Seistan. These lines will not be primarily 'threats to India.' But the possession of the Dardanelles will not make less necessary eventually, when the vast resources of Central Asia are fully developed, an outlet for Russian trade farther East.

Hirtzel and others felt that Russia would persist in her attempts to find an outlet in the Persian Gulf, even if she were to obtain control of Constantinople and the

Dardanelles, and that Kerman would continue to be the pivotal spot in railway development in Persia. An extension of the Quetta–Nushki line initially to Dalbandin would provide a strategic safeguard. For Hirtzel, the issue clearly had considerable strategic importance which transcended the current conflict and he was loath to let the opportunity slip to bolster Britain's position.

Added to these considerations were commercial factors to which Hirtzel and others pointed. Local experts suggested a steadily growing trade between India and Seistan prior to the war. Trade with Meshed was extremely good and trade between India and Khorasan was ripe for development.[32] According to General Barrow, Military Secretary at the India Office, there were further military factors in favour of the line. As Barrow noted, the northern flank of the proposed extension was protected by river, swamp and desert. Like his colleagues in the Political and Secret Department, Barrow did not seek to defend India from a 'few marauders with a sack full of combustibles', in other words the Germans and the Turks, but rather, from the possibility of a resurgent hostile Russia.[33]

At this point the discussion was at risk of escalating into a full blown debate of the strategic issues thrashed out by the CID from 1903 and Asquith, for one who was anxious to avoid this. To him it was a military matter and he therefore referred it to Sir William Robertson, Chief of the Imperial General Staff (CIGS), who, predictably, argued strongly against the extension on military grounds.[34] According to Robertson the extension would not help to prevent Turkish incursions, which were in his view unlikely. Furthermore, Robertson argued that as future political alignments among the Great Powers were unclear, he did not see any pressing strategic necessity to develop the line. However, no sooner had Robertson pronounced than Hankey, secretary of the CID, had circulated a potted history of the Trans-Persian debate, which he claimed must be read if any sense were to be made of the proposed extension beyond Nushki.[35] The discussions also attracted comment from Curzon.

Curzon's view was clear. The decision could not be taken purely on the basis of the present strategic situation or of the 'cogent military necessity' of the hour – the phrase used by the Indian authorities. Rather, Britain's future position in Persia must be considered, as must the future of British relations with Russia in Khorasan. The development of trade between India and Persia and the defence of India as a whole would also have to be considered. A railway from Quetta to Seistan would enable Britain to exercise a dominating influence beyond her frontier, an influence that might have spared her the experience of the past year when German and German inspired marauders had wandered about the Mekran and penetrated Afghanistan. Besides this, as Curzon continued, if the line were extended, then when trouble came in Afghanistan as inevitably it would, Britain would control the Helmand Valley up to Girishk. She would also be placed on the flank of a hostile power advancing from Herat on the Indian frontier. The extension would enable Britain to control more effectively illicit arms traffic between the Persian Gulf and Afghanistan and would have enormous benefits in terms of trade.[36]

Curzon's arguments in 1916 drew heavily upon the ideas which he and Kitchener had advanced in 1903. The only substantial difference in 1916 was that the line, if hastily constructed on a narrow gauge, might assist in attempts to curtail the activities of German emissaries and marauders, besides serving the broader strategic aims elaborated in 1903 with reference to Russia. For the purpose of having a forward move sanctioned, the latter country and its designs on India had, for the moment ceased to be a threat.

When the issue was next raised at the War Committee, it was most definitely presented as one of strategy. According to Austen Chamberlain, Secretary of State for India, it involved a 'survey of the whole future question of Persia'.[37] He, for one, felt uncomfortable with the proposed extension of the line. On this occasion, however, an extension to Dalbandin was sanctioned. Its detractors were swayed by assurances that the extension did not touch on the broader strategic issue. To drive home this victory and perhaps with an eye to posterity, on the same day Curzon wrote a memorandum on the Trans-Persian Railway scheme in which he demonstrated that, contrary to Hankey's assertion, Britain had never consented to it. According to Curzon, whatever commitments Russia might believe to exist had been nullified by the fact that she had, independently of Britain, proceeded to apply to the Persian Government for concessions which were to have formed part of the joint proposal.[38] Curzon, like Sir Arthur Hirtzel, was deeply interested in the longer term strategic position in Central Asia. If, as was anticipated, and Russia consolidated her hold on northern Persia, then Britain would counter this by strengthening her position in the south and east of Persia. Curzon took the opportunity provided by the discussion of strategic threats to press for the consolidation of British interests in South West Persia by means of railway construction. Specifically, he suggested that Britain should press on with a line from Bunder Abbas to Kerman, which would divert any future Trans-Persian line constructed by Russia to the south and towards the guns of a British fleet.[39]

The forward momentum established at the War Committee was partly sustained by evidence that Russia was seeking further concessions in northern Persia.[40] According to Curzon, whilst the development of these lines was inevitable, even if they would turn northern Persia into a Russian province, Russia was in effect attempting to rescusitate the Trans-Persian line.[41] Specifically, Russia had connected Julfa with Tabriz, had announced her intention to apply for a concession from Baku to Tehran, and had applied for a concession between Askabad and Meshed. In Curzon's view the whole issue would have to await peace as to do otherwise would simply 'prejudice the final issue and make a quite unnecessary sacrifice of British interests.' In short, Britain risked repeating the mistakes of the Baghdad Railway. The forward impulse was, ironically, also sustained by the increasing debilitation of Russia in the spring of 1917. Turco-German parties intent on intrigue in Afghanistan and Eastern Persia were able to proceed without opposition. According to Chelmsford, the efforts of those parties would be facilitated by instability in Persia and by virtue of the nomination of extremely able generals for key posts in Germany's drive to the east. In Chelmsford's view a recently proposed extension to Mirjawa would afford a more effective pivot, both offensive and defensive, from which to counter an enemy advance.[42]

Between them Russian and Turco-German activities fuelled the stronger approach to railway development favoured by Curzon. In his view, in May 1917 Russia was unlikely soon to conclude a separate peace and whilst her intrigues in northern Persia were hardly to be welcomed, they did at least show some indication of life. In fact, in order to prevent Russia's collapse Curzon had suggested a range of measures. Against this backdrop Curzon, as well as other imperial thinkers, was convinced that the only course was for the Allies to continue fighting. This would not necessarily preclude a receptive attitude towards future peace overtures from Germany's allies although the real danger was that such overtures might have the desired effect before Britain had secured her position in the east.

The issue was referred to Curzon's Mesopotamia Administration Committee which, on 22 August, on India Office advice, finally sanctioned the extension of the Nushki line to Mirjawa. The only reservations it expressed were that the line should not interfere with demands for railway materials, rolling stock or personnel in the theatres of war under the Government of India.[43]

When, 18 months later, in the spring of 1918 the line neared completion, the Government of India pressed for a further extension, deeper into Persian territory, to a place near Neh. It was recommended as a 'precautionary measure of paramount importance'.[44] According to Marling, Britain's Minister in Tehran, increased enemy activity was expected and the possibility of German forces crossing the Caspian also meant that they would at least try to gain control of the Trans-Caspian Railway for an advance on Afghanistan. Chelmsford and his advisers held that the extension would enable him to control the situation in East Persia and to counteract enemy agents. Further, the extension would enable his government to place a steadying influence on Afghan affairs and, in the event of a hostile advance on Afghanistan this might be countered from a forward position.[45]

Although surveys of the proposed extension were sanctioned, there was considerable opposition to it in Whitehall. The extension might offer military advantages but the War Office considered it most unlikely that the German/Turkish advance would continue along the Herat–Kandahar line on a significant scale. Whilst the chances of groups of marauders reaching Afghanistan and stirring up trouble was now increased because of conditions in Russia, a rising in Afghanistan directed against India was considered unlikely. In fact, even if such a rising were to occur, as Balfour had suggested in 1903 the War Office in March 1918 did not consider that British or Indian troops could be held indefinitely in Seistan.[46] For those reasons and as Chelmsford had apparently overlooked possible political repercussions with the Persian Government, besides those with the Amir of Afghanistan, Curzon's Eastern Committee vetoed the proposal. The line would extend to Mirjawa but no further.[47]

These objections to a further extension rested upon the perceived danger posed by the German–Turkish advance. By August 1918 the extent of that advance was such that General Smuts, the South African statesman confessed to having the 'gravest apprehensions' about the strategic situation in Persia.[48] Turkish and German troops were mustering in the Caucasus and on the approaches to Baku. A further concentration of Turkish troops was expected on the Hamadan–Resht road where British troops had formed a line against enemy penetration and advance. When the War Cabinet Eastern Committee discussed the position on 8 August, there appeared to be several alternatives in terms of strategic rail defence in Western Persia. However, each line entailed problems of construction in terms of topography or of difficult tribes. Curzon suggested a new construction that would link the Persian Gulf and Isfahan in Central Persia. However, should none of these ideas prove worthwhile, Curzon observed, it might then be necessary to extend the existing line from Quetta to Mirjawa and beyond.[49]

The idea was supported reluctantly by the Director of Military Intelligence at the War Office, George Macdonagh. He rejected a proposal from India to extend the line one third of the distance towards Meshed, but supported a more cautious extension. He did so essentially because the Government of India said that it could not adequately supply troops in eastern Persia. The notion put forward in 1903–6 at the CID in connection with Russia, that Britain must avoid any railway construction that shortened the distance between India and a potentially hostile force still held good, albeit in the context of the Turkish–German advance.[50] The extensions which had occurred had at each stage been carefully examined and were generally sanctioned by reference only to immediate military requirements. Precisely what would happen after the war remained unclear. However, it appeared that Britain would have to safeguard her position in Southern Persia and, possibly, more developed interests in Central Persia. According to Sir George Macdonagh that object might be achieved most effectively by constructing the line from Bunder Abbas to Kerman.[51]

From this point events began to move quickly. As the fate of Baku hung in the balance in the summer of 1918, Britain attempted to gain control of naval forces on the Caspian Sea. To the east, in Transcaspia, British intelligence officers had several months earlier been deployed via Meshed to destroy the Trans-Caspian Railway, in order to deny it to any hostile force advancing on India. Inadequately supported by the Home Government, in August 1918 the Transcaspian and Turkoman forces were being forced back by hostile Bolshevik forces upon North-western Persia.[52] When the Eastern Committee pondered this in August 1918 it seemed quite natural to play with the idea of a further extension of the Mirjawa line, albeit as a last resort and if Britain failed to hold her position in western and central Persia. Edwin Montagu, Secretary of State for India, believed that whilst events in north-west Persia might be decided soon, a long term challenge appeared to be emerging in Transcaspia. The official British support given to the Transcaspian Government was half-hearted and Britain's men on the spot were faced with what one of them described as a 'railway war'. With the British backed Transcaspian and Turkmen forces at one end of the line and, in time, hostile Bolshevik forces at the other end. A stalemate developed in which the locomotives controlled by each side would advance to within firing distance, discharge their weapons, and retreat.[53]

When, however, in January and again in November 1919, further extensions of the Quetta line, firstly into Persian territory, and then from the railhead at Duzdap were discussed by another of Lord Curzon's committees – the Interdepartmental Conference on Middle Eastern Affairs – it was twice turned down.[54] Yet the holding operation in Transcaspia, complicated by striking railway men and incompetent politicians, was doomed. With the Bolshevik capture of Orenburg and their southerly move on Persia, and in view of the broader context of British policy in the region it simply was not considered feasible (or as in 1903, wise) to extend the line towards a potential adversary. Late in 1919 Curzon claimed that Bolshevism was more of a political threat than a military one. This may have been due to a desire on his part to extend the line and promote the possibility of a British caretaking regime in Transcaspia as well as in the Caucasus.[55] Whatever the reality of the threat, Sir Henry Wilson, Robertson's successor as CIGS, would not sanction an extension unless the more expansive defence schemes of the War Office were approved.[56] So it seems that late in 1919 some strategists at least perceived an ambitious offensive function for the line that had not previously been explicitly stated. Besides the effects of retrenchment, in the case of some rail lines road traffic was becoming more competitive and this also tended to direct discussion away from railway construction.

Post-war thinking on railways in Persia was also closely linked to developments in Mesopotamia. There, the development of the Basra–Baghdad line was seen as a prerequisite. The building of a line from Baghdad to Khanikhin and Tehran was also a priority. Some, temporary building was also considered towards Mosul but, as in Eastern Persia, there was to be no construction that would lead to connections with Russian lines (in this case in the Caucasus). In Persia itself, there were renewed demands for the construction of the lines in which Britain had expressed an interest in 1911. Curzon, Hirtzel and his India Office colleague J.E. Shuckburgh argued for the extension of the Hamadan–Teheran line as the one most likely to facilitate British as well as Persian commercial interests. All of these proposals were, however, increasingly seen in the context of the inevitability of a continuous rail connection between Europe and India.[57] This idea, largely dormant during First World War was soon to be replaced by discussions about continuous air routes.

As to the role of the strategic railway in international diplomacy, it is probably true to say that for various reasons it diminished during First World War. With the sixteen or so Persian Cabinets that existed from 1914–19, Britain's key interest was to maintain peace in the country and to prevent Persia from siding with Germany and to prevent nationalists facilitating this and undermining British interests. In November 1917, J.E. Shuckburgh encapsulated British policy as being to secure the appointment of a government in Persia which 'was not anti-British or pro-German or a government whose policy it is to pinprick, thwart and annoy.'[58] Only in 1919, in the abortive Anglo-Persian Agreement, whereby, among other things, Britain and Persia were to have jointly developed communications in order to boost trade, did it again emerge from behind the screen of strategic considerations.

The future of the Nushki line was discussed on several occasions in the 1920s. In the aftermath of the Anglo-Russian Trade Agreement of 1921 especially, there were moves, resisted by successive Secretaries of State for India, as well as by Curzon, to pull up the line on Indian territory. Barrow was among its defenders, noting that on strategic and commercial grounds it would be 'short-sighted, pennywise folly' to dismantle it. Though recognizing that the line within Persian territory could not remain British, Barrow felt that some means could be devised to maintain it through a British syndicate. The syndicate might have a Persian façade and work with the Bank of Persia and with the backing of the Persian Government. As regards the section between Nushki and Mirjawa, Barrow suggested that it might be leased from the Government of India by the syndicate, thereby avoiding financial loss to India, whilst maintaining its value as regards trade with Central Asia.[59] Curzon also defended it on commercial as well as strategic grounds, noting in a letter to Viscount Peel, Secretary of State for India, that the Russians were reputedly about to send a consul to Kerman, 'admittedly for anti-British propaganda and intrigue.' Curzon argued that the existence of a motor road as well as the railway for part of the route had created some optimism about future trade prospects. At present, in the absence of Soviet Russian interest, Britain had the opportunity to press trade at Meshed and in Khorassan. That prospect was entirely dependent on the retention of the railway. Similarly, Persian exports via Quetta and Baluchistan were essential to finance dwindling imports.[60]

Critics of the line held that it had failed to deliver the promised commercial results. Increasingly, although military authorities in India acknowledged the principle of the strategic importance of Seistan in terms very similar terms to those of previous decades, they considered that in the event of conflict with the Soviet Union the extensive use of land forces anywhere in Persia would be impossible. From time to time intelligence was received that appeared to confirm previous ideas about Seistan. For example, in 1926 it transpired that Russia was surveying the Askhabad–Meshed line.[61] Yet the familiar arguments against extension still held good. In the protracted debates that occurred from 1926 on the defence of India, the Seistan issue had receded, being replaced by discussion about the defence of India from within Afghanistan. Certainly, Russia, if she were to take Herat, would utilize the Transcaspian line and, in anticipation of this, British strategists toyed with the notion of building strategic lines from India onto Afghan territory, something that Habibullah, the Amir of Afghanistan, had requested back in 1904 as part of an aggressive policy towards Russia.[62]

Just as Salisbury's vision of the railway in the development of Persia had failed to materialize, so in broader conceptions of geo-politics, in Central Asia the strategic railway enjoyed rather fleeting moments on the stage of international diplomacy during and after First World War.[63] Besides more routine discussion about their significance in the context of Anglo-Russian relations, periodically they were also considered in the context of passenger traffic and rail freight between Europe and India, and beyond.[64] From time to time, the Trans-Persian line was perceived as an element in the development of an All-Red route to India, or even in broader geo-political speculations.[65] In terms of actual development of railways in Persia itself, in April 1920, Cecil Harmsworth, Under-Secretary of State at the Foreign Office, recalled without too much exaggeration that during First World War it had been 'infinitesimal'.[66] Earlier that year the British government had apparently overlooked previous strategic concerns by supporting the formation of a syndicate to construct a line which would link Mesopotamia to the Caspian.[67] Several years later, in 1928 when discussions were commenced with Persia on a range of issues, the talk in strategic terms was increasingly of oil, British interests in Iraq, air power, and the greater importance of the Persian Gulf in British strategy in Persia. This reemphasis was assisted as the construction by the Persian Government of a Trans-Persian line from the Caspian via Hamadan to the Gulf got underway. It was expected that its future completion, together with the development of air power, would in time make that city the strategic pivot of western Persia, besides providing greater ease of access to the Persian Gulf for Soviet forces.[68]

Factors militating against greater progress on strategic railway construction were always likely to outweigh arguments, often linked to the circumstances of war, for their completion. Suspicions of Russian and then Soviet policies persisted especially but not exclusively in the minds of Indian and India Office officials. Dealings with successive Persian governments as well as the difficulty of attracting private sponsors to such an unstable country were added difficulties. Commercial considerations, whilst generally seen to favour construction of strategic lines, were not always so and soon after the First World War, arguments for the construction of roads rather than railways gained momentum.[69]

In the early 1890s Curzon had reflected as to why, given the widespread interest in and support for Persian railways, so few had actually been built. By way of explanation he pointed to certain topographical features of Persia. Far more obstructive, however, had been what he termed the 'selfish impulses of men' and, more especially, those in the cabinets and chancelleries of Europe and legations in Tehran. He continued: 'If the correspondence thereupon [Persian railways]… were collected, it would provide a bonfire that would blaze for a week.'[70] Fortunately we have been spared Curzon's pyromania and the subject remains a neglected but important aspect of Britain's interests in the region.

Notes

1 This chapter is based on a paper given to the International History Seminar at the Institute of Historical Research in 2002. I am grateful to the conveners of the seminar and to those who attended and contributed their ideas.

2 Cited in 'Notes on Persian Railways', JE F[errard], India Office, Political Department, 3 July 1911, C124, in L/P+S/10/793. All remaining references from L/P+S files (the Political and Secret Department of the India Office) are from the Oriental and India Office Collections (OIOC), of the British Library, London.

3 'Précis of Railway Projects in Persia, 1870–1910', secret, MO3c, War Office, W[ar] O[ffice] 106/52, The National Archives (TNA), formerly the Public Record Office (PRO). See also, J.S. Galbraith, 'British Policy on Railways in Persia, 1870–1930', *Middle Eastern Studies*, 25, 1989.

4 Minute by Hirtzel, 11 May 1914, L/P+S/10/416/P1832. Hirtzel was head of the Political and Secret Department of the India Office until the spring of 1917 when he became Assistant Under-Secretary of State. He subsequently rose to become Permanent Under-Secretary.

5 G.N. Curzon, *Russia in Central Asia in 1889 and the Anglo-Russian Question* (London, Longmans, Green & Co, 1889), ch. 8, passim.

6 Ibid., p. 262.

7 J. Fisher, *Curzon and British Imperialism and the Middle East, 1916–19* (London, Cass, 1999), 295.

8 Curzon, *Russia in Central Asia*, p. 275.
9 Curzon, *Persia and the Persian Question* (London, Longmans, Green & Co, 1892), 632–5.
10 S.A. Cohen, 'Mesopotamia in British Strategy, 1903–14', *Middle Eastern Studies*, 9, 1978, p. 177.
11 Note by Curzon on talk with Sir Arthur Nicolson, Permanent Under-Secretary for Foreign Affairs, 16 September 1913, Curzon Papers F112/251, OIOC.
12 For details of earlier Russian and British assessments of the rail line, see D.W. Spring, 'The Trans-Persian Railway Project and Anglo-Russian Relations, 1909–14', *Soviet and East European Studies*, LIV, 1, January 1976; J. Siegel, *Endgame: Britain, Russia and the Final Struggle for Central Asia* (London/New York, I B Tauris, 2002), 65–8.
13 Memorandum by Sir G. Buchanan on Sir A. Hirtzel's letter, 7 June 1913, annex 2, in Sir L. Mallet to the Members of the Inter-Departmental Committee on the Trans-Persian Railway, 13 June 1913, 27788, L/P+S/10/379.
14 Nicolson to Hardinge, 12 January 1910, 20/275 Hardinge Papers, Cambridge University Library. Hardinge wrote to Sir George Barclay, Britain's Minister in Teheran in precisely the same terms on 18 January; 21/1 ibid. See also, Nicolson to Hardinge, 9 February 1910, 20/286; 27 July 1910, 20/237 (both Hardinge Papers).
15 On this see Siegel, op. cit., 93. On the discussions about the Trans-Persian line also see K. Neilson, *Britain and the Last Tsar: British Policy and Russia, 1894–1917* (Oxford, Clarendon Press, 1995), pp. 334–6.
16 See n. 13, Mallet's letter. Debates had also occurred about the location of a break of gauge on the line, those suspicious of Russia's intentions holding that it must be as far from the Indian frontier as possible. For a more extended analysis of this point, see Siegel, op. cit., pp. 157–65.
17 Hirtzel to Crewe, 3 January 1913, C26 Crewe Papers, Cambridge University Library.
18 G.N. Curzon, *Russia in Central Asia and Persia and the Persian Question*.
19 Cited in 'Note on Persian Railways', J E F, India Office, Political Department, 3 July 1911, C124, L/P+S/10/793.
20 Minute of 28 October 1901 by Curzon, cited in 'Summary of Past History of Question and Telegrams From the Viceroy, Dated July 26 and 29, 1916, with Covering Minute by Mr Austen Chamberlain, 4 August 1916, Committee of Imperial Defence, Quetta–Seistan Railway, secret, 107-D, Cabinet Office CAB 42/17/2, TNA.
21 I am grateful to Professor Keith Wilson of the University of Leeds for drawing these discussions to my attention and for allowing me to read his draft article, 'Curzon outwith India: a note on the lost committee on Persia 1915–1916'.
22 'Second Installment of Draft Conclusions on Indian Defence by Mr Balfour, dealing chiefly with Seistan', secret, 21-D, 20 May 1903, reprinted for the Committee of Imperial Defence, August 1916, CAB 38/2/36.
23 'Memorandum By the Viceroy and the Commander-in-Chief on the Provisional Report of the Defence Committee on Indian Defence', 7 August 1903, CAB 37/65/48.
24 Ibid. Curzon and Kitchener did not preclude an extension of the line from Nushki to Robat and Bund-i-Seistan.
25 In this they agreed with the earlier, c1890, judgement of Sir H. Brackenbury, the then Director of Military Intelligence.
26 See n. 23; also 'Draft Reply to Memorandum by Lord Curzon and Lord Kitchener of August 7, 1903', A[rthur] J[ames] B[alfour], 23 November 1903.
27 As T.G. Fraser has suggested, the expeditions of German insurgents to Kabul in 1915–16 'were little more than token gestures': T.G. Fraser, 'Germany and Indian Revolution, 1914–18', *Journal of Contemporary History*, 12, 1977, pp. 259–60.
28 For an assessment of the interplay of these forces in the minds of British imperialists, see Fisher, *Curzon and British Imperialism*, passim.
29 'Summary of Past History of Question and Telegrams From the Viceroy, dated 26 & 29 July 1916', in 'Quetta–Seistan Railway', secret, CID-107-D, CAB 42/17/2. This summary may also be seen at E420/8, Barrow Papers (OIOC).

30 Ibid. Telegram from Viceroy, Army Department, 26 July 1916.

31 Ibid. Minute by Political Department, India Office, 27 July 1916.

32 See, for example, Crewe to Hardinge, 15 January 1915, C24 Crewe Papers.

33 See n.29, including Minute by General Sir Edmund Barrow, 28 July 1916, CAB 42/17/2.

34 Meeting of the War Committee, 10 August 1916, CAB 42/17/5; 'The Extension of the Quetta–Nushki Railway to Seistan', W.R. Robertson, 16 August 1916, secret, CAB 42/17/8.

35 'The Nushki–Seistan Railway: Note by the Secretary', M.P.A. Hankey, 17 August 1916, 109-D, secret, CAB 42/17/9.

36 'Nushki–Seistan Railway: Memorandum by Lord Curzon', secret, 110-D, 17 August 1916, CAB 42/17/10.

37 Meeting of the War Committee, 22 August 1916, secret, CAB 42/18/4.

38 'The Trans-Persian Railway', Note by Lord Curzon, secret, 22 August 1916, CAB 42/18/5. Curzon maintained his suspicions of Russian intentions even when her military efforts had withered: minute by Curzon, 22 June 1917, F[oreign] O[ffice] 371/2983/116.

39 'Bunder Abbas–Kerman Railway: Memorandum by Lord Curzon', 24 August 1916, C153, in L/P+S/10/417/P2917/16.

40 It was also sustained by the idea of creating a new line of supply to Russia via Central Asia; Minutes of the War Cabinet, 16 February 1917.

41 'Russo-Persian Railways', Note by Lord Curzon, 27 February 1917, CAB 24/12. An intelligence report by Major Redl at Meshed in November 1916 pointed to renewed investigations by Russian engineers on the feasibility of constructing lines to Meshed.

42 Viceroy to Secretary of State for India, 29 June 1917, 9614, L/P+S/10/595.

43 Minutes of the Mesopotamian Committee, ninth meeting, CAB 27/22. More detailed analyses of the proposed extension, encompassing political, military and commercial factors, had been undertaken. The risks connected with extending the line to Mirjawa, which was technically Persian territory, were outweighed by its advantages; 'A Memorandum Dealing With the Extension of the Quetta-Nushki Branch Railway Line to the Persian Frontier.

44 Viceroy, Foreign Department, 26 April 1918, EC 201, CAB 27/26.

45 Ibid., EC 201. It seems that two alignments were considered. The first was Mirjawar–Birjand, which was supported by the Government of India, and the second, Mirjawa–Nasratabad, which was supported by Sir H.V. Cox; minute by Shuckburgh, L/P+S/11/174/1539.

46 Note on Memorandum T21169 of 7 March 1918, circulated by the Secretary of State for Foreign Affairs, Henry Wilson, General Staff, War Office, 11 March 1918, WO 106/314.

47 Minutes of a meeting of the Eastern Committee, 3 May 1918, EC 6, CAB 27/24, secret.

48 Ibid. Minutes of 8 August 1918, EC 23.

49 Ibid.

50 This was also the message of a memorandum by Henry Wilson, CIGS, in which he argued for the maintenance of a 'wide no man's land' between the railheads of Britain and her adversaries in Asia; Henry Wilson, 24 July 1918, WO 106/315.

51 'The strategical aspect of railway construction in Persia, with special reference to the extension of the Sistan [sic] Railway', G. Macdonough [sic], 10 August 1918, WO 106/315; also at L/P+S/10/595.

52 See J. Fisher, 'The Caspian Experiment': British Policy in Trans-Caspia, 1918–20', *Journal of Central Asian Studies* (forthcoming).

53 R. Teague–Jones, *The Spy Who Disappeared: Diary of a Secret Mission to Russian Central Asia in 1918*, introduction and epilogue by P. Hopkirk (London, Victor Gollancz Ltd, 1990), 194–5. A more determined forward policy with regard to railway construction in Persia and its approaches after the war was reflected in a memorandum

by Colonel P.C. Young, 'Post-Bellum Railway Policy in Persia', 28 October 1918. Vol. 368 Milner Papers, Bodleian Library, Oxford. Young was Assistant Inspector-General of Transportation and had been in charge of the Quetta–Nushki line for a time.

54 Minutes of the Interdepartmental Conference on Middle Eastern Affairs, 11 January and 18 November 1919, Ms Eur F112/275 Curzon Papers, OIOC. The extension had also been turned down by the Indian General Staff (IGS) in December 1918 on the grounds that Britain had never intended to fight the Bolsheviks in Turkestan. The IGS also objected on more traditional grounds to the principle of bridging the gap between the British system and that of Bolshevik Russia.

55 See J. Fisher, ' "On the Glacis of India": Lord Curzon and British Policy in the Caucasus, 1919', *Diplomacy and Statecraft*, 8, 2, 1997, pp. 50–82.

56 Supporters of the line had continued to argue its commercial importance. Among these was Colonel Webb Ware, Political Officer in Chagai from 1896–1915, who argued for the connection by railway of Karachi with the Quetta–Nushki line; see his 'The Nushki Railway and Some of the Problems on Which it Bears', *Journal of the Central Asian Society*, 6, 1, 1919.

57 A further influence on strategic railway construction was the growing significance of oil; Frank Grove, 'A Railway Engineer's Journey's In Persia', *Journal of the Central Asian Society*, 2, 1922, p. 77.

58 Minute by Shuckburgh, 10 November 1917, Ms Eur F112/271, Curzon Papers, OIOC.

59 Note by Sir E. Barrow, 29 May 1922, L/P+S/10/784.

60 Curzon to Peel, Foreign Office, 15 July 1922, FO 800/156, Curzon Papers.

61 CO 732/21/2, TNA.

62 See, for example, minutes of the seventh meeting of the Interdepartmental Committee on Eastern Unrest, 14 January 1927, L/P+J/12/154, OIOC.

63 Among those who attached significance to the strategic railway were H.J. Mackinder and L.S. Amery. See Mackinder's 'The Geographical Pivot of History', *The Geographical Journal*, 4, 23, April 1904, pp. 434, 436–8, 441. Amery had also recognized the links between developing strategic railways and civil and military aviation; Amery to Curzon, 7 February 1917, Ms Eur F112/118a, Curzon Papers, OIOC.

64 See, for example, A.C. Yate in *The Times* of 25 May 1912, in which he envisaged the Trans-Persian line linking up with a further line to the east coast of China.

65 Writing to Sir Edward Grey in November 1911, Lord Ronaldshay had recorded his doubts about the Trans-Persian line. In his view it would be preferable for Russia to have Constantinople than access to the Persian Gulf; something which would place her on the flank of British communications with India, Australia and the Far East. In Ronaldshay's view, the Mediterranean could at least be 'sealed up' and South Africa replace Egypt as the 'strategical pivot of the Empire'; Ronaldshay to Grey *in* Tyrrell to Brown, 4 December 1911, I/2, Crewe Papers.

66 128 HC Deb, 27 April 1920.

67 125 HC Deb, 18 & 23 February 1920.

68 CAB 16/93, 5th meeting of the Persian Gulf Sub-Committee; 'An Appreciation of the Strategical Situation in the Persian Gulf' by the IGS, PG 20, A. Skeen, Lt General, CGS, Simla, 5 October 1928, CAB 16/94. On the broader issue of British strategic assessments in the region, see K. Neilson, ' "Pursued by a bear": British Estimates of Soviet Military Strength and Anglo-Soviet Relations, 1922–1939', *Canadian Journal of History*, 28, August 1993, 189–221.

69 In 1912 George Lloyd, later Lord Lloyd of Dolobran, who had considerable knowledge of international commercial interests in the Middle East, was equivocal about the commercial benefits to Britain of the Trans-Persian line, as well as sharing the strategic concerns of Hirtzel and others. Lloyd was asked to join the international consortium, the Société d'Études, which was to finance the line. On the commercial benefits to Britain and Russia, also see Siegel, op. cit., pp. 67–8, 84–7.

70 Curzon, *Persia and the Persian Question*, p. 614.

8   The Baghdad to Haifa railway

The culmination of railway planning for Imperial defence east of Suez

Keith Neilson

The Baghdad to Haifa railway was never built. First proposed in 1927, it remained on the drawing board when the Second World War began. However, this does not mean that its study is unrewarding. In fact, the Baghdad to Haifa line was the culmination of a long effort to defend the British Empire by means of railways. As such it provides a useful terminal point for the study of the impact of railways on British Imperial defence east of Suez.

Study of this topic is important. For the most part, historians have focused on the naval aspects of Imperial defence, rightly viewing the British Empire as a maritime polity in contrast to the land-based empires of such countries as Russia. In this context, at a theoretical level, studies have concentrated on the works of the historian and strategist Julian Corbett.[1] At a practical level, works on Imperial defence have looked at such things as how the Royal Navy dominated what Admiral Sir John Fisher termed the 'five keys [that] lock up the world' and the Suez Canal as the 'jugular vein of Empire'.[2]

However, late in the nineteenth century it became apparent that railways, as much as the Royal Navy, were an essential element in the maintenance of the security of the British Empire. This was particularly true with respect to the defence of India. The Russian building of the Trans-Siberian Railway (begun 1891), with a spur line reaching from Orenberg to Tashkent (scheduled to be completed in early 1905), meant that Tsarist troops would have easier (and quicker) access to the North West Frontier of India than ever before. The implications of this were manifest during the early phase of the Boer War, when it was feared that Russia would take advantage of the circumstances to threaten Persia and, hence, India. George Curzon, the Viceroy of India, was adamant that any Russian depredations against Persia should be resisted. However, Lord George Hamilton, the British Secretary of State for India, pointed out the difficulties that the new Russian railway construction had created for Britain. He informed Curzon in November 1899 that 'I have felt for a very long time past that we must, so far as Russia is concerned, acknowledge the changed conditions that the extension of railways has made in the relative fighting power of Great Britain and Russia'.[3] Sir Arthur Godley, the Permanent Under-secretary at the India Office, underlined his minister's point. 'It is also, I think, fairly plain', he informed Curzon, 'that a good many territories, such as India & China, which have hitherto been quasi-islands – being accessible by sea and difficult of access by land – are ceasing or will soon cease (whether we like it or not) to answer to this description, and that this must seriously modify our position & policy'.[4] Hamilton made this point even more plain some months later, when he argued against those who advocated a further expansion of India's frontiers:

> Mahan's writings, excellent as they are, I think, have put too much wind into the head of a good many of this school. He has, in my judgment, grossly exaggerated the influence and effective force of sea-power.[5]

The building of railways into Central Asia by Russia, Hamilton concluded, had led to a decrease in the importance of seapower and an increase in the threat of an invasion of Persia.

From this point onward, the defence of the British Empire east of Suez was inextricably linked to strategic railways. This was particularly evident in considerations of the defence of India. In 1903, the newly created Committee of Imperial Defence (CID) began a ten-month long examination of the topic.[6] Railways were an integral factor in the study. On 19 March, the CID discussed whether Afghanistan should be maintained as a buffer state between Britain and Russia and 'the advantages and disadvantages of extending the railway system into Afghanistan and Persia with a view to better counteract a Russian advance'.[7] This meeting 'came to no conclusion', but all were 'greatly impressed' with how much 'territory which, in certain contingencies, we may have to protect'.[8] This led, a week later, to a discussion of 'the scheme for railway extension from India through Beluchistan to Seistan with a view to counteract a Russian advance from the north'.[9] The key issue was the Perso-Russian Convention of 1900, by the terms of which Persia 'bound herself not to construct any railways or to allow any to be constructed by a foreign Company'.[10] As long as this Convention was observed, the British felt that the railway extension under construction from Quetta, on India's northern frontier with Afghanistan, westward to Nushki, would be sufficient to deal with any Russian advance against Persia. A Russian attack on Afghanistan provided another variant. Due to geographical factors, there were two possible invasion routes: in eastern Afghanistan through the mountain passes to Kabul and, in western Afghanistan, to Herat and hence to Kandahar.[11] The first of these routes depended on the Russian Orenberg to Tashkent line, with an extension from the latter to Termez on the Russo-Afghan border. The second threat originated with the Russian Trans-Caspian line. It began at Krasnovodsk (on the Caspian Sea), went inland to Ashkabad and then, via the Central Asian Railway, ran to Kushk, some 76 miles from Herat.

The possible British countermeasures to a Russian advance were twofold. In order to defend eastern Afghanistan, there was a need to move troops to the Indian border at the Khyber pass and from there to either Jalalabad or Kabul. As the Indian railway ended at Peshawar, Arthur Balfour, the prime minister and a leading light in Imperial Defence, asked the CID on 7 May to consider whether it would be necessary to build a railway line from Peshawar to the frontier.[12]

Defending western Afghanistan was another matter, since it was 'universally admitted' by British military authorities that nothing could be done to prevent the Russians from taking Herat.[13] In fact, as Hamilton pessimistically informed Curzon: 'The best defence that we can give to Herat is to make known to Russia that a movement of this kind entails war in all parts of the world with Great Britain'. However, with regard to any attempt by Russia to expand further after a seizure of Herat, it was believed that the British railway line reaching to Quetta would provide a logistic advantage over any Russian attempt to invade western Afghanistan via Kushk and Herat.

However, this was not the only menace to the region. Balfour raised the concern that, despite the Perso-Russian Convention, Russia would outflank Quetta by moving into eastern Persia. This would occur as much by infiltration as by military force. 'The Russians may peaceably and silently', Balfour wrote, 'Russsianise those portions of Persian territory which lie adjacent to the western frontier of Afghanistan, the Persian Government being a consenting party, and Persian sovereignty remaining nominally untouched'.[14] This having been done, the Russians could then build a railway from Ashkabad into Seistan, allowing them to utilize the latter territory as a springboard for an advance on Kandahar.

Balfour observed that, in order to counter this, Britain had to ensure 'that British influences [in Persia] shall filter in from the East faster than Russian influences filter in from the North. Each Russian move must be watched, and everything done to encourage the idea that we have interests in Seistan as predominant as those which Russia possess in Northern Persia'. How would Britain do this? This involved railway building: Britain could put pressure on both the Afghan and Persian governments to allow the Quetta–Nushki line to be extended through Afghanistan into Seistan and thus pre-empt any Russian move. However, this might lead, Balfour warned, to a railway war in Persia, in which Russia would release Persia from the Convention and build a competing line from Ashkabad to Meshed and southward into Seistan, raising the unpleasant possibility of 'through railway communication between St Petersburgh and Calcutta'. On the basis of this analysis, Balfour plumped for a political agreement with Russia to ban any railway building in eastern Persia.

Although Curzon termed any agreement with Russia 'one of those sentimental hallucinations that it is impossible to remove from the British mind', a political agreement with Russia was particularly important because it had become apparent that the Royal Navy could not guarantee a rapid transport of reinforcements to India.[15] The clash between naval power and railway power was evident. The nature of the Russian threat was particular and peculiar. Hamilton pointed out that, while any threat to Empire posed by France and Germany could be countered because they were 'both vulnerable to naval attack, both have Colonies, and both have a very large commerce', Russia was 'practically impenetrable to attack'.[16] Russia's 'want of communication', he continued,

> which, in the days of the Crimea War, rendered her external extremities liable to attack, is now passing away, and railroads are giving to her internally the

same advantages which we in the past, from our naval superiority, have had over the sea. It is for these reasons I should like, if possible, to come to some arrangement with Russia.

While there were arguments about the number of men that Russia's railways could support in any attempted invasion, the key point was that the defence of India was inextricably linked with Britain's comparative ability to move troops on railways to the frontier.[17] Lord Roberts, the Chief of the General Staff and a veteran of the Afghan frontier, wrote in May that the defence of India depended on 'two points': 'to keep Russia where she is, as long as possible, and to endeavour by every means in our power to extend our railway system, so that, when the time comes we may be able to meet the Russians with a sufficiently large army'.[18]

And, the size of the 'sufficiently large army' (with what that implied for railway transport) continued to grow. While the outbreak of the Russo-Japanese War in February 1904 meant that a Russian descent was not imminent (although some feared that Russia would attempt to recoup any setbacks against Japan with a strike against India), that did not mean that calculations about Indian defence ceased.[19] The CID met throughout March to discuss matters.[20] It was agreed that Russia could be stopped only by military force, and the number of reinforcements believed required to provide this force grew as the year progressed, from 135,614 in July to 143,687 in November to 211,824 by February 1905.[21] In March of the latter year, the CID reiterated that it was important to 'maintain, and if possible to increase, our influence at Teheran in order that we may be able to control railway construction in Persia' and confirmed that the 'extension of the railways to the frontier' of Afghanistan remained of 'great importance'.[22] However, as a result of Russia's on-going defeats in the Russo-Japanese War, no further decisions were taken in 1905, and only sporadic attention was paid to the details of the extension of India railways to the Afghan frontier.[23]

The Russian threat to Afghanistan was not the only concern of those who dealt with the implications of railway building for the defence of Britain's imperial interests in India and the Middle East. A similar threat was posed by the proposed construction of a railway to Baghdad and hence to the Persian Gulf. Such a railway first had been proposed in 1902 by a German consortium. The following year, the British had been asked to join in the project, but, for a variety of reasons, had decided not to do so.[24] The matter had not died there. In April 1905, the CID considered how a Baghdad railway would affect the defence of India.[25] In the opinion of the General Staff, such a line 'would not, as far as can be foreseen, exercise any detrimental effect, from a military point of view, either on our relations with Persia or on the defence of India'. However, this sanguine view was dependent on Britain's obtaining 'a share equal to that of any other Power in respect of [the] construction and management' of the line, 'more especially of that portion ... extending from Baghdad to the Persian Gulf, with a preponderating influence as regards the control of the terminus'. If these criteria were not met, then 'we should expect to see a diminution in those political rights and commercial interests' that Britain enjoyed in the region. Further, German control of the line from Baghdad to the Gulf would likely result in the port there being converted into a naval base, and it, 'combined with the use of the railway leading to it, would furnish Germany with more rapid means of communication' with her Pacific and East African colonies. Worse, this situation 'would also place her on the flank of our communications via Suez with India, and if in a war between England and Russia she were found, directly or indirectly, on the side of Russia our difficulty of reinforcing the Indian garrison, which is already a serious one, would be rendered still greater'. These views were reinforced by a study that Balfour had prepared.[26] As a result, the CID concluded that 'it was against our interests that the construction and control of the line should be entirely in German hands'.[27]

The importance of railway lines, and their relation to naval means of transport, was underlined by other matters. As a result of the provisions of the Suez Canal Convention of 1888, 'which have become effective in consequence' of the Anglo-French *Entente Cordiale* of 1904, the Canal and its approaches had become neutral waters.[28] This was to Britain's advantage if she were at war, as the Canal was an important line of communication to the Empire. However, the British needed to prevent others from utilizing Suez. This could be done most easily by improving the harbour at Alexandria such that it would accommodate deep-draft ships and thus allow the Royal Navy to be stationed there, to patrol the Mediterranean entrance to the Suez Canal and prevent its use by other belligerents. However, should the Germans have control over a Baghdad railway and a naval port on the Gulf, this would lessen the effectiveness of such a strategy.

The issue of the Baghdad railway was not taken up again until July 1906, when the new Liberal government took the matter under consideration.[29] Nothing had changed with regard to the strategical situation. However, as the new government was intent on negotiating what became the Anglo-Russian Convention, it was necessary to move carefully. The new Foreign Secretary, Sir Edward Grey, wanted to ensure that Britain moved in conjunction with France during discussions. Lord Cromer, the British Agent and Consul-General in Egypt, pointed out the need to 'avoid any suspicion of unfriendliness towards Russia', and suggested that the portion of any railway line running from Baghdad to the Gulf should be built under Anglo-Russian auspices. However, the means of effecting this were not apparent. As a result, the CID's conclusions echoed the earlier ones – 'it is most undesirable, from the military and commercial point of view, that the Baghdad Railway should be completed and controlled by a foreign Power or Powers' – but provided no blueprint as to how this should be prevented.

As a result, Grey established a body – the Baghdad Railway Committee – composed of leading members of the Foreign Office to consider the matter.[30] After a dozen meetings, in which leading experts were interviewed, the Committee issued a bleak report in March 1907. Even without British participation the likelihood of the line's being completed were 'considerable'. The result of this was entirely negative. 'From a political point of view, the possibility of the shortest route to India being exclusively under the auspices of Germany gives rise to serious anxiety'. In addition, the line was thought likely to be extended towards Persia, further weakening the British Imperial position. In the Committee's opinion, 'the completion of the Bagdad Railway to the Persian Gulf without British cooperation would inflict grave and irreparable injury upon British interests, both Imperial and Indian, in the Middle East'. How was this to be prevented? The Committee suggested that the British government 'take over, at their own cost and risk, the Mosul or Bagdad-Gulf sections of the railway'. While the Germans would likely oppose such a move, the Committee believed that eventually they would agree to the proposal. This was due to the fact that British participation would ensure a number of things: no British obstruction of the building of a terminus on the Gulf, cooperation from the Constantinople Quays Company (who controlled the vital docks in that city) and, 'above all', a financial certainty that would 'considerably accelerate the construction of the line' to the advantage of the German investors. As to Russia and France, the Committee believed that the former would be satisfied with being able to connect its own lines in northern Persia to Baghdad while the former would gain significant financial advantage for its railway interests in Turkey.

The matter rested there until 1908. In March, Herbert Asquith (soon to be Prime Minister) appointed a sub-committee of the CID and charged it 'to consider the effect that the completion of the Baghdad Railway may have on the situation – strategic, political, and commercial – in Southern Persia and the Persian Gulf'.[31] The sub-committee's findings echoed previous concerns. Britain's political position in the Gulf was dependent on its preponderant commercial position there. A railway from Baghdad to the Gulf under German control would diminish both. To counteract German advances, the Foreign Office returned to a previous theme: suggesting to the Russians that they connect their Persian line to Baghdad and from there – on a British line – to the Gulf.[32] But, despite Russian acceptance of this proposal, this scheme proceeded slowly, due to the fear of the Indian Government that such a connection would provide Russia with a means of circumventing the Afghan buffer state.

The Baghdad railway proposal also became bogged down in power politics. The Bosnian crisis delayed any further discussion of it until mid-1909.[33] At that time, the British reiterated their offer to the Russians, but the Germans offered London an alternative. In exchange for Britain's dropping all objections to the financing of the Baghdad railway, the Germans would permit Britain to have a half share in the line from Baghdad to the Gulf. However, this offer was also made contingent on a wider Anglo-German understanding, by which both countries would agree to remain neutral in any war with a third party. The political ramifications were obvious. The Baghdad railway was to be used as a lever to pry apart the Triple Entente. This raised the ire of St Petersburgh, as the Russians feared that Britain would sell out St Petersburg's interests in order to secure the line.[34]

They need not have worried. In December 1909, the British and Russians renewed talks. The Russians, once their *amour propre* was assuaged, did not prove unnecessarily stiff. In fact, British and Russian interests neatly dovetailed. The Russians, for commercial and financial reasons, did not wish to open up northern Persia to foreign (especially German) trade; the British, due to the strategic objections of the Government of India, merely wanted to 'earmark' lines in Persia that would likely not be built due to a Russian lack of funds.[35] Sir Charles Hardinge, the Permanent Under-secretary at the Foreign Office, put the situation clearly. As it was 'quite inevitable' that a Trans-Persian line would be built in the future, it would be best if it were an Anglo-Russian line. 'I have no fear', he informed the British Ambassador to Russia, Sir Arthur Nicolson, 'as to any military danger' to India. His opinion, however, did not move the Indian military authorities, who remained 'strongly opposed' to the project, much to the chagrin of Nicolson and Hardinge, who felt that such objections served only to increase Russian suspicions of Britain's good will, to the detriment of close Anglo-Russian relations.[36] As Nicolson put it, Germany's continued efforts to split Russia from Britain meant that in 'both Mid and Far East we should do our best to further the interests of Russia so far as they do not clash with our own.... If we continue to work the Convention as we have hitherto done, and are conciliatory as to the questions, railway and other, in Persia in which Russia is interested, all should go well'.[37]

These hopes were dashed. The Russians decided to pursue a policy of rapprochement with Germany.[38] Part of this change involved coming to terms about Persian railways.[39] At a meeting held in Potsdam in November 1910, the two sides agreed to cooperate with respect to the Persian lines: Russia dropped her opposition to the Baghdad railway and agreed to join her own Persian lines to it. British opposition to this was mostly on the political level, where it was feared that Potsdam foreshadowed a return to the Bismarckian system of close Russo-German ties. As to the defence of India, Hardinge, now Viceroy, remained confident that the arrangements made at Potsdam could be overcome:

> Personally I feel that we cannot make India an island like Great Britain, and that it would be very bad were we to succeed in doing so. The military side of the question could, I think, be safeguarded by branch lines from the Persian Gulf by which any force advancing along the line towards India could be taken in flank or rear.[40]

The matter rested here until the outbreak of the First World War, despite the efforts of some, like Curzon, to raise the spectre of a Russian threat to India via Persia.[41]

However, when hostilities began in 1914, the question of strategic railways and the defence of Empire came to the fore once again. This was a result of both events and alliance politics. In order to keep Russian eyes firmly focussed on Germany, the British formally promised Constantinople to St Petersburgh in any post-war settlement.[42] This required Britain to establish her own desiderata in the Ottoman Empire. To do so, a committee under the former British Ambassador to Vienna, Sir Maurice de Bunsen, was created in April 1915.[43] Already, the strategic issues surrounding the partitioning of the Ottoman Empire had come to the fore. Lord Kitchener, the Secretary of State for War and former commander-in-chief of the Indian Army, had argued that possession of Alexandretta was essential to British security.[44] Strategic railways bulked large. For Kitchener, Alexandretta could serve as a terminus for the Baghdad railway, allowing the British position on the Gulf to be linked with the Mediterranean. The Admiralty concurred. Harkening back to an argument that they had made in 1905, Their Lordships contended that possession of Alexandretta was essential to protect the Suez Canal from either France or Russia and to provide a conduit for Mesopotamian oil needed by the Royal Navy.[45]

At the de Bunsen Committee's meetings, these points were threshed out. As to how much of the Ottoman Empire Britain need acquire, opinions varied. Both the Indian government and the India Office were chary of extending British influence much beyond Basra and Baghdad.[46] Hardinge was insistent that the Baghdad railway, still not completed, must not be built, unless by the British, in order to ensure both the security and commercial prosperity of Basra. Arthur Hirtzel, the Secretary of the Political and Secret Department at the India Office, felt that any 'through line from Alexandretta via Aleppo and Mosul to Bagdad and Basra seems unnecessary and strategically undesirable'. He preferred, instead, shorter, unconnected lines: '*either* the Alexandretta–Mosul section... or the Mosul–Bagdad section', one of which seemed 'inevitable', with a line from Baghdad to Basra as a 'matter of urgent necessity in the early future'. These lines would increase the economic growth of the country, while dealing with concerns about defence. The War Office, however, was opposed to limiting the British sphere so tightly. In order to defend the territory against any future Russian depredations, a 'strategical frontier would be necessary', encompassing a region stretching from the Gulf to 'the range of hills to the north of the Mosul vilayet'.[47]

As Sir Charles Callwell, the Director of Military Operations pointed out, this latter would require Britain's possessing a base on the Mediterranean. This resulted from the fact that, in a war with Russia, 'it might be quite impossible to send reinforcements from India, as the whole of the Indian Empire might be fully occupied in another theatre of war'. Thus, reinforcements might have to come from Britain, and this required a railway port on the Mediterranean. There were concerns, political and strategic, about making Alexandretta this terminus. Politically, it was felt that the French would object to Britain's obtaining the port, as it was felt to be part of the natural French zone.[48] Militarily, the long line stretching from Alexandretta to Mosul would parallel the frontier with Russia, making the line insecure. Callwell preferred, as an alternative, making Haifa the Mediterranean end of the railway. For him, the 'only objection' to utilizing this port was that 'it would be necessary to build a strategic railway [from Haifa] to the Euphrates from which little return could be expected, and it would be commercially unprofitable'. The Admiralty's representative on the Committee, Admiral Sir H.B. Jackson, grudgingly accepted this line of argument, contending that, while Haifa was not a suitable naval base, it could serve as a port to off load troops and supplies. At the third meeting of the Committee, the Admiralty underlined its desire to ensure that the oil fields at Mosul were included in the British sphere, and agreed that Haifa could serve as well as Alexandretta as a Mediterranean terminus for a pipe line.[49]

The deliberations of the de Bunsen Committee were not the only time that strategic railways and Imperial defence were discussed during the war. Another resulted from the extension of the war by the Turks into Persia late in 1914.[50] This attack was unsuccessful, but was renewed in 1916. This raised all the pre-1914 fears for the defence of India, as it was felt that Turkish troops (likely reinforced by German units) would threaten Afghanistan and hence the Empire.[51] The railway situation had changed since 1910. At the latter time, the Anglo-Russian negotiations for a Trans-Persian line had reached an impasse. The Russians had proposed a line travelling from Baku to Julfa and hence through Tabriz to Teheran. From the latter, the line would proceed to Kerman and then eastward into Seistan to join a British line extending west of Nushki. London accepted the first part of this, but the Indian government rejected the idea of building a line west from Nushki, and preferred, instead, that the trans-Persian line from Kerman should travel south to Bunder Abbas on the Gulf and hence along the coast to Chahbar.

By mid-1916, the circumstances were different. On the outbreak of war, the Russians had linked Julfa with Tabriz. In the spring of 1916, St Petersburgh announced that it would seek a concessions from the Persians: first, to link Baku to Teheran and, second, to link the Trans-Caspian line with Meshed. This made the issue of whether to extend the Quetta–Nushki line towards Seistan more pressing. There were two reasons to construct the line: first, it would support the British troops operating in eastern Persia; second, it would establish a transportation system that would ensure the defences of Afghanistan against all comers in the future. But, this line of argument was rejected by the Chief of the Imperial General Staff (CIGS), Sir William Robertson.[52] For him, the German–Turkish threat was best met by improving the railway line from Bunder Abbas to Kerman, a move that would buttress the lines of communication for British forces in East Persia. This would also avoid all of the problems inherent in establishing a line into Seistan that could join up with the Russian Trans-Persian route in the future.[53] Curzon did not agree.[54] For the former Viceroy, the building of the railway was an imperative for Imperial defence. He did not think that the extension would be the precursor to a link to the Russian Trans-Persian line (thus negating Robertson's criticism) and would provide a valuable strategic tool at the present time for the British forces operating in eastern Persia. This argument was accepted, and, beginning in August 1916, the line westward from Nushki to Dalbandin was begun.[55] When the Russian revolution in March 1917 led to the collapse of the Russian forces operating in Persia, the line was extended further westward to Mirjawa.

The matter did not end there. In the dark days of 1918, when the German offensive in the West threatened Britain with defeat on the Continent and the treaty of Brest–Litovsk brought the Germans to the shore of the Black Sea (and hence provided new railway routes to Persia), a greater extension was begun.[56] This resulted in a decision, on 20 August, to attempt to solidify the 'ring fence' around Afghanistan by extending the existing line from Mirjawa some 90 miles towards Meshed.[57] This line was still under construction when the war came to its unexpected end in November. In December, the entire issue of railroads and the defence of India was reconsidered.[58] At that point, it was decided to stop work on the extension. As to general policy, there was a reversion to the point of view long held by the Government of India. In order to protect India, no attempt should be made to connect the Russian Trans-Persian line with the British Seistan line. And, if it were decided to link the two systems, the route to be adopted should be that going to Bunder Abbas, where British seapower could control the line.

Political changes in the region after 1918 changed the circumstances in which decisions about Indian defence and railway building were made. Anglo-Afghan and Anglo-Persian relations were rocky, and included a brief conflict between the Britain and Afghanistan in 1919.[59] By 1924, however, the situation had stabilized, with the British pursuing a policy of non-interference in Persia. In 1925, however, the threat of a Russian advance against Afghanistan once again brought the issue of the defence of India to the fore. At a meeting of the Chiefs of Staff Committee on 6 July 1926, General Sir Claud Jacob, the Secretary of the Military Department of the India Office, noted that a lack of strategic railways on the North-West frontier severely limited the British response to any Soviet incursion.[60] The entire issue became one for the CID. At a meeting on 25 November, that body decided to investigate the matter in conjunction with the Government of India.[61] When the views of the Indian government were received, railway construction was again at the centre.

The Indian General Staff (IGS) argued, as it had before 1914, that Afghanistan could not be defended in its entirety.[62] But, in sharp contradistinction to their earlier position, the IGS was opposed to the construction of new lines into Afghanistan, lest this result in Soviet Russia's doing likewise. In the opinion of the IGS, 'any railway move, Russian or Indian, risks the commencement of a railway race which must eventually bring Russia and India face to face whether in Afghanistan or on our Indian frontier'. Thus, the entire issue was best left alone. This view was 'in marked disagreement' with the opinions of the CIGS, General G.F. Milne.[63] In his views, the logistical difficulties mentioned by the IGS 'are the best arguments I can advance for adopting in peace time a policy of railway construction which will, if war be forced upon us, minimise these difficulties'. 'The adoption of a policy of railway construction in peace time', the CIGS concluded, 'is essential if we are to be prepared to take effective action again the Russians if and when they extend their existing territories into Afghanistan'.

The entire issue of the nature and seriousness of the Soviet threat to India could not be resolved. As a result, on 17 March 1927, a sub-committee of the CID under Lord Birkenhead, the Secretary of State for India, was created to discuss the issue.[64] The Birkenhead Committee held thirteen meetings, beginning in March and ending in November 1927.[65] The Committee concluded that protecting Afghanistan against any Soviet advance was still a necessity for the defence of India. As to railways, the difference of opinion noted above between the IGS and the British War Office remained. The decisive point in the discussion was the evidence given by Sir Francis Humphrys, the British Minister at Kabul.

Humphrys noted that the Afghan government, in the person of King Amanulla, was determined to introduce railroads into Afghanistan in order to modernize the country (a complete reversal of the pre-1914 attitude of Afghan rulers). While the

King preferred to begin with the routes originating in the south – Chaman (near Quetta) to Kandahar and Kandahar to Kabul – if the British attempted to 'deflect him from his purpose', Amanulla would begin with the northern routes – from Kushk (on the Russo-Afghan border) to Herat and Herat to Kandahar. Humphrys' conclusion gave support to the War Office's contention that Britain must initiate railway building. 'Railways in Afghanistan', he noted, 'are bound to come sooner or later, especially on the Kandahar side, and the Power which initiates them in response to the Afghan Government's request will be presented with a tactical advantage of the first importance'.

The Birkenhead Committee's recommendations, approved by the CID on 26 January 1928, reflected both the strategical and political points that had been raised.[66] It was agreed that 'we may regard railway extension in Afghanistan, provided that it takes the right form, at least with equanimity, if not with satisfaction'. Humphrys should not raise the matter of railway construction, but, if Amanulla were to do so, Humphrys should 'receive the proposal sympathetically'. He should also attempt to persuade the King that the first line to be built should be that from Landi Khana (near the Khyber Pass) to Kabul (this was the least disagreeable alternative for the IGS), while the second should be the Chaman to Kandahar passage. In addition, the Chiefs of Staff were tasked to find some means of attacking Soviet Russia.

Concerns about Indian defence did not end at the Afghan border. There still remained Persia. In order to deal with this, another sub-committee of the CID – the Persian Gulf Sub-Committee – was established on 25 June 1928.[67] This body held five plenary sessions before issuing an interim report in October. The point was quickly made that the defence of Afghanistan necessarily entailed protecting Persia, and that the latter was equally important to safeguard the British position in Iraq.[68] However, the issue of strategic railways, long at the centre of debate about Imperial defence and Persia, had nearly vanished. With the demise of the Russian Trans-Persian line, British concerns instead focussed on control of the Gulf and the establishment of air bases in the region, the latter because the Persian Gulf now formed what the Secretary of State for the Dominions, Leo Amery, termed 'an air Suez Canal'.[69] In fact, the defence of Persia was to be the province of the Royal Air Force.[70] The only point made about railways concerned the line from Nushti to Duzdab (modern Zahedan) built during the First World War to support the British troops operating in eastern Persia. Here, the Persian government was to be warned that the line would likely be dismantled.

With Persia safe from Russian attacks via rail, what about Britain's newly acquired mandatory territory in Iraq? Some of the debate at the de Bunsen Committee about possible railroad routes from Baghdad to the Mediterranean had been settled by the agreements worked out between Britain and France. The partition of Asiatic Turkey had left Alexandretta in the French sphere.[71] This made Haifa the preferred alternative terminus for any Baghdad–Mediterranean railway. The issue of building such a line was raised at the CID on 1 November 1927.[72] The driving force behind building the line was primarily economic.[73] Such a route would ensure that the products of the Anglo-Persian Oil Company's new fields in

Iraq would be able to reach the Mediterranean without passing through the Suez Canal, thus saving on the costs of the Canal fees. In addition, it would ensure that the proposed railway line in Persia from the Caspian to the Gulf would not divert trade away from Baghdad.

However, the line was still also a significant matter for Imperial defence. The War Office felt that the line had 'much to recommend it'.[74] As the Haifa to Baghdad railway would connect with the Baghdad to Basra line, it would provide a route to India 'alternative or additional to the Suez Canal. It would also considerably reduce the time taken to send reinforcements from Europe to Baghdad'. These advantages 'might assume considerable importance' for the defence of Persia, Afghanistan and India, as any conflict in these areas would require rapid reinforcement. The only caveat issued by the War Office was that it was important that the western portion of the line should be exclusively within the British territories of Palestine and Trans-Jordan: the 'further south the actual line can be located, the safer will it be from organise attack from the direction of Syria'.

In February 1928, the issue of the Baghdad–Haifa railway came before the Cabinet in order to determine whether government support should be given to the project.[75] The Prime Minister, Stanley Baldwin, appointed a Cabinet Committee to investigate the matter, and this Committee in turn referred the matter to a sub-committee of the CID.[76] The latter body asked the Chiefs of Staff for a further study, which was issued in May 1928.[77] The Chiefs considered the building of both the railway and an oil pipeline to Haifa. The construction of the latter increased the significance of the entire project. This resulted from the fact that the pipeline would ensure that the British 'Fleet will possess a source of oil supply upon which reliance can be placed in the future when the only other large British oil supply (in Persian territory) may, on account of political developments, become uncertain'. Further, if oil were available at Haifa, then in a war 'in the Home theatre' this supply 'would be 1,000 miles nearer than any other British source of supply'. This advantage would be multiplied in a conflict in the Mediterranean. Finally, should a war occur in the Far East, 'it would be on the direct line of communications ... with a resultant saving in tanker tonnage'. However, the sub-committee recommended that, despite the favourable strategic implications of the project, no 'action is necessary, or indeed desirable, at the moment'. This was due to the 'uncertainty' surrounding the economic prospects of the line. However, should the oil companies decide to take action then the British government should push for the Baghdad–Haifa line as against any alternative route (such as one leading from Baghdad to Alexandretta or Beirut).

The question of the significance of oil and the Baghdad–Haifa route was raised again in 1929. In its Third Annual Report, the Oil Board (a standing sub-committee of the CID), laid stress on the significance of a pipe line from Baghdad to the Mediterranean.[78] The points raised were similar to those put forward by the Chiefs of Staff. First, a Baghdad–Haifa pipe line would ensure the availability of at least 10 per cent of the total estimated Imperial needs for a war in 1937. Second, this oil would be under British control, and this 'would be of immense importance in time of war in the event of either (i) the United States of America being unfriendly, or (ii) the maximum output from the South Persian Fields being unobtainable for any reason'. Finally, should oil demand result in a further pipeline being built from the South Persian Fields to the Baghdad–Haifa line, then this would save 'a 6,400 miles' journey by sea and the Suez Canal charges'. It would also reduce the duration of the round-trip for oil tankers by some 16 days, effectively increasing the tonnage available to ship oil in time of war. Many of these advantages would also accrue if the pipeline from Baghdad went to a Syrian port. However, this latter would mean that the 'protection of a pipeline vital to the Empire would be in the hands of a Foreign Power'. The conclusion of the Oil Board was firm: 'it will be of first importance to the Empire in a maritime war that the oil pipeline from Iraq should have a terminal at Haifa'.

When this report was considered by the CID, it generated considerable discussion.[79] Sir Warren Fisher, the Permanent Secretary at the Treasury, opposed any expenditure on the line. He contended that the 'hypotheses on which the Sub-Committee had worked were distinctly alarmist'. Always concerned that the Admiralty were using the Japanese threat as a lever to extract more money from the Treasury, he argued that extra oil would be available from either the United States or the Dutch East Indies in time of war. The Secretary of State for Foreign Affairs, Austen Chamberlain, supported Fisher. Chamberlain observed that a 'war with Japan was so unlikely in present circumstances that this country need not in practice take any immediate measures of defence against such a contingency'. However, this did not mean that the Baghdad–Haifa project was dead. Instead, the CID called for the interested departments to obtain more information about projected oil needs.

Much of this was resolved over the next four years. In 1931, the Oil Board again recommended the building of a pipe line, but this time without the additional cost of a railway; its being assumed that the pipe line would be protected by air patrols.[80] This decision was confirmed in 1933. At that time, both the Air Ministry and the War Office reiterated their belief that the railway remained of great importance, the War Office for the reasons adduced in 1928, the Air Ministry because the construction and maintenance of the new air base near Fallujah would be facilitated by the line.[81] When these views were considered by the CID, the matter was deferred until it could be discussed with Sir Francis Humphrys, the British Ambassador in Iraq.[82] This discussion led to nothing. After 1933, the Baghdad–Haifa railway became a dead letter issue. The Far Eastern oil needs of British Imperial defence were solved by the construction of an oil pipe line to be defended from the air, not by troops shipped on railroads. The defence of India, the other justification for the Baghdad to Haifa railway, became only the third (and least) priority for Britain as a result of the deliberations of the Defence Requirements Sub-Committee, established in the autumn of 1933.[83]

However, study of the Baghdad–Haifa railway and its antecedents reveals a good deal about the impact of changing technologies on British Imperial defence. Before the end of the nineteenth century, British India was largely isolated from European influences, except by sea – a 'quasi-island' to use Godley's felicitous phrase. As long as the Royal Navy remained supreme, Britain could defend India by sending troops to the sub-continent by sea, secure in the knowledge that this method of transport would provide a decisive logistical advantage over any European opponent. However, the building of the Trans-Siberian railway changed matters. Now, the logistical balance swung towards Russia. Britain's only counter was to link her maritime lines of communication to strategic railways stretching to the Afghan frontier.

However, Britain's threat from Russia was not confined to the North-West frontier and Afghanistan. Russian railways threatened British India's security not only through Afghanistan but also through Persia. This meant that there was an on-going possibility that Britain's strategic railways in India would be outflanked to the west. The costs of combatting this were enormous, and the British hoped to eliminate the need for strategic railways in Persia by a political agreement with Russia. If this could not be obtained, the desire was to deflect Russian lines in Persia away from the vulnerable western frontier of Afghanistan and towards a coastal route that would allow Britain to utilize the Royal Navy against them in time of war. And, if Russian incursions in Persia threatened India, then so, too, did, German railway advances in the Ottoman Empire towards Baghdad. This meant the need for Britain to dominate any possible route from Baghdad to the Gulf. The Baghdad to Haifa line was the culmination of this web of railways stretching from India towards the Suez Canal. Only the advent of a new technology, aerial warfare, made the strategic significance of the Baghdad to Haifa railway decline, an ironic occurrence given that it was the earlier rise of the new railroad technology that had made the route significant in the first place. Thus, strategic railways for the defence of the British Empire east of Suez had enjoyed a relatively narrow window of predominance (or, at least, significance). But, however brief this period, the importance of such railway considerations as those raised by the Baghdad to Haifa line cannot be ignored if a proper understanding of Imperial defence east of Suez is to be obtained.

Notes

1 J.S. Corbett, *Some Principles of Maritime Strategy* (reprint ed., Annapolis: Naval Institute Press, 1988). For an analysis of Corbett, see Donald M. Schurman, *Julian S. Corbett 1854–1922* (London: Royal Historical Society, 1981).
2 A remark made in October 1904 and quoted in Aaron L. Friedberg, *The Weary Titan: Britain and the Experience of Relative Decline, 1895–1905* (Princeton, 1988), 200; Steven Morewood, 'Protecting the Jugular Vein of Empire: The Suez Canal in British Defence Strategy, 1919–1941', *War & Society*, 10, 1 (1992), 81–107.
3 Hamilton to Curzon, 2 Nov 1899, Curzon Papers, MSS Eur F 111/144.
4 Godley to Curzon, 10 Nov 1899, Curzon Papers, MSS Eur F 111/144.
5 Hamilton to Curzon, 26 Jan 1900, Curzon Papers, MSS Eur F 111/145.
6 For good accounts, see John Gooch, *The Plans of War: The General Staff and British Military Strategy c. 1900–1916* (London, 1974), pp. 198–237 and Friedburg, *Weary Titan*, 234–73.
7 Minutes, 7th meeting of the CID, 19 Mar 1903, Cab 2/1.
8 Hamilton to Curzon, 19 Mar 1903, Curzon Papers, MSS Eur F 111/162.
9 Minutes, 8th meeting of CID, 26 Mar 1903, Cab 2/1.
10 For the origins of the Convention, see appendix I to the minutes of the 67th meeting of the CID, 22 Mar 1905, 'British Position as Regards Railway Construction in Persia', Cab 2/1.

11 See the discussion in 'Memorandum on the Defence of India. Prepared for the Committee of Imperial Defence', CID 6-D, Intelligence Department, War Office, 10 Mar 1903, Cab 6/1.

12 Minutes, 12th meeting of the CID, 7 May 1903, Cab 2/1.

13 This and the following quotation are from Hamilton to Curzon, 24 Apr 1903, Curzon Papers, MSS Eur F 111/162.

14 'Second Instalment of Draft Conclusions on Indian Defence by Mr. Balfour, dealing chiefly with Seistan', CID D-19, Balfour, 20 May 1903, Cab 6/1. This paper was discussed at the CID, see minutes, 15th meeting, 27 May 1903, Cab 2/1.

15 Curzon to Selborne, 4 May 1903, Selborne Papers, 10; minutes, 9th meeting of the CID, 1 Apr 1904, Cab 2/1; 'Memorandum on the Despatch of Reinforcements from the United Kingdom to India', CID 15-D, Intelligence Department, Admiralty, 12 May 1903, Cab 6/1.

16 Hamilton to Curzon, 8 Apr 1903, Curzon Papers, MSS Eur F 111/162.

17 Kitchener (commander of the British Army of India) to Roberts, 23 Jul 1903, Kitchener Papers, PRO 30/57/29.

18 Roberts to Kitchener, 21 May 1903, Kitchener Papers, PRO 30/57/28.

19 For the possible Russian reaction, see Scott to Lansdowne, disp 71, 18 Feb 1904, FO 65/1678.

20 32nd-37th meetings of the CID, 2, 4, 10, 16, 24 and 30 Mar 1904, Cab 2/1. For a discussion, see Keith Neilson, *Britain and the Last Tsar. British Policy and Russia, 1894–1917* (Oxford, 1995), 130–1.

21 'Estimate of Forces required for the Defence of India during the First Year of a War with Russia, by Colonel H. Mullaly, R.E. With Comments by Viscount Kitchener', CID 64-D, 28 Jul 1904, Cab 6/2; 'Cavalry, Artillery and Infantry Reinforcements for India', CID 73-D, Nov 1905, Cab 6/2, and 'Demands for Reinforcements by the Government of India', CID 74-D, 20 Feb 1905, Cab 6/2.

22 For the quotations, see, respectively, minutes, 67th meeting of the CID, 22 Mar 1905 and minutes, 68th meeting of the CID, 27 Mar 1905, both Cab 2/1.

23 Minutes, 71st, 74th, 75th and 79th meetings of the CID, 19 Apr, 6 Jul, 13 Jul and 9 Aug 1905, all Cab 2/1.

24 For the project, see J.S. Galbraith, 'British Policy on Railways in Persia, 1870–1914', *Middle Eastern Studies*, 25 (1989), 480–505. For the British decision not to participate, R.M. Francis, 'The British Withdrawal from the Baghdad Railway in April 1903', *Historical Journal*, 16 (1973), 168–78.

25 Minutes, 70th meeting of the CID, 12 Apr 1905; 'Effect of the Baghdad Railway on our Relations with Persia and on the Defence of India', CID 45-B, General Staff, War Office, 16 Nov 1904, Cab 4/1.

26 'The Baghdad Railway' CID 47-B, G.S. Clarke (Secretary, CID), 26 Jan 1905, Cab 4/1.

27 Minutes, 70th meeting of the CID, 12 Apr 1905, Cab 2/1.

28 'The Necessity of a Temporary Naval Base Near the Suez Canal', CID 51-B, Admiralty, 21 Feb 1905, Cab 4/1.

29 Minutes, 92nd meeting of the CID, 26 Jul 1906, Cab 2/2; 'The Baghdad Railway. Note by the Secretary', CID 77-B, G.S. Clarke, 14 Jun 1906, Cab 4/2.

30 [Report of the Baghdad Railway Committee], R.P. Maxwell, R. Ritchie, W.H. Clark, W. Tyrrell and Alwyn Parker, 26 Feb 1907, Cab 37/87/36.

31 'Persia. Report of a Sub-Committee of the Committee of Imperial Defence appointed by the Prime Minister to consider Questions relating to the Persian Gulf and Baghdad Railway', CID 102-D, Morley, 26 Jan 1909, Cab 6/4. The report was approved by the CID; see minutes, 101st meeting, 25 Feb 1909, Cab 2/2.

32 D.W. Spring, 'The Trans-Persian Railway Project and Anglo-Russian Relations, 1909–14', *Slavonic and East European Review*, 54 (1976), 60–82.

33 What follows is based on Neilson, *Britain and the Last Tsar*, 310–12.

34 Nicolson to Grey, 19 Nov 1909, Grey Papers, FO 800/73.

35 Hardinge to Nicolson, 8 Dec 1909, Hardinge Papers, 17 for this and the following quotation. See also, Nicolson to Hardinge, 16 Dec 1909, Hardinge Papers, 16.

36 Hardinge to Nicolson, 5 Jan 1910, Nicolson Papers, FO 800/343; Nicolson to Hardinge, 12 Jan 1910, Hardinge Papers, 20; Hardinge to Nicolson, 18 Jan 1910, Nicolson Papers, FO 800/343.

37 Nicolson to Hardinge, 9 Feb 1910, Hardinge Papers, 20.

38 I.I. Astafev, *Russo-germanskie diplomaticheskie otnosheniia 1905–1911 gg. (ot portsmuskogo mira do potsdamskogo sogasheniia)* (Moscow, 1972), 219–48; Neilson, *Britain and the Last Tsar*, 313–16.

39 J.A. Head, 'Public Opinions and Middle Eastern Railways: The Russo-German Negotiations of 1910–11', *International History Review*, 6 (1984). 28–47.

40 Harding to Sanderson, 22 Dec 1910, Hardinge Papers, 92.

41 Spring, 'Trans-Persian Railway', 70–1; Chirol to Hardinge, 17 Jul 1912; Hardinge to Curzon, 12 Aug 1912, both Hardinge Papers 92.

42 Neilson, *Britain and the Last Tsar*, 358–9.

43 V.H. Rothwell, *British War Aims and Peace Diplomacy 1914–18* (Oxford, 1971), 26–8; 'British Desiderata in Turkey in Asia: Report: Proceedings and Appendices of a Committee Appointed by the Prime Minister', May 1915, de Bunsen, Cab 27/1. (Hereafter, 'De Bunsen Committee').

44 'Alexandretta and Mesopotamia', secret, Kitchener, 16 Mar 1915, Cab 24/1/G-12.

45 'The War: Alexandretta and Mesopotamia', Admiralty, 17 Mar 1915, Cab 24/1/G-13; H. Mejcher, 'Oil and British Policy towards Mesopotamia, 1914–18', *Middle Eastern Studies*, 8 (1972), 377–91.

46 'The Future Status and Administration of Basra', Hardinge, 24 Feb 1915; 'The Future Settlement of Eastern Turkey in Asia and Arabia', Hirtzel, 14 Mar 1915; 'Note by General Sir Edmund Barrow on the Defence of Mesopotamia', 16 Mar 1915, appendices V and VI, 'De Bunsen Committee'.

47 Testimony of Sir Charles Callwell, 2nd meeting, 13 Apr 1915, 'De Bunsen Committee'.

48 The British were right; see George H. Cassar, *The French and the Dardanelles. A study of failure in the conduct of war* (London, 1971), 54–60.

49 Testimony of Vice-Admiral Sir E.J.W. Slade, 3rd meeting, 15 Apr 1915, 'De Bunsen Committee'.

50 For this, see Edward J. Erickson, *Ordered to Die. A History of the Ottoman Army in the First World War* (Westport, CT, 2001), 65, 152–3.

51 What follows, except where otherwise noted, is based on 'Quetta-Seistan Railway', CID 107-D, A. Chamberlain, 4 Aug 1916, Cab 6/4.

52 'Extension of the Quetta–Nushki Railway to Seistan', CID 108-D, Robertson, 16 Aug 1916, Cab 6/4.

53 These are summarized in 'The Nushki–Seistan Railway', CID 109-D, M.P.A. Hankey (Secretary, CID), 17 Aug 1916, Cab 6/4.

54 'Nushki–Seistan Railway', CID 110-D, Curzon, 17 Aug 1916, Cab 6/4.

55 'The strategical aspect of railway construction in Persia with special reference to the extension of the Sistan [sic] Railway', EC 1116, Macdonogh (Director of Military Intelligence), Aug 1918, Cab 27/30.

56 For this, see Keith Neilson, 'For diplomatic, economic, strategic and telegraphic reasons: British imperial defence, the Middle East and India, 1914–18', in Greg Kennedy and Keith Neilson, eds, *Far Flung Lines. Studies in Imperial Defence in Honour of Donald Mackenzie Schurman* (London and Portland, OR, 1996), 108–13; for the gloom, see Brock Millman, *Pessimism and British War Policy 1916–1918* (London and Portland, OR, 2001), especially, 199–240.

57 Minutes, 27th meeting of the Eastern Committee, 20 Aug 1918, Cab 27/24; the term 'ring fence' derives from 'British Policy in Afghanistan and Turkestan. Note by the CIGS', General Sir Henry Wilson (CIGS), 21 Jun 1918, appendix to the minutes, 16th meeting of the Eastern Committee, 24 Jun 1918, Cab 27/24.

58 'Railway Policy in Relation to General Military Policy in the Middle East', EC 2677, General Staff, War Office, 8 Dec 1918, Cab 27/33.

59 For the situation, see G.H. Bennett, *British Foreign Policy during the Curzon Period, 1919–24* (London, 1995), 122–35.

60 Minutes, 35th meeting of the COS, 6 Jul 1926, Cab 53/1.

61 Minutes, 218th meeting of the CID, 25 Nov 1926, Cab 2/4.

62 'Afghanistan', CID 149-D, Birkenhead, 4 Mar 1927, Cab 6/5.

63 Ibid., Annexure D, 'Memorandum by the Chief of the Imperial General Staff on the Integrity of Afghanistan', Milne, nd.

64 Minutes, 223rd meeting of the CID, 17 Mar 1927, Cab 2/5. For the context, see Keith Neilson, ' "Pursued by a Bear": British Estimates of Soviet Military Strength and Anglo-Soviet Relations, 1922–1939', *Canadian Journal of History*, 28, 2 (1993), 201–3.

65 'Defence of India. First Report of Sub-Committee', Birkenhead, 19 Dec 1927, Cab 16/83.

66 Minutes, 232nd meeting of the CID, 26 Jan 1925, Cab 2/5.

67 See Neilson, 'Pursued by a Bear', 204–6; Uriel Dann, 'British Persian Gulf Concepts in the Light of Emerging Nationalism in the Late 1920s', in Uriel Dann, ed., *The Great Powers in the Middle East 1919–1939* (New York and London, 1988), 50–68. The minutes of the Committee are in Cab 16/93; the memoranda are in Cab 16/94.

68 'An Appreciation of the Strategical Situation in the Persian Gulf by the Indian General Staff', PG-20, Skeen (Chief of IGS), 4 Oct 1928, Cab 16/94.

69 For the report, see 'The Persian Gulf. Interim Report of a Sub-Committee', CID 169-D, Hailsham (Lord Chancellor), 29 Oct 1928, Cab 6/5. For Amery's remark, see minutes, 5th meeting of the Persian Gulf Sub-Committee, 24 Oct 1928, Cab 16/93.

70 David E. Omissi, *Air Power and Colonial Control: the Royal Air Force, 1919–1939* (Manchester, 1990).

71 Neilson, *Britain and the Last Tsar*, 361–3.

72 Minutes, 230th meeting of the CID, 1 Nov 1927, Cab 2/5.

73 See 'Construction of a Railway from Haifa to Baghdad', CID 828-B, Colonial Office, 27 Aug 1927; 'Construction of a Railway between Haifa and Baghdad', CID 833-B, Colonial Office, 25 Oct 1927; 'Construction of a Railway between Haifa and Baghdad', CID 837-B, Colonial Office, 29 Oct 1927, all Cab 4/16. There is a large literature done by business historians about the development of Middle Eastern oil and the debates about the possible pipeline routes. However, they do not take the defence considerations into account; see Edward Peter Fitzgerald, 'Business Diplomacy: Walter Teagle, Jersey Standard, and the Anglo-French Pipeline Conflict in the Middle East, 1930–1931', *Business History Review*, 67 (1993), 207–45.

74 'Construction of a Railway from Haifa to Baghdad', CID 830-B, War Office, 17 Oct 1927, Cab 4/16.

75 Minutes, Cab 12(28), 29 Feb 1928, Cab 23/57.

76 'Sub-Committee on the Construction of the Proposed Haifa–Baghdad Railway and/or Pipeline', CID 886-B, Stanhope (Civil Lord, Admiralty), 13 Jun 1928, Cab 4/17.

77 'The Baghdad–Haifa Pipeline and Railway', CID 894-B, COS, 14 May 1928, Cab 4/17.

78 'Oil Board. Third Annual Report', CID 937-B, Peel (President, Oil Board), 26 Apr 1929, Cab 4/18.

79 Minutes, 242nd meeting of the CID, 2 May 1929, Cab 2/5.

80 See 'Oil Board. Sixth Annual Report', CID 1068-B, 30 Sept 1931, Cab 4/21; minutes, 254th meeting of the CID, 7 Dec 1931, Cab 2/5.

81 'The Strategic Aspect of the Trans-Desert Railway from Baghdad to Haifa', CID 1105-B, Air Ministry, 8 Mar 1933; 'The Strategic Value of the Haifa–Baghdad Railway', CID 1110-B, War Office, 26 Mar 1933, both Cab 4/22.

82 Minutes, 258th meeting of the CID, 6 Apr 1933, Cab 2/5.

83 For this, see Keith Neilson, 'The Defence Requirements Sub-Committee, British Strategic Foreign Policy, Neville Chamberlain and the Path Appeasement', *English Historical Review*, 118, 477 (2003), 651–84.

9 Managing the hajj

Indian pilgrim traffic, public health and transportation in Arabia, 1918–1930

Martin Thomas

This chapter is less about a railway than about the consequences of the absence of one. More specifically, it traces the issue of a rail link to connect the port of Jeddah with Mecca's Arafat valley, the principal congregation point for the tens of thousands of Muslim pilgrims who journeyed to the Muslim holy places in Arabia during and immediately after the First World War. If completed, this route would have marked the first addition to the original Hijaz railway connecting the Ottoman Empire with Arabia's holy cities since the end of Turkish suzerainty over Central Arabia in 1918. The principal source used here are the records of the British consulate in Jeddah, which, together with the Government of India's dedicated 'Hajj Officer' in the port, submitted detailed pilgrimage reports each year to the Foreign Office Eastern Department. The consulate's detailed surveys of pilgrim numbers and experiences were published as discrete volumes in the early 1990s.[1] Taken together, these provide an interesting window onto the longer term ramifications of the annual influx to the holy cities for both Arabian and British imperial politics in the inter-war period. As Timothy Paris has recently noted, 'No aspect of Anglo-Hijazi relations represented a greater source of trouble than the annual pilgrimage to the Muslim holy places.'[2] Conversely, the internal dynamics of Arabian politics were increasingly critical to the successful management of pilgrimage in the 1920s. The years 1918 to 1930 witnessed massive political change in the Arabian Peninsula. The Arab Revolt and the end of Ottoman suzerainty signalled the intrusion of closer British imperial oversight. Meanwhile the contest between the Hashemite dynasty and the House of Saud for regional supremacy in the Hijaz, and the ultimate victory of Saudi forces, in part inspired by Muhammad ibn 'Abd al-Wahhab's unitarian doctrine of puritanical Islam, all impacted on the nature, scale and safety of the annual Muslim pilgrimage – the hajj.[3]

It is in this context of Arabia's shifting political sands that the question of the Jeddah to Mecca railway assumed such importance. The contest for regional supremacy between the the Hashemite ruler of the Hijaz, Husain ibn Ali, Sharif of Mecca, and the Amir of Najd, 'Abd al-'Aziz ibn Saud, always had a strong religious dimension to which the right to manage the hajj became central.[4] To the immediate north of the Arabian Peninsula, the end of Ottoman control over the Hijaz railway generated long-running controversy over the railway's religious status and the right of individual national governments and European mandate authorities to regulate its operation.[5] But, within the Hijaz itself, control over the railway, and any additional rail construction, was subsumed within the broader question of which rival dynasty should administer the holy places.

From its inception in 1900 the Hijaz railway was a source of local political controversy and international dispute. The railway's chief sponsor, the Ottoman Sultan Abdülhamid II, recognized religious sovereignty over the Hijaz as an important source of political legitimacy. A rail service for pilgrims to the holy cities added substance to the unifying power of Islam within the Ottoman Empire.[6] While there was undoubtedly some state coercion involved, Muslim financial support for the original Hijaz railway project between 1900–8 was proof of – and boost to – pan-Islamic sentiment. Not surprisingly, British imperial authorities in India and Egypt were unnerved by the extent of local voluntary donations to an Ottoman-controlled project, while the British Embassy in Istanbul actively opposed such gifts, suspicious that the funds might be diverted elsewhere.[7] It was while travelling overland from Jeddah, their main port of disembarkation, to the encampments at Arafat that Muslim pilgrims (Hajjis) from British India faced the most arduous leg of their pilgrimage. In the early years covered here, most travellers had little choice other than to join the long camel trains that undertook the journey during the pilgrimage season. In the years after 1925 and the imposition of Saudi control at Mecca, car and lorry traffic became more commonplace, although poorer hajjis were still reliant on camel hire. The journey was not a long one – fifty miles at most. But it was certainly a perilous one. Banditry, even murder of visiting pilgrims, was not uncommon, despite increasingly systematic efforts by both the Hashemite and Saudi authorities to prevent such attacks. But it was the combination of intense desert heat, lack of adequate drinking water, and the weakened condition of Indian and other foreign Muslim travellers after a cramped seaward journey across the Persian Gulf that took the heaviest toll. As we shall see, numerous deaths among visiting hajjis occurred during the final overland stage of their pilgrimage. A railway promised to end all that, making the trip from Jeddah to Mecca straightforward and routine rather than potentially life threatening.

The annual hajj was integral to the changing strategic and religious environment of the Arabian Peninsula in the decade after the First World War. Pilgrimage did not take place in a political vacuum, but was instead an essential element in the struggle for regional dominance between Arabia's rival dynasties and Sunni Muslim sects.[8] Sovereign control over Islam's holiest sites was a source of tremendous prestige, but brought with it onerous duties of management and protection. Administrative control over the holy places also conferred the right to levy taxes, road tolls and customs fees on visiting Hajjis. This, and the commercial revenue generated by the presence of tens of thousands of pilgrims, was critical to the economic solvency of, first, Sharif Husain's Hashemite government and, second, the Saudi regime that supplanted it after the surrender of Mecca and 'Abd al-'Aziz ibn Saud's enthronement as King of al-Hijaz and Sultan of Najd (the nucleus of Saudi Arabia) on 8 January 1926. In economies still dominated by

Oasis agriculture, tribal livestock production and market commerce, hajj traffic was financially indispensable. Moreover, pilgrimage revenue was more dependable than state revenues from an agricultural sector susceptible to recurrent problems of crop failure and high livestock mortality in the punishing climactic conditions of the Arabian peninsula.[9] With an average of 68,000 pilgrims visting the Hijaz each year in the early 1920s, and some, particularly Malayan and Javanese pilgrims remaining for several months in order to travel northward from Mecca to Medina as well, pilgrims provided the most important single source of income and foreign exchange to the Hashemite administration.[10] Central to this commercial dimension to the hajj were the caravan owners and pilgrim guides (*mutawwifs*) whose fees for overland transportation from Jeddah inland to the holy cities typically represented the largest single items of expenditure for foreign pilgrims.

Take, for example, the case of the Rashidi dynasty in Central Arabia. Before its overthrow by the Wahabi levies of Ibn Saud's *Ikhwan* in 1921, the Rashidi government at Ha'il used its control over the hajj caravan network to consolidate its authority as a regional emirate.[11] Guaranteed protection of the caravanserais conveying pilgrims back and forth to the holy cities against attack by Bedouin raids was both a political duty and a valuable revenue generator. A picture of this system in operation emerges from a retrospective account of pilgrimage traffic through Rashidi territory, written in 1928:

> Everyone of the pilgrims, who sometimes numbered ten thousand, had to pay for water and for his camels thirty megidijjat ($25) on the outward and fifteen megidijjat on the return journey. Furthermore a portion of all goods imported or transported by the pilgrims was expected as a toll. In this manner Mohammad [the *amir* of Ha'il] increased the prosperity not merely of the ruling house but of the settlers who acted as merchants and of the bedouins who were accustomed to hire out their camels to the caravans.[12]

The British government and the imperial Government of India were also alert to the symbolic and material importance of Muslim pilgrimage for the authorities *in situ*. The 'men on the spot' – consular staff, military advisors, and special envoys – recognized the prestige considerations and economic benefits that weighed heavily in hajj management. Perhaps more important from the British viewpoint, if the Empire was to be more closely aligned with Arabia's rulers, it was imperative that the thousands of Muslim colonial subjects that completed the hajj each year should be seen to receive more effective protection as a result of Anglo-Arab clientage.[13] It served Britain's own prestige interests that the hajj should become a safer, well-regulated occasion. From the mid-nineteenth century the Jeddah consulate played the leading role in monitoring the welfare of visiting colonial pilgrims and the substantial Indian trading communities in Mecca and the port of Jeddah itself. The killing of Europeans in the town (including the British vice-consul and the French consul) by Muslim rioters on 15 June 1858 and the punitive British naval bombardment that followed, heralded a more interventionist British policy in matters of Hijaz trade and pilgrimage traffic.[14] From the

1880s onward, the reportage of Jeddah consular personnel to the British Embassy in Constantinople was frequently exploited in justification of closer British oversight over Hijaz affairs, the argument being that Britain was imperial protector of a far larger Muslim population than the Ottoman Sultan.[15]

The pilgrimage protection dimension to British Imperial policy in Arabia has been eclipsed by the more infamous diplomatic and strategic objectives of its Middle East policy. As is well known, following the end of the First World War the British government struggled to reconcile the numerous contradictory pledges made to various Arab and other communal leaders across the Middle East during the war years. In the Arabian Peninsula, British envoys were hard pressed to square commitments to support the Hashemite authorities in Mecca with their 1915 alliance with Ibn Saud's Najd government in Riyadh. High-level British connections with each of these deadly rivals stemmed from the combination of short-term wartime expediency in the war against Ottoman Turkey and a longer-term imperial interest in regional supremacy, strategic control and exclusive commercial privileges from the Persian Gulf to the eastern Mediterranean. Ostensibly, the British relationship with 'Abd al-'Aziz ibn Saud seemed more tenuous. Between his capture of Riyadh in 1902 and Turkish entry to the First World War, Ibn Saud was repeatedly frustrated in his attempts to secure British backing as a lever to undermine Ottoman claims to suzerainty in Najd, so much so that he felt compelled to acknowledge his nominal subordination to the Ottoman Sultanate by treaty in May 1914.[16] And even the subsequent Saudi alignment with Britain in 1915 did not produce the same levels of cooperation as in the case of the Hashemites. In contrast, by 1921 British ties to the Hashemite dynasty appeared the stronger, cemented by their joint conduct of the Arab Revolt and the installation of Sharif Husain's sons, Feisal and Abdullah as, respectively, heads of state in the newly established Iraq and Transjordan mandates. But, within Arabia, the balance of power and religious influence was shifting decisively toward Ibn Saud. Relentless *Ikhwan* attacks on Rashidi territory and its loyalist tribes culminated in the 1921 capture of Ha'il. Conflict with the Hashemites escalated thereafter until the *Ikhwan's* bloody reduction of Ta'if on the Hijaz frontier in 1924 paved the way to the surrender of Mecca to Saudi forces.[17]

The Ikhwan's triumphal entry to Mecca confirmed their status as the most dynamic, single-minded and ruthless military force in Arabia. The Ikhwan movement's rise to prominence over the preceding two decades was engineered by Ibn Saud, for whom the Ikhwan served a number of complementary goals. The creation of settled *Ikhwan* communities composed of Najd tribesmen devoted to Wahabi unitarianism brought greater stability to Central Arabia and fostered popular loyalty to the Saudi authorities. The development of *Ikhwan* agricultural settlements reduced nomadism and inter-tribal conflict among the major clans and tribal confederations loyal to the House of Saud.[18] Effectively serving as envoys of Ibn Saud, the ulamas that preached strict adherence to the Wahabi code of Islamic puritanism in the *Ikhwan* settlements consolidated the bond between community members, *Ikhwan* leaders such as Ibn Bijad and Faysal al-Dawish, and their imam, Ibn Saud himself. And the religious zeal of the *Ikhwan* assured their constant readiness to embark on military attacks against non-Wahabi Muslims, especially those that served the Hashemite dynasty. The *Ikhwan's* fearsome reputation for unconditional bravery, uncompromising asceticism, and merciless killing of male opponents and prisoners added to their aura of invincibility. But it was this fundamentalism, as well as more worldly concerns over increasing state impositions, of the Saudi state, that would ultimately drive a wedge between the *Ikhwan* movement and their political master in Riyadh. Ibn Saud was anxious to limit the *Ikhwan's* appetite for forcible conversion to the populations and territory of what would become the Saudi Arabian state, a political system to whose modernization, bureaucratization and increasing fiscal demands the *Ikhwan* were poorly reconciled.[19] Suppression of the *Ikhwan* rebellion in 1930 marked the end of a decade of almost uninterrupted extension of the movement's influence to the southern margins of the British-controlled mandates of Transjordan and Iraq.[20] Inspired by Wahabism and thus resolved to eradicate the many heretical practices of non-Wahabi pilgrims, it was inevitable that the hajj would be an issue of burning concern to the *Ikhwan* throughout the 1920s. Implacably opposed to Wahabism and fearful of *Ikhwan* attacks, Husain's administration blocked access to Najdi pilgrims in the early 1920s.[21] During 1919–21 the British government was complicit in this, subordinating Saudi grievances at this exclusion to the requirements of an Anglo-Hijaz treaty. The Government of India followed suit. The Imperial authorities in Delhi were more consistently hostile to Hashemite administration and its repeated failures to safeguard Indian Hajjis than their partners in London. But it would not serve Raj interest to take issue with Hashemite administration as this was bound to add fuel to the Khalifat movement in India, which was itself sharply critical of Husain's pretensions to be Caliph.[22] Moreover, Husain's anxieties about Wahabi incursions were far from groundless. Sharifian control of the holy cities, the idolatrous decoration of Muslim holy sites, immodest attire, even the Egyptian buglers that accompanied the *mahmal* – the ceremonial caravan bearing the elaborate shroud (*kiswah*) for the Kab'ah stone in Mecca (a gift usually transported annually from Cairo) – were all targets of Ikhwan attack. And, of course, the Ikhwan vision of a properly devotional hajj was tied to Ibn Saud's installation as ruler of the Hijaz.[23]

The politics of pilgrim traffic, by sea, caravan, and, of course, rail was thus bound up with the wider contests for power between Arabia's dynastic leaderships. And the stronger British imperial influence in the Arab world, combined with paternalist imperial concern for colonial hajjis, ensured that the pilgrimage would be monitored closely year by year by a specialist network of Foreign Office, India Office and British military observers. But, in a sense, this was nothing new. Effective management of the Hijaz railway, a transportation system avowedly designed to facilitate mass pilgrimage, had been central to Ottoman claims of suzerainty in Arab territories since its initial approval in 1900. A working Hijaz railway was emblematic of the Caliph's duty to serve the interests of his Muslim subjects before 1918. Its financial basis in voluntary donations (as well as more coercive collection methods) across the Ottoman Empire and the Muslim world more generally symbolized the railway's principal role as a charitable, religious project rather than a commercial venture or a strategic transport link for easier troop deployment.[24] Furthermore, local and international competition for control over railway development in Arab territories bridged the divide between high politics, international diplomacy and the politics of the Middle East interior. Here, the British had tended to play a secondary role to their main European partners and rivals. By 1914 French financial investment in Ottoman Turkey and Paris financiers' grip over the Ottoman Public Debt was matched by the predominance of French-controlled railway companies in Anatolia and Greater Syria. By 1902 French firms operated five distinct railway lines in the Near East. But it was Germany's success in securing the principal concession to construct the Baghdad railway that drew more adverse international attention, not least from the French themselves.[25] Throughout the first two decades of the twentieth century the Fertile Crescent arcing south eastwards from Turkish Anatolia remained the epicentre of these commercial and strategic rivalries over railway construction. In Arabia the Hijaz railway remained the sole arterial railway in the early 1920s. So the construction of even a relatively short extension to the Hijaz line, connecting Jeddah into the Hijaz network, would have marked a major departure in the region's infrastructure development.

Not surprisingly, the 1918 hajj, beginning on 15 September, was the smallest on record in recent years. Political uncertainty, combined with the attendant shortage of overland transport and shipping, imposed formidable barriers to those wishing to make the trip. Even so, some 44,000 pilgrims made the journey to Mount Arafat. As usual, Hajjis from British-controlled territories figured large with two steamers arriving from India, one from Egypt and some 4,380 pilgrims from West Africa and the Sudan using the ten-day Khedivial shipping service from Suakin.[26] Medical staff of the Egyptian Public Health department, as well as specially trained Indian police inspectors monitored the observance of quarantine regulations for the Egyptian and Indian arrivals at Jeddah in conjunction with the Hijaz Quarantine Administration. With fewer pilgrims than usual, onward transportation, accommodation and water provision were all arranged without incident. But, as ever, Hajjis travelling inland from Jeddah were dependent on camel trains for the journey inland to Mecca.[27]

Pilgrimage traffic in the following year showed some signs of recovery. Numbers were up to between seventy and seventy-five thousand, and for the first time, the British intervened directly in the supervision of quarantine arrangements and medical provision, Royal Army Medical Corps personnel working in conjunction with Sherif Husain's Hijaz officials. The quarantine system, whose origins lay in the Ottoman period, became a politically charged issue in the succeeding decade of Hashemite rule. In May 1919 King Husain advised Britain's Jeddah consul, Major W.E. Marshall, that he intended to forbid the creation of any foreign-run institutions until the Hijaz had been fully independent for a full five years. This brought him into conflict with the Foreign Office and the Government of India, both of which were determined to establish a Pilgrimage Hospital to cater for the thousands of Indian Muslims who arrived each year. Once in place, the hospital was bound to cut across Hashemite administration of pilgrimage quarantine, undermining its *raison d'être* and highlighting the lack of any systematic medical care for Hajjis.[28]

The right of the independent kingdom of the Hijaz to impose quarantine regulations on British imperial subjects held great symbolic importance, even if pilgrims' actual experience of quarantine at Abu Sa'd island off Jeddah was anything but salubrious.[29] Indian pilgrims were typically assigned to Abu Sa'd island for one to three days' quarantine, often with minimal shelter and no supplies or bedding. British jurisdictional encroachment on the operation of the hajj was, however, unlikely to diminish. In 1919, for example, British staff at the headquarters of the Egyptian Expeditionary Force (EEF) supervised arrangements for some 2,000 Indian Muslim troops stationed across the Middle East to perform the hajj before returning to their garrisons.[30] As in 1918, so in 1919, pilgrims encountered few problems beyond the stifling heat on the overland journey from Jeddah to Mecca. But it was a different story during the onward trip inland to Medina. British consulate staff in Jeddah advised the Foreign Office that Bedouin tribesmen pillaged all caravan convoys at some stage during this section of the pilgrimage, and several murders were recorded. The Hashemite Crown made good any monies lost by pilgrims in this way. But this generosity caused problems of its own. Allegedly, exaggerated, even fraudulent, claims for losses incurred were, on occasion, submitted.[31]

Trouble continued on the eastward return journey made by Indian, Indonesian and Iranian Hajjis. Crowding on the Persian Gulf steamers operating from Jeddah became acute as a result of over-booking, a problem that generated hundreds of complaints from Iranian and Punjabi hajjis denied the opportunity to return home as planned. Whereas passengers with the Bombay–Persia Steam Navigation Company, the dominant Persian Gulf shipping line during and immediately after the First World War, typically bought return tickets prior to departure, those that travelled on the steamship *Zayani* of the rival Shushtri Company line were only sold single tickets. Ironically, the ensuing complications arose when the two companies agreed to accept tickets interchangeably. This, it seems, was done less in a spirit of cooperation than as part of a price-fixing agreement, the two shipping companies effectively controlling all westbound pilgrimage traffic into Jeddah.[32] In short, the first peacetime pilgrimage jointly supervised by the Hashemite authorities and British officials to the Hijaz was not counted an administrative success.[33]

Insecurity on the Hijaz road system persisted into 1920, threatening to undermine the success of that year's hajj.[34] The greatest concern of the EEF officers monitoring pilgrimage arrangements for Indian Hajjis therefore remained their inability to ensure the safety of pilgrims once they ventured inland from Jeddah. The need to safeguard visiting pilgrims travelling inland from Jeddah was sharpened by the acrimonious collapse in May 1920 of joint Hashemite–British control of the quarantine system in operation at Jeddah and Kamaran Island in the Red Sea.[35] British quarantine inspectors were convinced that Indian and other sea-borne Hajjis would face greater administrative abuses and physical hardships as a result. Providing clean water, better sanitation and medical facilities at the port and the holy cities was one thing, but only the completion of a railway was expected to make overland travel safe and healthy. No water was available to travellers for the first twenty-five miles of the Jeddah–Mecca trip, other than at small coffee shops at Bahra, the first significant stopping point en route. But the water sellers of Bahra could never cope with the volume of demand, and pilgrims collapsing with dehydration in and around the settlement were commonplace. A railway line would put an end to this. Its usefulness was not just to be measured in terms of public health. Improvements in hajj management might enhance the status of the Hashemite dynasty throughout the Muslim world. So advised the EEF's hajj observers in 1920.[36]

Hajj management in the late Hashemite period

The Hashemite authorities saw matters rather differently. For one thing, the Hijaz railway was associated with the former Ottoman regime. Its original religious purpose as a conduit for pilgrimage traffic had been subverted as the Turks came to rely on the railway as a strategic arterial route along which troops could be rapidly deployed to quell Arab dissent. As recently as 1914, King Husain had blocked Turkish plans to begin construction of the Jeddah–Mecca line, appropriating the construction materials sent to the region for other purposes. At root, however, the Hashemite hostility to the railway was less political than economic. Completion of a rail link between the port of Jeddah and the holy cities threatened to deprive the local population of an essential source of revenue from pilgrims currently reliant on local transport, accommodation and subsistence. Admittedly, a railway construction project offered the prospect of short-term manual employment for locally recruited construction gangs, as well as longer-term work for railway employees. But the relative benefits of this were unclear next to the known value of existing hajj traffic forced to rely on Arab service providers.[37]

Regardless of the lukewarm attitude of Husain's government, the Hashemites' British sponsors would not be easily dissuaded. The advantages to Britain in supporting a Jeddah–Mecca railway line were all too obvious. Whatever the official rhetoric about British respect for Islamic culture and the loyalty of its Muslim subjects, British imperialism in the Muslim world faced an uncertain future immediately after the First World War. Britain's part in the deposition of the Ottoman Caliph rankled with many, firing popular support for pan-Islamism from the Punjab to Egypt. Early Arab nationalism increasingly defined itself by opposition to the European imperial presence in the Middle East.[38] And during 1919–20 insurgencies, whether ethnic, tribal or national in origin, flared up in several British-ruled Muslim territories. Barely was the Zaglulist uprising in Egypt put down over the spring of 1919 than more intractable communal violence erupted in Iraqi Kurdistan and the Shia provinces of southern Iraq.[39] In 1920 the political status and territorial integrity of numerous predominantly Muslim territories from the Anglo-Egyptian Sudan through to the Transjordan and Iraq Mandates, was far from secure. Meanwhile, Pathan warlordism in and around

Waziristan on India's North-West frontier would pin down thousands of imperial troops in low intensity warfare for much of the inter-war period.[40]

Anything that could be held up as tangible evidence of more sympathetic British treatment of its Muslim imperial subjects could not be easily discounted. An estimated outlay of half a million Egyptian pounds to fund railway construction and rolling stock for the Jeddah–Mecca line was surely worth it. There were other, more practical benefits too. Rail travel would be affordable to all pilgrims, unlike the cost of motor transport, were a road to be built instead. Furthermore, other Muslim governments might well contribute to the expense of railway construction, regarding it as a charitable, religious venture of the same type as the existing Hijaz railway.[41]

But herein lay a problem. The Hijaz railway rapidly fell into disrepair after the dissolution of the Ottoman Empire. Western commercial investment in an extended rail network in the Middle East mandates established during 1919–21 shone an unwelcome light on Hashemite inability to fund the restoration of the Hijaz railway, itself a separate concern. The fact remained that, without a rail link, and with motor transport still virtually unknown, the pilgrims arriving at Jeddah in the immediate post-war years faced an extremely arduous overland journey by camel or on foot. For some of them it would prove fatal. According to figures compiled by British imperial observers, in 1920, 58,584 pilgrims disembarked at Jeddah. The figure was only marginally lower in 1921, with 57,255 arrivals recorded.[42] In these, as in subsequent years, the predominant ethnic groups were Indian, Indonesian and Malay Muslims, all of whom had spent an average of between three and seven days at sea prior to arrival. Those travelling from the Dutch East Indies, principally Javanese Muslims, enjoyed a distinct advantage over their South and South East Asian brethren. The Dutch and Blue Funnel line steamers that conveyed Javanese pilgrims to Arabia sailed more frequently from Batavia than the vessels travelling from Malayan and Indian ports, meaning that crossings were, in practice, less crowded. But, like all other pilgrims coming by sea to Jeddah, Javanese Hajjis had to endure cramped and unsanitary conditions during a compulsory period in quarantine on arrival. Most pilgrims were understandably keen to depart Jeddah immediately after passing through the port's quarantine islands, none of which had sanitary facilities or sufficient water to meet the demands of shiploads of new arrivals.[43]

The Hashemite authorities were also anxious to see Hajjis moved on from Jeddah to Medina as soon as they cleared quarantine. With so many visitors arriving over the space of a few days, it was imperative that a constant stream of pilgrimage traffic inland from Jeddah be maintained if camel trains were to cope. Furthermore, the threat to public health in Jeddah, a relatively small and enclosed port city of only 25,000 or so permanent inhabitants, was considerable the longer that thousands of pilgrims were detained there. A railway line would solve this bottleneck problem. It was also likely to end a major source of grievance among visiting pilgrims – the payment of exorbitant fees and the loss of baggage to unscrupulous *mutawwifs*.[44]

If the attractions of a Jeddah–Mecca railway for arriving pilgrims were obvious, the appeal of a rail service for returning Hajjis eager to depart as soon as possible after completing their pilgrimage was still more apparent. Large numbers of pilgrims were desperately short of money by the end of the hajj festival. Hundreds, even thousands, ended up destitute each year. West African and Somali Hajjis typically worked their passage home, providing casual labour and porterage services to fellow pilgrims. Large numbers of black Africans also found their way into the Hashemite and Saudi levies, whether as conscripts or volunteers. Malay and Indonesian pilgrims usually arrived weeks, sometimes months, in advance of the hajj, and some of the most elderly clearly did not intend to return to South East Asia at all. Indian Muslims generally stayed for shorter periods, but, in the immediate post-war years, often arrived without return tickets or sufficient cash to purchase one.[45] This problem was compounded by the fact that shipping rates tended to fluctuate with demand. The more pilgrims seeking passage home, the higher the on-the-spot ticket prices charged. Not all the practical problems of hajj travel were of the pilgrims' own making. Nor is it reasonable to ascribe their difficulties to inexperience or lack of planning. Religious devotion was, of course, central to the pilgrimage experience, and informed the outlook of travellers who were prepared to endure sustained hardships in order to complete their journey. Devout belief compelled many to travel regardless of their financial resources and the uncertainties inherent in itineraries that frequently stretched to thousands of miles over sea and land. For every Emir or sheikh completing the hajj there were thousands of Muslim pilgrims of far more limited means. Most made huge sacrifices and took extraordinary steps in order to make their journeys at all. Nigerians faced a gruelling overland journey via Sudan to Egypt or the Red Sea coast. After the Saudi takeover of Mecca, Iraqis were compelled to make their own travel arrangements, without official support, whether via Kuwait, Syria or Palestine or, more rarely, overland through the northern Hijaz. And for even relatively short sea passages from the Maghrebi ports of the southern Mediterranean, Alexandria, Beirut and Jaffa, the risk of contracting infectious illness aboard crowded tramp steamers remained high. In these circumstances, the stoicism and exemplary behaviour of most pilgrims is the more remarkable.[46]

But for all the goodwill and endurance of the pilgrims and their hosts, other more worldly problems intervened. Problems were most severe for travellers taking the main route between Mecca to Medina. Those Hajjis that made this additional pilgrimage faced additional charges, which were subject to arbitrary increase, as well as on-the-spot exactions from local tribal sheikhs through whose domains they passed.[47] Their problems were likely to continue on their return journey. The Hashemite authorities were suspected of restricting the availability of camel caravans from Mecca to the coast in order to maximize the opportunities for the local population to make money from the pilgrims. As a result, return journeys to Jeddah were not regulated in conformity with shipping companies, many of which either reassigned vessels temporarily to other routes, or were unable to cope with an unexpected glut of pilgrims demanding passage home to

India, Egypt, Malaya, or the Dutch East Indies. A timetabled railway was sure to diminish such problems. But it was also bound to reduce the possibilities of revenue generation for the Hashemite state, private traders, hostel managers, *mutawwifs*, and camel owners.[48] The introduction in 1922 of a new tax of forty Turkish piastres in 1922 for every camel travelling from Mecca to Arafat, plus a further eighty piastres payable for the return journey from Mecca to Jeddah seemed to confirm that Husain's government was determined to extract maximum wealth from the existing hajj transportation system rather than embark on fundamental change.[49]

Practical transportation difficulties, public health concerns, and the need to safeguard the traditional livelihoods of the local population gave rise to conflicting demands on King Husain's government. British diplomatic pressure for immediate improvement in the treatment of a pilgrim population of which well over 50 per cent were British imperial subjects added political complexity to the challenges of hajj management. British arguments with Husain over hajj administration in the four years after the First World War had tended to centre on public health questions in general and quarantine arrangements in particular.[50] By contrast, during the final years of Hashemite administration in the holy cities in 1923–4, one concern predominated above all others. This was the security of travellers on the main inland routes to Medina and Mecca.[51] Here, it became impossible to untangle the financial interests of the Hashemite state, the demands of caravan owners for an assured income, and pilgrims' mounting grievances over banditry, arbitrary road tolls, and the very real threats of dehydration, sunstroke or violent assault by Wahabi tribesmen. On the one hand, the Hashemite government wished to corral pilgrims along designated inland routes, both to facilitate security arrangements and tax collection. On the other hand, the knowledge that large numbers of Hajjis would be using a limited number of roads over a limited period increased the opportunity for extortion or outright robbery. No single solution could satisfy the conflicting requirements of locals and pilgrims.[52] A railway would undoubtedly drive an entire informal economy of guides, camel owners, water sellers and other traders out of business. And it was difficult to justify the capital outlay required for surveys, engineering and construction on a rail link that would only be intensively used for a matter of weeks each year.

The prospects of a Jeddah–Medina railway receded further in 1923 as international controversy over the management and maintenance of the Hijaz railway intensified. The immediate diplomatic pretext for this was the final regulation of a Turkish peace settlement at the Lausanne Conference.[53] The Turkish delegation at Lausanne raised the delicate question of how the Hijaz railway's distinctive Muslim character could best be conserved in a new era of Franco-British imperial dominance in the Fertile Crescent. Their suggestion of an all-Muslim management board with the Caliph as titular president marked a thinly veiled attempt to restore Turkish control over the railway. British and French responses were, inevitably, cool, although both declared their readiness to support an international management committee comprised of a single Muslim representative from Syria, Palestine, Transjordan and the Hijaz, and two further Muslim members from states with a strong record of participation in the hajj. This proposal was, in turn, rejected by King Husain, who insisted that the Hijaz railway be managed in Medina under direct Hashemite control. Unfortunately for the Hashemite authorities, the limits to their effective control over large swathes of the Arabian desert were laid bare by their efforts to strengthen their claim to manage the Hijaz railway. Repair work to the tracks conducted under the supervision of a Turkish engineer enabled a single train to complete the journey from Palestine to Medina in 1923. But the weight of the train in question caused the tracks to subside into the sand, requiring more substantial remedial work in future. Meanwhile, *Ikhwan* warriers loyal to King Saud were accused of undermining numerous stretches of the line by digging away at its sandy foundations.[54] On the one hand, these Wahabi attacks enabled King Husain to blame the Ikhwan for Hashemite inability to maintain the railway. On the other hand, the continuing deterioration of the line was an acute source of embarrassment to Husain's government – proof positive of his limited writ over the Hijaz heartland.[55] By the end of 1923 it was clear that the Hashemite government did not have the personnel or the administrative capability to maintain the existing Hijaz railway, still less to build an entirely new extension to it.[56]

The future of Sharifian management of the hajj became academic during the course of 1924, a year in which Husain made a series of politico-religious miscalculations that fatally undermined his authority in the Hijaz. Eager to revitalize his authority as guardian of the holy cities, Husain declared himself Caliph after Atatürk's republican regime formally abolished the Ottoman Caliphate in Istanbul. Soon afterward, Husain also assumed the title of King of the Arabs. Sure to affront Ibn Saud among others, these provocative measures were matched by Sharifian refusal to permit any *Ikhwan* community members to perform the hajj, a prohibition justified on the grounds of *Ikhwan* intolerance and their hostility to the Hashemite regime. Not surprisingly then, Husain's actions in early 1924 were instrumental in the agreement reached on 5 June 1924 between Najdi ulama, tribal chiefs, *Ikhwan* leaders and the Saudi royal family to overthrow Hashemite rule in the Hijaz. Denied their inalienable right to perform the hajj, the *Ikhwan* would form the spearhead of forces that marched on Ta'if in September.[57] Significantly, in spite of the massacre that attended the *Ikhwan* capture of the town, and which intimidated Mecca and Jeddah into capitulation a month later, news of the establishment of Saudi–Wahabi administration in Mecca and Medina seems to have been well received by foreign pilgrims, not least Muslims from British India exasperated the exploitation and administrative inefficiency that marred pilgrimage in the Sharifian period.[58] There may still have been no railway to transport sea-borne arrivals from Jeddah to Mecca, but at least the short inland journey would be less perilous and expensive under Saudi rule.

Hajj management under Saudi authority

From the outset of Saudi administration in the Hijaz, the hajj became a far more orderly affair.[59] The 1926 pilgrimage, the first conducted under Ibn Saud's undisputed authority, passed off without incident, in spite of the unanticipated presence of 35–40,000 Najdi pilgrims able to complete the journey for the first time since the installation of Husain's Hijaz government.[60] As usual, however, sea-borne pilgrims comprised the majority of hajjis in 1926. The ethnic and regional composition of the pilgrims arriving at sea at Jeddah in this, the first hajj year under full Saudi control, are listed below.

Regional composition of pilgrim arrivals (by sea) at Jeddah, 1926[61]

India	18,937
Egyptians	16,094
British Malays	5,500 (approx)
Dutch Malays	5,110 (approx)
Afghans	2,445
Hejazis	1,729
Bukharis	1,470
Sudanese (including West Africans)	1,377
Yemenis	565
Syrians	499
Iranians	475
Hadramis	360
Somalis (embarked at Djibouti)	215
Muscats	213
Iraqis	199
Palestinians	168
Turks	157
Maghrebis	115
Chinese	66
Others	31
Total	55,725

The greater efficiency of Saudi administration was underlined in the following year. Local and international observers judged the 1927 pilgrimage an unprecedented success. It was also the largest of the decade with some 240,000 Hajjis assembling at Arafat. Fears of a major epidemic consequent upon the far larger numbers of pilgrims proved ungrounded.[62] In this, as in subsequent years, crimes against pilgrims were reduced to a nugatory level, although numerous visiting Sunnis and Shi'ites faced arbitrary corporal punishment or even short prison terms for offence to Wahabi codes of acceptable Islamic prayer and forms of public devotion.[63] But perhaps the most obvious transformation in the conduct of the hajj under Saudi authority was the rapid introduction of motorized transport to convey pilgrims from Jeddah to the holy cities. Repairs to the Jeddah to Mecca road began in earnest in 1928 when a ten miles stretch was made more passable through the use of wire mesh to provide greater traction for lorries and other vehicles passing over its sandy surface.[64] By 1929 an officially sanctioned pilgrimage motor service, the Saudieh Motor Company, organized lorry transport for the great majority and cars for the wealthy few who disembarked at Jeddah.[65] And by 1930, in spite of an overall decline in pilgrim numbers, the availability of organized motor services from Jeddah increased still further with well over a thousand vehicles listed as engaged in hajj traffic. Lorries and cars, it seemed, had made an extended railway line, for the moment, irrelevant.[66]

The impetus to build a rail link from Jeddah was also diminished by the rapid improvement in standards of public health, brought about primarily by provision of affordable water supplies and outdoor shelters to assuage the impact of summer temperatures on fatigued travellers. There was no repetition in the late 1920s of the estimated 600 deaths among pilgrims encamped at Arafat in temperatures averaging 125° F in a single day of the 1920 hajj.[67] More rapid disposal of dead bodies and animal carcasses from pilgrimage routes and the main assembly centre at Arafat also cut the risk of epidemic illness. Lack of sanitation, the poverty and infirmity of numerous hajjis, and the extreme climate none the less exacted a heavy toll, and annual recorded mortality rates for the hajj seasons of 1926–32 fluctuated between 5 and 7 per cent.[68] It should be borne in mind that this figure included elderly hajjis that wished to die in the holy cities as well as pregnant mothers and newborn infants (principally Indonesians and Malays) who also travelled to the Hijaz to accrue the religious benefits of giving birth in the holy cities.

These figures notwithstanding, the Saudi authorities undoubtedly made strenuous efforts to make the pilgrimage a safer and healthier experience. Effective management of the hajj enhanced the reputation of the Saudi royal house throughout the Muslim world. The hajj also acquired stronger political and material significance in the late 1920s and early 1930s for several reasons. Saudi meetings with Muslim dignitaries during the hajj season and the House of Saud's patronage of visiting pilgrims in general took on a sharper political edge as Cairo and Jerusalem became more widely acknowledged as the key political centres of pan-Arabism. The absolute guarantee of pilgrim security offered the most tangible proof of the regional supremacy of Ibn Saud's government in the aftermath of the *Akhwan* revolt in northern Arabia during 1929–30 and the ongoing frontier disputes with the Yemeni and Iraqi regimes.[69] And the hajj remained the principal source of revenue in the Saudi budget.

The depression of the late 1920s and early 1930s hit the Saudi Treasury hard. Pilgrimage numbers tumbled in successive years from 1928 onward. The global collapse in commodity prices hit Asian colonial economies – and hence Asian Hajjis – particularly hard. Falls in the market price for rubber and tin, for instance, meant that far fewer Javanese and Malay pilgrims could afford the trip to the Hijaz in the depression years.[70] Tentative plans to expand Hijaz textile production to generate additional trade revenue were put on hold. A currency crisis hit the kingdom in autumn 1931 when Saudi silver riyal, previously linked at parity with sterling, was allowed to float after Britain's devaluation in September. And customs revenues collapsed during 1931–2 as regional trade levels plummeted.[71] Those Hajjis that still completed the trip generally spent less and stayed in the kingdom for a more limited period. By 1931 large numbers of hajj-related businesses in Jeddah, Mecca and Medina were struggling to survive. Business closures were commonplace and, by early 1933, government payment of state salaries was reportedly under threat.[72]

Conclusion

In these circumstances, it was little wonder that plans for a Jeddah to Mecca railway were shelved indefinitely. For one thing, the Saudi government had other, more urgent concerns. For another, the fall in pilgrimage numbers suggested that there was no longer any pressing need for such a rail link. Nor was it likely to be commercially viable. This was not simply a matter of few tariff-paying customers. The development of motor traffic along the Jeddah to Mecca road, and the vast improvement in security along all interior routes, afforded pilgrim travellers greater choice and peace of mind than in the years of Hashemite rule in the early 1920s. Evidently, then, the historical interest in an ephemeral railway line from Jeddah to Mecca cannot be measured in terms of opportunities lost. Nor is there much to be learnt about the undoubted strategic importance of railways or their immense commercial potential from what would – one has to admit – have been a quiet branch line for much of the year, only coming into its own as a vital, indeed life-saving service, during the hajj season.

Rather, the interest in the Jeddah to Mecca route lies elsewhere. Recurrent debate over the wisdom of this extension to the Hijaz line only makes sense in the context of pilgrimage politics, British imperial influence, and the contest for regional supremacy between the Hashemite authorities and Ibn Saud. The absence of a rail service from the principal port of entry to the Hijaz throws into sharp relief the mismanagement characteristic of the last years of Husain's rule. Hajjis making the arduous landward journeys to Mecca and Medina faced extortionate fees, numerous taxes and other arbitrary payments that were fundamental to Husain's exchequer and the clientage system that maintained a fragile peace among the Hijazis. Throughout the early 1920s the predations of the Ikhwan and the extension of Wahibite religious Puritanism that came with them presaged a wholesale change of power in the Hijaz as Ibn Saud's rule established itself across Central Arabia from its Najd heartland. The perils of pilgrimage were central to these transitions. The hajj was pivotal to the financial viability of government in the Hijaz. Protection of the holy cities and effective management of pilgrimage traffic were key measures of prestige and authority in the Muslim world. And the security and well being of tens of thousands of hajjis were important factors in Anglo-Hashemite and Anglo-Saudi relations during the 1920s and beyond. British imperial scrutiny of the conduct of the hajj played the same role in the diplomacy of 1920s Arabia was emblematic of the complex neo-colonial relationship between the region's rulers and the British Empire that would persist throughout the inter-war years. The Jeddah rail link may not have come to fruition in the decade studied here, bit its absence cast a long shadow over Hijazi politics.

Notes

1 See *Records of the hajj. A Documentary History of the Pilgrimage to Mecca*, especially *vol. 5: The Hashemite Period (1916–1925)* and *vol. 6: The Saudi Period (1926–1935)* both (London: Archive Editions, 1993). Inter-war pilgrimage reports during Ibn Saud's reign in the Hijaz, beginning in 1925, are collected together in *British Documents on*

Foreign Affairs, general editors Kenneth Bourne and Donald Cameron Watt, Part II, Series B, Robin Bidwell (ed.), Vol. 14: *Pilgrimage in the Reign of Ibn Saud, 1927–1939* (Public Record Office/University Press of America, 1989). Comprehensive political intelligence reports from the Jeddah Consulate, covering the period 1919–40, have also been published, see *The Jedda Diaries 1919–1940* five vols., (London: Archive Editions, 1990).

2 Timothy J. Paris, *Britain, the Hashemites and Arab Rule, 1920–1925* (London: Frank Cass, 2003), 311.

3 Regarding these dynastic-religious rivalries and the role of Wahabism, see John Habib, *Ibn Saud's Warriors of Islam: The Ikhwan of Najd and their Role in the Creation of the Saudi Kingdom, 1910–1930* (Leiden: Brill, 1978); Madawi Al Rasheed, 'Durable and non-durable dynasties: The Rashidis and Sa'udis in central Arabia,' *British Journal of Middle Eastern Studies*, 19:2 (1992), 149–57; David G. Edens, 'The anatomy of the Saudi revolution,' *International Journal of Middle East Studies*, 5:1 (1974), 51–5.

4 Paris, *Britain, the Hashemites and Arab Rule*, 299–313 *passim*; Joshua Teitelbaum, 'Pilgrimage Politics: The *hajj* and Saudi-Hashemite Rivalry, 1916–1925,' in Asher Susser and Aryeh Shmuelevitz (eds), *The Hashemites in the Modern Arab World: Essays in Honour of the Late Professor Uriel Dann* (London: Frank Cass, 1995), 65–84.

5 William Ochsenwald, 'A modern *Waqf*: The Hijaz railway, 1900–48,' *Arabian Studies* 3 (1976), 2–11; reprinted in William Ochsenwald, *Religion, Economy, and the State in Ottoman-Arab History* (Istanbul: Isis Press, 1998), 195–204.

6 Selim Deringil, 'Legitimacy structures in the Ottoman state: the reign of Abdülhamid II (1876–1909),' *International Journal of Middle East Studies*, 23:3 (1991), 346–7.

7 William Ochsenwald, 'The financing of the Hijaz railroad,' *Die Welt des Islams* 14 (1973); reprinted in Ochsenwald, *Religion, Economy, and the State*, 163, 172–6.

8 The links between temporal and religious authority in the region is succinctly described in Joseph A. Kechichian, 'The role of the ulama in the politics of an Islamic state: the case of Saudi Arabia,' *International Journal of Middle East Studies*, 18:1 (1986), 53–71.

9 Edens, 'The anatomy of the Saudi revolution,' 52–3.

10 Paris, *Britain, the Hashemites and Arab Rule*, 299.

11 Al Rasheed, 'Durable and non-durable dynasties,' 148; on the Ikhwan's role, see Joseph Kostiner, 'On instruments and their designers: the Ikh wan of Najd and the emergence of the Saudi state,' *Middle Eastern Studies*, 21:2 (1985), 298–323.

12 A. Musil, *Northern Nejd* (New York: American Geographical Society, 1928), cited in Al Rasheed, 'Durable and non-durable dynasties,' 148.

13 Al Rasheed, 'Durable and non-durable dynasties,' 154.

14 Regarding the massacre and the strained inter-communal relations in nineteenth-century Jeddah, see William Ochsenwald, 'The Jidda Massacre of 1858,' *Middle Eastern Studies*, 13 (1977), 314–26; and Oschsenwald, 'Muslim–European conflict in the Hijaz: The slave trade controversy, 1840–1895,' *Middle Eastern Studies*, 16 (1980), 115–26; both reprinted in Ochsenwald, *Religion, Economy, and the State in Ottoman-Arab History*.

15 Saleh Muhammad Al-Amr, *The Hijaz under Ottoman Rule 1869–1914: Ottoman Vali, the Sharif of Mecca, and the Growth of British Influence* (Riyad University Publications, 1978), 171–88.

16 Jacob Goldberg, 'The 1914 Saudi-Ottoman Treaty – myth or reality?,' *Journal of Contemporary History*, 19:2 (1984), 290–1, 306–9.

17 Edens, 'The anatomy of the Saudi revolution,' 59.

18 Habib, *Ibn Saud's Warriors of Islam*, chaps. 5, 6, and 9.

19 Kostiner, 'On instruments and their designers,' 314–17.

20 For a more sceptical assessment of the novelty and exclusivity of the Ikhwan than Habib's standard account, see Kostiner, 'On instruments and their designers,' 298–308.

21 Paris, *Britain, the Hashemites and Arab Rule*, 312.

22 Ibid., 304–7.

23 Habib, *Ibn Saud's Warriors of Islam*, 118–19.

24 Ochsenwald, 'The financing of the Hijaz railroad,' 163–83.

25 William I. Shorrock, 'The origin of the French Mandate in Syria and Lebanon: the railroad question, 1901–1914,' *International Journal of Middle East Studies*, 1:2 (1970), 133–53.

26 These ships also carried pilgrims from Morocco, Algeria, the Dutch East Indies and Eritrea, see *Records of the hajj. A Documentary History of the Pilgrimage to Mecca, vol. 5: The Hashemite Period (1916–1925)* (London: Archive Editions, 1993), 'Summary of arrivals and departures of pilgrims by sea, 1918,' p. 107.

27 Ibid., *vol. 5*, Captain W.P. Cochrane, 'Report on the hajj of 1336AH (1918),' pp. 105–6.

28 *The Jedda Diaries*, vol. 1: 1919–1921 (London: Archive Editions, 1990), E7445/455/16, Major W.E. Marshall (Jeddah) to Earl Curzon, Enclosure 1: 'Jeddah Report for the period 21 May to 10 June 1921.

29 Ibid., E15806/38/44, Enclosure 2: Captain Nasiruddin Ahmed, 'Report on the Hadj (Pilgrimage) for the year 1338 AH, i.e. 1920 AD,' received in FO registry, 8 October 1920, pp. 262–5.

30 Ibid., E15806/38/44, Viscount Allenby to Lord Curzon, 4 December 1920, p. 261.

31 Ibid., 'Extracts from a report on the Pilgrimage 1919, by Lt. Col. Vickery, British Agent, Jeddah,' pp. 159–61.

32 Ibid., E15806/38/44, Enclosure 2: Captain Nasiruddin Ahmed, 'Report on the Hadj (Pilgrimage) for the year 1338 AH, i.e. 1920 AD,' 8 October 1920, p. 263.

33 Ibid., 'Extracts from a report on the Pilgrimage 1919, by Lt. Col. Vickery, British Agent, Jeddah,' pp. 159–61.

34 Ibid., Captain Agub Khan, 'Intelligence Report up to 29 March 1920,' pp. 214–15.

35 Paris, *Britain, the Hashemites and Arab Rule*, 300–1.

36 *Records of the hajj, vol. 5*, E15806/38/44, Enclosure 2: Captain Nariruddin Ahmed to British Agent, Jeddah, 8 October 1920, p. 262.

37 Ibid., p. 265.

38 Good introductions include C. Ernest Dawn, *From Ottomanism to Arabism. Essays on the Origins of Arab Nationalism* (Urbana, Ill., 1973); Israel Gershoni, 'Rethinking the Formation of Arab Nationalism in the Middle East, 1920–1945. Old and New Narratives', in James P. Jankowski and Israel Gershoni (eds), *Rethinking Nationalism in the Arab Middle East* (New York, 1997), pp. 3–25; Said Amir Arjomand (ed.), *From Nationalism to Revolutionary Islam* (Albany, NY, 1984); Rashid Khalidi (ed.), *The Origins of Arab Nationalism* (New York, 1991).

39 Hanna Batatu, *The Old Social Classes and the Revolutionary Movements of Iraq* (Princeton, N.J.: Princeton University Press, 1978); Mohammad Tarbush, *The Role of the Military in Politics. A Case Study of Iraq to 1941* (London: KPI, 1982); Eliezer Tauber, *The Formation of Modern Syria and Iraq*, (London: Frank Cass, 1995); and two key articles by Saad Escander, 'Britain's Policy in Southern Kurdistan: The Formation and the Termination of the first Kurdish Government, 1918–1919', *British Journal of Middle Eastern Studies*, 27:2 (2000), pp. 139–63; Escander 'Southern Kurdistan under Britain's Mesopotamian Mandate: From Separation to Incorporation, 1920–23', *Middle Eastern Studies*, 37:2 (2001), pp. 153–80.

40 Tim Moreman, 'Watch and ward: the Army in India and the North-West Frontier, 1920–1939' in David Killingray and David Omissi (eds), *Guardians of Empire. The Armed Forces of the Colonial Powers c. 1700–1964* (Manchester: Manchester University Press, 1999), pp. 137–56.

41 Ibid., p. 265.

42 Ibid., E1120/113/91, Major Marshall (Jeddah Consul) to Marquess Curzon, 30 January 1922, Enclosure 1: 'Pilgrimage report, 1921.'

43 Ibid., p. 318–19.

44 *Records of the hajj, vol. 5*, E25/11/91, Consul Bullard (Jeddah) to Marquess Curzon, 18 December 1923, Enclosure 1: 'Pilgrimage report, 1923,' pp. 452–3.

45 The problem of destitution diminished, but did not disappear, in the first years of Saudi administration, see *Records of the hajj. vol. 6: The Saudi Period (1926–1935)*, E4387/249/91, Consul Stonehewer-Bird (Jeddah) to Sir Austen Chamberlain, 24 September 1927, Enclsoure 1: 'Report on the pilgrimage, 1927,' pp. 123–4.

46 Ibid. E25/1191, Consul Bullard (Jeddah) to Marquess Curzon, 18 December 1923, Enclosure 1: 'Pilgrimage report, 1923,' pp. 456–60.

47 *The Jedda Diaries*, vol. 1, E9617/455/91, Major Marshall (Jeddah) to Curzon, 31 July 1921, Enclosure 1: Jeddah Report, July 11–31, 1921.

48 Ibid. E15806/38/44, Enclosure 2: Captain Nariruddin Ahmed to British Agent, Jeddah, 8 October 1920, p. 272.

49 Paris, *Britain, the Hashemites and Arab Rule*, 302.

50 See, for example, *The Jedda Diaries*, vol. 2: 1922–1927 (London: Archive Editions, 1990), E4085/656/91, Acting Consul L.B. Grafftey-Smith to Curzon, 31 March 1922, Enclosure 1: Jeddah Report for the period 11–31 March 1922.

51 Ibid. E25/1191, Consul Bullard (Jeddah) to Curzon, 18 December 1923, Enclosure 1: 'Pilgrimage report, 1923,' p. 453.

52 Ibid., 453–4.

53 For an excellent sketch of British perspectives on Lausanne, see Erik Goldstein, 'The British official mind and the Lausanne Conference, 1922–23,' *Diplomacy and Statecraft*, 14:3 (2003), 185–CHECK.

54 *The Jedda Diaries*, vol. 2, E1532/424/91, Consul R.W. Bullard (Jeddah) to Mr MacDonald, 29 January 1924, Enclosure 1: Jeddah Report, January 1–29, 1924.

55 Ibid.

56 *Records of the hajj. Vol.5*, E25/1191, Bullard (Jeddah) to Curzon, 18 December 1923, Enclosure 1: 'Pilgrimage report, 1923,' p. 455.

57 Habib, *Warriors of Islam*, pp. 110–15.

58 *British Documents on Foreign Affairs (BDFA)*, general editors Kenneth Bourne and Donald Cameron Watt, Part II, Series B, Robin Bidwell (ed.), vol. 4: *The Expansion of Ibn Saud, 1922–1925* (Public Record Office/University Press of America, 1985), doc. 159, R.W. Bullard (Jeddah Consul), 'Report on the capture of Taif,' no date, pp. 190–5.

59 *Records of the hajj. vol. 6: The Saudi Period (1926–1935)*, E4942/103/25, Sir Andrew Ryan (Jeddah) to FO, received in FO registry, 27 September 1932, pp. 488–91.

60 *Jedda Diaries*, vol. 2, E4434/367/91, Vice-Consul Jordan to Sir Austen Chamberlain, 5 July 1926, Enclosure 1: Report on events in the Hedjaz for the period June 1–30, 1926. Ibn Saud had advised his Najdi subjects not to perform the hajj in 1926.

61 Figures based on UK Jeddah consulate disembarkation returns.

62 *BDFA*, Part II, Series B, vol. 14, doc. 1, E4387/249/91, Consul F.W.H. Stonehewer-Bird, Pilgrimage Report, 1927, 24 September 1927.

63 *Records of the hajj. vol. 6*, E4867/58/91, Stonehewer-Bird (Jeddah) to Lord Cushendun, 'Report on the pilgrimage, 1928,' 12 September 1928, see especially section 7: Religious intolerance, pp. 195–6. (Also reproduced in *BDFA*, Part II, Series B, vol. 14, doc. 2.)

64 *BDFA*, Part II, Series B, vol. 14, doc. 2, E4867/58/91, Stonehewer-Bird (Jeddah), Pilgrimage Report, 12 September 1928.

65 *BDFA*, Part II, Series B, vol. 14, doc. 3, E2421/54/91, W.L. Bond (Jeddah), Report on the Pilgrimage of 1929.

66 *BDFA*, Part II, Series B, vol. 14, doc. 4, E3460/100/25, Sir Andrew Ryan (Jeddah), Report on the Pilgrimage of 1930.

67 *Records of the hajj, vol. 5*, E1120/113/91, Major Marshall (Jeddah Consul) to Marquess Curzon, 30 January 1922, Enclosure 1: 'Pilgrimage report, 1921,' p. 323.

68 *Records of the hajj. vol. 6*, E4867/58/91, E2421/54/91, E3460/100/25, E5140/100/25, E4942/103/25: Pilgrimage reports on public health and sanitation, 1928–32. It should

be borne in mind that this figure included elderly Hajjis that wished to die in the Holy Cities as well as pregnant mothers and newborn infants (principally Indonesians and Malays) who also travelled to the Hijaz to accrue the religious benefits of giving birth in the Holy Cities. It should be borne in mind that this figure included elderly hajjis that wished to die in the Holy Cities as well as pregnant mothers and newborn infants (principally Indonesians and Malays) who also travelled to the Hijaz to accrue the religious benefits of giving birth in the Holy Cities.

69 Ibid., E2421/54/91, Consul Bond (Jeddah) to Arthur Henderson, Enclosure 1: 'Report on the pilgrimage of 1929,' 3 April 1930; E3460/100/25, Bond to Henderson, Enclosure 1: 'Report on the pilgrimage of 1930,' 13 May 1931; E4942/103/25, Ryan (Jeddah) to FO, received in FO registry, 27 September 1932.
70 See *BDFA*, Part II, Series B, vol. 14, docs. 2–5, Pilgrimage Reports, 1928–31.
71 Ibid., E4942/103/25, Ryan (Jeddah) to FO, received in FO registry, 27 September 1932; E4704/30/25, Consul A.S. Calvert (Jeddah) to FO, received in FO registry, 16 August 1933.
72 Ibid., Calvert (Jeddah) to FO, received in FO registry, 16 August 1933.

10 Barometer of war

British views of imperial security in the far east, Russo-Japanese relations and the Chinese Eastern railway, 1929–1935

Greg Kennedy

When is a railway more than just a strategic, logistics or mobility issue? One answer to that is when it assumes an aspect of international relations.[1] In military terms, railways are usually associated with the movement of troops, industrial goods and the material of war, or seen as a means of achieving strategic lift – a mathematical equation of modern warfare requiring calculations in support of strategic and operational planning.[2] Railways have seldom, therefore, been seen as barometers of war. Instead, they have been viewed as indicators. Such things as troop movements by rail, the increased traffic of coal, steel, timber or any other strategic resource, the laying of extra tracks or diversion of rolling-stock to support operations are the usual strategic and operational weights given to the worthiness of railways in pointing towards the likelihood of war.[3] The Chinese Eastern Railway (CER), as far as British Imperial Defence in the Far East in the 1930s is concerned, was a different sort of railway.

The sale of the Chinese Eastern Railway by the Soviet Union to Japan in March 1935 was a significant event in the balance of power between the Great Powers – the Soviet Union, Japan and Great Britain – vying for influence in China[4]. However, the importance of the sale was not only linked to any strategic lift capability it bestowed on or removed from either Japan or the Soviet Union, but rather what this important strategic accommodation between the bitter rivals meant for Britain's security interests in the region.[5] Until its sale, the CER was used as a barometer by British observers for measuring the stability of Russo-Japanese strategic foreign relations in the Far East from 1929, at the time of greater Japanese expansion in Manchuria and Mongolia. This chapter will look at how British strategic foreign policy makers read the CER barometer over the six year period from 1929 to 1935 with respect to Russo-Japanese relations, Anglo-Russian relations and Anglo-Japanese relations. This triangular relationship did not provide security for China, but was the essence of stability for the balance of power which existed between the three Great Power rivals in the Far East. Any instability in that relationship was thought to have the capability of creating the conditions necessary for war, an eventuality fraught with peril for British Imperial interests in the area. Therefore, the CER was one critical predictor used by the British strategic foreign policymaking elite to gauge whether or not another

Russo-Japanese war was a serious possibility or not in this period. More importantly for the purposes of this study, British observations of the CER situation was a litmus test for British perceptions regarding the balance of power dynamic in the Far East and its evolution in the period under investigation. Was a Russo-Japanese non-aggression pact a possibility? Was the USSR a serious military power in the Far East? Did Japan feel sufficiently strong militarily to risk a war with Russia in order to further its position in China? And, could Britain benefit strategically in the Far East from the tensions existing in Russo-Japanese relations? All these questions were intertwined with the conditions surrounding what the CER symbolized to the Soviet Union

From July 1929, until the end of that year, the Soviet Government and the National Government of the Chinese Republic in Nanking were embroiled in a bitter dispute over control of the CER. On 10 July reports began to reach Moscow of Chinese troops and authorities seizing the entire network of rail and telegraph lines. In rapid order, further information began to filter back to the Soviet capital regarding demands from the Chinese that complete management of the railway be given over to their authority. As well, Manchurian troops were being brought to a state of military preparedness and positioned along the frontier, with sporadic exchanges of gunfire taking place.[6] As a counter to the threatened use of major military force, the Soviet Union created the Special Far Eastern Army on 6 August, under the command of Comrade (Marshal) V.K. Blücher. By the end of the month formal relations between the two countries had come to an end.[7] Furthermore, despite the instigation of talks between Moscow and London aimed at the normalization of Anglo-Soviet international relations, the Soviet Vice-Commisar for Foreign Affairs, M.M. Litvinov, held the British Government, as well as the American and Japanese Governments, responsible for the state of affairs existing between China and the Soviet Union. His logic operated on the belief that China, afraid of military and economic retaliation by the Imperialist Powers if it tried to displace their imperial interests in China, was thus forced by those powers instead to seek to undermine pacifist Russia's place in the region: 'There is no doubt at all that without the implicit or even the active encouragement of other Powers in the early stages of the conflict, and without this reliance on widespread anti-Soviet hostility, Nanking would never have decided on the provocative policy which has led to the present situation.'[8] So, while on the one hand the capitalist nature of those nations was to blame for that Far Eastern predicament, the restoration of formal and trade relations with Great Britain and the United States was seen as being of great import for the future development of the Soviet Union on the world stage. The Soviet Minister expressed this dual perspective regarding the place of Great Britain in the Soviet Union's strategic considerations to the Central Executive Committee on 4 December: 'On our side there is good will, the sincere desire to establish friendly relations with the peoples of Great Britain, to remove those misunderstanding which have up to now been deliberately created by certain circles in order to estrange the two States. It is, however, to be regretted that the relations just established have already been somewhat darkened by the British association with the American démarche in the Manchurian conflict.'[9]

Unsurprisingly, Great Britain's strategic foreign policy makers viewed the situation in China through a different lens and in a different light entirely.

Some early global views on how the Chinese seizure of the CER was being perceived by other Powers, with regard to the protection of the various interests of those nations in the region, began to come the British foreign policy makers in the summer of 1929. One of the first indicators in favour of the Soviet actions came from Sir Esme Howard, the British Ambassador in Washington, in July 1929.[10] Henry Stimson, the American Secretary of State, informed Howard that he thought the strong Russian stand being taken against the Chinese illegal seizure was good for British and American interests. In Stimson's view, such a robust reaction was a useful demonstration that the Anglo-Americans could use as a coercive point, showing the Chinese the dangers that could befall them if they threatened American or British interests in a similarly rash and unreasonable fashion.[11] Both western Powers, however, were at a severe disadvantage when compared to the Soviet Union, as neither had a sizeable and credible military force in mainland China able to back up such a 'intolerant' policy. Japan, however, was not at such a disadvantage. But Tokyo wished to see diplomacy allowed to work in order to solve the CER incident and wished for that solution to be a cooperative one, arrived at with not only with China and the Soviet Union, but also with Great Britain and the United States playing a role. However, none but Japan should play a direct or influential role. The Japanese Government hoped that local Chinese authorities, favourably disposed to Japanese interests in that area, would be left to negotiate directly, with the Soviet Government, a settlement regarding management of the CER in August 1929.[12] The CER incident, and any resolution respecting its future operations, were causing the strategic foreign policy making elites in the various Powers to pay some closer attention to the dynamics that existed between the Soviet Union, China, and Japan, and to consider what any actions in the incident might mean for their own policies, if faced with such a violation of treaty rights by China in the future. For the British elite, the events of 1929 in the Far East were not yet instructive or decisive in allowing those observers to gauge Soviet international intentions in the region and whether those intentions were a destabilizing influence in the theatre.

In January 1930, the Foreign Office (FO) paid little attention to the role of the Soviet Union in the China. An extensive Departmental memorandum outlining Britain's options in China did not give any weight to the Soviet Union's place in the balance of power in the region. While acknowledging a linkage between Moscow and the Canton Kuomintang government, set up in 1923 through discussions with Sun Yat-sen, the view held by the FO was that Nationalist Chinese forces under Chiang Kai-shek were decided anti-Soviet. This meant that since July 1927 Central and Southern China, the main areas of British interest, had been free of Soviet meddling: 'Since that date Russian influence in China has been practically dead.'[13] However, while not directly acknowledging the Soviet Union's future use of military force, the report acknowledged that Britain's place in China had been carved out by the use of force and that 'It was maintained up to the Great War on prestige, but the Chinese have now come to realize that unless there is force behind it mere prestige is another word for bluff.'[14] This declaration reflected the fact that the Soviet Union and Great Britain faced similar decisions: whether to arm themselves in preparation for the use of force to protect their Chinese interests or to find other means to do so. As well, there was another, more dangerous potential threat to both Soviet and British interests in the region: Japan. Parallelling Litvinov's fears of Japan's place in Manchuria, and on mainland China in general as being a most probable source of future armed conflict, the FO memorandum pulled no punches in designating Japan as the main threat to British interests in China:

> But notwithstanding the outward show of harmony among the Powers in their relations with China, it has been impossible to ignore the underlying divergence of interests which renders co-operation in practice so difficult. The chief disturbing element in this respect is Japan. There is no gainsaying the fact that Japan, though she may not like chaos in China, does not, for very obvious reasons, want a strong and united China; while, unfortunately, Great Britain and America, though in essentials pursuing the same ends, often do not act in complete harmony owing to a fundamental difference of political outlook. France has considerably less interest in the East than any of the other Great Powers concerned. Her co-operation is unreliable, and she is prone to use her position to seek her owns ends rather than pursue an enlightened policy.[15]

The strategic picture in the FO at the beginning of 1930 regarding possible British friends and allies interested in making a common front in China to contain Japan, did not yet see any evidence that the Soviet Union was important. However, with diplomatic relations with that country now normalized there was some hope that a greater knowledge and sense of the Soviet Union's pursuits in the Far East could be obtained.

By February 1930, Sir Esmond Ovey, the British Ambassador to the Soviet Union, had only been in Moscow a little over two months. His still immature views of Soviet Russia's intentions were preliminary in nature, but he believed that his arrival coincided with a genuine rise in the Soviet political temperature concerning international relations.[16] As well, a common theme was emerging in those disgruntled Soviet sensibilities. The Soviet Union believed itself encircled by the capitalist Powers, not only in Europe but in the Far East as well. This was a global containment of the Communist dream. Ovey was sceptical of such a simplistic explanation for all Soviet international woes, seeing such rhetoric as being part of the communist creed. However, he did think that a combination of events had conspired to make a legitimate feeling of injustice in the Soviet strategic foreign policy making elite and the CER was a part of that ill-feeling. In particular, the United States was seen as having meddled in that affair to the detriment of Soviet interests. As any good Ambassador would, Ovey made the diplomatic rounds in Moscow to confirm his own suspicions through the sources of others.

After his factfinding exercise, Ovey informed the FO that he was certain that the Soviet Union's bark in the Far East was much worse than its bite and that any threatened actions or warlike talk was just talk.[17] In particular, on 8 February, he ended his report on the Soviet strategic position in the world to Arthur Henderson, the Secretary of State for Foreign Affairs, by quoting the views of the Ambassador Tanaka, the Japanese representative to the Soviet Union. Tanaka had offered Ovey the opinion that: 'The attention of the Soviet Government, he [Tanaka] said, was riveted to the internal situation. They did not wish to fight anyone, nor did anyone wish to fight them. Friendship with them was impossible, but enmity was of no avail. Mr. Tanaka, too, expressed his unsolicited opinion that, when trouble comes, it will be in the direction of Bessarabia.'[18] With such reports and opinions coming in from the Far East and Russia, the Foreign Office had little evidence of any reason to consider the Soviet Union an expansionist power or a destabilizing influence on the balance of power in the Far East.

In early July, 1930, the British Minister to China, Sir Miles Lampson, compiled a complete report on the CER incident and its ramifications that questioned that benign assessment to some extent.[19] Lampson declared that the terms stipulated in the negotiations between China and the Soviet Union to end the crisis marked a 'complete capitulation' by the Chinese. This reversal had been brought about by the successful use of the force of arms by the Soviets and a successful diplomatic strategy, which '...combined of ruthless realism and semi-Asiatic subtlety, has proved itself admirably suited for dealing with the Chinese race.' Even when assured of absolute victory, the Soviets had shown restraint and common sense regarding their position in the region *vis-à-vis* Japan, China, and the European nations, including Great Britain. Pointing out that the incident was merely one in what he believed was a long-term policy by the Chinese central government to oust foreigners from vital positions, particularly those who controlled the country's key economic, financial and technical resources, Lampson felt that 'Only on the Chinese Eastern Railway, China is unlikely, after last year's decisive trial of strength, to resort again, at least for some time to come, to such crude and drastic methods.'[20] Therefore, in the British minister's eyes, the Soviets had retained their position in the region through the threat of the use of military force and were now able to expect a more cooperative, or at least a neutral, stance from the Chinese. Other nations involved in China, such as Great Britain, might not in the future be able to expect treatment similar to the new Soviet position. The FO concurred with Lampson, conveying to the service Chiefs and Cabinet the opinion that law and order was now expected to prevail in China, that British interests were safe in the near future from any sort of aggressive, armed take-over by Chinese authorities, but that considerations about how to combat the future spread of Communistic influences in the country required serious consideration.[21] It was not, however, the spread of Soviet sponsored Communism that began to threat the British interests in the region throughout the rest of 1930 and 1931, but the growing aggressiveness of Japanese actions on mainland China.

Part of the problem concerning growing tensions between China and Japan revolved around railways, in particular the South Manchurian Railway (SMR), which was linked to the Chinese Eastern Railway issue. In July 1931, British diplomatic representatives reported an increasing tension in Sino-Japanese relations in Manchuria. Citing a collection of issues for which the increased tensions could be blamed, M.E. Dening, the Acting-Consul in Dairen, informed Sir Francis Lindley, the British Ambassador in Tokyo, that one of the main topics was railways. Dening reported that the Nanking Government was particularly agitated about regaining the CER and then wished to turn its attentions to recovering the South Manchurian Railway.[22] British intelligence sources in the region had for some time been pointing to a dangerous buildup of tensions between the two countries and voiced concerns that the increases in Japanese military power in the area pointed to a Japanese intention to take over Manchuria.[23] Lindley, concerned with the slipping prestige of Great Britain in the Far East, was loath to acknowledge that there was any mounting danger to British interests.[24] The Far Eastern Dept. of the FO, however, was not so sanguine about the events in Manchuria which were linked to railway issues. F.K. Roberts, a senior clerk in that department, prepared a large memorandum on the issue. This was sent to Lindley in order to bring him up to speed on the overlapping strategic issues at stake in the SMR debate.[25] Of concern to the FO was that Japan would emulate the proven Soviet method of using military force to protect and advance its strategic railway interests in China. If such a thing occurred, British interests could begin to appear to be the least protected and thus the most vulnerable in the region. As well, such a use of force could destabilize China by increasing the Japanese military presence in Manchuria and posing a threat to the Soviet position. Lindley agreed with the FO's assessment of the role of the Soviet Union in Japan's plans, confirming that his conversations with the Japanese Minister for Foreign Affairs, Baron Shidehara, led him (Lindley) to believe,

> Apart from the Chinese aspect of the situation, there is the possibility of Soviet intervention, which is certainly very present in the minds of the Japanese. Many people believe that any move of troops into South Manchuria by the Japanese would be followed by an advance of the Russians in the north. There are obvious objections to such a movement from the Soviet propaganda point of view and it might never take place. But I am inclined to think that a serious effort would be made to come to some understanding with Moscow before anything serious in a military way was undertaken by the Japanese in South Manchuria.[26]

Reports from Dening in Dairen did not support the Ambassador's optimistic view. Dening's observations supported the FO fears that local Japanese authorities were looking to use force as the only remedy for Japanese problems in Manchuria. He believed that a peaceful resolution of the tensions was unlikely.[27] Sir Miles Lampson's reports also informed the FO that rising Sino-Japanese tensions were taken by many in China, both communist and non-communist alike, as a sign of the need for closer military links between China and the Soviet Union.[28] The issues of railways, international tensions between China, Russia and Japan, and maintaining a balance of power in China, were all beginning to combine to create a new regional strategic reality for British strategic foreign policy makers to have to consider.[29]

On 18 September, 1931, the rate of change in that strategic environment was accelerated. An explosion on the SMR killed Japanese troops and civilians, sparking an escalation in the use of military force by the Japanese in Manchuria. The feared Soviet reaction to such an increased Japanese presence in Manchuria did not, however, materialize. Indeed, reports from both Russia and China indicated that the Soviet Union was quite happy with the increased Japanese embroilment in China. William Strang, the new British chargé d'affaires in the Soviet Union, forwarded to London a picture of a smug and self-satisfied Litvinov and Soviet foreign policy making elite. Seeing the Chinese suffer at the hands of the Japanese, while at the same time the Japanese were lashed by world opinion into moderation, was an ironic condition for the Soviets and one which they enjoyed mightily.[30] Strang put greater weight on Soviet economic plans, and the need for that nation to avoid any large-scale military operations due to its focus on internal economic programmes, as being a limiting factor on Russian interest in the Manchurian situation. The Soviet Foreign Ministry was keeping in close contact with its Japanese counterpart during the crisis and any potential clashes between the two in areas such as Harbin were being carefully managed and avoided. Neither nation, according to Strang, wished the Manchurian punishment raids to escalate into a greater conflict.[31] The Japanese actions had been careful to avoid any threatening movements north along the SMR toward the junction with the CER at Harbin. Secure in their belief that the Japanese actions were not a threat to Soviet interests in the area, the Soviet Union was happy to stand aside as China was once more 'taught a lesson'. British observers in the region agreed that so long as Japan did not create a direct threat to Soviet interests in the Eastern Provinces during its expansionist drive, the likelihood of intervention by the Soviet Union was slight. Also, all agreed that Japan took such a cautious approach due to a fear of arousing 'the Soviet menace', implying that Japan feared a military showdown with Russia in China.[32] As one of the few potential brakes on Japanese actions in the area, just how much respect Japan really had for Soviet military power in Manchuria was becoming a more important question for British policy makers to answer.[33]

In Tokyo, Ambassador Lindley blamed the Russian attacks on China over the CER in 1929 for providing the blueprint for the current Japanese line of action. He reasoned that the Japanese had observed the way in which the international community had allowed the Soviets to use military force without intervention or reprisal. While recognizing that the Soviet and Japanese geographic and political realities were not similar, Lindley was concerned that neither the League of Nations' moral and ethical arguments, nor Western economic pressures, would be enough to stop Japan's transgressions in Manchuria.[34] Therefore, if moral and economic levers (traditional tools of British strategic diplomacy) would not work in containing Japan, what would? The Soviet Union was one possible answer. With the Japanese occupation of Changchun, in October 1931, Lindley and the other British observers were able to consider a possible rationale for a greater

Soviet effort to contain Japanese plans in Manchuria. In November the movement of troops by the USSR to its eastern frontier gave greater heart to those British policy makers who pinned some hope of containing Japan on a substantial Soviet military presence in the region. Those expectations were dashed by January 1932, when reports of talks between Japan and the Soviet Union over a possible non-aggression pact began to filter into the wider international community.[35] Therefore, by the end of 1931, the question for British strategic foreign policy makers was: what was the state of Russo-Japanese relations in mainland China and what did that mean for British imperial security?

Reports from Moscow were beginning to paint a different picture of the Soviet interests in Manchurian affairs. Ambassador Ovey had asked the Soviet Foreign Minister directly, in mid-January 1932, whether Litvinov believed the Japanese promises that their actions in seizing other key railways and junctions in Manchuria were only temporary and did not threaten Soviet CER interests. Indeed, Ovey inquired whether the Soviets considered the Manchurian question closed. Litvinov's reply was that it 'had only really just begun.' In Ovey's view Litvinov believed that Japan and Russia would engage in open conflict perhaps over the CER or some other question of control in that area. This clash was not imminent, but almost inevitable in the medium to distant future.[36] Litvinov had mentioned to Ovey his discussions of the possibility of a non-aggression pact with Yoshizawa, the new Japanese Minister for Foreign Affairs, who had passed through Moscow in late 1931. Ovey was not convinced that such a pact with Japan was a likely proposition, at least not in Litvinov's eyes, and that such talk was just part of the greater Soviet attempt to negotiate such non-aggression pacts with all its neighbours, both in the Far East and Europe.[37] However, the Far East did hold a special place in the Soviet Foreign Minister's planning for the future. Ovey told the FO that such a pact would serve two purposes for Litvinov:

> It is, therefore, evident that a very strong additional reason in favour of concluding these pacts is the desire on the part of Russia to be entirely secure on her western frontier in the event of trouble in the Far East. ... If the Japanese accept, so much the better. But this manoeuvre would also have its advantages were the Japanese to refuse the offer. In such case the Soviet Government would be in a position to construe any 'act of violence' which may occur on the Far-Eastern frontier as an aggression within the meaning of the pact on the part of the Japanese Government and thus to ensure non-aggression in the West.[38]

To some in London, Litvinov's fear of Japan was a beacon of hope at a time when British imperial defence planning in the region called out for the need to find a counter-weight to the growing Japanese menace. At the end of January the Sino-Japanese conflict had spread to the key British interest of Shanghai. By March of that year many FO officials, such as Sir Robert Vansittart, the Permanent Under-Secretary, were exasperated by the Japanese attitude towards foreign powers in China, fearful of further, bolder attacks on British interests by either Chinese or Japanese forces and desperate to find some leverage or ally that might deter any further Japanese invasion of China.[39]

Unfortunately, Soviet concerns about the CER or Japanese aggression in Manchuria did not appear to be enough of a catalyst for creating useful, concerted actions by the USSR. Lindley's assessment of the Soviet attitude towards Japan was that, in order to protect the 30 to 40,000 Soviet citizens who were dependent on the CER, Russia would be willing to go a long way towards not creating any antagonisms with Japan. This view was informed by talks between the First Secretary of the British Embassy, T.M. Snow, and Mr. Spilwanek, the former Soviet Consul-General at Habarovsk, who, in March of 1932, was now the Counsellor at the Soviet Embassy in Tokyo. Lindley considered Spilwanek an intelligent and reliable source of information on the Soviet intentions and put good stock in the intelligence gathered from him. It was also Spilwanek's view that the Soviet Union was not interested in the commercial success of the CER and that its commercial prospects were not considerable and therefore not vital to the Soviet's Five Year Plan. Lindley thought that the Soviet Government would use its citizens in a propaganda war for world opinion against any Japanese aggression towards the CER but was not ready to contemplate protecting the railway at the risk of starting a major war with Japan.[40] But in the FO, that estimation by British sources in Tokyo of a cautious Russia was countered by continued, contradictory reports from Moscow.

In mid-March Ovey was informing the FO and War Office (WO) of the despatch of sizeable numbers of Soviet troops, modern aircraft, and other war material to the Far East. Teams of Soviet engineers had also been sent to Italy to purchase war material for a possible Far Eastern conflict. Finally, Ovey knew that Litvinov had been having important strategic discussions with Stalin, and, in the aftermath of those talks, was repeating the message in the press and through diplomatic channels that the Japanese would do well to be wary of going too far in threatening Soviet interests associated with the CER and the areas linked to that railway.[41] Later that same month, Ovey and his staff compiled a report on just exactly how large the Soviet reinforcement of the Far East had been. It was their opinion that at least 100,000 troops had been redeployed to that theatre as a result of Japan's actions, making the total strength available to the Soviet commander approximately 200,000 men. Tensions between the Japanese and Soviet authorities were being exacerbated as well by the Japanese attempts to limit the movement of cereals and grains eastward along the CER in the belief that those supplies would be used by the growing Russian contingent threatening to strike at the Japanese forces. Factories in the Soviet Union were also reported to be on a war mobilization footing, with increased production in small arms, artillery and ammunition being noted.[42] British observers on the ground in Manchuria confirmed that Japanese intentions towards the CER appeared very aggressive. The Soviet Union's continued denial of the CER to Japan for use in troop redistribution in the region between Harbin and Hailin, as well as the insistence that the CER's administration remained split 50–50 between Chinese and Soviet personnel, was causing some high-ranking Japanese officers in China to contemplate the temporary seizure of the railway and a declaration of martial law in its subsequent adminis-tration. These observers also confirmed the growing military strength of the Soviet Union in the region as well as the reallocation of CER rolling-stock for the stockpiling of strategic materials necessary if the Soviets were contemplating seriously the use of military force against the Japanese incursions.[43]

In April, Ambassador Lindley confirmed that the local Soviet authorities had indeed succeeded in saving much of the CER rolling-stock from falling into Japanese hands, as the latter continued to take greater control of the railway for their own purposes. Lindley, from Japanese and other sources in Japan, con-firmed the vast increase in Soviet military strength in Manchuria, putting the Russian strength at around 250,000 men, as opposed to the 60,000 present in the previous September. Bombings along the CER aimed at Japanese troops were being blamed on Bolshevik agents, raising tensions between the two nations to even greater heights.[44] Given this intelligence and the recent developments in Russo-Japanese relations on mainland China, the British Ambassador in Japan was now very concerned about the prospects for continued stability, and the subsequent consequences for British imperial defence, in China:

> While we have reason to believe that the Soviets are most anxious to avoid becoming embroiled in the Far East and while the Japanese certainly have not up to now contemplated hostilities with them, I am bound to admit that I am becoming uneasy at the turn events have taken during the past month. The arrogance of the Japanese military is such that, if they become convinced that the Russians mean to harass them in Manchuria, they are capable of forcing the issue. In such an event I should be sorry to prophesy what the Soviet would do. There are many alternatives, of which the most probable is, perhaps, acceptance of a rebuff coupled with promises of good behaviour in the future. But it is at least possible that the Soviets, with the strength which they have quietly built up in the Far East, might think the moment was ripe for a great world-revolutionary move. The temptation to come out as the champions of the toiling millions of China against the Militarist Japanese and the Imperialist League of Nations, led by Great Britain, must be extraordinarily strong to Bolshevik mentality. But these are mere speculations. What is not a speculation is that the Japanese General Staff, and wide circles outside the Army, are convinced that, sooner or later, there will be a second Russo-Japanese campaign in Manchuria. Such a state of mind is not reassuring.[45]

For Lindley, the most important concern was whether local Japanese commanders in China would create an incident that could ignite the powder-keg of bad Russo-Japanese feeling that existed at that point in time into a larger conflagration, '... starting another war which is no war'.[46]

The differing answers issuing from the three imperial, strategic observation-posts (the embassies and attached Legations and Consuls in China, Japan and Soviet

Union) concerning whether the Soviet Union would fight over the CER and whether Japan would risk a war with the Soviets while China remained unsubdued, reflected Britain's overall confusion regarding the role of the Soviets in the Far East. At the Committee of Imperial Defence (CID) and at Cabinet/Ministerial levels no clear consensus regarding the strategic 'weight' of the Soviet Union in Great Power affairs in that region had been established.[47] The FO, following the lead of such Far Eastern experts as Sir John Pratt, a senior official usually attached to the Far Eastern Department, held a general consensus that the Japanese would not be so foolish as to press their military adventure recklessly to the point of starting a war with the Soviets. Considering information and intelligence garnered not only from British sources in Japan, China and the Soviet Union, but also from discussions with such Soviet representatives to the League of Nations as Karl Radek, a member of the editorial board of the Soviet newspaper *Izvestiya*, Pratt surmised that Japanese expansion would stop at the Amur river and there was little the Soviets would do to interfere with Japanese plans so long as the later did not cross that boundary.[48] All important British strategic decision making bodies, however, were still waiting to see how future relations between Russia and Japan, particularly over the CER issue, would develop before any concrete Imperial Defence policy was constructed.

By August of 1932 more information was making its way into the British strategic foreign policy making machinery. Ovey had confirmed some of the views put forward by Spilwanek. The British Ambassador in Moscow was not prone to crediting Soviet foreign policy with having any greater humanitarian motives regarding the defence of Russian citizens associated with the CER than had its Tsarist predecessor. However, he agreed absolutely with the Soviet official in Japan that '...the present government are much more realistic in the foreign policy than were the later Imperial Government and that so far as the Chinese Eastern Railway and Manchuria in general are concerned they are more likely to be weighted by material considerations than by considerations of mere prestige.'[49] The WO in London was also beginning to take notice of the strained state of Russo-Japanese relations and watched the CER as a litmus test for any important changes in attitude from either side. That department's assessment of the situation was that Japan was moving towards a more independent, aggressive stance and set to leave the League of Nations upon the establishment of the Japanese puppet state of Manchukuo. However, as far as any prospect of a Russo-Japanese war being in the offing, the WO's view was that such an event was very unlikely. Indeed, its greatest suspicion was that the two Asian powers had struck a bargain and over June and July had settled on the terms which would allow a non-aggression pact to be signed, if one had not already been agreed to.[50] Ultimately, the WO did not feel that there was any immediate danger of a Russo-Japanese war breaking out. More importantly, instead of seeing the Soviet Union as a possible balance against Japanese expansion in Asia, as was the want of the FO, the WO was distinctly anti-Soviet in its opinions regarding the Russo-Japanese question. In September 1932, MI2, the strategic intelligence wing of the WO, highlighted the advantages to be had from a strong Japanese presence in Manchukuo. Such a development would not only rob the Soviet Union of the assurance of being able to use the CER for any redeployment of troops, but, more importantly, would create a strong and persistent, nagging contention for the Soviet strategic foreign policy makers to have to consider. Such a condition would, in the WO view, help ensure that the USSR would be reluctant to undertake any adventures against British interests in India, the British Army's main strategic pre-occupation in the interwar.[51] Maj. General W.H. Bartholomew, the Director of Military Intelligence and Operations [DMO&I] and his deputy, Maj. General A.C. Temperley, agreed that Japan was the better choice as far as strategic friendships went. If Russia were allowed to spread the poison of communism into China, no one could predict the disasters that could befall the British Empire.[52] For the WO, Japan as still a former ally and a nation worthy of martial consideration. Once it had thrown off the momentary cloak of madness that had created so much global disgust and loathing over its actions in China, and as soon as sanity had been restored once more to Japanese national life, was to be courted as a potential partner in the global quest to counter the insidious spread of Communism. But, in the autumn of 1932, the announcement of the League-sponsored, and British supported, Lytton Report, which denounced the Japanese actions in China over the last year,1933 promised little for the WO's hoped for Anglo-Japanese reconciliation.[53]

Indeed, by supporting the publication of the Lytton report, the British Cabinet had crossed a Rubicon in Far Eastern matters. Most British Cabinet officials gave little consideration to Far Eastern affairs at the best of times. The crisis in China over the last year had changed all that. A threat to the League and the liberal notion of collective security, a threat to British Imperial interests, and a threat to a stable balance of power in the region, Japanese aggression had now become a known, as opposed to a suspected, threat. For most British strategic foreign policy making officials, events in Manchuria and the creation of the illegitimate state of Manchukuo represented '... an anxious and unhappy business.'[54] Anthony Eden, the British representative to the League of Nations in 1933, summarized the views of many British politicians when he wrote to Prime Minister Stanley Baldwin: 'Manchuria is an anxious and unhappy business... but I hope, now that it has become apparent that we are as determined as anybody else to carry out the recommendations of the Lytton Report and to stand by the Covenant, that the position will improve for us in China. It is however obvious the longer the business is dragged out the more harm must be done to our interests in the Far East.'[55] If calm and stability was to be brought back to the balance in China, then the worth of the Soviet Union as a strategic counter-weight to the dangerous Japanese ambitions would be take on a greater importance in British strategic considerations. War would wreak havoc on British interest. But, the threat of war could work to the Empire's advantage, if the fears created by that tension were properly utilized.[56] Therefore, given the complexities and sensitivities surrounding the Russo-Japanese relationship, the issues attached to the CER remained an even more important strategic barometer than ever at the end of 1932.[57]

In 1933, there were differing departmental views as to how to maintain stability in Manchuria. The WO held the view that Britain's strategic foreign policy should centre around the idea of appeasing or wooing Japan with economic terms and conditions that would alleviate some of the sting delivered by the Lytton Report.[58] With no significant naval or military forces of note in the region and no foreseeable increase in the defence budgets in sight, the British Army was inclined to pin its hopes on Japanese self-restraint and budgetary limitations, rather than any idea of closer ties to Soviet Russia, as the solution most likely to thwart Japan's plans. The FO, however, held other views about how the quagmire of Manchukuo could work to Britain's advantage. Sir George Sansom, the unrivalled expert on Japan and all things Japanese, instructed the FO not to expect Japan's adventures in Manchuria to bankrupt the Asian nation economically. He did, however, point out the huge deficit present in the 1933 Japanese budget and highlighted the vast amounts being spent on defence projects. One of the biggest drains on that budget was the Manchurian campaign.[59] The Soviet Union's increased military power along its eastern frontiers had to be met, and, so long as Japanese building programmes and troop deployments were aimed at that area of Asia, Britain's interests would not be in serious danger.

Another old Asian-hand, T.M. Snow, was in London in December 1932, about to return to Japan. He counselled the FO that Japan was not likely to give up its Manchurian adventure under any League of Nations' pressure due to Tokyo's belief in the need to remain in Manchuria to block communist expansion.[60] Indeed, by January of 1933, with the Japanese almost assuredly leaving the League of Nations on the 16th of that month and British military power at a low ebb, Sir Robert Vansittart saw only Japan's 'own capacities for absorption and the fear of Russia, with whom she may anyhow eventually come to a second round [of non-aggression pact talks]'[61] as being the only things restraining Japan. Sir John Pratt, writing not just as an expert on Chinese issues but also from his vantage point as advisor to Anthony Eden in Geneva, appraised the FO in late December 1932 that China was well on its way to closer strategic ties with the USSR now that diplomatic relations between the two nations had been normalized. Seen by Pratt as a warning to Japan that it would find allies wherever it could to continue the fight against Japanese aggression, the Chinese restoration of normal relations with the USSR confirmed the end of any hope of collective security working in the region.[62] It also confirmed the continued growth of the worth of the Soviet Union in the balance of power system that now appeared to be at work in the Far East. Vansittart summed up the FO view, calling Japan a nuisance in the League, a nation with 'playboy'-like qualities of 'a fine natural savagery', and a country that was not 'housebroken' to a degree sufficient to allow it to co-habitat with other nations in such an international environment. Finally, he believed that dealing with Japan from a position of diplomacy and strength was preferable to appeasing such a rapacious nation in the fashion suggested by the WO. And the worth of the Soviet Union and its relationship with Japan informed his views to a large degree concerning Britain's dealings with Japan in the future: 'There is... little chance of any lasting Russo-Japanese bloc, especially as the decomposing or reviving mass of China will always provide them with bones of contention. It is not an alluring future, but neither is her future presence in the

League;'[63] Clearly, Vansittart, senior members of the FO entrusted with Britain's Far Eastern strategic policy, as well as the Ambassadors to Moscow, China and Japan, were already considering how to play the Soviets off against the Japanese in order to protect British interests in the new security environment that existed in the Far East in the aftermath of the Lytton Report.[64] The question now was to ascertain to what degree Russo-Japanese tensions could be utilized to best British advantage.

By the end of January 1933 the idea of a possible Russo-Japanese non-aggression pact had passed. The USSR seemed content with the situation regarding the CER's administration and protection and was allowing Japan to still use the railway in an almost unlimited fashion, except for the rolling-stock. However, the Soviet Government was not allowing Japan to have things all its own way in the debate about who was the more respectable nation in terms of international affairs. The Soviet Foreign Office and Litvinov took the opportunity to embarrass the Japanese further on the stage of global public opinion by publishing documents in late January related to the non-aggression pact discussions, documents which insinuated that Japan was in the hands of a military-controlled government bent on imperial conquest in China. In such circumstances, China was of course justified in seeking Soviet aid for its fight for freedom.[65] The tactic was to paint the Soviets as the concerned nation, aiding the underdog China in the face of a merciless and uncaring aggressor.[66] Reports from Lindley at the end of January indicated the Count Uchida, the Japanese Minister for Foreign Affairs, was annoyed at the Russian tactic, but, overall the two nations seemed to be on amicable terms, with the CER issue remaining a tense but manageable affair.[67] However, British observers were becoming more concerned over the influence of the Japanese Army on that nation's strategic foreign policy and in particular that organization's belief that a war with Russia was inevitable.

Lt Col E.A.H. James, the British Military Attaché in Japan, filed a report to the War Office in January that pointed to the Japanese response to the Soviet military buildup along its Far Eastern frontiers. The military mobilization taken in order to safeguard that nation's claims to the CER had prompted an escalation in Japanese armament production and general readiness for war. As James explained

> There is no question but that the officers of the army, and notably some of the senior officers, feel convinced that in a few years' time Japan will find herself at war with Russia. How long this opinion has been held I have no means of saying, nor do I yet know whether it is a sudden conviction brought about by the present Manchuria incident, or whether it has been one long held. ...I am of the opinion that the present activity and the decision to undertake the rearmament of the Japanese army are directed mainly against Russia, though other possibilities cannot be excluded altogether. All available information up to the present has pointed to there being little likelihood of a conflict in the immediate future, but Japanese army circles believe that there is an undoubted danger of war, say, in three to five years' time.[68]

Sir George Sansom confirmed the dangers outlined in James' report with his own intelligence derived from the departing Soviet Ambassador to Japan. Ambassador Troianovsky told Sansom that the non-aggression pact idea had been sabotaged by the younger officers of the Japanese Army. It was that same faction which was now, in late January, inciting anti-Soviet articles in the various Japanese newspapers in an attempt to retaliate for the Soviets' use of the news agencies to embarrass the Japanese Government for failing to come to terms over the non-aggression agreement. This group, said Troianovsky, was committed to eliminating the Soviet Union's presence in the Far East once and for all.[69] By mid-March British sources in Japan were adding to the strategic picture outlined by James and Sansom. The Soviet Military Attaché, Col Rink, told the British Attaché that Japan feared the recent buildup of Soviet military power, particularly the bomber force in Vladivostok which now could threaten Japanese cities with aerial bombardment. For that reason, Japan was interested in evicting the Soviets from the Maritime Province of Siberia.[70] A possible first stage of isolating Siberia and restricting Soviet strategic mobility was the seizure and control of the CER. Contemporaneously with Colonel James' discussions with Rink, the British Army officer was also provided with intelligence from the American Military Attaché, Major Bratton, who had gleaned information from the Soviet assistant Military Attaché, Major Panoff, concerning the fate of the CER. Panoff had revealed that the Soviet military were worried,

> If the Japanese removed the troops guarding the line it would be ruined, and would even physically disappear in a very short time, for the sleepers would be stolen for fuel and the rails sold for scrap. In fact the Japanese had it in their power to force some arrangement on the Russians for the final disposal of the railway, which would be in favour of Japanese interests. Negotiations for the sale of the southern branch of the line between Harbin and Changchun had, indeed, already been begun. In this connexion M. Panoff drew the attention of Major Bratton to the news which had recently appeared in the press that the South Manchuria Railway Company was to control the whole of the railways in Manchuria.[71]

Charles W. Orde, the head of the FO's Far Eastern Dept., confirmed Rink and Panoff's views. He, too, thought that the Japanese intention would be to oust the Soviet Union from Siberia in order to nullify the air threat to mainland Japan and that the Soviets would resist such actions with military force. As well, he believed that it was a very real possibility that 'The Chinese Eastern Railway from Harbin eastward seems inevitably doomed to decay and disappearance.'[72] When queried by Sir Victor Wellesley, the Deputy Under Secretary of State in the FO responsible for Far Eastern matters, as to what the Japanese increase in armaments meant and whether it indicated a more potentially dangerous rise in tensions between the Soviet Union and Japan, Lindley gave voice to the evolving strategic option such tensions provided for the defence of British imperial interests in the Far East: 'From the point of view of British interests, it is obvious that Japanese expansion in the Maritime Provinces is much to be preferred to expansion south of the Great Wall or, indeed, anywhere else in the world.'[73] A Japanese attempt to oust the Soviet Union would ensure British interests remained secure while such an operation took place. Indeed, the ill-will created by such an attempt could provide the desired strategic impetus for the creation of a balance of power condition that provided a counter-weight to Japan's ambitions and provided cheap, long-term protection of Great Britain's Far Eastern possessions, as well as placing Britain in the position of holding a decisive strategic position of neutrality in any circumstance. And, if the Japanese Army was bent on forcing the Soviet forces from the Maritime Provinces, control of the CER was a necessary pre-requisite for such an adventure.

Faced with the potential re-combination of international relations affecting the strategic situation in the Far East, by the middle of 1933 the CID began to reconsider plans for the defence of empire. The formation by the Cabinet of the Defence Requirements Committee (DRC) in the summer of that year was an event driven by the primacy of Far Eastern concerns facing the British imperial strategic foreign policy making elite.[74] And a vital consideration of that quest for a new security policy was the need for an accurate assessment of Russo-Japanese relations, a part of which pertained to the CER issue. However, by April 1933, with the Japanese concentrating on resolving their invasion of Northern China and the Soviets refusing to act as the aggressor in any CER-related actions, the issue seemed benign. All that changed in May when news of a Soviet offer to sell the CER to Japan reached British observers.

Early FO reactions to the event were sceptical, seeing the offer as a shot to nothing, with the Soviets knowing full well that Japan would refuse the conditions of sale stipulated.[75] But, the British embassy in Moscow proposed that Litvinov's offer was a genuine and 'humiliating confession of the inability to resist pressure from Japanese who have succeeded in forcing Soviet Government to A. to proclaim their reluctance to defend their rights in railway, B. To take fresh step towards recognition of Manchukuo. C. To draw away from [China] and even embroil themselves with Nanking Government'. They also opined that it was unlikely that Japan or the puppet Manchukuo Government would actually pay anything for the CER.[76] Protests by the Chinese Government against the sale were swift and unequivocal. In their view such a sale was illegal, as the agreement in place stipulated that the USSR was obligated to sell its interests in the CER to China. More importantly, such a sale was seen as the first step in the USSR's recognizing the Manchukuo Government as a legitimate entity, a precedent that could have even greater negative ramifications for the ability of the Nanking Government to recover its lost territory. If the USSR recognized Manchukuo as the legal holder of the CER concessions, it was also free to renegotiate the agreement with that government, perhaps to greater advantage.[77] From China, Lampson learned from the Soviet Ambassador there that the Soviet Government had recognized the increased potential for conflict now that Japan and not China was the *de facto* ruler of Manchukuo. The CER was a flash point for war that could be eliminated at no real loss for the Soviet Union.[78] In June, the British embassy in Tokyo informed the FO that discussions between the Manchukuo and Soviet Governments for the sale of the CER were to begin soon. Their sources added another point for reflection, in that the Soviet Ambassador in Tokyo, Yureneff, had intimated that the offer was a probe by Litvinov to test the Japanese militarist's intentions. If they refused to negotiate or consider the offer, then the Soviet Foreign Minister could assume that there was little hope of avoiding conflict with Japan in the region. An acceptance of the offer and a negotiated settlement would auger well, however, for peace in the future.[79] While the two sides probed each other's position, British policy makers were considering the ramifications of this new role for the CER, as olive branch, and what such a development boded for Britain's imperial defence of interests in the region. One of the main considerations was to try and establish who was the dominant power: Japan or the USSR.[80]

Towards the end of October, the FO sought out the WO's expert evaluation of how a potential Russo-Japanese war in Manchuria would develop and what the expected outcome would be. W.R. Connor-Green, a member of the Far Eastern Department (FED), wrote to Lt. Col. E.G. Miles, MI 2(c), putting forward the FED's opinion on the situation. He told the WO representative that it was the FO's contention that Russia was in no condition to fight a real war with Japan and that the latter could take the Maritime Provinces any time it liked. In two or three years time, however, things could be different. Russian reinforcements to the area and the headway made in the industrialization of the Soviet Union as a whole could make such a Japanese attack too risky. As well, even if initial Japanese success was achieved through the elimination of Vladivostok as a strategic base for submarine and air strikes against the Japanese mainland, such an extension of Japan's frontiers would leave it vulnerable to counter-attacks from not only the USSR but also from China. Overall, Connor-Green contended that, 'the idea of seizing the Maritime Provinces would appear to be most dangerous and short-sighted from Japan's point of view. Nevertheless, we cannot exclude the possibility of this being done.'[81] Three days later, Miles replied, stating that the WO view was generally in line with the points put forward by the FO, but: 'In the recent bickering over the question of Japanese activities on the Chinese Eastern Railway, Russia even seems to have assumed the offensive; and from that it may be deduced that Stalin's slogan, "not an inch of Soviet soil will we yield", was not mere bluff.'[82] The WO also demurred from the FO's view of the Soviet military being an easy opponent for the Japanese Army, citing mobilization, transportation and morale improvement in the Soviet forces as being significantly improved to make any Japanese aggression already a risky venture. Everything hinged on the all-important issue of railways and strategic lift into the theatre from external sources of supply and manpower:

> The main problem for both sides is likely to be the lack of adequate rail communications. In this respect, the position of Russia may, at first sight, appear to be far worse than that of Japan. But, although the Japanese Army have several alternative lines of communication from the coast too Harbin and Tsitsihar, thence onwards to the frontier they would be confined to a

single track railway – a position exactly similar to that of the Russian forces across the frontier. It will be apparent, then, that this would result in an equal limitation of the numbers that could be employed and that it would preclude the concentration, by either side, of a force numerically superior to that of its opponent. In addition, the Japanese would, at the present time, have to contend with the difficulty of a change of gauge between the Chinese Eastern Railway and the other Manchurian railways. Railway communications are, indeed, likely to play a predominant part in operations in this theatre. It seems to us, therefore, that before Japan can hope to launch a successful attack against the USSR, she will have to improve her railway communications towards the Russian frontier – a procedure on which, incidentally she already seems to be busily engaged. On the other hand, Russia is unlikely, within the next few years at any rate, to be able materially to increase the maintenance capacity of the Trans-Siberian Railway.[83]

If Japan was to improve her railway communications towards the Maritime Provinces, however, it did not appear in December 1933 as if it would be done through negotiation. The talks begun in June regarding the sale of the CER were at a complete standstill, with no foreseeable break in the impasse likely. Indeed, the level of brinksmanship between the two nations had increased over the intervening six months, with punitive layoffs of workers on the CER, Japanese military aircraft threatening Vladivostok's airspace, the release of various embarrassing documents related to the non-aggression pact talks, and further sabre-rattlings concerning troop deployments and mobilizations coming from both Moscow and Tokyo in attempts to gain the initiative in the negotiations.[84]

As 1933 came to a close, the FO and WO were agreed on a number of factors related to the Russo-Japanese relationship and Britain's imperial defence questions in the Far East. The first point of agreement was that Russia's increase in her military power, and a demonstrated willingness to use such force after a certain period and process of escalation, had gained it strategic leverage in her dealings with Japan. Therefore, as a lesson for possible British courses of action in Anglo-Japanese relations in the future, until British naval power was fully established through the establishment of Singapore as an operational base and improvements had been made to Hong Kong for supporting naval operations, Britain would not have the military power available in the region to force the respect of any nation. Therefore, diplomacy would have to be the weapon of default. And that diplomacy, in terms of any coercive or deterrence value, was, without credible military forces available, a house made of straw. The second area of agreement was that Russia and Japan were not likely to engage in any war in the near future. Questionable returns for such efforts, serious questions about limited abilities to concentrate and sustain forces, and the ever-present danger of China regaining ground on a weakened Japan, all combined to indicate that the CER issue was all part of a period of strategic manoeuver. Lastly, both British strategic foreign policy making bodies concurred that strategic tensions, such as those caused by the CER issue, but not an open Russo-Japanese conflict, was a condition that was of benefit to the overall defence of British interests in the region. Worries about a potentially hostile Soviet Union in the North would keep the militarist government of Japan fully occupied. It would continue to consume valuable economic and military resources that otherwise might be marshalled against British interests. Therefore. in the eyes of the FO and WO, the Russian bear rampant in the Far East, while a potential threat to British interests in China due to the spread of communism into that country, in sum was a greater strategic benefit because of the distraction and deterrence it created in the minds of their Japanese counterparts.[85] Orde summarized the Japanese situation nicely in a seminal memo for the FO in December.

> There is more to be gained and less to be lost in a war with Russia than with the United States or the British Empire.... but if, on consideration, Japan feels it more discreet to hold her hand, the Russian strategic position north and east of Manchukuo will greatly hamper her in undertaking warlike adventures against other Great Powers. It is difficult to conceive of an understanding between the two countries which would alter this position. The Soviet Government, in a crisis for Japan elsewhere, would surely exact a price which it would not be worth while to pay when the gains to be expected in other directions are so limited.[86]

Where the two departments did differ was on the question of how to utilize Japan itself. The FO was wary and reluctant to follow any course that seemed to promise a return to the days of the Anglo-Japanese alliance. Worries about public reactions to courting a known aggressor state, a League of Nations rogue, as well as American reactions to any closer, formal Anglo-Japanese relations, informed the independent, centrist path promoted by the FO. The WO, on the other hand, desired to alleviate some of the strategic risk through the re-establishment, even on a limited scale, of closer Anglo-Japanese ties. The latter did not proved to be the eventual course of action taken by Great Britain's strategic foreign policy making elite.[87]

Peace between the Soviet Union and Japan did prevail for the next two years and the CER was eventually sold to Japan in early 1935. Throughout 1934, the British elite continued to follow the negotiations over the CER.[88] However, given the Soviets' continued expansion of their military capability in the region, as well as their upgrading of the Trans-Siberian railway and non-Manchurian lines to Vladivostok, the issue lost a good deal of its previous worth as a barometer of Russo-Japanese tensions. Now alerted to the changed conditions governing the balance of power dynamic between the relevant Great Powers in the region, British decision makers were monitoring a more global network of such strategic indicators. Considerations of American, as well as Chinese, Japanese and Soviet involvement and reaction were now taken into account. Throughout the year, the FO became more convinced of the benefits of all continued Russo-Japanese tensions short of war.[89] In particular, British trade talks with Japan were credited as being more amiable than was expect because of the Japanese need to curry favour with Great Britain. That attitude was seen as a direct result of Japan's fearing a Anglo-Soviet Bloc being formed against Japanese trade and territorial interests.[90] By October of that year, the new British Ambassador to Japan, Sir Robert Henry Clive, was confirming the calming effect on Anglo-Japanese relations that the new balance of power in the region was creating. Progress was being made on the CER negotiations and a detente was in the offing.[91] Such hopes for a detente were as unfulfilled as those which had looked for a war between the two nations a few years earlier. Despite the sale of the CER, Russo-Japanese relations remained tense, combative and advantageous for British imperial defence purposes.[92] By the time of its sale, the worth of the railway, in both logistical and national terms, for the Soviet Union had passed. Determined to remain a Far Eastern power, the USSR, with or without the CER, continued to grow and exert great pressures on the relations between all Great Powers in the region, as the British observers had predicted earlier. The CER episode had signalled a potential swing in the barometric pressures governing the rise and fall of Great Power relations in 1929. By 1935 it had run its course as such a useful tool for British strategic foreign policy makers and was replaced by other, more comprehensive methods of measurement regarding the growing crisis in the Far East.

Notes

1 A good starting place for a wider conceptualization of the idea of railways within a national security context is Robert Lee, 'Tools of empire or means of national salvation? The railway in the imagination of western empire builders and their enemies in Asia' *Institute of Railway Studies*, at *http://www.york.ac.uk/inst/irs/irshome/papers/robert1.htm*, Feburary, 2003; Akira Iriye, *After Imperialism: The Search for a New Order in the Far East, 1921–1931*, (Cambridge, MA, 1965).

2 Some of these more traditional approaches can be found in: Walker D. Hines (Director-General of Railroads, 1919–1920), *War History of American Railroads*, (New Haven, 1928), Edwin A. Pratt, *British Railways and the Great War: Organisation, Efforts, Difficulties and Achievements*, 2 Vols, (London, Selwyn and Blount, 1921), John Lyn ed., *Feeding Mars: Essays on Logistics and Resource Mobilisation in Western Warfare from the Middle Ages to the Present*, (Boulder, Colorado, 1993), Paul Kennedy ed., *War Plans of the Great Powers, 1880–1914*, (London, 1979).

3 One of the earliest strategic thinkers to recognize the new strategic consequences, in terms of lift, tempo, and the mobilization of national resources provided by the railway was the 19th century geo-strategic thinker Halford Mackinder. See Paul Kennedy, 'Mahan versus Mackinder: two interpretations of British sea power', in Paul Kennedy ed., *Strategy and Diplomacy*, (London, 1983); W.H. Parker, *Mackinder*, (Oxford, 1982). Mackinder was aware of the counter to maritime strategic lift given over to land powers with the advent of extensive national rail systems.

4 On the pre-1929 conditions surrounding the CER and Russo-Japanese relations see Bruce A. Elleman, 'The Soviet Union's Secret Diplomacy Concerning the Chinese Eastern Railway, 1924–1925', *The Journal of Asian Studies*, 53, No.2, (May 1994), pp.459–6; Richard A. Florez, 'Vladivostok and the Primorye Krai: A Look at Far Eastern Economies in Transition' at *http://acad.bryant.edu/~ehu/h385nis/2000/proj98rich.htm*; David Wolff, *To the Harbin Station: The Liberal Alternative in Russian Manchuria, 1898–1914*, (Stanford, SUP, 1999); Roberta A. Dayer, *Bankers and Diplomats in China, 1917–1925*, (London and Portland, OR, 1981).

5 For works which look at Britain's perceptions of various aspects of the Russo-Japanese relationship in the Far East see: Greg Kennedy, *Anglo-American Strategic Relations and the Far East, 1933–1939*, (London, 2002), Ch.2; Keith Neilson, 'The Anglo-Japanese Alliance and British Strategic Foreign Policy, 1902–1914', in Phillips Payson O'Brien ed., *The Anglo-Japanese Alliance*, (London and New York, 2004), pp.48–63; idem, 'Unbroken Thread: Japan and Britain and Imperial Defence, 1920–1932', in Greg Kennedy ed., *British Naval Strategy East of Suez, 1880–2000*, (London and Portland, OR, 2004), pp.97–143; idem, *Britian, Soviet Russia and the Collapse of the Versailles Order*, 1919–1939 (Cambridge, 2006), which is an extensive study of Britain's perceptions of Soviet Russia in the world security system in the period from 1919 to 1939; Antony Best, *British Intelligence and the Japanese Challenge in Asia, 1914–1941*, (Basingstoke, Hampshire, 2002); Ibid., *Britain, Japan and Pearl Harbor: Avoiding War in East Asia, 1936–1941*, (London, 1995); Phillips Payson O'Brien ed., *The Anglo-Japanese Alliance, 1902–1922*, (London and New York, 2004). For the question of perception management at the strategic foreign policy formulation level see, E. Waltz, *Information Warfare: Principles and Operations*, (Boston and London, 1998); and Michael Handel, *Master of War: Classical Strategic Thought*, 3rd edition, (London, 2001).

6 Jane Degras ed., *Soviet Documents on Foreign Policy*, Vol.II 1925–1932, (Oxford, 1952), 'Extracts from a note from Karakhan to the Chinese Chargé d'Affaires in Moscow on the Chinese attempt to seize the Chinese Eastern Railway', 13 July 1929, pp.384–7.

7 Ibid., 'Decree of the Revolutionary Military Council on the Formation of the Special Far Eastern Army', 6 August 1929, p.391; 'Press statement by Karakhan on the Situation on the Chinese Eastern Railway', 15 August 1929, p.392; 'Decree of the Central Executive Committee and the Council of People's Commissars breaking relations with China', 16 August 1929, p.392; 'Reply to the Chinese proposal for joint declaration of the terms of settlement of the Soviet-Chinese dispute', 29 August 1929, pp.393–4; 'Extracts from a press statement by Litvinov on the Soviet reply to the Nanking proposals for a settlement', 6 September 1929, pp.394–5.

8 Ibid., 'Report by Litvinov, Vice-Commissar for Foreign Affairs, to the Central Executive Committee', 4 December 1929, pp.408–32, p.413.

9 Ibid., p.427. Well over half of this address is given over to the CER/China/Great Britain question.

10 On Howard's career in America see B.J.C. McKercher, *Esme Howard: A Diplomatic Biography*, (Cambridge, 1989).

11 Documents on British Foreign Policy, 1919–1939 (hereafter *DBFP*), Second Series, Vol.VIII, telegram from Howard to A. Henderson (Arthur Henderson, Sec. of State for Foreign Affairs), 23 July 1929, p.119.

12 *DBFP*, Vol.VIII, 'Record by Victor Wellesley of a conversation with the Japanese Ambassador', 31 July 1929, pp.124–6.

13 *DBFP*, Second Series, Vol.VIII, 'Chinese Questions, 1929–1931', Foreign Office Memorandum of January 8, 1930, on British Policy in China, pp.1–26, p.10; Ibid., telegram from Lampson to A. Chamberlain, 5 June 1929, p.65.

14 *DBFP*, Vol.VIII, 'Chinese Questions, 1929–1931', p.1.

15 Ibid., p.4.

16 *DBFP*, Second Series, Vol.VII, telegram from Ovey to A. Henderson, 6 February 1930, p.94.

17 *DBFP*, Vol.VII, telegram from Ovey to Henderson, 8 February 1930, pp.97–9.

18 Ibid., p.99.

19 *DBFP*, Second Series, Vol.VIII, Appendix 1, 'Despatch from Sir M. Lampson dealing with the Sino-Russian dispute over the Chinese Eastern Railway', 2 July 1930, pp.1011–28.

20 Ibid., p.1026.

21 *DBFP*, Second Series, Vol.III, 'Foreign Office Memorandum respecting the Prospects of Stable Government in China', 19 July 1930, pp.384–8; Best, *British Intelligence*, p.80.

22 *DBFP*, Second Series, Vol.III, despatch and enclosure from Lindley to Henderson, 16 July 1931, pp.634–8.

23 Best, p.98.

24 *DBFP*, Second Series, Vol.III, despatch and enclosure from Lindley to Henderson, 16 July 1931, pp.634–8; Ibid., despatch from Lindley to Henderson, 23 July 1931.

25 *DBFP*, Second Series, Vol.III, 'Memorandum by Mr. Roberts: Sino-Japanese Relations in Manchuria and the Mukden Negotiations on Manchurian Railway Problems', 27 July 1931, pp.646–50.

26 *DBFP*, Second Series, Vol.III, despatch from Lindley to the Marquess of Reading, 17 September 1931, pp.655–8.

27 Ibid., enclosure Dening to Lindley, 26 August, 1931.

28 *DBFP*, Second Series, Vol.III, telegram from Lampson to Marquess of Reading, 29 September 1931, pp.691–2; Ibid., telegram from Lampson to Marquess of Reading, 30 Sept., 1931. p.695.

29 On events in China concerning Britain, China, Japan and the Soviet Union, see Michael Barnhart, *Japan Prepares for Total War: The Search for Economic Security, 1919–1941*, (Ithaca, Cornell University Press, 1987); Paul Haggie, *Britannia at Bay: The Defence of the British Empire Against Japan, 1931–1941*, (Oxford, Clarendon. 1981); Akira Iriye, *The Origins of the Second World War in Asia and the Pacific.* (London, 1987); W.R. Louis, *British Strategy in the Far East, 1919–1939*, (Oxford, Clarendon, 1971); Ian H. Nish, *Japan's Struggle with Internationalism: Japan, China and the League of Nations, 1931–33*, (London, 1993); Y.-L. Sun, *China and the Origins of the Pacific War, 1931–1941*, (New York, 1993); Christopher Thorne, *The Limits of Foreign Policy: The West, the League and the Far Eastern Crisis of 1931–1933.* (London, 1972).

30 *DBFP*, Second Series, Vol.III, telegram from Strang to Marquess of Reading, 28 September 1931, pp.685–6.

31 Ibid., Strang to Marquess of Reading, 1 October 1931, pp.697–8.

32 *DBFP*, Second Series, Vol.III, despatch from Lindley to Marquess of Reading, 1 October 1931, pp.698–702; Ibid., telegram from Lampson to Marquess of Reading, 3 October 1931, p.706; Ibid., telegram from Lampson to Marquess of Reading, 8 October 1931, pp.724–5.

33 Neilson, *Britian, Soviet Russia*, pp.43–87; Max Beloff, *The Foreign Policy of Soviet Russia, 1929–1941*, (Oxford, 1963), pp.70–89.

34 *DBFP*, Second Series, Vol.III, telegram from Patteson to Vansittart, 13 October 1931, note 1, pp.761–2.

35 Beloff, pp.77–80.

36 *DBFP*, Second Series, Vol.II, despatch from Ovey to Sir John Simon (Foreign Secretary), 14 January 1932, pp.227–8.

37 Ibid.

38 *DBFP*, Second Series, Vol.II, despatch Ovey to Simon, 19 January 1932, pp.229–30.

39 CAB[inet] 27/482, CJC(32), 5th meeting, 8 March 1932.

40 *DBFP*, Second Series, Vol.X, confidential despatch from Lindley to Simon, 12 March 1932, pp.108–10.

41 *DBFP*, Second Series, Vol.X, confidential despatch from Ovey to Simon, 15 March 1932, p.128.

42 *DBFP*, Second Series, Vol.X, despatch from Ovey to Simon, 28 March 1932, pp.201–5.

43 Ibid., *DBFP*, Second Series, Vol.X, despatch from D.F. Garstin, British Consul-General in Harbin to Sir Miles Lampson, British Minister in China, 23 March 1932, pp.181–3.

44 *DBFP*, Second Series, Vol.X, confidential despatch from Lindley to Simon, 14 April 1932, pp.306–8.

45 Ibid.

46 *DBFP*, Second Series, Vol.X, telegraph from Lindley to Simon, 19 April, 1932, pp.328–9.

47 For overall state of Britain's views regarding the Russo-Japanese condition at this time see Neilson, *Britian, Soviet Russia*, pp.70–4; A. Best, *British Intelligence and the Japanese Challenge*, pp.93–101.

48 *DBFP*, Second Series, Vol.X, despatch from UK Delegate (A. Eden) to FO, 26 April 1932, with two enclosures, confidential enclosure, note of Conversation with Karl Radek, 20 April and Minute by Sir J. Pratt, 23 April, pp.356–59; Ibid, Memorandum regarding the Soviet Union and Japan in relation to the Sino-Japanese Dispute, Far Eastern Dept., 20 May, 1932.

49 *DBFP*, Second Series, Vol.X, despatch from Ovey to Simon, 23 May 1932, pp.452–3.

50 War Office [WO] 106/5395, Memo I, Attention of CIGS by Director of Military Intelligence and Operations [DMO&I], Major General W.H. Bartholomew, 8 September 1932.

51 Ibid., Memo III by Col. A.G.C. Dawnay, MI2, 'The Situation in the Far East', 20 October 1932; WO 106/5397, untitled minute by Dawnay, 9 September 1932.

52 WO 106/5397, Temperley minutes, 23 September, 1932 and Bartholomew minutes, 29 September 1932.

53 On the Lytton report and its place in British Far Eastern policy see: Louis, *British Strategy in the Far East, 1919–1939*, pp.199–201; Ann Trotter, *Britain and East Asia, 1933–1937*, (Cambridge, 1975), pp.1–22; Ian Nish, *Anglo-Japanese Alienations, 1919–1952*, (Cambridge, 1982), Ch.2; *DBFP*, Second Series, Vol.X, notes in No.674, telegram from Lindley to Simon, 12 September 1932, pp.749–50.

54 Avon Papers, Birmingham University Library, AP 14/1/127–153, letter from Eden to Baldwin, 10 February 1933.

55 Ibid.

56 *DBFP*, Second Series, Vol.X, despatch from Lindley to Simon, 31 August 1932, pp.725–6; *DBFP*, Second Series, Vol.X, despatch from Strang (Moscow) to Simon, 15 September 1932, pp.735–7.

57 *DBFP*, Second Series, Vol.X, despatch from E.M.B Ingram (Peking) to Simon, 16 September 1932, pp.769–77.

58 WO 106/5397, Dawnay minute, 17 February 1933.

59 F[oreign] O[ffice] 371/17073/73/33/10, Sansom memo and covering note by Lindley, 7 December 1932.

60 FO 371/17073/81/33/10, Snow Memo, 23 December 1932.

61 FO 371/17073/74/33/10, Vansittart minute, 30 December 1932. See other instructive minutes here by FO members, as well as Sir John Simon for views on Japan.

62 Ibid., Pratt memo, some time late December 1932. Ambassador Lindley saw the Soviet motivation for the agreement as being in part as punishment of Japan for the latter's refusal to agree to the earlier offer of a Russo-Japanese non-aggression pact. See FO 371/17117/512/512/10, confidential despatch from Lindley, 22 December 1932.

63 FO 371/17073/74/33/10, Vansittart minute.

64 FO 371/17152/154/154/23, despatch from Lindley to FO, 29 December 1932, and associated minutes.

65 FO 371/17117/512/512/10, confidential despatch from Lindley to Simon, 22 December, 1932. Lt Colonel E.A.H. James, the British Military Attaché in Tokyo, informed Lindley and the WO that it was his opinion that the Sino-Soviet renewal of ties had made the Japanese military only more determined to speed up their preparations to be able to prosecute a large-scale war against both parties in the future.

66 FO 371/17151/468/116/23, confidential telegram from Ovey to Simon, 20 January 1933; Ibid., Victor Mallet minute, 20 January 1933; FO 371/17151/599/116/23, telegram from Ovey to Simon, 25 January 1933.

67 FO 371/17077/1152/33/10, confidential despatch from Lindley to Simon, 25 January 1933.

68 FO 371/17149/747/11/23, secret despatch from Lindley to Simon, 5 January 1933; FO 371/17149/1653/11/23, report No.3 on Japanese Army by Lt. Col. James, 7 February, 1933.

69 FO 371/17151/1634/116/23, confidential despatch from Lindley to Simon, 30 January 1933.

70 FO 371/17151/2550/116/23, confidential despatch from Lindley to Simon, 14 March 1933, confidential report by Lt. Col. James, 10 March. For WO assessment of Soviet strategic lift via railways in Far East in support of major operations at this time see, CAB 21/395, 'USSR Present Capacity of the Railways to Maintain an Armed Force in the Far East,' ICF 14, 4 April 1933.

71 Ibid.

72 Ibid., Orde minute, 21 April 1933. Pratt, Wellesley and Simon had all read this material as well.

73 FO 371/17149/2615/11/23, letter from Lindley to Wellesley, 24 March 1933.

74 Neilson, 'Unbroken Thread: Japan and Britain in Imperial Defence, 1920–1932'; idem, 'The Defence Requirements Sub-Committee, British Strategic Foreign Policy, Neville Chamberlain and the Path to Appeasement', *English Historical Review*, CXVIII, 477, (June, 2003), pp.651–84; FO 371/17148/5189/5189/61, Ashton–Gwatkin Memo 'Far East – Changing Situation' and minutes, 3 August 1933.

75 FO 371/17133/3182/2463/10, Randall minutes, 13 May 1933.

76 FO 371/17133/3194/2463/10, telegram from Strang to FO, 13 May 1933.

77 FO 371/17134/3386/2463/10, telegram from Strang to FO, 17 May 1933.

78 FO 371/17134/3507/2463/10, telegram from Lampson to FO, 24 May 1933; FO 371/17134/3588/2463/10, confidential telegram from Lampson to FO, 28 May 1933.

79 FO 371/17134/3739/2463/10, telegram from Snow (Tokyo) to FO, 6 June 1933; FO 371/17134/3926/2463/10, despatch from Snow to Simon, 12 May 1933.

80 FO 371/17151/6925/116/23, FO minute and attachments from WO, 30 October 1933; FO 371/17152/7301/116/23, very confidential despatch from Snow to Simon, 13 October 1933; FO 371/17152/7317/116/23, very confidential despatch from Snow to Simon, 25 October 1933 (both above despatches contained extensive reports from Col. James on talks with Soviet, French and Japanese military officers concerning state of Russo-Japanese relations and chance of war between the two in the near future.

81 FO 371/17151/6925/116/23, letter from Connor-Green to Miles, 30 October 1933.

82 Ibid., letter from Miles to Connor-Green, 2 November 1933.

83 Ibid.

84 FO 371/17135/6521/2463/10, confidential despatch from Strang to Simon, 10 October, 1933; FO 371/17135/7755/2463/10, despatch from Chilston (Moscow) to Simon, 11 December 1933; FO 371/17152/8022/116/23, confidential despatch from Snow to Simon, 24 November 1933.

85 WO 106/5396, 'A Review of the Far Eastern Situation', Lt. Col. Miles, MI 2(c), 31 December, 1933; FO 371/17148/7818/5189/61, 'Memorandum on British Policy in the Far East', John T. Pratt, 1 December, 1933 and associated minutes; FO 371/17152/7824/128/23, confidential 'Memorandum respecting our Relations with Japan', C.W. Orde, 14 December 1933.

86 FO 371/17152/7824/128/23, confidential 'Memorandum respecting our Relations with Japan', C.W. Orde, 14 December 1933.

87 This strategy has been termed the 'No-bloc' policy. See Greg Kennedy, '1935: A Snapshot of British Imperial Defence in the Far East', in Keith Neilson and Greg Kennedy eds, *Far Flung Lines: Studies in Imperial Defence in Honour of Donald*

Mackenzie Schurman, (London, 1997), pp.190–216; Neilson, 'The Defence Requirements Sub-Committee', pp.682–4.

88 What follows, unless otherwise noted, is based on Kennedy, *Anglo-American Strategic Relations and the Far East*, Ch.2.

89 FO 371/18180/964/373/23, Vansittart minute, 27 Feb., and Simon minute, 2 March 1934.

90 FO 371/18176/823/316/23, FO Memo by A.W.G. Randall, 9 February 1934.

91 FO 371/18177/6388/316/23, confidential despatch from Clive to Simon, 28 September, and associated minutes, 1934.

92 FO 371/19347/6298/13/23, despatch from Alexander Cadogan (British Minister to China) to Simon, 26 August 1935.

11 Swiss trans-Alpine railway lines

Strategic railways and the strategy of deterrence

Neville Wylie

There can be few geographical features in Europe of greater strategic or political significance than the valleys and passes which thread their way through the Alps connecting the northern Italian plain with the lands of central and western Europe. The economic value of these routes was already well established by the thirteenth century, but Hannibal proved their military worth as early as 218 BC, and this continued to be recognized well into the modern era, with Napoleon Bonaparte using the St Bernard pass to particularly dramatic effect in the early summer of 1800. The importance of the Alpine routes explains the willingness of the European great powers to affirm Switzerland's 'permanent' neutrality in 1815, and accept joint responsibility for upholding Swiss independence thereafter. Preventing these assets falling under the exclusive control of one power was in the interests of the entire community of states. Writing in late 1847, the British diplomatist Stafford Canning probably had the Alpine passages in mind when he suggested that Switzerland could not be 'enfeebled, convulsed or mutilated without suggesting dangerous fears or guilty hopes to the great monarchies which nearby surround it'.[1]

While the events of the 'year of revolutions' in 1848 reminded European statesmen of the truth of Canning's observation, it was the threat of economic isolation that probably posed the greatest danger to the Swiss confederation from this time. By the middle of the nineteenth century, the arrival of the railway had led to renewed political and commercial interest in the Alpine passages and triggered a race to capitalize on Europe's burgeoning international trade. With ownership of Swiss railways divided between a dozen independent companies, and development hitherto reliant on foreign, primarily French, capital, Switzerland was poorly placed to meet the challenges ahead. Indeed, the opening of the Brenner pass in Austria to railway traffic in 1867, followed four years later with the completion of the Mont Cenis tunnel, between France and Italy, led many to fear that Switzerland would slip back into an economic backwater. Discussion over which route to develop split Switzerland along linguistic lines and was complicated by Switzerland's decentralized political system, in which power resided with individual cantons, and by the need for prospective parties to secure financial backing from abroad.

The final decision to develop the St Gothard route, taken in 1869, was as much a reflection of the rising stature of Prussia–Germany within Europe as it was a response to the merits or feasibility of the engineering project itself. Moreover, although the line was eventually opened in 1882, and agreement was reached in 1878 to work on the 'French' line – through the Simplon – concern at the scale of foreign influence over Switzerland's trans-Alpine railway system gathered apace over the last decades of the century. The national assembly, conscious of these fears, agreed in 1898 to buy out the individual companies and nationalize the Swiss railway system. Nevertheless concern remained. In 1909, debate over the renewal the St Gothard convention, concluded initially in 1869 and renewed in 1882, provoked a political crisis, with many people fearing that Swiss independence was being mortgaged to foreign commercial interests. The 1909 convention essentially gave Germany and Italy most favoured nation status and guaranteed free transit of goods across Switzerland in all circumstances except those in which Swiss neutrality was endangered.[2] Further steps however were taken to 'protect' the railway lines from disruptive foreign influences in 1916 when the collapse of coal imports, upon which Swiss industry depended, encouraged the government to agree to have the rail network electrified.[3]

The development of Switzerland's trans-Alpine railway lines were then, very much in keeping with the country's historical experiences. On the one hand, the Swiss had once again shown their talent for improvisation and exploiting their country's meagre natural resources to good effect. As in the thirteenth century, when the Alpine passes were first opened up to commercial traffic, the opening of the St Gothard (1882), Simplon (1906) and Lötschberg (1913) railway lines re-established Switzerland's pivotal position within the European transportation system, and 'guaranteed the prosperity of the country'.[4] Nevertheless, the frantic scramble to construct the complex system of tunnels, viaducts and cuttings had thrown up technical and financial demands that Switzerland found difficult to meet with its own resources. Switzerland may have been given nominal authority over the Alpine passes in 1815, but their exploitation was of interest to Switzerland's neighbours as much as itself, and the need to strike a balance between their legitimate economic interests and the requirements of Swiss sovereignty was encountered at almost every stage of the process. The events of the Second World War, which we will turn to in the remainder of the paper, continued this trend, and exposed some of the inherent difficulties in trying to harness the strategic railways for the benefit of Swiss political and military interests.

I

In strategic terms, the value of Switzerland's railways in the 1930s and 1940s lay in their importance to the Italian economy. The dearth of indigenous sources of raw materials and solid fuel supplies meant that by the 1930s the Italian government was dependent on the importation some 12 million tons of coal every year to keep its industry working. In the early part of the decade, well over half of Italy's needs were supplied by Britain. The sharp deterioration in Anglo-Italian relations in the mid-30s however, persuaded Rome to switch her sources of supply, and by 1938, 6.8 m tons of coal purchased from Germany, a quarter being transported overland by means of rail freight across the Swiss and Austrian Alps, with the remainder handled by sea-borne traffic via Rotterdam. To Rome's good fortune, these facilities were barely affected by the outbreak of war in September 1939. London's desire to maintain Italian non-belligerency meant that while Britain progressively reduced the amount of coal it was prepared to allow through the blockade for Italian consumption, Italy's coal imports were neither entirely suspended, nor were serious efforts made to interdict Germany's sea borne traffic. Circumstances changed during the spring of 1940, when doubts over Mussolini's aggressive intentions, coupled with the signing of a German–Italian agreement on 24 February, in which Germany promised to meet its partner's energy needs, persuaded London that more draconian measures were required. Nevertheless, even though Italian coal imports were increasingly obstructed over the spring and early summer, it was only after Italy's declaration of war on 10 June that London finally prohibited all German collier traffic to Italian ports.[5]

The interruption of its sea-borne imports at precisely the time when the demands of war placed ever greater burdens on Italy's fragile economy posed the Italian government with an urgent and pressing problem. In short, if Italy failed to expand its rail-borne imports of coal and other raw-materials from Germany and other European sources of supply, it faced the very real prospect of seeing its economy grind to a halt. Not surprisingly, Rome and Berlin looked to the Swiss to relieve the pressure. The Swiss lines were modern, fully electrified and were serviced by ample rolling stock. They were also well positioned to satisfy the needs of the two Axis partners, lying as they were between the major centres of industry in northern Italy, and Germany's western coal fields in the Saar and Ruhr.[6]

The federal government in Berne was fully aware of the importance of its trans-Alpine lines to Italy's economic health, and kept a wary eye on Britain's shifting blockade policy towards Italian sea borne trade over the course of the Phoney War.[7] Any question of making life difficult for the Italians, by restricting Italian use of Swiss railway facilities was however, rejected. For one thing, since the traffic did not directly affect Swiss neutrality – a judgement the Swiss alone could make – the federal authorities were legally obliged, under the terms of the 1909 Gothard Convention, to permit a free flow of transit traffic across its railways. For another, the Swiss Federal Railways (the Chemins de fer fédéraux, CCF), which was responsible for the Simplon and Gothard routes, and the BLS Lötschberg Railway were only too pleased to see the proceeds from any increased transit activity flow into their coffers. The Depression in the 1930s had hit Swiss railways particularly hard, and no one was inclined to forgo the obvious financial benefits that accrued from Switzerland's fortuitous wartime position. More particularly however, as Gilles Forster has recently shown, after the summer of 1940 the CCF leadership became increasingly wary of any action that might rebound against Switzerland's long-term interests, especially if Hitler's New Order led to a restructuring of the European transport system.[8] Foreign political considerations also weighed heavily in Swiss policy. For the past two decades, Switzerland had placed the cultivation of amicable relations with Rome at the forefront of its foreign political agenda. Rome was seen as Berne's principal sponsor amongst the great powers, and, more importantly, its unofficial guardian in its dealings with Nazi Germany. It was largely out of concern to protect Swiss standing in Rome that Berne distanced itself from the League of Nations and returned to a policy of strict neutrality in early 1938.[9] The outbreak of war only inflated Swiss sense of reliance on Italian patronage. Berne was only too ready to curry favour in Rome and Berlin by responding promptly to requests for transit traffic quotas. Not unnaturally, the sudden collapse of France in June 1940, which at a stroke made Berlin arbiter of Switzerland's economic and political fate, strengthened this trend. Together with the provision of generous credit arrangements, the trans-Alpine transit traffic became the central element in Berne's efforts to appease its overbearing northern neighbour.[10] Over the following years, the federal government studiously avoided any direct involvement in railway policy, and instead left it to the CCF and BLS to make arrangements with German railway and government authorities as they saw fit. On only two occasions before late 1943 did the CCF approach the Swiss foreign ministry (the federal political department, FPD) for its opinion on transit matters.

On 9 August 1940, after weeks of fraught and testing negotiations, Berne signed a trade and credit agreement with Berlin, granting Germany widespread economic, financial and transit concessions in return for guaranteed access to German energy and raw material supplies.[11] From this date, over 1,800 wagons would cross Switzerland every day from Germany to Italy. Transit traffic, which had been insignificant in 1880, and accounted for barely 20 per cent of Switzerland's total rail usage in 1900, reached a staggering 56 per cent by 1941.[12] The vast quantity of this traffic consisted of wagons drawn from Axis countries or originated from countries under Axis occupation. By far the most significant commodity transported was coal. Some 14.8 m tons of coal was shipped across Swiss railways for Italy's use between January 1941 and December 1943, compared with little over 3.7 m tons of other raw materials. What this meant for the Italian economy – and the Axis war effort – can be gauged from the fact that Swiss railways transported over 50 per cent of all Italian coal imports during the middle years of the war, and reached as much as 62 per cent in 1944.[13] The significance of this traffic was repeatedly confirmed by statements made by Italian and German officials over the course of the war. In June 1942, according to the state secretary in the German foreign ministry, the free passage of goods across Switzerland was of 'vital importance to the Axis powers'.[14] The collapse of Axis military fortunes in North Africa that winter, and the Allied invasion of Italy the following summer, only went to deepen German concern over the security of Switzerland's trans-Alpine railways. Carl Clodius, Germany's senior economic negotiator, tellingly remarked in September 1943 that 'even a brief interruption of German supplies [across the Alps] by enemy action would bring about a complete paralysis of the Italian economy and lead to a catastrophe'.[15] These views were echoed seven months later, after the German occupation of northern Italy, in a report written by Major Gäfgen, head of the *Deutsche Industriekommission* in Berne. Switzerland's transit traffic was, according to Gäfgen, one of the most important advantages Germany gained from its relations with neutral Switzerland: 'Switzerland maintains the north-south transit traffic in spite of the demands of the enemy, and conveys [...] over the Gothard the important raw material supplies from Germany to Italy, for example coal, scrap iron etc. These supplies were the prerequisite for keeping the Italian industry going, and are now the prerequisite for sustaining the industry in [occupied] northern Italy.' As we shall see, Germany's systematic plundering of northern Italy prompted Berne to introduce restrictions on north bound traffic in late 1943, but as Gäfgen's report shows, these measures did little to diminish the importance of Switzerland's trans-Alpine railway lines in German eyes.[16]

II

While Berne's political authorities were content to appease its Axis neighbours by adopting a relaxed attitude towards the use of Swiss railways, the Swiss army's views were distinctly less altruistic. During the First World War, despite the opening of the Italian front in 1915, Switzerland's railways had been of little direct strategic value to either belligerent camp.[17] Little thought appears to have been given to the railways in Swiss contingency planning during the inter-war period. Instead, Swiss defence plans were predicated on the belief that the army would be required to defend the frontiers against the encroachments from whatever quarter. The emergence of an aggressive and expansionist regime in Germany finally convinced the Swiss general staff of the need to coordinate Swiss defence policy with the French, and over the final years of peace, tentative steps were made to this end.[18] The *Wehrmacht's* stunning successes in May and June 1940 not only made Switzerland's pre-war plans obsolete, but also compromised the standing of the Swiss military leadership, especially the commander-in-chief, general Henri Guisan, whose involvement in the Franco-Swiss military discussions was exposed when German forces stumbled upon secret French military papers that summer. The Swiss military staff was thus forced back to the drawing board at the moment at which Switzerland confronted the most serious threat to its national existence since William Tell and his compatriots took on the Hapsburgs six hundred years before.

It did not take Swiss planners long to realize the value of the trans-Alpine railways in the new strategic environment. Their potential appears to have been first muted by Karl Kobelt, a staff officer in 4th corps, on 9 June 1940, hours before Mussolini brought Italy into the war. In a letter to the chief of the general staff, Kobelt pointed out that since Germany had a vital interest in keeping its Axis partner supplied with coal, any German attack on Switzerland would have to include, as one of its primary objectives, the seizure of Switzerland's trans-Alpine railway lines intact. 'If however', Kobelt opined, 'the attacker has to reckon with the fact that we would contrive to cause such enduring damage to the Gothard railway that weeks or months would be needed to put it back into operation, this would represent a weighty argument against an attack.'[19] Kobelt's views took on added importance after Italy's entry into the war on 10 June and France's military collapse the following week, made the Axis encirclement of Switzerland complete. When General Guisan met with his senior staff on 22 June, two days after the signing of the Franco-German armistice, the transit lines offered one of the few glimmers of hope on an otherwise gloomy horizon.[20] Undeterred, Swiss planners got to work, and over the following three weeks concocted what became known as the Réduit strategy: a strategy which entailed withdrawing the bulk of the Swiss army from the frontiers and redeploying them into a defensive redoubt (Réduit) in the central Alpine region. The pivot of the strategy rested on the expectation that the Alpine-railway lines could be prevented from falling into enemy hands. Bernard Barbey, Guisan's influential personal staff officer, summarized the strategic logic of the Réduit in his diary on 9 July, when the final touches were being put on a draft directive for submission to the Federal Council:

> Finally ... a decisive point. It must be made clear [to the Federal Council] that the Réduit, amongst other trump cards we hold, guarantees the surveillance of the Alpine passes, which connect the two Axis partners to the south and the north, and ensures that everything is in place for their destruction. As soon as we have these controls really in our hands the 'Réduit policy' can begin.[21]

While the audacious use of the Alpine railway lines had obvious merits, there were various reasons why, in the summer of 1940, a full deterrent strategy was less than appealing. Since the majority of Switzerland's population and industry lay in the northern cantons, any retreat by the army into the mountains might, it was feared, appear dishonourable. Civilian morale, already badly shaken by the summer's events had taken a further tumble when the Federal President, Marcel Pilet-Golaz, had made a radio-address on 25 June which was heavily laced with defeatist tones. From a technical point of view too, there was considerable doubt as to whether the fortifications, storage and supply facilities in the central Alps were capable of sustaining the Swiss army if put to the test by a German invasion. There was, finally, a natural reluctance, especially amongst the Swiss railways authorities, to embrace a policy of deterrence which, if Switzerland was forced to carry out, would merely result in the destruction of one of the country's most important commercial assets.[22]

From July 1940 therefore, while a section of the army was held in the Alpine valleys, astride the railway lines, the rest was dispersed along the frontier and in the northern cantons. This position was maintained until May 1941 when improvements in Switzerland's political position within Europe permitted the adoption of a full deterrent strategy and the complete withdrawal of the army into the Réduit. From this moment on, the country's security rested on the twin pillars of holding central Switzerland against an Axis attack and denying any attacker the benefits of Switzerland's railways, by destroying the main lines and tunnels before they fell into enemy hands.[23] The instructions to troops which were appended to the new strategic dispositions pronounced in May 1941 left this in no doubt; 'The principal Alpine passages, the Gothard, Grimsel and Lötschberg, are the best assets we have in our hands. We will defend these bastions and preserve them at all costs.'[24]

The importance of the trans-Alpine railways for the creation of a credible defensive strategy, capable of seeing the country through the most perilous period of its history, can hardly be under-estimated. Guisan's Réduit strategy naturally occupies a cherished place in the long and illustrious annals of Swiss military history. What the country lacked in military hard-wear was more than made up for the plucky defiance of its citizen-soldiers and Guisan's imaginative use of the country's natural resources. In some quarters the strategy is widely accepted as saving Switzerland from inevitable German invasion and occupation.[25] Swiss military papers from the period however, suggest that there were serious difficulties in transforming what appeared as a perfectly attractive and feasible draft-board exercise into a credible military strategy. In particular they demonstrate that the possession of strategic railway lines was not in itself able to guarantee Swiss security.

If push came to shove, the Swiss had to be able to inflict lasting damage on the railway lines, and it was here that the most intractable problems arose. The first full assessment of what would be necessary to sabotage the Swiss railway system was carried out in June 1940. The stimulus came from Gottlieb Duttweiler, a prominent businessman, national councillor, leader of the 'Alliance des Independents' party, and member of the parliamentary commission established at the start of the war to oversee the use of the federal council's emergency war powers.[26] To its dismay, the Swiss general staff discovered that Duttweiler's proposal for preparing the three main tunnels for destruction was fraught with problems. It was calculated that some two years work would be required to ensure the successful sabotage of the principal railway tunnels, entailing the services of some two thousand mining engineers and staff, working round the clock. What was more, at least 15,500 tons of explosive would be required at a cost of nearly 59 mSF; a sum equal to half the pre-war federal military budget.[27] Political difficulties also loomed large. France's decision to grant Germany unrestricted transit facilities through the French Alps eroded the strategic value of the Swiss railway lines, and any ostentatious mining activity in the Gothard would more than likely be construed in Berlin as a provocation and might precipitate just the sort of attack it was designed to deter.

The Réduit strategy was then, not without its difficulties, and it was therefore by no means a foregone conclusion that the proposed strategy would be followed through in every detail. Indeed, although momentum behind some form of deterrent strategy gathered pace over the autumn of 1940, it was the election of Karl Kobelt, one of the earliest promoters of the project, as federal councillor for the military department in December 1940, that did much to enhance the tunnels' profile in Swiss strategic thinking. Under the watchful eye of Jacob Huber, the chief of the general staff, planning began for the partial demolition of the tunnel system in the event of an invasion. The demolition project was however so dogged with delays that it was only completed several months *after* the most acute danger of invasion had passed. Since Duttweiler's project was considered too expensive, further studies were needed to ascertain whether and in what form a demolition project could be carried out. Before long, it became evident that the project would have to be limited to the two most important tunnels, the St Gothard and Simplon, but it was only in April 1941 that the Council finally gave its blessing to a series of financial estimates, totalling 3.2 mSF, for this work.[28] In the meantime, with the exact nature of the tunnels project still in the balance, the army concentrated its engineering resources on the numerous railway viaducts and bridges leading through the Alps. Poor weather, atrocious working conditions and the shortage of explosives, manpower and resources all meant that it was not until March 1941 that the preliminary sites were finished. Secondary objects were not ready until the end of May 1941. These were completion dates which, given Switzerland's precarious strategic situation, struck the head of the army's technical corps as 'awfully late'.[29] Work on the St Gothard and Simplon tunnels began in earnest in the summer of 1941 but was also bedevilled with delays. As late as October 1941 the army engineering department complained that 'since the beginning of the project, progress has considerably suffered from the lack of qualified workers (miners and assistant miners) for tunnel construction'.[30] As a result the mines at north entrance of the Gothard were only completed in early 1942, those in the south entrance were ready by April 1942, while demolition devices in the Simplon tunnel were only in place later that summer.[31]

There is no question that by early 1942, Switzerland possessed a formidable strategic deterrent, with a demolition plan covering not only the country's railway lines, tunnels and viaducts, but also rolling stock, repair facilities, and energy supplies.[32] But there is little doubt that the obstacles to achieving this goal weighed heavily on the minds of Swiss military officials. Debates over whether the existence of German invasion studies for Switzerland reflected a genuine desire to occupy Switzerland, and whether these studies were sufficiently detailed to act as operational plans, are still unresolved.[33] In all the studies known to have existed, the problem of tying the Swiss army down to a decisive engagement before retreating to the Alps clearly worried German planners, as did the security of the trans-Alpine railway lines. However it is clear that until early 1941 Switzerland's railways were anything but prepared for a German assault. Indeed had German forces invaded Switzerland in the late summer or autumn of 1940, all major tunnels would have fallen into their hands intact, and the small number of sabotaged viaducts, ramps and bridges would not have posed insuperable difficulties for German engineering companies. By January 1941, the Swiss had in place only eighteen demolition points on the St Gothard line, with a further twenty four in preparation. What is more, the absence of precise orders over who was responsible for the demolition charges leaves in doubt whether those mines prepared by this date would indeed have been detonated.[34] Guisan's hesitation in embracing a full deterrent strategy until May 1941 therefore in part reflected the difficulties encountered in establishing a credible sabotage system for the Alpine railways, upon whose destruction the whole strategy ultimately hinged. It took another eight months or more before Swiss officers could sleep soundly in their beds, confident in the knowledge that the real lynch-pin, the St Gothard tunnel, was readied for destruction.[35]

III

Swiss officers and politicians naturally portrayed the Réduit, and the railway lines that ran through it, as the embodiment of Swiss determination to resist foreign invasion. In reality of course, so long as Axis rolling stock was allowed to pass unhindered across the Alps, Germany had no reason to challenge Swiss independence. Swiss soldiers were defending installations not so much against the Germans as against the British, for it was London, not Berlin, which had most to fear from Germany's unrestricted use of Swiss railways. No sooner then, had the last pack of explosives been neatly set in place in the Alpine mine shafts, than German and Swiss officials began to consider the possibility of Allied sabotage against the railway lines and tunnels. The main stimulus for this was the intensification of fighting in North Africa over the course of 1942. The year saw the military fortunes of both sides ebb and flow, with German troops threatening Britain's hold on Egypt in the summer, and then suffering what proved to be a terminal reverse in November with the opening of the El Alemein offensive and the landing of American forces in French North Africa. The mounting significance of events in the western desert, and the obvious attention given by Allied planners to interdicting the supply routes to Rommel's *Afrika Korps*, inevitably raised concern in Berlin over the security of its rail communications with Italy. From the middle of 1942, German diplomats began prodding the Swiss for assurances that their defences were capable of coping with Allied air attacks both against Swiss factories working on German contracts and Switzerland's railway infrastructure. They were also worried about the possibility of a paratrooper or glider assault to seize vital installations, including sections of the Swiss railways.[36]

Both the federal council and the Swiss army spent a great deal of time evaluating these possibilities, assessing possible future scenarios and constructing suitable defences.[37] Countermeasures against British covert activities were intensified and while the Swiss had by July 1942 found 'no indications of English sabotage preparations concerning the railways', such operations could not be ruled out 'because, owing to the development of military events, the destruction of the north-south links could critically damage the Axis'. Three Swiss factories working for Germany were already known to be under surveillance by British diplomats, and whenever British bombers jettisoned their bomb-loads in Switzerland, numerous Swiss blithely – though mistakenly – believed their country to be under direct and deliberate attack.[38] Although Guisan was more aware than most of the difficulties of navigating at night across a blacked-out continent, and more inclined, as a result, to take British excuses at face value, he thought it wise, nonetheless, to express the hope to Britain's air attaché in early 1942 that the increase in the number of Canadian pilots manning British aircraft would not result in a rise in the number of 'accidents'! Guisan's suspicions about the quality of geography teaching in North American high schools were confirmed the following years when American aircraft repeatedly bombed Swiss targets by mistake.[39] Swiss concerns over the menace to the railway-lines increased after the establishment of air bases in North Africa following the American landings in late 1942. The possibility of facing attacks from the south, as well as from the north, persuaded Guisan to redeploy several heavy (75 mm) anti-aircraft batteries from the frontier districts to Réduit to protect the principal Alpine railway lines. By the end of the year preparations were put in motion to strengthen the defences of strategic air fields considered vulnerable to a sudden Allied *coup de main*, and black out regulations in railways and trains were enforced were greater vigilance. All this frantic activity was sufficient at least to convince the German minister by early December 1942 that 'the Swiss government believed more in a violation of Swiss neutrality through the Allied airforce attacking, perhaps with paratroopers, the German-Italian links through Switzerland, than an attack from the side of the Reich'.[40]

The records show that the Swiss and Germans were much more imaginative in their appraisal of Allied military options than the Allies themselves. So far as one can tell, at no time did the British ever consider bombing Swiss industries, or occupying the country, even as a pre-emptive strike against a possible German invasion. This did not mean however, that London, or later Washington, were blind to the importance of the Germany's coal traffic across Switzerland. There is some evidence to suggest that in the autumn and winter of 1940 Britain contemplated taking military action to hamper this traffic. One of the first tasks given to the Special Operations Executive (SOE) in July 1940 was the interdiction of German coal transports across Swiss territory. Action directed against the tunnels was ruled out at an early stage as unfeasible, however blocking the railway lines, marshalling yards and bridges through 'accidents' or landslides, or sabotaging the water pipelines feeding hydroelectric power stations could conceivably result, SOE's planners believed, 'in holding up [Italy's] coal deliveries…military supplies or even, in certain circumstances, offensives'. Despite the obvious dangers of attacking Swiss targets, SOE's plans received the guarded approval of London's political authorities in September, and an 'Italian' expert on SOE's staff, Jock McCaffery, was despatched to Switzerland early the following year, to take control of operation. The plan even attracted the attention of the Prime Minister, Winston Churchill, who expressed himself in favour of 'impeding' German coal shipments 'in every way'.[41] The archives are tantalizingly vague on exactly how close SOE came to putting its operations into effect. While the backing of the Foreign Office was never wholehearted, SOE is known to have had contacts in the CCF, capable of doing London's bidding. It is probable however, that the delay in establishing an SOE station in Berne, and the upturn in Italy's military fortunes in April – with Hitler's invasion of Yugoslavia and Greece saving Mussolini from humiliation – convinced London that the moment for military action against the transit-traffic had passed. By the following winter, Britain's stake in the maintenance of Swiss neutrality had grown, and there is no evidence that SOE seriously considered reactivating aggressive operations in Switzerland. All covert measures against German rail traffic were therefore carried out on trains as they left Swiss territory, with teams stationed in the marshalling yards in Basle and Ciasso from early 1942, to immobilize Axis rolling-stock by applying abrasive powder to their axles and brakes.[42]

The possibility of bombing Swiss railways from the air appears to have been debated in the Air Ministry in the autumn of 1940, but was turned down as being technically unfeasible. The nearest that the Allies came to using aerial action to halt German–Italian transit traffic came in late 1944, when the commander in chief of Allied forces in Italy warned that if Berne failed to reduce the traffic, he would cut the lines leading into Italy by air or partisan action. None of the schemes discussed after the winter of 1940 entailed either a major violation of Swiss neutrality or undertaking operations in Switzerland itself. Paradoxically, the only serious sabotage threat to Switzerland's railways came from the Germans. In early December 1944, SS units holding the Ossola valley started excavating demolition mines at the end of the Simplon tunnel. The CCF and intelligence service used various techniques to hamper the progress of this work. By mid-April 1945, with German preparations nearing completion, they finally called upon the services of Italian partisans, and had the explosive supplies destroyed before they could do any harm.[43]

IV

It was ultimately through political and diplomatic means, rather than direct military action, that the Allies tried to tackle the problem posed by Swiss transit traffic over the last two years of the war.[44] Despite German and Swiss fears to the contrary, apart from a flurry of activity in late 1940/early 1941, British interest in Switzerland's transit facilities before the summer of 1943 was negligible. The general impression in Whitehall was that the Swiss had strong legal grounds for justifying their resistance to external interference in the level of transit traffic. An assessment of Switzerland's likely position in a future war written in January 1939 tellingly commented that 'in wartime it might be impossible to stop any goods but arms in transit between Germany and Italy', and no one thought fit to challenge this view when war broke out eight months later.[45] The only people outside SOE concerned with the matter were officials in the Foreign Office, but they tended to guided by the views of the British minister and military attaché in Berne, who saw the Alpine railways in the same light as the Swiss army: as Switzerland's key strategic assets rather than indispensable components in the collective Axis war effort. As a result whenever British diplomats were invited to raise the matter in Berne, they were instructed to limit their enquiries to simply reminding the Swiss to keep their eye on the ball and finger on the button. The one time Britain hinted at Germany's possible misuse of transit facilities in May 1941, an approach that was probably triggered by the realization that SOE's military option was now firmly off the agenda, the assurances of foreign minister Pilet-Golaz were accepted without demur.[46]

It was only in 1943 that a more sceptical view of Switzerland's transit traffic crept into official thinking. But even then British officials tended to play down the value of these facilities. On 31 May, the War Cabinet agreed to the dispatch of a 'general communication' to the federal authorities, which included a request for oil shipments to be suspended on the grounds that, although not technically war material, any oil dispatched in the current circumstances, with Allied forces mopping up the last pockets of Axis resistance in North Africa, was bound to be destined for military purposes.[47] Foreign Office minutes suggest however that the action was primarily geared towards placing the matter on the diplomatic agenda for future discussions, rather than picking a fight with the Swiss government. Few considered a Swiss climb-down likely. The minuscule quantity of oil transported over Switzerland – Italy received most of its oil from Romania, not Germany – and the existence of alternative routes across the French and Austrian Alps were all taken as sufficient reason to let the matter rest. Besides, most of Britain's economic leverage was being used to force reductions in Switzerland's exports to Germany. The Allied landings on mainland Italy in September and the Swedish decision to embargo oil shipments in early October did nothing to change these views. As a Foreign Office official noted on 6 October, nobody thought 'the cessation of this comparatively small oil traffic through Switzerland would adversely affect German military supplies to Italy. [...] Nothing would therefore be gained and goodwill might be lost if we pursued this matter further'.[48]

Unbeknown to the British, Berne took the occasional nonchalant remark about their transit traffic very much to heart. This was partly due to the fact that Berne had indeed permitted *war* material, though not soldiers or military equipment, to cross Swiss territory since the summer of 1940. As a 1944 report by the customs department noted, the 1907 Hague convention, governing neutral conduct in war, allowed the federal authorities to waive any right of 'initiative or obligation to search for war material on trains passing through Swiss territory which remained under the custody of German railway authorities'.[49] As a consequence small quantities of German war material were allowed to pass across Switzerland into Italy over the first years of the war. London appears to have been completely unaware of this practice, although interest at this stage centred on Germany's shipments of coal, which could hardly be considered war material. Nevertheless, London's casual enquiry in May 1941, while not exposing Swiss practices, did provoke alarm in Berne, and led to the federal authorities insisting that cargoes be assessed on a case by case basis thereafter.[50] Two years later, when London requested a suspension in the transport of German oil supplies in the early summer of 1943, the Swiss responded with even greater sensitivity. Their concern at the apparent awakening of Allied interest in this subject was almost certainly fanned by their exaggerated fear of the possibility of Allied aerial attacks on the railway lines, particularly now that American planes were regularly to be seen beyond, and sometimes above Swiss borders, by this date. Nevertheless, the federal authorities clearly judged the Allied request as sinister in itself. 'For the first time', Pilet-Golaz warned his colleagues in mid-June, 'a demand has been presented that really contradicts our neutrality'.[51] The council's bland response to the Allied memorandum, reiterating its determination to remain loyal to Switzerland's *'politique traditionelle'*, while remaining silent over the specific question of oil transports, thus hid a deep and profound anxiety. Despite Berne's best endeavours, by the middle of 1943, the transit issue had emerged as an issue on the diplomatic agenda, and a potent one at that.

Over 1944, as German defences crumbled in Russia, Italy, and later France, Allied pressure against the neutrals became increasingly intense. While Switzerland was exempted from many of these pressures, Berne's fear that its transit facilities would attract Allied attention was soon realized.[52] Half a dozen memoranda calling for the reduction or suspension of Switzerland's transit traffic were presented to the federal authorities over the course of the year. The military rationale behind this action was sound enough. Interdiction of German supply lines to German forces in Italy had been made a priority for Allied airforces in the Mediterranean theatre and it was clearly illogical to expend valuable resources bombing the Brenner Pass, when traffic was allowed to pass unhindered across Switzerland.[53] Fortunately for the Allied governments, many of the legal devices used by Berne to defend the high level of transit traffic were negated by military or political developments on the continent. Italy's surrender in September 1943, and subsequent declaration of war against Germany the following month inevitably cast doubt over the validity of the St Gothard Convention in justifying the transit traffic. Drafters of the convention had not envisaged a time in which free access to the Swiss facilities would be to the detriment of one of the main signatories; however, by late 1943, the Royal Italian government could legitimately maintain that Berlin's use of the Swiss lines to strip northern Italy of its industrial plant and keep its army of occupation supplied with the resources of war contradicted the spirit of the agreement. Any transiting of requisitioned material from Italy, even when not strictly war material, was clearly open to question. The Allies also expanded the definition of 'war material' and made great play out of Sweden's earlier acceptance of these terms, including its willingness to define oil as a war material. Finally, there was a strong case for viewing even a restriction of traffic to pre-war levels as inadequate, since an increasing part of Italy's population and industry lay in Allied hands and was therefore no longer dependent for its sustenance on goods ferried across Switzerland.

In the face of these arguments, Berne gradually backed down and reduced German transit. The transportation of liquid fuels to Italy was restricted to 1,000 tons a month from December 1943, and suspended altogether the following June.[54] In the opposite direction, the federal authorities agreed in December 1943 to limit all traffic to pre-war levels, so as to meet the charge that Swiss facilities were aiding Germany's despoliation of northern Italy. Restrictions on a range of commodities were introduced in April 1944, and the measures were progressively extended and tightened in August, September, October and November. In all these decisions, Berne made a show of transparency, providing the Allies with comprehensive statistics on the rail traffic, and responding conscientiously to all requests. It also insisted that all restrictions were fully within Switzerland's legal rights, and commissioned its most eminent international lawyers to scrutinize all proposals prior to taking a decision. These efforts to play the honest broker however were constantly marred by rumours of infringements in Swiss customs practices. The Allies repeatedly claimed that quotas were exceeded and illegal goods allowed to slip through Swiss controls. Berne reacted to each accusation with consternation, but it is telling that criticism of lax Swiss customs practices was also voiced within the federal authorities themselves.[55] Nor were surveillance measures as flawless as the CCF ardently maintained.[56] Before November 1943, 'only statistics on the basis of groups in the tariff positions were specified [in train manifests] but not over the individual goods categories [themselves]'. As a result it was not always possible 'for the customs organs to confirm which quantity of the individual goods categories are to be considered permissible or impermissible'.[57]

In January 1944, Berne took a conscious decision to maintain the utmost flexibility in the face of Allied demands.[58] Berne's primary concern was for the health of Swiss neutrality, but other considerations also impinged on their thinking, which made a supple policy on transit issues a wise approach to take. The first was financial. Regardless of the political aggravation caused by the inflated transit levels, the CCF was slow to abandon a perspective on the problem that was essentially driven by commercial considerations. The revenue this traffic generated for the Swiss railways was a life-saver for an industry which had been hard hit during the economic downturn in the 1930s, and seen some of the country's most bitter labour-relations disputes of the inter-war era. From an average of 386,5 mSF in the 1920s, annual revenue from the railways had plummeted to 325,8 mSF by the mid-1930s.[59] Italy's urgent wartime raw material requirements radically changed this situation. By 1941 and 1942, the Swiss railway network generated well over 450 mSF a year, and carried over 50 per cent more cargo goods (32 million tons per annum) than during the 1930s. Figures for the trans-Alpine railway lines, those most heavily used by the Italo-German transit traffic, show even greater increases. Between 1933 and 1938 the Lötschberg-Simplon line transported some 1.5 m tons every year. In 1940 this had more than doubled to 3.25 m tons, while in 1941 and 1942 the figure exceeded a staggering 4.25 m. A little under 3.50 m tons passed along the route in 1943, and despite the restrictions imposed in 1944, the 2.2 m tons carried that year was still almost double the pre-war average.[60] Suspending all transit traffic across Swiss railways therefore had significant financial implications that no government in Berne could ignore.[61]

The handling of the transit issue also had grave implications for the state of the Swiss economy. Just as Rome needed the unfettered use of Swiss transit facilities, so too Berne depended on free transit across German controlled territory in order to maintain trade links with other neutral countries in Europe. With the collapse of France, Switzerland's overseas trade evaporated and Berne was compelled to expand its trade with other neutral states in Europe; by 1944, these countries accounted for one fifth (236,9 mSF) of Swiss imports and a quarter (277,4 mSF) of its exports.[62] In such circumstances, the Swiss were hardly likely to welcome Allied demands to put all transit traffic on pre-war, or 'courante normaux', levels, since Switzerland's pre-war trade with the neutrals had been minuscule (2.2 per cent imports and 3.5 per cent exports). Moreover, trade with the Iberian peninsula and Sweden, which had swollen by over 500 per cent and 480 per cent between 1938 and 1943 respectively, contrasted unfavourably with the Italo-German transit traffic through Switzerland which by 1944 stood at 'only' 287 per cent of its pre-war level.[63] Berne then, did not enjoy an entirely free hand in its transit discussions with Rome and Berlin.[64]

Finally, it was obvious that behind Berne's defence of Swiss neutrality lay the more immediate imperative of maintaining stable relations with its northern neighbour. Nothing had occurred to diminish Berlin's interest in Swiss railway facilities; on the contrary, the eruption of fighting in Italy only went to heightened German determination to exploit all available means to keep its rolling stock moving. In recognition of this, the Swiss transferred responsibility for transit issues to the Federal Political Department (foreign ministry), and became very agitated if Allied diplomats were caught trying to approach Swiss railway authorities directly.[65] Repeated British press reports during the winter of 1943/44, about irresistible German demands for augmented transit rights over the Swiss Alps, were vigorously denied at every opportunity. Berne's embargo on the transportation of Italian labourers in September 1943 and requisitioned goods three months later made any undue publicity on the transit traffic distinctly unappealing. Germany did indeed inquire whether 'labourers' could cross Switzerland, and tested Swiss resolve in maintaining its embargo on war materials. In mid-October 1943 Albert Speer, minister of war and armaments production, even went so far as to recommend blockading Switzerland, if Berne refused to relax its transit restrictions. Fortunately for the Swiss, the German foreign ministry defeated the proposal by pointing out that such a measure had no guarantee of achieving immediate results because of the high levels of Swiss raw material reserves. Nevertheless, Speer continued to take a lively interest in Swiss transit traffic, and to a large extent made decisions on all bilateral trading issues contingent on receiving satisfaction on this issue.[66]

Berne ultimately sought to weave itself between the competing exigencies of the belligerents by linking the transit issue to the country's commercial needs. So long as Berlin met Switzerland's coal and other raw material requirements as stipulated in a series of arrangements thrashed out over 1944, Berne was prepared to turn a deaf ear to Allied complaints. Germany supplied some 1.3 m tons of coal to Switzerland over 1944, representing over 97 per cent of Switzerland's entire coal imports that year. But, when over the winter, Berlin started to renege on its coal deliveries, Berne seized the opportunity to placate Allied criticisms by suspending the transit of coal to Italy until Berlin made up the arrears.

Swiss tactics turned out to be notably less effective with the Allies. Allied impatience at the glacial pace of Swiss concessions was particularly damaging since it merely fuelled suspicions that the Swiss were seeking to extract the last ounce of profit from its commercial relations with Germany while opportunities remained. While the British were prepared to be forgiving, the Americans proved harder to convince, and it was largely Switzerland's failure to show sufficient alacrity and grace in meeting Allied demands that ultimately prevented the British from convincing their American allies to negotiate transit reductions in return for raw material import guarantees, as the Swiss proposed. By the autumn of 1944, with sizeable reductions in Swiss transit traffic already in place, and Allied troops blocking Germany's principal rail line into Switzerland through Basle, neither the Ministry of Economic Warfare, Foreign Office nor the Chiefs of Staff believed that further pressure justified the likely gains. It was feared that Swiss humanitarian services and intelligence facilities might all be lost if Switzerland was forced to abandon its neutrality by severing all transit traffic. But no bargaining with the Swiss on future supplies could begin without Washington's approval, and this proved impossible to obtain.

The dispatch of a high powered Allied economic mission to Berne in February 1945 did not fundamentally alter this situation. Indeed, despite efforts over the winter to soften Washington's views, it was the British rather than the Americans who changed their tune. In the weeks leading up to the discussions, Swiss diplomats perceived a noticeable stiffening in British attitudes on the subject. When negotiations began in Berne in February, led by the parliamentary secretary for economic warfare, Dingle Foot, it was the maximum Allied demands, for the unconditional and total suspension of all traffic, that were placed on the negotiating table.[67] Foot commented after the negotiations, and historians have largely followed his reasoning ever since, that the decisive moment in the talks came with the intervention of the Italian minister in Berne, who pressed the Swiss to accept the St Gothard as null and void in the present circumstances.[68] Swiss records suggest however that while the Italian letter was certainly considered at length, and used freely in discussions with the Germans, its significance and place in Swiss thinking has been misconstrued.[69] The Royal Italian government had voiced its views before, without result, and its intervention in February 1945 seems to have been seen by the Swiss as a valuable face saving device, rather than an irresistible line of reasoning forcing them into a policy which they would otherwise have avoided.

The real pressure on the Swiss came not from the Italians but from the Anglo-Americans, and the arguments were political in nature, rather than legal. From the first session, Dingle Foot brushed aside Switzerland's legal defence of the transit traffic, and attacked Swiss neutrality head on. 'Neutrality has been treated very elastically in this war', Foot insisted, recalling Berne's repeated refusal to establish an air service with neutral Spain or Portugal. 'It is not an unreasonable demand that now the Swiss should be no "more rigid" than they were before.' The Allies were not interested in a legal solution to the transit problem. The members of the delegation 'were lawyers but in the first line belligerents'.[70]

The Swiss had set out their legal position with respect to the transit traffic at the outset of the negotiations. Restrictions could only be countenanced when they were kept within the limits of Switzerland's rights and obligations as a neutral country.[71] By the end of the discussions, Berne had clearly retreated from this position. Much was made of the fact that an absolute suspension of all traffic had been avoided, and that some of the reductions could be legally justified. However slashing the transit quotas to token levels – 8,200 tons southbound and 5,900 tons northbound per month – and agreeing to a complete embargo on the transport of coal, iron, scrap steel and steel nevertheless contradicted the principles of Swiss neutrality. It was more than anything the 'disregard for obligations towards' Germany which these concessions entailed, that placed the agreement, in the words of the Federal Council at the 'extreme limit of solutions compatible with political neutrality'. The linkage which Berne had tried to forge between its transit traffic and import requirements was disregarded. All the Swiss received in return for their concessions on economic and financial matters were vague promises that Switzerland's future import requirements would be viewed sympathetically by the Allied authorities. The Federal Council insisted that the agreement constituted 'an act of political realism' required to create 'the necessary contact between our economy and those of the Allies', but the contacts were more imaginary than real. More than anything, the accord was in reality a political agreement, designed to promote political relations with the victorious powers for the post-war era.[72]

V

In many respects Switzerland's trans-Alpine railways embodied its historical role within the European state system. For the great powers, Swiss neutrality was a diplomatic necessity precisely because it guaranteed free access to the Alpine trade routes. Conditions in the 1940s tested these assumptions. Switzerland's northern and southern neighbours were locked together in alliance, and Italy's economy was critically dependent on over-land fuel imports from Germany. These factors inevitably compounded Switzerland's difficulties in trying to maintain an equilibrium in its relations with the two belligerent camps, since the advantages of its transportation facilities flowed so disproportionately in one direction. Paradoxically the rapid demise of British military fortunes in 1940, which left Switzerland so cruelly exposed to German demands, also meant that it was not until 1943 that the inequality in Switzerland's transit traffic came to haunt the Swiss government. In the meantime, Berne reaped handsome financial, economic and strategic rewards from the Swiss railways, creating a deterrent strategy, which while not as immediately realizable as historians have assumed, nevertheless gave the Swiss a valuable card to play in their relations with the Axis.

Swiss attitudes towards the right of free transit across the Alps was neatly encapsulated in a remark of the federal foreign minister in October 1941: 'En droit, la situation est claire. En politique, elle depend des circonstances.'[73] The circumstances, rather than the law, go a long way to explain Swiss policy. Unlike the Swedes, who permitted an entire German division to pass across their country in July 1941,[74] Berne could legitimately claim that its policy was driven by a determination to live up to Switzerland's legal obligations under the Gothard and Hague conventions. (Although it is certainly open to question whether the Swiss military would have welcomed the passage of German soldiers and military equipment through the heart of the Réduit, whatever the word of the law.[75]) The Swiss took a distinctly 'light' touch towards their duties of surveillance, and their reading of what constituted 'war material'. By 1944, it was the sheer scale of Switzerland's rail transit traffic that provoked the Allies into making demands that were 'incompatible' with Swiss neutrality. In reality, the issue which had gone such a long way to save Swiss neutrality in 1940, proved to be the issue upon which it was sacrificed five years later.

If the Second World War was an exceptional era for the trans-Alpine railway lines, creating a unique set of problems – and opportunities – for the Swiss government, their existence nevertheless continued to have a powerful place in shaping Swiss history. Though the vast bulk of the population lived on the dissected bloc plateau in the north and the west of the country, the Alps played an important role in defining Swiss identity. Over the course of the nineteenth century in particular, as foreigners flocked to marvel at the country's natural beauty, the sense of Switzerland being a 'Gotthardstaat', forged on the Alpine anvil, became increasingly popular. The centrality of the Alps to Swiss national consciousness was, if anything, strengthened by the events of the war, especially the part played by the Réduit and the strategic railways that passed through it. Moreover, for all the changes that Switzerland has undergone in recent years, with its wartime conduct pilloried in the world's press, and its claim to neutrality brought into question by its entry into the United Nations, the trans-Alpine railways continue to exercise a profound influence over the country's identity and economic life, even if their strategic role has declined. Public concern at the environmental impact of the increasing volume of heavy transit traffic on Swiss roads was ultimately assuaged by insisting that foreign lorries wishing to traverse Switzerland had to go by rail. In taking heavy goods vehicles off the roads, Switzerland's trans-Alpine railways are once again coming to the country's aid, ensuring its economic prosperity, protecting its image as a mountainous-idyll and enabling the Swiss to enjoy a standard of living and a quality of life that is the envy of their neighbours.

Notes

1 Cited in Ann G. Imlah, *Britain and Switzerland, 1845–1860* (London, 1966), 183.
2 See Karl Weber, 'Die Staatsverträge zwischen der Schweiz und dem Ausland', in Eidgenössische Post- und Eisenbahen Department (ed.), *Ein Jahrhundert Schweizer Bahnen, 1847–1947. Jubiläumswerk, vol. 4* (Berne: Eidgenössische Post- und Eisenbahen Department, 1947), 690–3.
3 For Swiss railway development see Roland Ruffieux, 'La Suisse des radicaux (1848–1914)', in *Nouvelle Histoire de la Suisse et des Suisses* (Lausanne: Payot, 2nd edn. 1986), 599–681 (esp. 618–20, 650–53, 661–2).
4 Jean-François Bergier, *Histoire économique de la Suisse* (Lausanne: Payot, 1983), 290–2. The Lötschberg tunnel linked the central Swiss railway network to the Valais, where trains could continue their journey to Italy through the Simplon tunnel.
5 For British attitudes see W.N. Medlicott, *The Economic Blockade. Vol. 1* (London: H.M.S.O., 1952), 280–311.
6 See Gerhard Schreiber, Bernd Stegemann, Detlef Vogel, *Germany and the Second World War vol. 3* (Oxford, Oxford University Press, 1995), 30–1, and in general, Vera Zamagni, 'Italy: how to lose the war and win the peace', in Mark Harrison (ed.), *The*

Economics of World War II: Six Great Powers in International Comparison (Cambridge: Cambridge University Press, 1998), 177–223.

7 See for example Swiss intelligence report, 'Das deutsch-italienische Kohlenabkommen und die wirtschaftspolitischen Perspektiven für die Schweiz', 19 March 1940. *Documents Diplomatiques Suisse 1848–1945*, (hereafter *DDS*) vol. 13 (Berne: Benteli Verlag, 1991), No. 254/1.

8 Gilles Forster, *Transit ferroviaire à travers la Suisse (1939–1945)* (Lausanne: Payot, 2001), 123–47. Forster's work updates the earlier work of Richard Ochsner, 'Transit von Truppen, Einzelpersonen, Kriegsmaterial und zivilen Gebrauchsgütern zugunsten einer Kriegspartei durch das neutrale Land', in R.L. Bindschedler, (*et al.*, eds), *Schwedische und schweizerische Neutralität im Zweiten Weltkrieg* (Basle: Helbing und Lichtenhahn, 1985), 216–235 and Neville Wylie, 'Neville Wylie, 'Le rôle des transports ferroviares en Suisse, 1939–1945: les aspects militaire, économique et politique'. *Relations internationales*, 95 (Autumn, 1998), 361–80.

9 For Swiss–Italian relations see Mauro Cerutti, *Le Tessin, la Suisse et l'Italie de Mussolini: fascisme et antifascisme* (Lausanne: Payot, 1988) and Stephan Winkler, *Die Schweiz und das geteilte Italien: Bilaterale Beziehungen in einer Umbruchphase 1943–1945* (Basle: Helbing & Lichtenhahn, 1992).

10 See 'Procès-verbal de la réunion de la Délégation financière du Conseil fédéral et de la Délégation suisse pour les négociations économiques avec l'Allemagne', 21 June 1940. *DDS*, vol. 13, No. 314/1.

11 The most comprehensive survey of this topic is R.U. Vogler, 'Die Wirtschaftsverhandlungen zwischen der Schweiz und Deutschland 1940 und 1941', PhD dissertation, Zurich, 1983, 118–57, although this can be supplemented with Klaus Urner, *Let's Swallow Switzerland: Hitler's plans against the Swiss Confederation* (Langam: Lexington Books, 2002. German original, 1991), 77–107, and Daniel Bourgeois, *La Troisième Reich et la Suisse* (Neuchâtel: La Baconnière, 1974), chap. 9.

12 Bergier, *Histoire économique*, 292.

13 This was up from 11–12 per cent in the final years of peace. Forster, *Transit ferroviaire*, 59 (Table 3).

14 Ernst von Weiszäcker (German Ministry of Foreign Affairs) to Otto Köcher (German legation, Berne), 29 June 1942. Auswärtiges Amt (ed.), *Akten zur deutschen auswärtigen Politik, 1918–1945*. (hereafter ADAP) Ser. E, 1941–1945 Vol. 3 (Göttingen: Vandenhoeck & Ruprecht, 1969–79), No. 48., p. 79.

15 Carl Clodius to German Foreign Ministry, 7 Sept. 1943. *ADAP* Ser. E Vol. 6 No. 281. p. 488.

16 The report, dated 1 April 1944, is cited in Daniel Bourgeois, 'Les relations économique Germano-Suisses pendant la seconde guerre mondiale: un bilan allemand de 1944', *Revue suisse d'histoire*, 32 (1982), 563–73.

17 For Swiss political and security issues in the First World War see Max Mittler, *Der Weg zum Ersten Weltkrieg: Wie neutral war die Schweiz?* (Zurich: Neue Zürcher Zeitung Verlag, 2003) and H.R. Fuhrer, *Die Schweizer Armee im Ersten Weltkrieg: Bedrohung, Landesverteidigung und Landesbefestigung* (Zurich: Neue Zürcher Zeitung Verlag, 1999).

18 See Georg Kreis, *Auf den Spuren von La Charité. Die schweizerische Armeeführung im Spannungsfeld des deutsch-französischen Gegensatzes 1936–1941* (Basle: Helbing & Lichtenhahn, 1976), Willi Gautschi, *Le général Guisan. Le commandement de l'armée suisse pendant la Seconde Guerre mondiale* (Lausanne: Payot, 1991), 113–40.

19 Karl Kobelt to Jakob Huber, 9 June 1940. *DDS*, vol. 13, No. 301.

20 'Compte-rendu de une conférence tenue à Berne' 22 June 1940. *DDS*, vol. 13, No. 317.

21 Bernard Barbey, *Fünf Jahre auf dem Kommandoposten des Generals. Tagebuch des chefs des persönlichen Stabes General Guisans, 1940–1945* (Berne: Herbert Lang, 1948, trans. from French), 28 (entry for 9 July 1940).

22 See the opinions of Maurice Paschoud, vice-president of the CCF, quoted in Forster, *Transit ferroviaire*, 119.

23 See Hans Senn, *Der Schweizerische Generalstab/L'Etat-major Général suisse, vol VII. Anfänge einer Dissuasionsstrategie während des Zweiten Weltkriegs* (Basle: Helbing & Lichtenhahn, 1995), 305–25 and Gautschi, *Le général Guisan*, 284–310.

24 Cited in Gautschi, *Le général Guisan*, 310.

25 For this view see Hans Rudolf Kurz, *Operationsplannung Schweiz. Die Rolle der Schweizer Armee in zwei Weltkriegen* (Thun, 1974) and Stephen Halbrook, *Target Switzerland: Swiss* Armed Neutrality in Second World War (New York, 1998).

26 Swiss Federal Archives (hereafter SFA), E27/12899, G. Duttweiler to Guisan 16 June 1940.

27 SFA, E5795/152, J. Huber to Guisan 4 July 1940.

28 SFA. E27/12899, Guisan to Kobelt 21 Feb. 1941; Kobelt to Guisan 25 Apr. 1941.

29 SFA, E27/12903, 'Besprechung mit Oberstlt von Gunten, Oberst I Gst. Kaufmann', 8 Feb. 1941. E27/12899, Report 'Betr Zerstoerung Gothard und Lötschbergbahn', Oberstlt. von Gunten, 17 Jan. 1941.

30 SFA. E27/12901, Chef du Génie de l'Armée to Kriegs-Industrie-und-Arbeits-Amt, 30 Oct. 1941.

31 The exact completion dates are not available. These are estimates calculated on dates given in May 1941 and the disruption known to have been caused. SFA, E27/12899, Huber to Guisan 10 May 1941.

32 See summary of the general staff's 'Weisungen für die Zerstörung der Bahnen und ihrer Anlagen', 18 June 1942, in Maurice Paschoud, 'Das Militäreinbahnwesen bis zum Ende des Zweite Weltkriege', in Eidgenössische Post- und Eisenbahen Department, (ed.), *Ein Jahrhundert Schweizer Bahnen, 1847–1947. Jubiläumswerk vol. 4.* (Berne: Eidgenössische Post- und Eisenbahen Department, 1947), 200.

33 See Urner, *Let's Swallow Switzerland*, 37–73.

34 See reports by von Gunten, 17 Jan. 1941, Strueby, 20 Jan. 1941, and Lardelli, 22 Feb. 1941, in SFA, E27/12899, and E27/12903, 'Notiz für den Herrn Unterstabschef Front betr. die Minen-Objekt im Lötschbergtunnel', Oberst. I Gst. Kaufmann, 10 Dec. 1940.

35 These views support the thesis advanced by Philippe Marguerat that Swiss strategy was defective before May 1941. Philippe Marguerat, *La Suisse face au IIIe Reich. Réduit national et dissuasion économique, 1940–1945* (Lausanne: Editions 24 heures, 1991), 39–44.

36 The British attack on the French Renault works at Billancourt in March 1942 was widely thought to herald a broadening of the air war. See in general, Alfred C. Mierzejewski, *The collapse of the German war economy, 1944–1945: Allied air power and the German National Railway* (Chapel Hill: University of North Carolina Press, 1985), and *idem, The Most Valuable Asset of the Reich: a history of the German National Railway* (Chapel Hill: University of North Carolina Press, 1999).

37 See Gautschi, *Le général Guisan*, p. 315.

38 SFA, E2809/2, Special report for Pilet-Golaz, 22 July 1942 by Roger Masson, head of the Swiss intelligence service. See Neville Wylie, 'Keeping the Swiss Sweet' Intelligence as a factor in British policy towards Switzerland during the Second World War', *Intelligence & National Security*, 11/3 (July 1996), 442–67.

39 See Peter Kamber, *Schüsse auf die Befreier. Die 'Luftguerilla' der Schweiz gegen die Alliierten, 1943–1945* (Zurich: Rotpunkt, 1993).

40 Otto Köcher (German minister in Berne) to Berlin, 7 Dec. 1942, cited in Daniel Bourgeois, 'L'image allemande de Pilet-Golaz, 1940–1944', *Études et Sources*, 4 (1978), 69–125 (106). Forster, *Transit ferroviaire*, 111–22.

41 The National Archive: Public Record Office (hereafter TNA) HS6/1010. Minute by Churchill, 27 Jan. 1941; Hugh Dalton (SOE) to General Sir Hastings Ismay (War Cabinet Office), 28 Sept. 1940.

42 See Neville Wylie, *Britain, Switzerland and the Second World War* (Oxford: Oxford University Press, 2003), 184–6, and *idem*, 'SOE and the neutrals' in Mark Seaman (ed.), *Special Operations Executive. Proceedings of a conference held at the Imperial War Museum* (London, 2005), forthcoming.

43 For this affair see papers in SFA, E27/12902 and E27/12896.

44 This is discussed in Wylie, *Britain, Switzerland and the Second World War*, 186–94.

45 TNA, FO371/23860 R2744, Industrial Intelligence Centre 'General Survey: Switzerland', 27 Jan. 1939, by Desmond Morton.

46 Britain's minister in Berne, David Kelly, thought the suggestion that the Swiss were doing anything improper preposterous, and found the whole experience rather embarrassing. See Pilet's recollections of his meeting with Kelly in Barbey to Guisan 4 Feb. 1944. SFA, E5795/448. See also SFA, E2809/3, Note par Bonna 20 Aug. 1941.

47 TNA, CAB65/23 Minutes of the War Cabinet, 31 May 1943. *DDS*, vol. 13., No. 380., note 3.

48 TNA. FO371/34890 C11456 Minute by Reay (FO) 6 Oct. 1943.

49 See SFA, E6100 (B) 1973/141/88 'Der Transitverkehr durch die Schweiz in den Kriegsjahren 1939/1944', Oberzollinspektor Widmer (Swiss customs service) 22 Dec. 1944. I am indebted to Daniel Bourgeois for kindly drawing my attention to this important memorandum.

50 Berne rejected any prohibition on the transit of war material. For these discussions see Forster, *Transit ferroviaire*, 77–90, and Markus Heiniger, *Dreizehn Gründe. Warum die Schweiz im Zweiten Weltkrieg nicht erobert wurde* (Zurich: Limmat Verlag, 1989), 56–7.

51 *DDS*, vol. 13, No. 380. Procès-verbal de la séance du conseil fédéral, 25 June 1943. For a discussion of the council's deliberations see Edgar Bonjour, *Histoire de la neutralité Suisse pendant la seconde guerre mondiale, vol. 5* (Neuchâtel: La Baconnière, 1970), 338–9.

52 For the waxing Allied, particular American, pressure on Switzerland see Jürg Martin Gabriel, *The American Conception of Neutrality after 1941* (Basingstoke: Palgrave, 2nd edn, 2002), 42–54; William Slany (coordinated by Stuart E Eizenstat), *Preliminary Study on U.S. and Allied Efforts To Recover and Restore Gold and Other Assets Stolen or Hidden by Germany During Second World War* (Washington, May 1997).

53 For military pressure to have the transit traffic reduced see, Sir. W. Jackson, *The Mediterranean and Middle East; vol. VI. 'Victory in the Mediterranean'. Part III* (London: H.M.S.O., 1988), 60–6.

54 *DDS*, vol. 15 (Berne: Benteli 1992), No. 16, Bonna (DPF) to R. Furrer (Swiss customs service) 30 Dec. 1943.

55 SFA, E6100 (B) 1973/141/88 R. Furrer (Swiss customs service) to Federal councillor Ernst Nobs 22 Dec. 1944. I am indebted to M. Bourgeois for drawing my attention to this letter. See also Jean Ziegler, *La Suisse, l'or et les morts* (Paris: Le Seuil, 1997), 169–171, and Felix Auer, *Das Schlachtfeld von Thun, oder: Dichtung und Wahrheit bei Jean Ziegler* (Zurich: Stäfa, 1997).

56 See *DDS*, vol. 13, No. 359. Notice by Pilet-Golaz, 22 May 1943.

57 SFA, E 2001 (D) 3/349. Notice by Hohl, 10 Nov. 1943.

58 See minute by Pilet-Golaz 21 Jan. 1944. *DDS*, vol. 15, No. 72, Note 1, and, 'Compte-rendu d'une séance des négociations économiques ... sur la question du transit', 5 April 1944. *DDS*, vol. 15, No. 117.

59 H. Siegenthaler & H.R. Blickenstrofer, (eds), *Historical Statistics of Switzerland* (Zurich: Chronos, 1996), Figure N8., p. 774.

60 Eidgenössischen Amt für Verkehr (ed.), *Schweizerischer Eisenbahnstatistik*, vols 61 (1933) to 73 (1945). From October 1944 the Simplon tunnel only remained open for the use of Swiss citizens in the Italian town of Domodossola.

61 Forster has revealed however that Italy's reneging on its payments meant that in effect the federal authorities footed much of the bill (SF89 m). Forster, *Transit ferroviaire*, 147.

62 Jean Hotz, 'Division du commerce et politique commerciale pendant la guerre', in Centrale fédérale de l'économie de guerre (ed.), *L'économie de guerre en Suisse 1939/1948* (Berne: Centrale fédérale de l'économie de guerre, 1951), 65.

63 SFA, E 2001 (D) 3/349, Notice by the Federal Political Department 14 Sept. 1944. 'Certains aspects du trafic de l'Italie vers l'Allemagne à travers la Suisse'.

64 As the federal foreign minister remarked in early 1944, 'si nous voulions l'abondoner, [freedom of transit], nous nous exposerions à des conséquences fort désagréables'. 'Notice sur le trafic de transit' by M. Pilet-Golaz, 4 Feb. 1944. *DDS*, vol. 15, No. 77.

65 SFA, E2001 (D) 3/303, Pilet-Golaz to M. Paschoud (CCF, military director) 29 June 1943.

66 See D. Bourgeois, 'Les relations économiques germano-suisses pendant la seconde guerre mondiale: un bilan allemande de 1944', *Revue suisse d'histoire*, 32 (1982), 563–573: SFA, E 2001 (D) 3/349. 'Notes sur un entretien chez M. Pilet-Golaz le 15.2.44' by M. Merminod; SFA, E2001 (D) 3/347 Minute by P. Bonna (FPD) 21 Oct. 1943.

67 The transit issue has tended to be overlooked by historians examining the Currie mission, who have tended to focus attention on its trade and financial aspects; see Marco Durrer, *Die schweizerisch-amerikanischen Finanzbeziehungen im Zweiten Weltkrieg* (Berne: Haupt, 1984), 184–214.

68 The Italian note of 14 Feb. 1945 to the FPD is printed in *DDS*, vol. 15, Docu 364. TNA, FO371/49674 Z3529 memo. by Dingle Foot (MEW) 15 Mar. 1945, printed in Edgar Bonjour, *Geschichte der schweizerischen Neutralität, vol. XI* (Basle: Helbing & Lichtenhahn, 1976), No. 129. See Medlicott, *The Economic Blockade, vol. II*, (London: H.M.S.O., 1959), 620–39; Heinz K. Meier, *Friendship under Stress, US–Swiss Relations 1900–1945* (Berne: Lang, 1970), 342–6.

69 *DDS*, vol. 15, No. 364, Italian legation, Berne, to the Federal Political Department 14 Feb. 1945.

70 SFA, E2001 (D) 3/348 'Compte-rendu du séance', 14 Feb. 1945.

71 See *DDS*, vol. 15, No. 362. 'Exposé sur la question du trafic de transit à travers la Suisse', 12 Feb. 1945.

72 *DDS*, vol. 15, No. 386, Minutes of the Federal Council, 6 Mar. 1945.

73 Pilet-Golaz to Gassmann (director-general of the Swiss customs service) 7 Oct. 1941. *DDS*, vol. 14 (Berne: Benteli, 1997), No. 112, p. 333.

74 See K. Zetterberg, 'Le transit allemand par la Suède de 1940 à 1943', *Revue d'histoire de la Deuxième Guerre mondiale* 109 (1978), 59–80.

75 See remarks of the Swiss minister in London: Thurnheer to Pilet-Golaz 5 Oct. 1940, printed in Bonjour, *Geschichte der schweizerischen Neutralität, vol. XI*, No. 101.

Index